GW00319954

EUTHANASIA AND ASSISTED SUICIDE

Examining the evidence from Belgium – one of only five countries where euthanasia is practised legally – an international panel of experts considers the implications of legalised euthanasia and assisted suicide. Looking at the issue from an international perspective, the authors have written an invaluable in-depth analysis of the ethical aspects of this complex area. The discussion forms a solid foundation for informed debate about assisted dying. With contributors from a broad range of disciplines, this is ideal for students, academics, legislators and anyone interested in legal, medical, social and philosophical ethics. This book is a vital and timely examination of a growing phenomenon and one of the most challenging ethical questions of our time.

DAVID ALBERT JONES is Director of the Anscombe Bioethics Centre, Oxford and a Research Fellow at Blackfriars Hall, Oxford. He is also a Research Fellow at St Mary's University, Twickenham. He is Vice-chair of the Ministry of Defence Research Ethics Committee.

CHRIS GASTMANS is a Professor of Medical Ethics and Director of the Centre for Biomedical Ethics and Law, Faculty of Medicine, KU Leuven, Belgium. He was a member of the Bureau of the European Association of Centres of Medical Ethics and held the positions of Secretary-General, Treasurer and President.

CALUM MACKELLAR is Director of Research at the Scottish Council on Human Bioethics, Edinburgh and a Member of the Advisory Board of the Centre for Bioethics and Emerging Technologies at St Mary's University, Twickenham.

CAMBRIDGE BIOETHICS AND LAW

This series of books was founded by Cambridge University Press with Alexander McCall Smith as its first editor in 2003. It focuses on the law's complex and troubled relationship with medicine across both the developed and the developing world. Since the early 1990s, we have seen in many countries increasing resort to the courts by dissatisfied patients and a growing use of the courts to attempt to resolve intractable ethical dilemmas. At the same time, legislatures across the world have struggled to address the questions posed by both the successes and the failures of modern medicine, while international organisations such as the WHO and UNESCO now regularly address issues of medical law.

It follows that we would expect ethical and policy questions to be integral to the analysis of the legal issues discussed in this series. The series responds to the high profile of medical law in universities, in legal and medical practice, as well as in public and political affairs. We seek to reflect the evidence that many major health-related policy debates in the United Kingdom, Europe and the international community involve a strong medical law dimension. With that in mind, we seek to address how legal analysis might have a trans-jurisdictional and international relevance. Organ retention, embryonic stem cell research, physician assisted suicide and the allocation of resources to fund health care are but a few examples among many. The emphasis of this series is thus on matters of public concern and/or practical significance. We look for books that could make a difference to the development of medical law and enhance the role of medico-legal debate in policy circles. That is not to say that we lack interest in the important theoretical dimensions of the subject, but we aim to ensure that theoretical debate is grounded in the realities of how the law does and should interact with medicine and health care.

Series Editors
Professor Graeme Laurie, *University of Edinburgh*
Professor Richard Ashcroft, *Queen Mary, University of London*

EUTHANASIA AND ASSISTED SUICIDE

Lessons from Belgium

Edited by

DAVID ALBERT JONES
Anscombe Bioethics Centre

CHRIS GASTMANS
Catholic University of Leuven

CALUM MACKELLAR
Scottish Council on Human Bioethics

CAMBRIDGE
UNIVERSITY PRESS

CAMBRIDGE
UNIVERSITY PRESS

University Printing House, Cambridge CB2 8BS, United Kingdom

One Liberty Plaza, 20th Floor, New York, NY 10006, USA

477 Williamstown Road, Port Melbourne, VIC 3207, Australia

314-321, 3rd Floor, Plot 3, Splendor Forum, Jasola District Centre, New Delhi - 110025, India

79 Anson Road, #06-04/06, Singapore 079906

Cambridge University Press is part of the University of Cambridge.

It furthers the University's mission by disseminating knowledge in the pursuit of education, learning and research at the highest international levels of excellence.

www.cambridge.org
Information on this title: www.cambridge.org/9781107198869
DOI: 10.1017/9781108182799

© Cambridge University Press 2017

This publication is in copyright. Subject to statutory exception and to the provisions of relevant collective licensing agreements, no reproduction of any part may take place without the written permission of Cambridge University Press.

First published 2017

A catalogue record for this publication is available from the British Library

Library of Congress Cataloging in Publication data
Names: Jones, David Albert, editor. | Gastmans, Chris, 1966- editor. | MacKellar, C. (Calum), editor.
Title: Euthanasia and assisted suicide : lessons from Belgium / edited by David Albert Jones, Anscombe Bioethics Centre; Chris Gastmans, Catholic University of Leuven; Calum MacKellar
Description: Cambridge [UK] ; New York : Cambridge University Press, 2017. | Series: Cambridge bioethics and law | Includes bibliographical references and index.
Identifiers: LCCN 2017016930 | ISBN 9781107198869 (hardback : alk. paper) | ISBN 9781316648353 (pbk. : alk. paper)
Subjects: LCSH: Euthanasia–Law and legislation–Belgium. | Right to die–Law and legislation–Belgium. | Assisted suicide–Law and legislation–Belgium. | Euthanasia–Law and legislation.
Classification: LCC KJK4058 .E98 2017 | DDC 344.49304/197–dc23
LC record available at https://lccn.loc.gov/2017016930

ISBN 978-1-107-19886-9 Hardback
ISBN 978-1-316-64835-3 Paperback

Cambridge University Press has no responsibility for the persistence or accuracy of URLs for external or third-party internet websites referred to in this publication, and does not guarantee that any content on such websites is, or will remain, accurate or appropriate.

To Kevin Fitzpatrick, who showed what it can be both to live well and to die well and whose contribution to this book is much more than the sum of his words.

CONTENTS

    an End to Interminable Discussion   235
    DAVID ALBERT JONES

15 Psychiatric Patients and the Culture of Euthanasia in
    Belgium   258
    WILLEM LEMMENS

    Final Conclusions on Final Solutions   278
    DAVID ALBERT JONES, CHRIS GASTMANS AND
    CALUM MACKELLAR

    Appendix I   *Wet Betreffende de Euthanasie 28 Mei 2002*
                  (The Belgian Act on Euthanasia,
                  Dutch-language Version)   284
    Appendix II   *Loi Relative à L'Euthanasie 28 Mai 2002*
                  (The Belgian Act on Euthanasia,
                  French-language Version)   295
    Appendix III *The Belgian Act on Euthanasia of*
                  28 May 2002 (Unofficial Translation)   305
    References   316
    Index   352

TABLES

AUTHORS' AFFILIATIONS

DAVID ALBERT JONES, Anscombe Bioethics Centre, Oxford, United Kingdom, and the Centre for Bioethics and Emerging Technologies, St Mary's University, Twickenham, United Kingdom.

CHRIS GASTMANS, Centre for Biomedical Ethics and Law, Catholic University of Leuven, Belgium.

CALUM MACKELLAR, Scottish Council on Human Bioethics, Edinburgh, United Kingdom, and the Centre for Bioethics and Emerging Technologies, St Mary's University, Twickenham, United Kingdom.

HERMAN NYS, Centre for Biomedical Ethics and Law, Catholic University of Leuven, Belgium.

ETIENNE MONTERO, Faculty of Law, University of Namur, Belgium.

DANIEL P. SULMASY, Departments of Medicine and Philosophy, the Pellegrino Center and the Kennedy Institute of Ethics, Georgetown University, USA.

PAUL VANDEN BERGHE, Federation of Palliative Care Flanders, Belgium.

ARSÈNE MULLIE, Federation of Palliative Care Flanders, Belgium.

MARC DESMET, Federation of Palliative Care Flanders, Belgium.

GERT HUYSMANS, Federation of Palliative Care Flanders, Belgium.

SIGRID STERCKX, Bioethics Institute Ghent, Ghent University, Belgium.

KASPER RAUS, University Hospitals and Bioethics Institute Ghent, Ghent University, Belgium.

BENOIT BEUSELINCK, Department of Oncology, University Hospitals, Catholic University of Leuven, Belgium.

TREVOR STAMMERS, Centre for Bioethics and Emerging Technologies, St Mary's University, Twickenham, United Kingdom.

KEVIN FITZPATRICK, Disability Rights Commission for Wales, United Kingdom (2000 to 2007) and Euthanasia Prevention Coalition International (2014 to 2016).

JORIS VANDENBERGHE, Department of Neurosciences, University Hospitals and University Psychiatric Center, Catholic University of Leuven, Belgium.

STEFAAN VAN GOOL, Immunology-Oncology Centre, Cologne, Germany.

JAN DE LEPELEIRE, Academic Centre for General Practice, and University Psychiatric Center, Catholic University of Leuven, Belgium.

RAPHAEL COHEN-ALMAGOR, School of Law and Politics, University of Hull, United Kingdom.

WILLEM LEMMENS, Department of Philosophy, University of Antwerp, Belgium.

~

Introduction

DAVID ALBERT JONES, CHRIS GASTMANS
AND CALUM MACKELLAR

Belgium is one of very few countries in the world where one can assess the impact of legalising euthanasia or assisted suicide. Attempts to legalise euthanasia or physician-assisted suicide date back at least to the 1930s, with the founding of the Voluntary Euthanasia Legalisation Society in London in 1935. However, it was only in the 1980s that organised forms of these practices were legally tolerated in Switzerland and in the Netherlands and the first statute law to provide for medically assisted death was not passed until the mid-1990s, in Oregon. Twenty years later, the number of jurisdictions with extensive experience of euthanasia or physician-assisted suicide remains very small: only Switzerland, the Netherlands, Belgium, Luxembourg and a handful of States in the United States. There are some other jurisdictions where such practices are now, or have been, legal, but in all other cases their experience is much more limited in time or in extent.

Euthanasia in Belgium is the subject of a large body of empirical research and there is also a set of biennial official reports from 2002. However, until the present volume no study has sought to draw this research together into a coherent narrative and present it to an English-speaking readership. Without prejudice to work that has been done on euthanasia in the Netherlands and physician-assisted suicide in the United States, such evidence is always partial. With so few exemplars it is essential also to consider in depth and in detail the experience of Belgium for what it may have to teach in relation to the impact of medically assisted death. The best guide to what *could* happen is what *has* happened.

It can be useful to compare Belgian law and practice with those of other countries, with the Netherlands or Luxembourg, or with the United Kingdom or the United States. Several of the chapters contain such comparisons. Nevertheless, the focus of interest for this volume remains Belgium. By considering the experience of one country in depth and from different perspectives it is possible to explore the diverse ways in which a change in law in this area can have an impact on society. The aim is to consider what lessons the Belgian experience may hold for other countries that are contemplating a similar move.

The book begins with an account of the Belgian euthanasia law, comparing the law with similar legislation in the Netherlands and in Luxembourg, and examining amendments and interpretations of the law. The author, Herman Nys, is Professor of Health Law at the University of Leuven and is well known in Belgium for his interpretation of the euthanasia law. In the second chapter, Etienne Montero, Professor in the Faculty of Law at the University of Namur, considers the implementation of this legislation. This chapter draws on official reports and independent research to explore the pattern of euthanasia practice in Belgium.

After two contrasting Belgian perspectives, the third chapter provides a viewpoint from the United States. It focuses on areas of overlap between experience in Oregon and that in Belgium, in relation to psychiatric dimensions of the practice. The author is Daniel Sulmasy, professor at the Pellegrino Center and the Kennedy Institute of Ethics, Georgetown University, USA.

A key concern in relation to euthanasia is the impact of a change in the law on the shape of end-of-life care. A palliative care perspective is set out by Paul Vanden Berghe and Gert Huysmans, who are director and president, respectively, of the Federation of Palliative Care Flanders. Their co-author Marc Desmet is both a Jesuit and a medical doctor working in palliative care. The current volume reprints a paper these authors wrote in 2013 on the experience of euthanasia embedded in palliative care, together with a postscript reflecting on that paper in the light of subsequent developments up to 2016. This contribution is followed by a chapter by Sigrid Sterckx and Kasper Raus on the practice of continuous sedation. Professor Sterckx and Dr Raus of the University of Ghent took part in an international collaborative research project on sedation and have edited a scholarly volume on the topic. They examine the contrast between sedation practice in Belgium and that in the United Kingdom. Another clinical contribution, from Benoit Beuselinck, provides an individual perspective from a clinician with fifteen years of experience in oncology who is very critical of the impact of the law.

The last chapter in the Part II is by Trevor Stammers, a former general practitioner in the United Kingdom and currently editor of a bioethics journal and former programme director of a masters in bioethics. The chapter considers the topic of organ transplantation after euthanasia. The subject functions as a bridge to other debates in bioethics, not least the ethics of novel forms of organ procurement.

The five subsequent chapters consider groups of patients who, it has been alleged or might be supposed, could be affected adversely by such legislation. Kevin Fitzpatrick, a philosopher and former Disability Rights Commissioner for Wales explores the relationship of disability to the practice of euthanasia as this is performed in Belgium. He died before he could finish writing this chapter and, with his prior agreement, the chapter was completed by David Albert Jones.

Joris Vandenberghe, a psychiatrist at Leuven University Hospitals and Associate Professor in the Faculty of Medicine, considers the highly controversial practice of euthanasia in patients suffering from psychiatric illnesses. Such cases are much less prevalent than euthanasia in terminally ill patients, but the numbers are increasing both in absolute terms and as a proportion of the total. In contrast, the extension of the euthanasia act to children, which generated international controversy when the law was amended in 2014, has yet to be applied in practice. This issue is examined by Stefaan Van Gool, a professor in paediatric neuro-oncology and Jan De Lepeleire, a general practitioner who chaired an ethical forum on euthanasia at the University of Leuven. They ask whether the extension of the law was needed and whether it is workable in practice.

Raphael Cohen-Almagor, Professor of Politics in Hull in the United Kingdom, has written extensively on euthanasia in the Netherlands and in Belgium. His chapter considers the practice of euthanizing people who are 'tired of life'. The last vulnerable group to be considered in this section are people with dementia. Currently the Belgian law does not permit euthanasia of people with dementia on the basis of an advance euthanasia directive. However, this is permitted in the Netherlands and there have been repeated attempts to extend the Belgian law to cover such cases. The difficulties with such proposals are explored by Chris Gastmans, Professor of Medical Ethics at the University of Leuven.

Part IV considers conceptual or philosophical issues. Calum MacKellar, the Director of Research of the Scottish Council on Human Bioethics, explores the phenomenon of 'normalisation' applied to euthanasia in Belgium. David Albert Jones, Director of the Anscombe Bioethics Centre in Oxford and Research Fellow in Bioethics at St Mary's University, Twickenham, considers the difficulty of applying empirical data to ethically contested questions in public policy. The empirical evidence from Belgium is examined from three distinct ethical and philosophical perspectives and it is argued that this process shows convergence to a common conclusion.

A final paper in this section, by Willem Lemmens, Professor of Modern Philosophy at the University of Antwerp, returns to the example of euthanasia for patients with psychiatric disorders. This example is used to explore the relationship between autonomy and vulnerability. A genealogical reading of this issue is presented which highlights some features of the euthanasia debate as it has unfolded in Belgium. Professor Lemmens' considerations relate first to psychiatric patients. However, these considerations provoke critical observations on the Belgian euthanasia practice more generally, and have application to a much wider category of patients.

These fifteen chapters by nineteen authors include contributions from bioethicists, philosophers, lawyers and clinicians. They provide perspectives from outside as well as inside Belgium. Many are critical of some aspect of end-of-life care in Belgium but not all are opposed to medically assisted death in principle or to the Belgian law in particular. Furthermore, even among those who are opposed in principle, almost all clinicians express a willingness, albeit reluctant, to work within the system for the sake of supporting patients.

The book, therefore, represents a collection of different perspectives which are not only diverse in relation to focus and method but also in relation to the author's ethical stance on euthanasia and assisted suicide. There is no consensus view that would represent appropriately all the contributors.

As editors, we believe the book is stronger because it includes such a diversity of views. Nevertheless, the principal aim of the book is to help readers come to an overall view for themselves about what has happened in Belgium with respect to euthanasia.

The editors' own views are presented at the end as they seek to draw some clear conclusions or lessons from the chapters of the volume taken together. Social and ethical understanding rarely comes from a single argument, or a few isolated pieces of evidence, instead it is a reflective process whereby 'light dawns gradually over the whole'.

PART I

Euthanasia Legislation in Belgium and Its Applications

1

A Discussion of the Legal Rules on Euthanasia in Belgium Briefly Compared with the Rules in Luxembourg and the Netherlands

HERMAN NYS

Introduction

On 28 May 2002, the Belgian House of Representatives, the lower house of Parliament, passed the *Act Concerning Euthanasia* (2002) (the Belgian Act)[1] which had already been approved, a year earlier, by the Belgian Senate. This legislation then came into force on 23 September 2002 and has since been amended twice: by a law of 10 November 2005 (aiming at offering legal security to the pharmacist who delivers so-called *euthanatica* to be used by a physician who practices euthanasia) and by a law of 24 February 2014 to make euthanasia possible on so-called non-emancipated, capable minors. This contribution offers a description and discussion of the revised Euthanasia Act and makes, where relevant, brief comparisons with the Dutch *Termination of life on request and assisted suicide Act* (2002)(the Dutch Act)[2] and the *Act on euthanasia and medically assisted suicide* (2009) of Luxembourg (the Luxembourg Act).[3] These three countries form together the so-called Benelux. This is an economic union in Western Europe that includes three neighbouring monarchies: Belgium, the Netherlands and Luxembourg, and is particularly active in the field of intellectual property. It is a remarkable twist of fate that these

---

[1] An English translation of the original version of this Act is available in the *European Journal of Health Law*, 10.3 (2003): 239–255; it is also available in Ethical Perspectives 9 (2002)2–3: 182–188. A version, incorporating the 2014 amendments, is reproduced as an appendix to the current volume.
[2] An English translation of this Act is available in the *European Journal of Health Law*, 2001, 183–191.
[3] An English translation of this Act is available on www.sante.public.lu (Luxembourg Act on euthanasia).

three countries also have their liberal euthanasia policies in common although the legal rules on euthanasia differ sometimes in an important way as our analysis will demonstrate.

This contribution starts with a presentation of the legal definition of euthanasia and how the law relates to other end of life decisions, in particular (medically) assisted suicide. It is followed by a description of the rules concerning the two main parties involved in euthanasia: the physician and the patient. The four different scenarios that can be distinguished in the Belgian Act will then be presented and discussed. The first scenario is euthanasia practiced upon an *incurable and terminally ill adult or emancipated minor patient* who unbearably suffers physically or mentally. The second scenario is euthanasia practiced on *an incurable and terminally ill non-emancipated minor* who unbearably suffers physically. The third scenario is euthanasia practiced upon *an incurable and not yet terminally ill adult or emancipated minor patient* who experiences unbearable physical or mental suffering and the fourth and final scenario is euthanasia practiced upon *an adult or emancipated minor patient who is in a state of permanent unconsciousness.*

The discussion of each of these four scenarios will concentrate on the legal conditions regarding the validity of the request by the patient, the required health status of the patient and the legal conditions that must be respected by the physician when he or she practices euthanasia. This will be followed by a discussion of the obligation of the physician who has practiced euthanasia to notify each case to the Federal Control and Evaluation Commission on Euthanasia. The provisions regarding the conscientious objections of physicians and other health care providers will be treated and will also be discussed at the most convenient place. Throughout this contribution we will also deal briefly with possible developments in the future: particular attention will be paid to the topics that have already been, in the past, the subject of parliamentary bills introduced by members of Parliament to amend the law of 28 May 2002 but which have not been approved until now: euthanasia on patients who are in a late stage of dementia; a legal obligation for a physician who refuses to practice euthanasia to refer a patient to a colleague who is willing to do so and the validity without any limitation in time of an advance request for euthanasia. Finally, we will draw the main legal conclusions in a comparative perspective.

Practices Regulated

Euthanasia

Section 2 of the Belgian Act defines euthanasia as intentionally terminating life by another person than the person concerned, at this person's request. The definition is commonly known as the 'Dutch' definition of euthanasia because it was put forward by the Dutch State Commission on euthanasia in 1985. Ironically, the Dutch Act does not contain this definition and even the term 'euthanasia' is not mentioned. This Act always refers to 'the termination of life on request' without giving a definition of this notion. Because termination of life on request coincides with the act labelled as euthanasia in the Belgian Act, both acts have the same field of application in this respect. Moreover, section 293 §1 of the Dutch Criminal Code defines a crime that strongly resembles the definition of 'euthanasia' in the Belgian Act: a person who terminates the life of another person at that person's express and earnest request is liable to a term of imprisonment of not more than 12 years and/or a fine of the fifth category. Section 1 of the Luxembourg Act defines euthanasia basically in the same way as the Belgian Act but instead of referring in a neutral way to 'another person than the person concerned', the Luxembourg Act refers to a physician. This has no practical consequence however because under the Belgian Act only a physician may legally practice euthanasia (see later in this chapter). The conclusion is that, in this respect, the three acts have the same field of application.

Assisted Suicide

At this point, there is an important difference between the Belgian Act on the one hand and the Dutch and Luxembourg Act on the other. The Belgian Act is not applicable to assisted suicide, whereas the Dutch and the Luxembourg Acts regulate assisted suicide in the same way as euthanasia. Section 1(b) of the Dutch Act defines assisted suicide as intentionally helping another person to commit suicide or providing him or her with the means to do so as referred to in section 294, paragraph 2, second sentence, of the Criminal Code. Section 1 of the Luxembourg Act contains a comparable definition. The Belgian legislature deliberately left assisted suicide out of the field of application of the Euthanasia Act. In its advice to the Government on the proposed Act, the Council of State pointed to the fact that there is no difference in principle between euthanasia and assisted suicide and recommended to include assisted suicide in the proposed Act. Also, from within the parliamentary majority itself, different amendments have been proposed with the same purpose. By not approving these proposals, the legislature has clearly opted not to regulate assisted suicide under the same conditions as euthanasia. One motive could be that in the current state of Belgian criminal law, assisted suicide is not expressly prohibited, whereas it has been in the Netherlands for many years (section 294 of the Dutch Criminal Code). Because assisted suicide was not a (separate) crime, whereas ending another person's life, even at his/her request, was (and still is) a crime, the Belgian legislature could limit itself to regulating euthanasia. However, this reasoning can easily be reversed: because assisted suicide is not a crime and the difference between euthanasia and assisted suicide is minimal, both should be submitted to the same legal norms and procedures to prevent physicians from using assisted suicide to circumvent the detailed legal procedure that regulates euthanasia. Regulating euthanasia and assisted suicide under the same conditions is exactly the position taken by the Luxembourg legislature although aiding suicide is not prohibited expressly in Luxembourg criminal law, just as it is not prohibited expressly in Belgium. The status of assisted suicide by a physician in Belgium remains legally ambiguous, to say the least. To complicate things even more the Federal Control and Evaluation Commission on Euthanasia (FCECE or Commission), established by the Euthanasia Act (see later in this chapter), in its first biannual evaluation report, published in September 2004, stated that it considered assisted suicide to fall within the definition of euthanasia and consequently under the Euthanasia Act (FCECE 2004). The Commission would consider a reported case of assisted suicide as a legitimate case of euthanasia if all the conditions of the Euthanasia Act are respected. According to the Commission, assisted suicide can be regarded as falling under the Act because the Act does not define the means to be used to practice euthanasia nor does it define exactly how the drugs should come into the patient's body. Although this is as such a correct statement, the legal conclusion the Commission draws from it is manifestly wrong: the Act clearly requires *that another person than the patient himself or herself* has to intentionally shorten the life of the patient (see the definition of euthanasia in the Belgium Act). If it is the patient him- or herself who shortens his or her life with the aid of a physician, this condition is not fulfilled and the Euthanasia Act cannot be applicable. It is odd that a

Commission that is only competent to control and evaluate the practice of euthanasia is also interpreting the rules as if it were a court.

Other 'Life-Shortening Medical Action'

None of the three acts on euthanasia in the Benelux countries regulate other forms of life-shortening medical actions, such as pain relief and withholding or withdrawing life-prolonging treatment. This has attracted some criticism: since euthanasia can be camouflaged as pain control, any official supervision of euthanasia is impossible if not all end-of-life decisions and actions are regulated. The question is whether such broad supervision is viable in practice, since it would possibly lead to an unmanageable bureaucracy that defeats its purpose. The best way of remedying this would, apparently, be to guarantee patient autonomy through the enactment of legislation on patients' rights. The three countries all approved an Act protecting the rights of patients that is applicable to all other life-shortening medical actions other than euthanasia and assisted suicide.

Persons Regulated

The Physician

According to section 3 §1 (dealing with the so-called [actual] request for euthanasia) and section 4 §2 (dealing with the so-called [advance] directive for euthanasia) of the Belgian Act, *the physician* who performs euthanasia 'does not commit a criminal offence' when the norms and procedures prescribed by this Act have been followed. This has two important legal implications: first, euthanasia remains in principle a crime, and second, only a physician may practice euthanasia which is not an offence if he or she ensures that all the legal conditions are respected. Section 293 of the Dutch Criminal Code, amended by section 20 of the Dutch Act, provides that terminating another person's life at this person's request is not a criminal offence if it is committed by *a physician* who fulfils the due care criteria set out in section 2 of this Act. In Luxembourg, the requirement that euthanasia must be practiced by a physician is already included in the definition of euthanasia (supra). Moreover, section 2 of the Luxembourg Act repeats this requirement. The three acts have in common that they reserve euthanasia to the medical profession as a legal monopoly. An interesting point of discussion is what conclusion can be drawn regarding the legal status of euthanasia from the requirement that euthanasia must be practiced by a physician. In the Netherlands, there is a consensus among health-care lawyers that euthanasia is not a 'normal medical act', although it must be administered by a physician. In Belgium, there is much more discussion on the legal status of euthanasia in this regard. Some regard it as a 'normal medical act' and the legal requirement that euthanasia be performed by a physician is used as an argument for this point of view. This argument is not very convincing: if euthanasia is a normal medical act, then, according to the Act governing the practice of medicine, only a physician may perform it. So, the explicit requirement in the Euthanasia Act would have been superfluous in that case. This dispute masks a more fundamental discussion regarding the obligation of a physician who refuses to practice euthanasia to refer the patient to a physician who is in principle willing to do this. I will come back later to this issue.

None of the three acts requires additional conditions regarding the physician who performs euthanasia: he or she need not be the patient's treating physician nor is any special knowledge (in the field of palliative care, for instance) explicitly required. What can make a difference in this respect is that one of the due care criteria provided for in the Dutch Act is that the physician has terminated the patient's life 'with due medical care and attention'. The Belgian and the Luxembourg Act do not contain such a prescription. It was debated in the Belgian parliament but the majority considered such a requirement superfluous since a physician is always required to exercise due medical care.

Section 14 of the Belgian Act and section 15 of the Luxembourg Act expressly provides that no physician is under an obligation to practice euthanasia (and assisted suicide in Luxembourg); a physician may always refuse to practice euthanasia on grounds of conscience or for medical reasons. In such a case, however, the physician must inform the patient or the 'person of confidence' of the patient (see later in this chapter), within a reasonable time (according to the Belgian Act) or within 24 hours (according to the Luxembourg Act) of his refusal and explain the reasons to refuse to practice euthanasia. If the physician's refusal is based on medical grounds, then it must be noted in the patient's medical record. Moreover, at the request of the patient or his or her 'person of confidence', the refusing physician must transmit the patient's medical record to the physician appointed by the patient or his or her 'person of confidence'. Also, in the Netherlands, it is generally accepted that a physician may refuse to practice euthanasia although the Dutch Act does not explicitly provide for this. The Dutch parliamentary proceedings – though not the Dutch Act itself – establish that in such a case a duty exists to refer the patient to another physician. Neither in Belgium nor in Luxembourg does a legal duty to refer to another physician exist in the status of the law. In Belgium, section 27 of the Act governing the practice of medicine provides for a so-called obligation to guarantee the continuity of care by physicians: if a physician is not able to guarantee the continuity of care him- or herself, he or she should guarantee that another physician takes over the responsibility for the patient. Those who consider euthanasia as a 'normal medical act' because it should be practiced by a physician believe this obligation to guarantee the continuity of care also obliges a physician who refuses to practice euthanasia to refer the patient requesting euthanasia to a colleague who is in principle willing to practice it. However, exactly because euthanasia cannot be regarded in legal terms as a 'normal medical act', different political parties have in the past introduced bills in the Belgian Parliament to amend the Euthanasia Act to impose a referral duty upon refusing physicians. But until now, none of these bills have been able to find a majority in Parliament to approve them.

Apart from providing that no physician is under an obligation to practice euthanasia, section 14 of the Belgian Act and section 15 of the Luxembourg Act also stipulate that 'no other person may be compelled to assist' in practicing euthanasia (and assisted suicide in Luxembourg). The Dutch Act does not contain such an explicit prohibition but it is a generally accepted policy.

The Patient

In this paragraph, we will discuss only the legal status of the patient requesting euthanasia. His or her required health status will be dealt with below. The question is whether not only adults but also minors can express a valid request.

I start with the Luxembourg Act because it is the strictest and therefore also the simplest of the three acts with regard to the person who can request euthanasia: only an adult patient (which means having reached the age of 18 years or older; see section 2.1 of the Luxembourg Act for euthanasia following an [actual] request and section 3.1. following an [advance]directive).

In Belgium, the situation was from the very beginning more complicated. In the original version of the Belgian Act (2002), minors did not have the right to request euthanasia. This was a deliberate choice by the legislature since the subject of euthanasia for minors turned out to be so controversial during the parliamentary proceedings that including it would have threatened approval of the euthanasia bill entirely. And although both the Committee for Public Health of the Chamber of Representatives, which wrote an advisory report for the Chamber Commission of Justice, and the Order of Physicians (comparable with the General Medical Council in the United Kingdom) were critical of the exclusion of minors from the euthanasia bill, this did not lead to any amendments of the bill. However, as a kind of compromise between the proponents and the opponents of giving minors a right to request euthanasia the so-called emancipated minors were given this right. Given the specific legal status of 'emancipated minors', this is, however, only an apparent exception to the rule that only adults have the right to request euthanasia. Emancipation of a minor (which has become a very exceptional procedure) requires a decision by a judge and results in the biological minor becoming legally an adult with (almost) all the rights of an adult person: the emancipated minor becomes 'the master over himself'. (Foreign writers not acquainted with Belgian law have misunderstood the concept of *emancipated minor* which is a narrowly circumscribed legal notion in Belgian law, by mixing it up with the purely factual notion of mature minor [Khorrami 2003; Cohen-Almagor 2009a]. Cohen-Almagor refers to personal communications with nonlegally trained Belgian academics who 'explained' that *emancipated minors* 'relates to boundary cases of 16–17-year-old patients' and 'that the legislators made the phrase vague on purpose, as a matter of principle, in order to defend the autonomy of as young patients as possible'.) Ironically, also without an explicit reference to emancipated minors in the Euthanasia Act, they would have the right to request euthanasia, given their legal status as adults. Until now no cases of euthanasia practiced on an emancipated minor have been reported to the FCECE. As already stated, the 24 February 2014 law has amended the Belgian Act to give a (non-emancipated) minor the right to request euthanasia. Also, his or her parents should agree with this request (see later in this chapter for more details on this). The amended Act does not provide for a minimal age but the minor must be 'factually capable' of making a valid request for euthanasia.

From this perspective, the Dutch Act is completely different, as can be seen from section 2, §3 and 4 of the Act. If a minor aged between 16 and 18 is deemed to have a reasonable understanding of his or her own interests in the matter, then he or she can submit a legitimate request for euthanasia if, at least, the parent(s) (or the legal guardian) who exercise authority over the minor are included in the decision process. Moreover, if a minor patient aged between 12 and 16 is deemed to have a reasonable understanding of his or her own interests in the matter, then the physician may consent to the minor patient's request if the parent(s) (or guardian) who exercise authority over the minor are able to reconcile themselves with the request.

None of the three laws contain requirements regarding the nationality of the person requesting euthanasia in one of the three countries nor regarding his/her domicile. However, so-called euthanasia tourism to these countries has not been reported until now.

Different Scenarios of Euthanasia Being Regulated

Euthanasia after an [Actual] Request on a Terminally Ill Adult Patient or Emancipated Minor Patient (Section 3, §1–§2 Belgian Act)

A physician who practices euthanasia (which will be abbreviated as 'the physician' or 'the attending physician') must ensure that the patient is legally competent and conscious at the moment of making the request. There is some controversy whether the patient must still be conscious at the moment that euthanasia is practiced. This is not explicitly provided for in the Act and therefore the FCECE concluded that this is not required. Once again, the Commission is doing more than just controlling and evaluating the application of the Act by giving this rather liberal interpretation.

The Act regulates in detail the formal and material requirements for a request. Such a request must be 'voluntary', 'well-considered' and 'repeated'. Moreover, it must not be 'the result of any external pressure'. The reference to 'external pressure' adds almost nothing, since any request that is the result of external pressure cannot, by definition, be considered voluntary. It is not clear what 'repeated' here means exactly, other than that the request should be made more than once. Section 3 further stipulates that the physician must verify that the request is 'persistent', ascertaining this by means of several discussions. The question arises how the physician can verify whether the request is still 'persistent' before he or she practices euthanasia when the patient is no longer conscious at that moment. For this reason, the viewpoint of the FCECE in this regard is questionable. Section 3 further provides that the physician must inform the patient beforehand about his or her state of health and his or her life expectancy, discuss with the patient his or her request for euthanasia and discuss any remaining therapeutic options including those offered by palliative care, as well as their consequences. Finally, the request must be in writing. In principle, a request must be drafted, dated and signed by the patient himself. It is not required that he or she has written it by hand; it can be typed or written on a computer and printed out. If, because of a physical disability, for example, the patient is incapable of writing down the request, then it is to be written down by an adult person who has been chosen by the patient and who has no material interest in the patient's death. This person must record the fact that the patient is not able to formulate the request in writing, and give the reasons why. In such a case, drafting the request must take place in the presence of the physician, and the person drafting it must record the name of the physician in the document. The patient's request must be appended to his or her medical record. The patient may revoke the request at any time, in which case it must be removed from the medical record and returned to the patient.

Section 3 of the Belgian Act further requires that the physician ascertains that the patient who makes a request is in a 'medically hopeless situation' characterised by 'persistent and unbearable physical or mental suffering that cannot be alleviated' which is the result of a 'serious and incurable disorder caused by illness or accident'. This requirement provoked copious and confused debates in the Belgian Parliament.

One can distinguish a more objective and a more subjective element in this requirement. The more objective element is that a patient must suffer from a 'disorder' that is of a *serious* and *incurable* nature and caused by illness or accident. The Act makes no distinction between disorders of a physical or mental nature or origin. This, combined with the fact that mental suffering without physical suffering in this scenario is a sufficient condition, has led recently to the relatively common acceptance of euthanasia on the request of psychiatric patients. This demonstrates that the Act contains a certain dynamic, making practices possible that were considered as being prohibited when the Euthanasia Bill was discussed in Parliament. Indeed, the president of Chamber Commission of Justice (Fred Erdman, a respected lawyer belonging to the Flemish socialist party) concluded that psychiatric patients would never be entitled to ask for euthanasia because mental suffering is not compatible with the condition of a free and voluntary expression of will (Chamber Commission of Justice). Of course from a legal point of view, this was mistaken because a mental illness does not automatically make someone incompetent to make valid legal decisions. Also, this broader medical practice is not *contra legem per se;* it rather brings to surface the dynamics and flexibility of the terms used in the Belgian Act and the role played in the interpretation of them by the medical profession. Moreover, the notion of 'incurable disorder' seems less objective than one might think at first glance. The Act does not require a patient to undergo alternative treatment if this is available. It stipulates only that the physician must *discuss* with the patient 'his request for euthanasia and any *remaining* therapeutic options, including that of palliative care'. One might conclude from this that the patient may refuse a treatment with the result that his or her disorder becomes 'incurable'. A physician could then legitimately agree to such a patient's euthanasia request. The sole objective requirement of the Act – of a serious and incurable condition caused by accident or illness – could in this way, in effect, be created by the patient. Of course, when a patient refuses a standard treatment for his or her disorder so that it becomes incurable, any physician may for medical reasons refuse to practice euthanasia on him or her. Consenting to a request from a patient for whom there is still a genuine treatment alternative might, from such a perspective, be considered a non-subsidiary or disproportionate action on the part of the physician, given the existence of other treatment possibilities.

Regarding the persistent and unbearable physical or mental suffering that cannot be alleviated it is the patient, and the patient alone, who determines whether he or she is suffering from it. The physician's task is simply to be certain that *the patient finds him- or herself* in such a situation.

Before carrying out a request for euthanasia, the physician must consult another physician regarding the serious and incurable nature of the patient's condition, and inform him or her of the reason for such a consultation. A negative opinion towards euthanasia of the physician who is consulted is not binding. The physician consulted must be independent both of the patient and of the consulting physician and he or she must be qualified to assess the patient's condition. In principle, every doctor is legally competent, but the term is also used here in the sense of professionally competent. The French version of the Belgian Euthanasia Act uses the term 'compétent', which encompasses both meanings. He or she must review the medical record, examine the patient and make sure that the patient's suffering is persistent and unbearable and cannot be alleviated in another way. He or she must make a written report of his or her findings. The attending physician must inform the patient of the results of the consultation. If nurses are in regular contact with the patient, then the patient's request must be discussed with them as well. Should the patient so desire, the request must also be discussed with relatives or friends whom the patient indicates. Of course, the opinions of the relatives or friends consulted are not determinative of the legitimacy of euthanasia. But this does not prevent the physician from being influenced by these opinions in deciding whether to agree to a euthanasia request. Once euthanasia has been practiced the physician must offer the possibility of psychological assistance to all persons concerned.

Finally, section 3 §2 allows the physician to require additional conditions next to the legal conditions. For instance, he or she can require the patient to consult a physician with special experience in palliative care. There is no evidence whether and how this possibility is used in practice.

Section 2 of the Luxembourg Act is almost literally a copy of section 3 §1 and § 2 of the Belgian Act in this regard (with a notable exception being that the possibility to require additional conditions does not exist in the Luxembourg Act). It is, however, too early to make comparisons regarding the application in practice between both acts.

The Dutch Act, by contrast, is much more concise. According to section 2.1., the attending physician must:

- be satisfied that the patient has made a voluntary and carefully considered request;
- be satisfied that the patient's suffering is unbearable and that there was no prospect of improvement;
- have informed the patient about his or her situation and prospects;
- have concluded that there is no reasonable alternative in the light of the patient's situation;
- have consulted at least one other, independent physician, who must have seen the patient and given a written opinion on the due care criteria already mentioned;
- and have terminated the patient's life or aided with suicide with due medical care and attention.

Euthanasia after an [Actual] Request on a Terminally Ill Non-Emancipated, Factually Competent Minor Patient (Section 3, §1–2 Belgian Act)

As already stated, the 24 February 2014 law has amended the Euthanasia Act in Belgium to make it possible for a non-emancipated minor who is factually competent of making a valid request for euthanasia, to express such a request. When this happened, all the conditions that have been presented under III a) must be respected. But there are some important different and additional conditions. The most important difference relates to the medical condition of the minor patient: he or she should be in a medically futile condition of constant and unbearable physical suffering (the Act makes no mention here of mental suffering which means that mental suffering alone is never a sufficient condition in this scenario) that cannot be alleviated and that results from a serious, incurable disorder caused by illness or accident *that will cause death within a short period of time.* Moreover, the following additional conditions must be respected by the attending physician. He or she must consult with a psychiatrist or psychologist specialised in child or youth psychiatry to verify the factual capability of the minor to make a valid request (section 3 §2,7°) (The Constitutional Court decided in a judgment of 29 October 2015 that the result of this consultation is binding for the attending physician). Apart from the written request of the minor, the written agreement of both of his or her parents is also required (article 3 §4). Until now two cases of euthanasia practiced on a non-emancipated minor have been reported to the FCECE.

In this regard, the three acts of the Benelux countries differ substantially: the Luxembourg Act does not allow euthanasia on minors; the Belgian Act allows the practice but requires stricter conditions than with adults; sections 2.3 and 2.4 of the Dutch Act enable euthanasia on minors under the same conditions as adults (with the involvement, however, of the parents in the decision-making process; see earlier in this chapter).

Euthanasia after an [Actual] Request on a Non-Terminally Ill
Adult Patient or Emancipated Minor Patient
(Section 3, §1–§2 Belgian Act)

If the attending physician believes that a patient is not going to die within a foreseeable period (which is, in practice, called non-terminally ill) he or she must, apart from respecting the conditions mentioned under III a), fulfil two additional requirements. First, he must consult a *second* physician, who is a psychiatrist or a specialist in the condition in question, and inform him or her of the reason for such a consultation. This second physician must then review the medical record of the patient, examine him or her and make certain of the persistent and unbearable physical or mental suffering which cannot be alleviated, as well as the voluntary, well-considered and repeated nature of the request. This physician must also report on his or her findings, and must be independent of the patient, of the attending physician and of the first physician consulted. In this case as well, the attending physician is obliged to inform the patient of the results of this consultation. Second, in the case of a non-terminally ill patient, at least one month must elapse between the patient's request and the act of euthanasia. This scenario is not applicable in the case of a non-emancipated minor patient (see second scenario).

Regarding euthanasia on a non-terminally ill adult patient, the Belgian Act contains two additional requirements; the Dutch and the Luxembourg Acts, however, do not make this distinction between terminally ill and non-terminally ill patients: in both cases the same requirements must be respected.

Euthanasia after an (Advance) Directive (Section 4 Belgian Act)

Article 4 of the Euthanasia Act regulates in detail the formal requirements for a valid advance directive for euthanasia. An advance request may be drafted at any time by an adult person or an emancipated minor to address the situation when he or she is no longer able to express his or her will. The latter may not be misunderstood. It does not mean that euthanasia may be practiced after a directive when the author is no longer able to express his or her will. The patient must moreover be irreversibly unconscious. In the directive, one or more 'person(s) of confidence' can be designated in order of preference, who inform(s) the attending physician about the patient's will. Each person of confidence replaces his or her predecessor as mentioned in the directive in the case of refusal, hindrance, incompetence or death. The patient's attending physician, the physician consulted and the members of the nursing team may not act as persons of confidence. The directive must be drafted in the presence of two adult witnesses, at least one of whom has no material interest in the patient's death, and it must be dated and signed by the author, by the witnesses and by the patient's person of confidence, if any has been appointed in the request. The directive may be modified or revoked at any time. If a person who wishes to draft a directive is permanently physically incapable of doing so, he or she may appoint an adult who has no material interest in his or her death to write down his or her request, in the presence of two adult witnesses, at least one of whom has no material interest in his or her death. The directive must note that the person concerned is incapable of signing the document and give the reasons why. The directive must be dated and signed by the person who writes it down, by the witnesses and by the person(s) of confidence, if any, of the person concerned. A medical certificate is to be appended to the directive as proof that the author is permanently physically incapable of writing and signing it.

Finally, the Euthanasia Act provides that a directive is only valid 'if it has been drafted or confirmed fewer than five years before the moment at which the person in question can no longer express his wishes'. Section 3 of the Royal Decree of 3 April 2003 more clearly stipulates that a directive must be confirmed within five years to remain valid. Several bills have been introduced in Parliament to prolong the term of validity of the directive until 10 years or even to make a directive valid for an undetermined term but, until now, none have been approved in Parliament. The annex to the Royal Decree of 3 April 2003 contains a model advance directive for euthanasia. There is, however, no requirement to use this model. The Euthanasia Act has delegated to the Crown the competence to regulate the way a directive is registered and made available to the physicians concerned. These rules are laid down in the Royal Decree of 27 April 2007. Only directives made according to the model annexed to the Royal Decree of 3 April 2003 can be registered by the local authorities of the place where the person concerned has drafted a directive. These authorities are obliged to register the directive and transmit it to a database kept at the Ministry of Health. The attending physician of a patient, who is no longer able to express his or her will and who might be eligible for euthanasia according to the conditions laid down in section 4 of the Euthanasia Act, should consult the register after due identification and authorisation.

Section 4 of the Act contains specific requirements regarding the patient's state of health who has made up a directive: the patient must be affected by a serious and incurable condition caused by accident or illness and he or she must be 'irreversibly unconscious according to the current state of science'. In this scenario, there is no requirement of unbearable physical or mental suffering, since the legislature assumes that patients who are irreversibly unconscious are no longer capable of suffering. Had such a requirement been imposed, the fear was that euthanasia in such cases would have been impossible in practice. There is a consensus in Belgium that 'irreversibly unconscious' has a very limited meaning and is synonymous to the so-called persistent vegetative state (PVS). Also, this scenario is the result of a compromise between members of the majority who were in favour of euthanasia after a directive and those who opposed it: the proponents obtained recognition of the validity of an advance directive in the Act while the opponents saw the field of application of the directive reduced to an almost symbolic significance. There is also a consensus nowadays that patients in a late stage of dementia are not irreversibly unconscious so that euthanasia practiced on these patients, who made up a directive, remains prohibited in Belgian law. In the past, several bills have been introduced in Parliament by different political parties to broaden the field of application of a directive but, until now, without any success. One of the reasons for this lack of success is that the political parties that favour a change of the Act in this respect, have different opinions on how to formulate the broader scope.

Regarding euthanasia after a directive, the Luxembourg Act is almost a copy of the Belgian Act. The Dutch Law, however, differs importantly from the Belgian Act because it does not require for specific conditions regarding the health status of the patient in case of a directive: section 2.2 that deals with the directive states that 'the due care criteria referred to in section 2.1 (that regulates the request) shall apply *mutatis mutandis*'. This means that the potential field of application of a directive is much broader in the Netherlands than in Belgium and Luxembourg and encompasses patients in a later stage of dementia. Another difference is that a minor aged 16 or over can make up a directive for euthanasia in the Netherlands. This is not possible in Belgium or Luxembourg. A final difference is that the Dutch Act does not limit the validity of a directive to a determined period (unlike the Belgian and Luxembourg Act: five years), making it valid in principle for an undetermined period.

The Reporting Procedure

Section 5 of the Belgian Euthanasia Act stipulates that a physician who has performed euthanasia must complete a registration document and submit it within four working days after the act of euthanasia to the FCECE. By virtue of section 8 of the Act, the Commission must review the completed registration document, which consists of a non-anonymous and an anonymous part, and determine based on the anonymous section of the registration document whether or not the euthanasia was performed in accordance with the conditions and procedures provided for in the Act. The Commission – which is composed of 16 members (eight physicians, four lawyers and four members 'from groups charged with the problem of incurably ill patients') – can, in cases of doubt, decide by simple majority to suspend anonymity. The Commission must then inspect the non-anonymous part of the registration document. The Commission may request from the attending physician any part of the patient's medical record that concerns the euthanasia. The Commission must pronounce judgement on the matter within two months. If the Commission holds, in a decision taken by a two-thirds majority, that the conditions provided for in the Act have not been fulfilled, it must refer the dossier to the public prosecutor of the jurisdiction in which the patient died. Until recently this had not yet taken place; on 27 October 2015 the Commission referred unanimously a case to the public prosecutor of Antwerp. The reporting procedure in the Luxembourg Act is inspired by the procedure in the Belgian Act and only differs in some details (e.g., the composition of the Commission).

Chapter III of the Dutch Act establishes 'regional review committees for the termination of life on request and assisted suicide' of which five are currently functioning. They were already set up in 1998 and comprise three members each (and three substitutes): a physician, an expert in ethical questions and a lawyer, the latter acting as chair. If euthanasia or assisted suicide is performed, the physician in question submits a report to the review committee in his or her region. This committee is tasked with reviewing compliance with the due care requirements as provided for in the Dutch Act. The committee's motivated judgment, taken by simple majority vote, must be communicated to the physician within six weeks. Either the committee or the physician may request the judgement to be clarified. In the event of a negative judgment, the committee must notify the public prosecutor as well as the health inspectorate.

There are many striking similarities between the Belgian and Luxembourg Acts, on the one hand, and the Dutch Act, on the other, regarding the reporting procedure. In both systems only suspicious cases are referred to the public prosecutor and the reporting committees function as a kind of buffer between physician and prosecutor, based on the idea that a physician does not want to (nor should) be dealt with in an atmosphere of criminality. The intention, of course, is to make the reporting rate as optimal as possible. Also, in both systems the public prosecutor's office is still empowered to launch an independent investigation in accordance with that authority's autonomy. There are, however, also several striking differences. The Dutch reporting procedure builds on the physician's duty to report suspected deaths, which existed long before there was any talk of regulating euthanasia. A similar duty to report suspected deaths has never existed in Belgium. Indeed, Belgium is

notorious for the high number of exhumations that take place, probably
due to the lack of an efficient system for registering deaths. Moreover,
whereas it is accepted in the Netherlands that euthanasia is not a natural
death, in Belgium this is not the case at all. Section 15 of the Belgian Act
states that a person who dies because of euthanasia performed in accordance with the conditions established by the Act, is *deemed* to have died a
natural death for the purposes of the execution of any contracts to which
he or she was party, in particular insurance contracts. Also, the administrative organisation of the Belgian Federal Commission is not without
problems. Can one Commission composed of 16 non-fulltime members
possibly give serious consideration to all the files, especially now that
there are a few thousand per year? Finally, compared to the Dutch
regional committees, the Belgian Commission is working in a non-
transparent climate.

Conclusions

Our analysis of the Belgian Act on euthanasia is based on the provisions
of the Act itself, in a permanent confrontation with its homologues in
Luxembourg and the Netherlands. A first and superficial look on the Acts
regulating euthanasia in the three Benelux countries may give an impression of great similarity between them. Indeed, on closer inspection, this
first impression corresponds with the law in the books in Belgium and
Luxembourg. This is not surprising because it is crystal clear that the
Belgian Act was a model for the Luxembourg legislature when drafting
the Euthanasia Act. French being one of the official languages in both
countries makes this more understandable. Belgium and Luxembourg
were also in a very comparable position when they started to debate the
legalisation of euthanasia: both countries had (and still have) no case law
regarding euthanasia that could be used as building blocks for an Act on
euthanasia, as was the case in the Netherlands. That also made the
Belgian Act, with its detailed and extensive regulations, a much more
attractive model for the Luxembourg legislature than the Dutch Act to
achieve the optimal legal certainty for physicians, patients and society.
Nevertheless, when comparing the original version of the Belgian Act
with its Luxembourg counterpart there are two striking differences:
assisted suicide (not covered by the Belgian law) and euthanasia when
the patient is not terminally ill, in which case the Belgian Act requires
additional conditions to be respected. However, with the recent amendment of the Belgian Act giving non-emancipated minors a right to

request euthanasia, the difference between both Acts is now wider than before. To my knowledge there is no intention in Luxembourg to adopt the Belgian model in this respect. This recent amendment of the Belgium Act has brought it more in line with the Dutch Act although, at the same time, it reinforced the existing differences because the Dutch Act requires a minimal age while the Belgian Act does not. The same norms and procedures for euthanasia or assisted suicide in case of terminally and non-terminally ill patients; the same norms and procedures for euthanasia or assisted suicide practiced on adults and minors (except for the involvement of parents/guardian in the latter case); the same norms and procedures for euthanasia or aiding suicide after an (actual) request and for euthanasia after an (advance) directive, this all makes the Dutch Act much less detailed and complex than the Belgian one. To make it more concrete: for a, hopefully, clear oversight of the Belgian Act, I needed to distinguish four scenarios; for the Dutch Act, two scenarios would have sufficed. This all taken together with the deficient transparency of the Belgian procedure to evaluate and to control the practice of euthanasia underpins my conclusion that the acts are not comparable in their details. And as everyone knows: the devil is in the details.

The Belgian Experience of Euthanasia
Since Its Legal Implementation in 2002

ETIENNE MONTERO

Introduction

The questions raised by the prospect of life's end are complex and delicate. It would take many words to express how deeply aware I am that situations exist of great suffering, where patients cannot take it any longer, feel cast down, sometimes humiliated by painful symptoms of their disease, tired of living in conditions that have become unbearable in their eyes – and they are tempted to 'end it all' and ask for euthanasia. We should also add to this the occasional burnout of health professionals and the physical and emotional exhaustion of families. Unfortunately, it is not possible in a few pages to treat the subject comprehensively with the appropriate sensitivity and subtlety it demands.

This chapter focuses on a single question: What lessons can we learn, with respect to the legal standpoint, from a review of euthanasia 'in action' since 2002, as we have lived and practised it in Belgium? (see Montero 2013 for other matters and references). This question can be reformulated as follows: Have the strict legal conditions laid down in 2002 for euthanasia been rigorously respected and is this practice under control?

Sources and Method

To maximise objectivity, I am basing my remarks primarily on figures, data, findings, statements and analysis drawn from scientific studies and mainly official documents such as the text of the Belgian Act on euthanasia, the (extensive) preparatory parliamentary work for the Act and the reports of the Federal Control and Evaluation Commission on Euthanasia (hereinafter, FCECE or 'Commission'). Another source is the direct testimony of protagonists who have spoken out on television or in the press before being euthanised, thus *providing first-hand information*. These cases, and the resulting comments made by the members of the FCECE, are enlightening in that they illustrate the interpretation of certain legal conditions in the Commission's reports.

Lastly, to provide an overview of the movement that has been emerging in Belgium since the inception of the Act on euthanasia, I will discuss the status of the numerous new legislative initiatives aimed at relaxing or extending this Act that have passed into law or are currently before Parliament.

As for the working methodology, it consists in a *comparison* between, on the one hand, the text (the letter) of the Act on euthanasia (2002) and the statements made before drafting the law during preparatory parliamentary proceedings which reveal the intentions of Parliament, and, on the other hand, interpretations and assessments of the Commission, which has published a report every two years beginning in 2004.

Accordingly, this study is split into two parts. The first examines whether the path to euthanasia is adequately signposted in Belgium and its application strictly controlled according to the criteria established by the Act on euthanasia. The second part probes the sense and logic of the resulting observations and analysis.

Interpretation and Control of the Legal Requirements for Euthanasia

This section covers eight topics. First, I will show that the control system is questionable and that several requirements are in fact uncontrollable (1). Then, I will discuss how the FCECE interprets two fundamental conditions of the law: the requirement of 'a serious and incurable disorder' (2) and the requirement of 'physical or mental suffering' (3). Other developments and trends can still be identified: the factual decriminalisation of physician-assisted suicide (4), the increasingly official evolution from exception to 'legal right' (5) and the trend to question the 'conscience clause' and the health care institution's freedom (6). As we shall see, the extension of the Act on euthanasia to minors is already a reality since 2014 (7). Finally, we will give some indications about the (possible) future by examining several proposals regarding euthanasia (or ending of life) for the mentally incompetent (8).

About the Reliability of the Control Mechanism

We should begin by assessing the efficiency and reliability of the control mechanism.

First, it is obvious that a control system, which operates after the fact [*a posteriori*], is not capable of protecting patients against euthanasia procedures that violate the statutory conditions. The monitoring is based on self-reporting; it depends completely on trusting information supplied by the physician who has carried out the euthanasia. It is at best naive to assert that physicians will report their own failure to comply with the fundamental conditions or procedures prescribed by law. It is more likely that a physician will fail to report euthanasia that did not meet the statutory conditions or will report them in such a way that he or she cannot be faulted.

In successive reports, the Commission confesses to feeling powerless: it states quite realistically that it does not have the ability of assessing the number of reported euthanasia cases versus the number of euthanasia cases actually performed (FCECE, First report 2004, p. 14; Second report 2006, p. 22; Third report 2008, p. 22; Fourth report 2010, p. 22; Fifth report 2012, p. 14; Sixth report 2014, p. 14). In this regard, independent research carried out in Flanders presents evidence of around 50 per cent underreporting (Chambaere et al. 2015a). This figure confirms what had already been observed in earlier research (Cohen-Almagor 2013[1]; Cohen et al. 2012[2]; Smets et al. 2010[3]; Chambaere et al. 2008[4]).

Yet, in 2002, the goal of taking euthanasia out of the shadows was a strong argument made by those who were in favour of its decriminalisation. Ever since its first official report, the Commission stated that it is 'aware of the limitations of the controls on the enforcement of the Act of 22 May 2002, which control is the Commission's task'. The Commission acknowledges that: 'It is clear that the effectiveness of its [the Commission's] mission relies, on the one hand, on medical professionals' compliance with the requirement to report performed cases of euthanasia and, on the other hand, on how these reports are prepared' (FCECE, First report 2004, p. 23). In other words, the Commission sees only what the physicians it oversees decide to show it. One should not be surprised that in 15 years, only one single case has been taken to the public prosecutor. This case concerns an old lady who was euthanised on June 2015 for 'reactive depression' (she had lost her daughter three months before). The last days of Simona were filmed by an Australian journalist who

---

[1] 50 per cent of euthanasia cases allegedly are not reported.
[2] 73 per cent of euthanasia cases were reported by Flemish physicians to the FCECE, whereas 58 per cent of cases by their Walloon counterparts.
[3] Approximately 50 per cent of euthanasia cases reported in Flanders.
[4] 53 per cent of euthanasia cases were reported in Flanders.

THE BELGIAN EXPERIENCE OF EUTHANASIA 29

made a documentary on euthanasia in Belgium broadcasted on SBS News Channel ('Belgian euthanasia doctor could face criminal charges' 2015). It is evident that the media coverage of the Australian documentary has influenced the unanimous decision of the FCECE to communicate the case to justice and that this case is only the visible part of the iceberg.

A second observation concerns the practical impossibility for the Commission to verify whether most of the 'strict legal conditions' for euthanasia have been met. Several examples suffice to illustrate this.

How can we verify after the act of euthanasia that the request was fully voluntary, well-thought-out and not due to external pressure? Many people who live in situations of chronic suffering express two opposite wishes: to live and to die, to obtain relief or to 'end it all'. How can we be sure that they received support not just for their wish to die? Obviously, we cannot control that the information on diagnosis, prognosis, possible treatments and options provided as part of palliative care is accurate and complete, and was provided in an appropriate climate of dialogue and empathy.

Similarly, we cannot verify and be sure that the physician who agrees to a request to perform euthanasia, the second physician consulted and especially the members of the Commission really are able to take the full measure of the constraints and pressures, including the subconscious ones that most patients face.

It also seems impossible, in practice, to verify that the compulsory consultation of a second physician does not become a routine performed for form's sake [pro forma] with physicians who are particularly open to the practice of euthanasia, which is necessarily the case for EOL (End-of-Life Doctors) and LEIF (LevensEinde [End-of-Life] Information Forum) to whom recourse is usual?[5] In fact, not all physicians are convinced of the usefulness of a second opinion, and it sometimes happens that it is not requested or that euthanasia is performed despite a negative opinion (Cohen et al. 2012[6]; Cohen-Almagor 2013[7]).

---

[5] The forum EOL was created in 2003 in the French Community of Belgium, as an initiative and with the logistical support of the *Association pour le Droit de Mourir dans la Dignité* (ADMD) [Association for the Right to Die with Dignity], which campaigns for the right to euthanasia. LEIF is the Flemish counterpart of EOL, which arose from the RWS association (Flemish counterpart of ADMD).

[6] 55 per cent of the physicians in Wallonia and 71 per cent of those in Flanders find it useful to consult a second physician.

[7] In 35 per cent of the cases, the opinion of the second independent physician was apparently not solicited and in 23 per cent of the cases, euthanasia apparently was performed despite a dissenting opinion.

These remarks may appear perfectionist. Perhaps it is possible to believe that all legislation may be affected by the difficulty of identifying unlawful activity. It is true but, in this matter, the issue is especially serious for two reasons. The first is as follows: it was clear in 2002 that euthanasia loses its criminal character only *through exceptions* and *lax legal conditions*. During the parliamentary discussion and public debate, it has been stated again and again that the legal requirements were extremely strict. If this were not the case, the Bill would probably not have won a parliamentary majority in 2002. The control of legal conditions is fundamental for a second reason. The Act on euthanasia is unusual and even quite unique: it means considering as lawful an act that in principle is criminal if and only if the requirements are met. Any good lawyer knows that legal conditions that cannot objectively be verified are not true conditions.

The Requirement of a Serious and Incurable Disorder

To access euthanasia, the patient must manifest a *serious and incurable disorder* caused by illness or injury.[8] Such a condition seems objective and verifiable. However, the notion of 'incurable disorder' is imprecise and not defined, and the list of incurable diseases is practically endless such as diabetes, rheumatism, arthritis, heart failure, emphysema, chronic bronchitis, chronic renal failure and hepatitis (e.g., Hearing of Prof. W. Distelmans, Appendix to the Report of the Joint Commissions for Justice and Social Affairs 2002, p. 664). This observation helps us put the legal requirement into perspective: officially, it will almost always be possible to state that it has been met.

For the Commission, however, the seriousness of the patient's condition may be the result of 'multiple disorders', none of which, taken individually, is *serious and incurable*. This expression was invented by the Commission: there is no trace of it in the thousands of pages of reports of the parliamentary discussions.

Members of the Commission acknowledge that the absence of a serious and incurable disorder poses a problem. Nevertheless, they specify that in elderly people, the cumulative effect of a combination of ailments may cause unbearable suffering and justifies euthanasia.[9]

---

[8] Article 3, § 1st, third point, of the law.
[9] J. Herremans, member of the FCECE and President of ADMD [Association for the Right to Die with Dignity] (Belgium) quoted by Saget 2008. Englert, member of the FCECE and of the ADMD, quoted in 'L'euthanasie des patients âgés' 2016.

The public was apprised of the notion of 'multiple disorders' through the extensive media coverage of the controversial cases of Jeanne[10] and Amelie Van Esbeen.[11]

The Commission is thus increasingly approving euthanasia cases at the request of people who, although unable to prove that they have a serious and incurable disorder, suffer from various ailments related to old age. For example, people suffering from polyarthritis, who have reduced mobility, and have an ailing eye sight and hearing impairment.[12]

The first report to the legislative chambers identified three cases of 'multiple disorders', the second report 20 cases, the third report 16 cases, the fourth report 30 cases, the fifth report 39 cases, the sixth report 166 cases and the seventh report 385 cases (FCECE, First report 2004, p. 8; Second report 2006, p. 16; Third report 2008, pp. 16–17; Fourth report 2010, p. 16; Fifth report 2012, pp. 8–9; Sixth report 2014, p. 8; Seventh report 2016, p. 5).

In its seventh report, the Commission points out that the number of euthanasia cases because of 'multiple disorders' has again increased significantly both in numbers and as a percentage of all euthanasia cases. Indeed, in 2015 more than one in ten euthanasia deaths were from multiple disorders (209/2022). The fourth, fifth and sixth reports highlight the divergent views that have arisen within the Commission with respect to the justification for euthanasia for very old persons with multiple disorders; some members thought that this suffering was more related to *the natural consequences of old age* (FCECE, Fourth report 2010, p. 22; Fifth report 2012, p. 14; Sixth report 2014, p. 15). The seventh report emphasised that neither old age nor being tired of life justify euthanasia in the absence of a serious and incurable disease. However, they admitted that the older a patient is, the more likely he or she is to develop multiple disorders (FCECE, Seventh Report 2016, p. 26).

It is remarkable that the Commission agreed to collapse into a single condition, the two conditions that are distinct in the legislation: (1) the

---

[10] This 88-year-old woman apparently did not suffer from a serious and incurable illness. That was the conviction of both her son and her personal physician (Gruber 2008; Delpierre 2011; Saget 2008).

[11] This 93-year-old woman did not suffer from any serious and incurable illness and her physician had refused to approve her request for euthanasia. Cf., e.g., Lamensch 2009; Lamensch and Soumois 2009; 'Les leçons d'un cas très médiatisé' 2009; Hovine 2009; and Keuleneer 2009 (an alternate member of the FCECE).

[12] Englert, member of the FCECE in 'L'euthanasie des patients âgés' 2016; Prof. W. Distelmans, President of the FCECE (Distelmans 2013a).

Table 1 *Euthanasia cases declared for 'multiple disorders'*.

2004	2005	2006	2007	2008	2009	2010	2011	2012	2013	2014	2015
9	11	6	10	12	18	16	23	57	109	176	209

necessity of demonstrating a serious and incurable disorder that (2) results in constant and unbearable physical or mental suffering that cannot be relieved. This approach, combined with the absence of a definition of a 'serious and incurable disorder' and the fact that euthanasia is legally possible for patients who are not expected to die in the short term seem tailor-made to permit euthanasia for patients who claim to be suffering unbearably because of their old age, social isolation or world weariness (an expression used overtly by Distelmans 2013a).

While this point of view is of course understandable, we must nonetheless point out that it contradicts the *principle of strict interpretation of penal texts* and the frequently reaffirmed will of the legislators to grant permission to euthanise only under 'strict conditions'.[13] This represents a slippage in the required indications for euthanasia, which have come to include euthanasia for older persons who would like to end their lives. Even if they cannot prove that they have a serious and incurable disorder, or truly unbearable suffering, they should be able to 'benefit' from medical assistance to die. A 'quality of life' deemed to be insufficient seems to be gradually replacing the medical indications and legal conditions for euthanasia.

The Requirement of Physical or Mental Suffering

Among the conditions for euthanasia, Belgian law requires the presence of constant and unbearable physical *or* mental suffering that cannot be alleviated (Article 3, § 1st, of the Act). From the beginning, the Commission felt that the assessment of the *unbearable* nature of the suffering was largely 'subjective and depends on the patient's personality, ideas and values' (FCECE, First report 2004, p. 16). As for the suffering that *cannot be alleviated*, the Commission stated that it had to consider the fact that 'the patient has the right to refuse treatment for pain, even palliative treatment, for example, when the patient deems the side effects or

---

[13] See, e.g., *Proposition de loi relative à l'euthanasie* [Proposed law on euthanasia], 20 December 1999, Doc. parl., Sénat, sess. 1999–2000, n° 2–244/1: 3.

methods of treatment to be unbearable' (FCECE, First report 2004, p. 16). In reality, any notion of a 'palliative filter procedure' (e.g., Gastmans et al. 2004; Broeckaert and Janssens 2003) is scorned by partisans of euthanasia. Physicians must limit themselves to giving information on the possibilities provided under palliative care, which admittedly is not the same as experiencing the benefits provided by this type of care. How can we assert that the patient's suffering 'cannot be alleviated' if he or she refuses any type of palliative care? In practice, the Commission exercises very lax control over the unbearable nature of the suffering that cannot be alleviated, criteria that are nevertheless central in the legislation.

When the Belgian Act on euthanasia was being developed, it was stated repeatedly that *patients with psychiatric disorders, dementia or depression were excluded from the Act* (Report of the Chamber Commission of Justice 2002, pp. 52, 56, 217, 243, 244, 245, etc.; see also Chapter 1). Logically, the neuropsychiatric condition of these patients pointedly raises the serious issue of the validity of their requests, as it is difficult to confirm the voluntary, well-thought-out and lucid nature of the request. However, the *Commission approves an ever-increasing number of euthanasia cases for patients with psychiatric disorders, dementia or depression.* In a recent paper, 100 cases of euthanasia requests by psychiatric patients are analysed (Thienpont et al. 2015).

The euthanasia in 2012 of a 48-year-old prisoner with psychiatric problems,[14] in 2013 of Nathan, a transgender 44-year-old, after a botched sex change operation,[15] or in 2012 of Ann G., who suffered from anorexia and a psychiatric condition (Beel and Bergmans 2013) are paradigmatic examples.

The Belgian experience demonstrates how *extremely difficult it is to stick to the initial statements and intentions of the legislators* and to ensure that the original very strict statutory conditions have been met.

In 2013, the President of the Commission announced that in Belgium, several dozen people had been euthanised because of their 'mental

---

[14] Dr Marc Moens President of ABSyM, asks whether 'the inmate would have taken this decision under appropriate psychiatric treatment' (*'Un prisonnier belge a été euthanasié'* 2012). Since then, euthanasia requests from long-term prisoners have multiplied (Ide 2013). More recently, many requests were made following the media coverage of the case of F. Van Den Bleeken.

[15] According to Distelmans, who has supervised euthanasia, the interested candidate could clearly demonstrate unbearable psychological suffering (*'Une euthanasie après une opération ratée de changement de sexe'* 2013). But what incurable illness did he have? One might ask.

Table 2 *Euthanasia cases declared for neuropsychiatric disorders.*

2004	2005	2006	2007	2008	2009	2010	2011	2012	2013	2014	2015
6	3	5	4	13	21	25	33	53	67	61	63

suffering' (Distelmans 2013b). Confusion between mental suffering and mental illness remains common. Recently, the euthanasia of Laura, a 24-year-old, was authorised by three physicians for only chronic depression (but on the scheduled day, she refused). One can question the legality of such euthanasia in the absence of incurable disease and being unable to appreciate the unbearable nature of psychiatric suffering. There are no measurable parameters for objectivity. In any case, the characteristic of depression and other similar forms of mental suffering is precisely the loss of any life force and perspectives for the future. Therefore, the feeling of lack of prospects and the expression of death wish says nothing on the prognosis of mental suffering.[16]

In its second report, the Commission approved nine cases of euthanasia for patients with a neuropsychiatric disorder: one case of Creutzfeldt-Jacob disease, three cases of Alzheimer's disease, one case of Huntington's disease and four cases of untreatable depression (FCECE, Second report 2006, p. 16, p. 22). A Flemish association that actively supports people suffering from depression (*Netwerk Depressie Vlaanderen* [*Flanders Depression Network*]) was upset by this, stating that it sets a dangerous precedent: 'The door to euthanasia is open for thousands of depressed and suicidal people to kill themselves legally' ('*Quatre cas pour dépression majeure irréductible*' 2007). In later reports, these figures continued to rise. They have declined slightly since 2013 but still account for more than 60 deaths a year (FCECE, Third report 2008, p. 16, p. 22; Fourth report 2010, p. 16; Fifth report 2012, p. 8; Sixth report 2014, p. 8).

Starting with its third report, many Commission members, following lively debate, decided that 'a *foreseeable* dramatic change ... suffices to constitute unbearable, unrelievable mental suffering within the terms of the Act' (FCECE, Third report 2008, p. 24).

The fourth and fifth reports indicated that certain members of the Commission believed that mental suffering had been interpreted too

---

[16] On this topic, see the opinion expressed and signed by a large number of psychologists and psychiatrists (Bazan et al. 2015).

broadly, because a foreseeable dramatic change could not constitute unbearable, unrelievable mental suffering in the here and now [*hic et nunc*], as required under the terms of the Act on euthanasia. However, most Commission members did not share this point of view (FCECE, Fourth report 2010, p. 33; Fifth report 2012, p. 16).

In other words, the degree of suffering required to gain access to euthanasia could include *anticipated future suffering*.

Since the case of Hugo Claus, the famous Flemish writer who chose euthanasia at the age of 78 (in 2008), from the appearance of the first symptoms of Alzheimer's disease,[17] dozens of people have apparently been euthanised preventively (*sic*), at an early stage of dementia (Distelmans 2013b, p. 60). From among many other cases of *euthanasia out of fear of future suffering*, the cases of the Verbessem twins (euthanised together in 2012)[18] and of Emiel Pauwels (euthanised in 2014)[19] clearly illustrate this questionable and much discussed interpretation of the condition of constant and unbearable suffering.

From Euthanasia to Physician-Assisted Suicide

The Belgian legislator very clearly intended to exclude physician-assisted suicide from the scope of the Act on euthanasia. This intention was criticised and extensively debated when the Act was being developed.

---

[17] See e.g. APPF 2008; Rotman and Beal 2008; see also the opinions and analyses published in *De Standaard* between 22 and 24 March 2008 and 21 May 2008. The case was declared to the Commission, which deemed it acceptable with respect to the legal requirements. The dossier was not sent to the public Prosecutor.

[18] See De Ceulaer 2013. The request for euthanasia of the twins Eddy and Marc Verbessem, who were born deaf, was due to the diagnosis of glaucoma, which apparently would have gradually led to blindness. It was the expectation of a future loss of autonomy that motivated their request. This latter request is understandable and deserving of respect, but one might wonder if society provided them with sufficient support. On this topic, see the opinion piece written by L. Walraedt, director of '*Bastide*'; (in Namur), with the approval of his colleague, director of '*Spermalia*', in Bruges, the only two Belgian specialised institutions in supporting deafblind people ('*L'euthanasie de deux frères sourds et aveugles bouleverse*' 2013).

[19] Emiel Pauwels was a 95-year-old athlete who had just received a diagnosis of stomach and intestinal cancer. Given his excellent physical condition, radiation therapy was feasible and had been proposed. He refused: '*I opted for euthanasia because I did not wish to suffer*'. It is *future* suffering that is invoked and, certainly, now when euthanasia took place (after a party where champagne flowed freely and many relatives, friends and journalists attended), the man did not appear at that moment [*hic et nunc*] prey to a 'constant and unbearable physical or mental suffering that could not be relieved', in the words of the law.

(Report of the Chamber Commission of Justice 2002: 55 and 57; Report of the Joint Commissions for Justice and Social Affairs, pp. 545f, pp. 581f, pp. 613f). Several amendments seeking to incorporate physician-assisted suicide into the law were tabled, but they were all rejected[20], to the surprise of the Council of State.[21] After the Act was passed, some members of parliament deemed it necessary to amend the Act on euthanasia to include physician-assisted suicide performed under the same conditions as those that had been specified for euthanasia.[22] In their minds, physician-assisted suicide is clearly not covered by the Act on euthanasia.[23]

Therefore, it is remarkable that the Commission regularly approves reports of physician-assisted suicide and has been doing so since its first official report (2004, p. 17), stating that the practice 'falls within the scope of the Act, as it is currently written, according to which the physician is in control of the process of dying until the end, regardless of the means' (FCECE, First report 2004, p. 24). In its second report, the Commission appears to identify ten cases of physician-assisted suicide (FCECE, Second report 2006, p. 24) and specifies that its interpretation is in line with the position of the National Council of the College of Physicians (2003). The third (FCECE, Third report 2008, p. 24), fourth (2010, p. 24), fifth (2012, p. 17) and seventh (2016, p. 48) reports indicate 24, 14, 12 and 29 cases of physician-assisted suicide, respectively. Since physician-assisted suicide complies with the conditions of the Act on euthanasia, it seems logical and reasonable to handle it in the same way. Nonetheless, it must be noted that a practice that the legislator intentionally excluded from the scope of the Act has been endorsed. This suggests

---

[20] See, e.g., the discussion on page 190 of the Report of the Chamber Commission of Justice 2002.

[21] Proposed law on euthanasia, Opinion of the Council of State, 2 July 2001, n° 2-244/21, pp. 14–15. The Council of State infers this clear intention of the legislature to reject the amendments 5, 24 and 97, p. 14, footnote 3.

[22] See, e.g., Bill to amend the law of 28 May 2002 on euthanasia and to introducing the concept of assistance for self-euthanasia, 26 May 2008, Doc. parl., Senate, sess. 2007–2008, n° 4-7841/1. This bill incorporates, with some modifications, the text of a bill that had been previously tabled in the Senate on 2 October 2003, Doc. parl., Senate, sess. extr. 2003, n° 3-220/1.

[23] See the memorandum explaining the bill to amend the Act of 28 May 2002 concerning euthanasia and the Royal Decree of 2 April 2003 laying down the conditions on which the advance directive of euthanasia should be written, confirmed, revised or withdrawn, 18 October 2007, Doc. parl., Senate, sess. 2007–2008, n° 4-301/1. This bill incorporates, with some modifications, the text of a bill that had been previously tabled in the Senate the 25 April 2006, sess. 2005–2006, n° 3-1671/1.

slippage, as it is neither for the National Council of Physicians nor for the Commission to decide that they are above the law (see also Chapter 1). In addition, it is not clear that physicians feel legally obliged to report to the Commission the situations in which they helped a patient to end his or her own life, given that the Act requires only 'the physician who has performed euthanasia' to report it to the Commission (article 5 of the Act). This also means that we cannot rely on the figures for 'physician-assisted suicide' provided by the Commission.

From Exception to 'Legal Right'

In 2002, euthanasia was presented as an ethical transgression, an exceptional act, a last resort for extreme cases (e.g., Masson 2005). But now it is being stated that 'euthanasia is neither an exception nor an ethical transgression and its practice, properly regulated, is part of end of life care' (Lossignol 2012, p. 24). Yet if the legislator chose not to adapt the Penal Code, it was to signal the fact that euthanasia remains a criminally punishable form of homicide. It is only *by exception*, under the conditions laid down by the law, that it loses its unlawful character. During the development of the future Act, all the stakeholders – parliamentarians and experts who were heard – agreed that the Bill should not provide a 'right to euthanasia', and the Bill limited itself to decriminalising, under certain conditions, the action of a physician who freely accesses a request for euthanasia (Report of the Chamber Commission of Justice 2002, pp. 34, 176, 153, 337, 347, etc.).

Twelve years later, there are countless news articles, websites,[24] official documents,[25] information brochures[26] and bills[27] stating that a 'right to euthanasia' exists. This preponderant focus generates troublesome misunderstandings because patients apparently believe that they have a right to euthanasia and that they can determine when it will take place without any input from the physician.

During the development of the Act, it was often argued that euthanasia – even if it is entrusted to the doctor – is not a 'normal

---

[24] www.admd.net/international/la-belgique.html (accessed 24 October 2016).
[25] Cf. Portail Belgium.be, www.belgium.be/fr/sante/ (accessed 24 October 2016, topic to choose on the site: soins de sante/fin de vie/euthanasie).
[26] Brochure published by one of the largest mutualities (health insurance companies) in Belgium, available at: www.mutsoc.be/ (accessed 24 October 2016).
[27] Proposed law amending the Act of 28 May 2002 on euthanasia, 7 July 2004, *Doc. parl.*, Senate, sess. 2003–2004, n° 3-804/1, p. 1.

medical procedure' but intrinsically an infraction (Report of the Chamber Commission of Justice 2002, pp. 172–173, 151, 159, 172, 173, 183, etc.). Indeed, the law took away its unlawful character as soon as the fundamental conditions and procedural requirements had been met. Nonetheless, the law provides such a special act to be subject to social control. How else can we explain that the act of euthanasia, and it alone of all the actions of a physician, must be reported to the Commission?

In current publications, euthanasia and physician-assisted suicide are considered medical procedures or acts of health care. In the so-called Belgian model of integral palliative care, they are classified without any special distinction as acts of health care among others in the set of end-of-life health care acts (Bernheim, Distelmans et al. 2014; Id. 2012; Id. 2008). Opinion polls indicate that the majority of the Belgian population (85 per cent to 93 per cent) support euthanasia (Cohen-Almagor 2009a). However, at least in certain environments, since euthanasia has insinuated itself into palliative care, the image of the latter has become blurred: some people, at the end of their lives, are afraid to go to a palliative care unit because of the possibility of 'euthanasia' or life-ending without request – that has not disappeared (Cohen-Almagor 2015). Moreover, patients sometimes fear the use of opioids that have legitimately been proposed to alleviate their pain and are even more afraid of palliative sedation to treat refractory symptoms that is in keeping with established clinical practice. This implies that the law concerning euthanasia has an impact on palliative care (Dopchie 2014: e38). There was already an awareness that this mixture might alter the perception, effectiveness and public confidence in palliative care (see Pereira et al. 2008a, and the references).

Health Care Institutions' Freedom

The Euthanasia Act explicitly states that 'the request and the advance directive' for euthanasia 'are not compulsory in nature' (art. 14, para. 1). Similarly, a refusal clause, also called a 'conscience clause', has been written into law. The result is that 'no physician may be compelled to perform euthanasia' and 'no other person may be compelled to assist in performing euthanasia' (art. 14, para. 2 and 3). According to the standpoint of the legislator in 2002, the Act upholds 'the measured faculty to make a request [for euthanasia]' and states that no criminal offence is committed by the physician 'who freely agrees to respond positively' (Schamps and Van Overstraeten 2009, p. 352). No obligation is associated with this request, other than that imposed on the physician who refuses to perform euthanasia, to inform 'in a timely manner' the patient or the persons taken in confidence, and to explain his or her reasons for such a refusal. At most, at the request of either of these people, the physician must communicate the patient's medical record to the physician designated by the patient or person taken in confidence (art. 14, para. 4 and 5).

Several amendments tabled in Parliament seek to oblige a physician who refuses to approve a request for euthanasia to forward the file to another physician favourable to this practice.[28] If this type of proposal were adopted, it would constitute a serious breach of the physician's freedom of conscience because it would compel him or her to collaborate indirectly in an act that his or her conscience condemns.

The intention is also to oblige physicians to warn the patient at very short notice of their refusal to perform euthanasia.[29] In practice, things are not so simple, since the refusal may result not from an objection of principle, but from the physician's inability to arrive, with the patient, at the conviction that there is no reasonable alternative (art. 3, § 2, 1°, of the law). It is especially common today for a patient, immediately upon learning of a disturbing diagnosis, to make a vague request for euthanasia; it is understandable that the physician wants to start by reassuring him or her, indicating for example that the disease is in the very early stages, that its evolution can be slowed or that the disease is curable or that therapies are available.[30]

---

[28] E.g., Bill to amend the Act of 28 May 2012 on euthanasia, tabled the 23 February 2016, *Doc. parl.*, Chamber of Representatives, 2015-2016, 54-1677/001; Bill to amend the Act of 28 May 2012 on euthanasia, 9 May 2012, *Doc. parl.*, Senate, sess. 2011-2012, n° 5-1611/1; Bill, tabled the 16 August 2010, *Doc. parl.*, Senate, sess. extr. 2010, n° 5-22/1; Bill to amend the Act of 28 May 2002 concerning euthanasia to introduce an obligation for the doctor who refuses to perform euthanasia to refer the patient to a colleague, 5 October 2012, *Doc. parl.*, Senate, session 2011-2012, n° 5-1798/1 (according to this latter proposal, the obligation would devolve on the social service of the institution).

[29] E.g., Bill to amend the Act of 28 May 2012 on euthanasia, tabled the 23 February 2016, *Doc. parl.*, Chamber of Representatives, 2015-2016, 54-1677/001; Proposed law amending the Act of 28 May 2002 concerning euthanasia to introduce an obligation for the doctor who refuses to perform euthanasia to refer the patient to a colleague, and to send the patient's medical file to a commission in the case that he or she has refused the patient's request, 26 June 2013, *Doc. parl.*, Senate, session n° 5-2172/1; Proposed law mentioned above, 10 January 2013, *Doc. parl.*, Senate, sess. 2012-2013, n° 5-1919/1. See the Flemish Government Decree of 14 September 2012 relating to programming, under the conditions of approval and the scheme for subsidising the organisations that offer health care and housing services and associations of users and close caregivers, their offering of family support services and complementary home care and day care centres – Appendix IX – Day care centres, *M. B.*, 14 November 2012, p. 68342.

[30] Information drawn from converging witness statements of medical oncologists.

Ultimately, these proposals intend to 'associate the request for euthanasia with an additional binding condition' and thus 'give more body to
the right, cautiously established in 2002, to request death' (Schamps and
Van Overstraeten 2009, p. 353).

The claim, initially surreptitious (through manipulation of the
language), but later more blatant, that there is a real 'right to euthanasia'
has been accompanied by a growing controversy about the institutional
dimension of the 'conscience clause'.[31]

It seemed clear, during the preparatory work on the Act on euthanasia,
that health care institutions would be able to refuse to lend their assistance in the practice of euthanasia after the Bill came into force. In the
Report of the Justice Commission, for example, the following is stated:
'The speaker ... is expressly asking all members of the Commission
whether they agree with the stance that the Bill under review will give
hospitals the option of prohibiting the practice of euthanasia. The chairperson has concluded that, based on the correct interpretation of the
Bill under review, hospitals have the right to prohibit the practice of
euthanasia within their walls. *No member* disputed the chairperson's
interpretation' (Report of the Chamber Commission of Justice, p. 178.
The words in italics are in the text).

Today, however, hospitals and nursing homes that are reluctant or
refuse to practice euthanasia are often pilloried and threatened with
losing their public funding.[32] An amendment recently tabled in Parliament specified: 'No doctor can be prevented from practicing euthanasia
under an agreement. If appropriate, such a prohibiting clause shall be
deemed unwritten'.[33]

It is true that most health care institutions have integrated – with more
or less restraints – the practice of euthanasia (e.g., Lemiengre et al. 2009;
Lemiengre et al. 2008). And many physicians put up with it (Smets et al.
2011). In any case, an institution may no longer prohibit euthanasia

---

[31] For a summary of the debate, see Tack 2013 and Bioethics Advisory Committee of
Belgium 2014, especially 13–43.

[32] Publicly well-known: often repeated on the radio and on television. In the written press,
see, for example, the proposals of Prof. W. Distelmans (Distelmans 2011b) and the
interview with Senator P. Mahoux (Mahoux 2014a). Cf. also the bill to amend the Act
of 28 May 2002 on euthanasia and the associated Act of 10 July 2008 on hospitals and
other health care facilities, with the intention of ensuring respect for the conscience
clause, 26 June 2013, *Doc. parl.*, Senate, sess. 2012–2013, n° 5–2173/1.

[33] Bill to amend the Act of 28 May 2012 on euthanasia, tabled the 23 February 2016, *Doc.
parl.*, Chamber of Representatives, 2015–2016, 54–1676/001.

within its walls (Heneghan 2016). Physicians and nurses who are critical of euthanasia testify to pressures (e.g., Dopchie 2014), despite the existence of the conscience clause. Here too, we are imperceptibly departing from the legislator's initial intentions. Whatever anyone may say, the assertion of 'the ultimate freedom' for some goes hand in hand with constraints and pressures exerted on the freedom of others (health care workers and health care institutions).

Extension of the Law to Minors

In 2002, euthanasia was limited to adults (and emancipated minors). Since the Act of 28 February 2014,[34] euthanasia is now available to minors, *regardless of age*, if they can show that they are subject to constant and unbearable physical suffering that cannot be relieved and which results from a serious, incurable injury or pathological condition and which will result in death in the short term. In addition, on the one hand, it is necessary for a child psychiatrist or psychologist to certify that the child has the mental *capacity for discernment*, and on the other, that the parents agree.

This text, whose form and substance have been criticised by many, carries the seed of discrimination that will immediately be challenged; the text limits euthanasia to cases of 'physical' suffering and 'death in the short term', whereas these conditions do not apply to adults.

This reform was passed quickly, without any real social demand for it, despite the opposition of numerous paediatricians, professors of paediatrics and other practitioners experienced in caring for seriously ill children.[35] Moreover, the extension to minors was adopted without going before the Public Health Commission of the Senate, after having refused to conduct all the expert hearings requested at the House of Representatives and, finally, without a request for an opinion from the Council of State. Until recently, two cases of euthanasia conducted in a minor had been reported. Several newspapers on 17 September 2016 indicated that, for the first time in Belgium, euthanasia of a minor had been notified to the FCECE.

---

[34] Act of 28 February 2014 amending the Act of 28 May 2002 on euthanasia, with the intention of extending euthanasia to minors, *Moniteur Belge*, 12 March 2014, p. 21053.

[35] Opinion signed by 38 paediatricians, (Van Gool et al. 2014). The list of signatories grew in just a few days to nearly 200 paediatricians (Cf. Hovine 2014, p. 9). Information published in numerous other newspapers.

Euthanasia of the Mentally Incompetent

Euthanasia for persons with dementia According to article 4, § 1 of the Act of 28 June 2002, any capable adult or emancipated minor may draw up an advance directive to request euthanasia in circumstances where he or she can no longer express his or her wishes. Euthanasia may be performed based on such a directive if the physician confirms that (1) the patient suffers from a serious and incurable disorder caused by illness or injury and (2) the patient is in a state of irreversible unconsciousness.

Some amendments tabled at Parliament have aimed at simplifying the wording and the confirmation of the *advance directive* by reducing the number of witnesses required, extending its period of validity and even removing the obligation to confirm the directive.[36]

Several new bills aim to extend the decriminalisation of euthanasia based on an advance directive for the case where the physician believes that the patient, while not in an *irreversible coma* (whose criterion is a strict and objective test that is currently in force), is progressively losing his or her cognitive abilities and is no longer self-aware.[37]

Regularly, there are calls to extend the law to adults who are incapable of expressing their informed wishes, and in whom moments of consciousness fluctuate, that is, people affected by degenerative mental illnesses (Alzheimer's disease and other forms of dementia).[38] Certain bills combine this standpoint with permitting an unlimited validity period for advance directives.[39] It is intriguing to note how far these

---

[36] I shall limit myself to mentioning just the most recent bills: Bill to amend the Act of 28 May 2002 on euthanasia, removing the limitation on the validity of the advance declaration to five years and permitting the patient to specify the validity period, 26 June 2013, *Doc. parl.*, Senate, n° 5-2171/1; Bill to amend the Act of 28 May 2012 on euthanasia regarding the registration process for advance directives, 24 January 2013, *Doc. parl.*, Senate, sess. 2012-2013, n° 5-1942/1; Bill to amend the Act of 28 May 2002 on euthanasia, 10 January 2013, *Doc. parl.*, Senate, sess. 2012-2013, n° 5-1919/1; Bill to amend the Act of 28 May 2002 on euthanasia, removing the limitation on the validity of the advance declaration, 5 October 2012, *Doc. parl.*, Senate, sess. 2011-2012, n° 5-1799/1. Cf. also the Bill tabled 9 May 2012, *Doc. parl.*, Senate, sess. 2011-2012, n° 5-1611/1, Bill tabled 16 August 2010, *Doc. parl.*, Senate, sess. extr. 2010, n° 5-24/1.

[37] E.g., Bill to amend article 4 of the law of 28 May 2002 on euthanasia, 8 April 2008, *Doc. parl.*, Senate, n° 4-676/1, which incorporates the text of a bill previously tabled 14 December 2005, *Doc. parl.*, Senate, sess. 2005-2006, n° 3-1485/1.

[38] Cf. statements by W. Distelmans in '*Steeds meer Belgen willen levenseinde zelf bepalen*' 2015; Mahoux 2014b, p. 24.

[39] E.g., Bill to amend the Act of 28 May 2002 concerning euthanasia, with the intention to extend this to people affected by an incurable and irreversible brain disorder, and who have expressed their will in an advance directive on euthanasia, 3 July 2013, *Doc. parl.*,

new amendments ignore the prudential considerations stated during the development of the 2002 Act (e.g. Report of the Joint Commissions for Justice and Social Affairs 2002, pp. 80, 329–334, 386 ff., etc.; Report of the Chamber Commission of Justice 2002, p. 249).

Ending the life of newborns Some parliamentarians are also arguing for the legalisation of neonatal euthanasia. This would involve newborns with a fatal disease or those who are very premature. It is apparent from one amendment that it is 'urgent to extend the Act on euthanasia to minors' by providing that 'where the child does not have the capacity to discern' the parents may request euthanasia.[40]

Others favour adopting a protocol, outside of the Act (e.g. Report of the Joint Commissions for Justice and Social Affairs 2002, p. 13), based on the model of the Groningen Protocol adopted in the Netherlands for ending the life of newborns (Verhagen and Sauer 2005).

Ending the life without request There are currently calls to legalise life-ending without request. As one critical care physician stated in a news article in 2014, it is not a matter of increasing doses of analgesics to relieve pain or other symptoms, 'but rather a matter of administering significant doses of sedatives to hasten death when the quality of life has become insufficient'.[41] The Belgian Society of Intensive Care Medicine published an article clearly favouring the practice of 'shortening the dying process' without an explicit request, 'with use of medication, such as analgesics/sedatives, even in the absence of discomfort', in 'due consideration of the wishes of family members' (Vincent et al. 2014).

Sense and Logic of the Resulting Observations

Fifteen years of experience in Belgium have demonstrated, that by various means, indications for euthanasia are constantly multiplying, despite the legislator's initial statements and intentions. This predictable evolution will inevitably continue not only because of the symbolic

---

Senate, n° 5-2184/1; Bill to amend the Act of 28 May 2002 on euthanasia, 9 May 2012, *Doc. parl.*, Senate, session 2011–2012, n° 5-1611/1.

[40] Bill complementing, with respect to minors, the Act of 28 May 2002 on euthanasia, 9 May 2012, *Doc. parl.*, Senate, sess. ord. 2011–2012, n° 5-1610/1. Going in the same direction, previously, see *Doc. parl.*, Senate, n° 3-1993/1 and n° 4-431/1; *Doc. parl.*, Ch. repr., n° 2553/1 and n° 611/1.

[41] J.-L. Vincent, Professor of intensive care, Free University of Brussels (Vincent 2014, p. 26). This physician used the expression 'unrequested euthanasia'.

force of the law and its immanent dynamic, but also for obvious logical and psychological reasons.

The Symbolic Force of Law

The law, general and abstract, disposes for the future. It conveys social, moral and cultural values; it structures social behaviour. The laws on health, life and death have a considerable impact on the mentality and *ethos* of a society. So it is with the law on euthanasia which, far from being neutral and referring each person to his or her own autonomy, carries a specific anthropological vision and imposes it on one and all. From the moment that such a law leads to a substantial change in the mission entrusted to physicians, the conception and image of medicine are at stake. One cannot emphasise strongly enough the eminently symbolic, pedagogical and institutive functions of the law, particularly in the field of criminal law.

The Belgian experience illustrates this. Initially, euthanasia was presented as an ethical transgression, an exceptional act. Rapidly, by blurring the standards, euthanasia became a norm: it became one medical procedure among many, and then a right to be claimed.[42] 'We are simply asking that our view be respected: we want to let people choose to stay in control of their body, their life and their death'.[43]

As was predictable and as we observe today, supply creates demand which is then multiplied artificially. We are even seeing a spurt: five euthanasia cases a day were declared in 2013 and that is without counting all those that are not declared. Year after year, the number of euthanasia cases declared to the Commission continues to rise dramatically. In addition, in an interview, Wim Distelmans, chairman for the FCECE, stated: 'Remember, the number of euthanasias performed but not declared remains in the shadows, which prevents us from having a real view of the magnitude of the phenomenon' ('*Plus de 2,000 déclarations d'euthanasie en* 2015' 2016).

---

[42] Cf. Lossignol 2012, p. 24; Thirion et al. 2013, p. 14: 'In the longer term, normalizing the practice of euthanasia in institutions should be encouraged by the government . . .'; Cf. the opinion of Dr M. Cosyns, who opposes all conceptual distinction between legislation on euthanasia and that on patients' rights and palliative care (Beel and Sioen 2013, p. 58).

[43] Joint statement by a group academics and physicians, '*Dix ans d'euthanasie: un heureux-anniversaire!*' (Alaluf et al. 2012), in response to a critical opinion previously published by another group academics and physicians, '*Dix ans d'euthanasie: un heureux anniversaire?*' (Ars et al. 2012).

Table 3 *Registered euthanasia cases.*

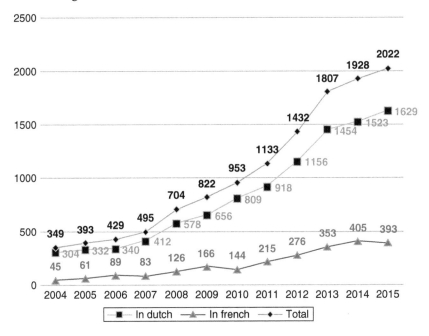

Table 4 *Euthanasia reported based on the expected time of death.*

2015	299/1723	14.8/85.2
2014	295/1633	15.3/84.7
2013	266/1541	17.2/82.8
2012	167/1265	13.2/86.8
2011	114/1019	11.1/88.9
2010	80/873	8.2/91.8
2009	67/755	8/92
2008	49/655	7/93
2007	28/467	6/94
2006	26/403	6/94
2005	27/366	7/93
2004	24/325	7/93
2003	19/216	8.7/91.3
	not short term/short term	%

It is also striking that an increasing number of people ask to be euthanised although their death is not expected in the short term: 17 per cent of the total number of euthanasia cases declared in 2013 and 13 per cent in 2012 (FCECE, Sixth report 2014, p. 8) versus 6 per cent in 2006 and 2007 (FCECE, Third report 2008, p. 15). The seventh report shows that the percentage of euthanasia cases where death was not expected in the short term has declined since its peak of 2013, but it remains higher than at any time before that year. Furthermore, the actual number of non-terminal cases has increased every year.

The Immanent Dynamics of Law

This evolution of euthanasia, from its inception as an exceptional practice and an ethical transgression into a practice that is ever more readily accepted (so-called normalisation of euthanasia), also for scenarios where it was initially not permitted, makes it necessary to seriously consider the *logic that operates in the dynamics of law-making and implementation.*[44]

Indeed, the legal provisions do not have autonomous lives that play out solely in accordance with the will of the legislature that created them. They are part of the legal system, which, like any system, has its own dynamic determined by macro principles (hierarchy of rules, principles of interpretation, principles of equality and non-discrimination, principles drawn from logic or common sense, such as 'He who can do more can do less', etc.). It is legitimate to draw attention to real cases for which the law does not provide satisfactory solutions and to ask that the law be amended to achieve desirable results for those cases. But we should ask, at the outset, whether the proposed approach will result in injecting a dynamic into the system that will have unforeseeable and unwanted effects.

In our constitutional systems, the fundamental principles of equality and non-discrimination have acquired an importance that is not lost on anyone. They dictate that similar legal treatment must apply to objectively similar situations and different legal treatments to objectively different situations. But we know that the assessment of situations (are

---

[44] The following reflection takes its inspiration from the explanation of Mr. F. Keuleneer in the context of his audition, Report of the Chamber Commission of Justice pp. 159f.

they similar or not?) and the qualification of their legal treatment (are they similar or not?) are controversial questions. With the decriminalisation of euthanasia under certain conditions, there is a natural tendency to consider very similar or even 'slightly different' situations as similar and to invoke the principles of equality and non-discrimination to request euthanasia. For example, in the name of these principles, euthanasia, initially reserved for adults, has been made available to minors. As was foreseeable, the limit of 18 years was soon attacked as being arbitrary and a source of unjust discrimination. Another example was the requirement for constant and unbearable physical or mental suffering resulting from a serious and incurable disorder. However, in the name of the same principles, it quickly becomes difficult to refuse euthanasia to a person who reports only unbearable psychological suffering, but is not able to show a serious and incurable disorder. The Belgian experience attests to that.

The Logic of Autonomy

Finally, in keeping with the philosophy of autonomy as the foundation of the law, it seems logical and even natural that, sooner or later, the 'strict' legal conditions weigh less than the firm and specific wishes of the patient.

Not surprisingly, euthanasia supporters assert: 'Who, other than the person in question, can reasonably determine [the severity of his or her condition]?' (Jaeken 2009, p. 10). Similarly, a member of the FCECE wrote: 'Again, it comes down to the heart of the legislation that decriminalises euthanasia: respect for an individual's autonomy' (Herremans and Galand 2009, p. 14, published also in the *Bulletin de l'ADMD* (*Belgique*), n° 112, June 2009, p. 13). Although these views are rooted in common sense, they seem to disregard the other 'strict conditions' of the law.

Conclusion

Since euthanasia was legalised in Belgium, in 2002, experience demonstrates that it is an illusion to believe that euthanasia can be permitted as a narrowly circumscribed, well-defined exceptional practice to which 'strict conditions' apply and which is under rigorous control. Once euthanasia is allowed, the limiting conditions established under the law fall away, one after the other, and it appears practically impossible to maintain a strict interpretation of the statutory conditions and to prevent the extension of the law.

We have seen that many euthanasia cases are not declared and that we have only a very piecemeal view on the practice. Therefore, it is inappropriate to state, bluntly, that euthanasia is under control in Belgium and that the conditions for applying the law are fully respected.

It is of concern that, unwittingly, society may be ready to put euthanasia forward as the most humane solution or the most dignified exit, as the level of tolerance for illness or suffering decreases and the bonds of solidarity wither. Indeed, this phenomenon is already perceptible.

3

Ethics and the Psychiatric Dimensions of Physician-Assisted Suicide

A View from the United States

DANIEL P. SULMASY

Introduction

Suicide occurs most often in the setting of psychiatric diseases such as depression. By contrast, physician-assisted suicide (PAS) is proposed as a form of rational suicide. To be legally eligible, one must be judged free from the irrationality and distortions of will that sometimes accompany psychiatric disease. Whether there can be such a thing as rational suicide is a matter of debate among philosophers. Kant, for instance, thought suicide unreasonable, a performatively self-refuting act inasmuch as respect for autonomy cannot be proposed as the grounds for the elimination of autonomy (Kant 1785). Other philosophers have disagreed (Hume 1783).

In this brief chapter, I will not address the philosophical question of whether there can be such a thing as rational suicide. Rather, I will explore some of what is known about the psychology of PAS, a practise that is regarded as one form of rational suicide, describing what is known about the psychology of those who seek it, those who provide it, and those who are left behind. I will explore what is understood about PAS in light of current understandings of the psychology of the patient–physician relationship. I will treat these psychiatric aspects of PAS (whether pathological or not) as data for moral deliberation rather than as empirical answers to moral questions. I will focus on observations from the United States (and therefore on PAS), but make special reference to Belgium and the Netherlands, where euthanasia (and not just PAS) is taking place, and where psychiatric diseases can be considered legally permissible indications for these practices.

49

Those Who Seek PAS

Contrary to popular rhetoric, those who seek PAS generally are not suffering from intractable physical symptoms such as pain or seizures (Suarez-Almazor et al. 2002). Empirical studies demonstrate that those who seek PAS report no more pain than similarly ill patients who do not seek PAS (Smith et al. 2015). Rather than pain or other physical symptoms, the top reasons for seeking PAS in Oregon are loss of autonomy, loss of 'dignity', decreased ability to enjoy life, loss of control of bodily functions, and being a burden on others (Oregon Department of Public Health 2015).

This reasoning appears to be an international phenomenon. In the Netherlands, for example, the top reasons for seeking euthanasia are 'pointless suffering', 'loss of dignity' and even include 'tiredness of life' (Jansen-van der Weide et al. 2005). Similarly, a Belgian survey showed that 'suffering' and 'loss of dignity' were far more important than pain as reasons for making a request for euthanasia (van Wesemael et al. 2011). In light of these facts, it seems important to think more clearly about both the psychiatric and social factors that lead to requests for PAS rather than ascribing the phenomenon a failure on the part of medical care to provide adequate symptom control.

Being sad when one is dying is understandable, normal and not patho-logical. Diagnosable depression, however, is not normal and represents a medical condition that can respond to treatment (Cassem 1995; Chochinov et al. 1995; Wilson et al. 2009; Breitbart et al. 2010). Unsurprisingly, terminally ill persons frequently think about death and entertain thoughts of suicide. A desire to hasten one's death must be distinguished from the acceptance of an inevitable natural death (Balaguer et al. 2016). Chochinov et al. (1995) have shown that 45 per cent of terminally ill patients express at least a transient desire for death. Those terminally ill patients whose desire for death is persistent harbour a significant burden of psychiatric disease. Of the 9 per cent whose desire for death is persistent, 59 per cent meet criteria for depression. Among cancer patients already receiving palliative care, 18 per cent express transient wishes for death and 12 per cent persistent wishes for death. Fifty-two per cent of patients in this latter group have a diagnosable mental disorder, mostly depression (Wilson et al. 2014).

Depression and Referral

Differentiating between 'rational' suicides and those due to depression or other mental illnesses is challenging, especially because suicidal ideation is itself one of the major diagnostic criteria for depression, and because depression itself does not automatically confer a lack of decisional capacity (Cohen et al. 2000; Nash et al. 2009). Rates of screening for depression or other psychiatric disorders among patients who request PAS are not known definitively, but appear to be quite low. There are no data on any screening for depression by the physicians who provide PAS in the United States. All that is known are rates of psychiatric referral. State laws in the United States recommend but do not require formal psychiatric evaluation. In 2014, only 3 of 105 patients who died of lethal ingestions under the PAS law in Oregon underwent psychiatric evaluation; since the passage of the law only 5.5 per cent have had such evaluations (Oregon Department of Public Health 2015). If rates of depression among the terminally ill who desire death are as high as those described, this proportion seems low. Moreover, while referral bias likely has resulted in an underestimation of the rate of depression in their sample, Ganzini and colleagues (2008a) have reported that at least three of the 18 patients they interviewed who received a lethal prescription under the Oregon law were clinically depressed, yet none had seen a psychiatrist and all three completed their suicides.

While depression itself does not render a patient decisionally incapacitated and preclude legal access to assisted suicide, it would nonetheless seem prudent to try to treat any depressed patient who requests assisted suicide (Moskowitz 1997). Such a policy both would avoid the error of overestimating the patient's capacity and would leave open the possibility that the patient might withdraw the request were the suffering caused by depression abated.

A Personality Type

There is a small number of Americans who do not suffer from any diagnosed psychiatric disorder, but seek a physician's assistance with suicide for reasons they argue are rational, such as the anticipation of not being able to cope with physical symptoms, or to preclude the possibility of a future physical and/or mental state characterized by lack of control, dependence on the assistance of others, or disfigurement. Their number is estimated to be less than 0.5 per cent of the US population (Emanuel 1999; Oregon Department of Public Health 2015). When they become sick, these are the persons who best fit the legal parameters for being considered candidates for PAS. Emerging data suggest that they represent a distinct personality type. They tend to have personalities with a dismissive attachment style and are fixated on being in control (Oldham et al. 2011; Smith et al. 2015). Psychiatrists who have interviewed patients who have requested PAS have observed that the request appears almost to represent the culmination of a lifelong pattern of concern with issues such as control, autonomy, self-sufficiency, distrust of others, and avoidance of intimacy (Oldham et al. 2011; Ganzini et al. 2003). These observations suggest that it is the personalities of a small group of individuals who face chronic, progressive, eventually fatal conditions rather than anything about the conditions themselves, or the attitudes of the other 99.5 per cent of the population facing these same conditions, that drive the actual demand for PAS in the United States.

Those Who Provide PAS

PAS, by definition, requires a patient–physician interaction. Little attention has been paid, however, to the psychological aspects of the physician side of this interaction.

Intentionally precipitating the deaths of patients through assisted suicide and euthanasia exacts a significant price from practitioners. In a survey from the Netherlands, 75 per cent of physicians who had performed euthanasia reported psychological discomfort afterwards (Haverkate et al. 2001). In a survey of US oncologists, 24 per cent expressed frank regret over having done so even once in their careers (Emanuel et al. 1998). These studies suggest that physicians sense that there is something about euthanasia and PAS that causes them moral angst.

Family members who witness the assisted suicides of their loved ones have rates of Post-Traumatic Stress Disorder (PTSD) as high as 20 per cent (Wagner et al. 2012). While the psychological impact on clinicians who perform euthanasia or assist with suicide has not been investigated with formal psychiatric testing, it is unlikely that clinicians are immune from such effects.

Perhaps, however, it is this psychological impact on clinicians that really undergirds the American preference for PAS over euthanasia – physicians typically do not witness the suicides of the patients they assist in PAS, and may be relatively shielded from the emotional impact. From a moral perspective, however, one can question whether this is a good consequence. Those who oppose PAS could argue that it is not good to immunize physicians from the psychological consequences of a deed that is at least universally acknowledged to be ethically controversial. The distress itself might represent an initial moral evaluation.

Yet again, those who favour euthanasia could argue that it is self-serving for physicians rather than patient-centred to permit PAS but not euthanasia, if euthanasia is actually better for patients. If physicians were to practice euthanasia more often, they could argue, their distress would diminish over time. Physicians should not let their moral qualms stand in the way of good patient care.

Those who oppose PAS and euthanasia could counter that this diminution in distress with repeated action is exactly the problem with dropping the legal barrier to these actions. Like other human practices, once one overcomes one's moral resistance to an act and performs it, a strong human tendency kicks in to justify the action to oneself and to others (Callahan 1991). Repetition of the act becomes, of itself, a powerful means of such justification. As Dutch euthanist Dr Herbert Cohen reported to Dr Herbert Hendin, 'The first time you do it, euthanasia is difficult, like climbing a mountain' (Hendin 1998). This is what is meant by the psychological slippery slope. Once one crosses a moral barrier, a practice that is initially difficult becomes easier. The scope of those who are seen as eligible recipients for the action widens.

Countertransference

A number of psychiatrists have warned of the potentially troubling role that countertransference might play in the patient–physician relationship with respect to the questions of euthanasia and PAS. Countertransference refers to the unconsciously determined responses of a clinician to the specific characteristics and behaviours of the patient based upon the doctor's previous patterns of behaviour and emotional responses in the significant relationships in his or her life. These responses subconsciously affect how the clinician interacts with the patient (Nash et al. 2009).

Multiple authors have pointed out the subtle ways in which legalization of PAS can become a medium through which negative countertransference reactions by clinicians, which once were held in check by law and professional norms, can be enacted (Wesley 1993; Miles 1994; Miles 1995; Varghese and Kelly 2001; Kelly et al., 2003; Stevens 2006).

One possible source of countertransference derives from physicians' feelings of inadequacy. Physicians want to fix things, sometimes almost obsessively. They can often feel helpless and inadequate in the face of illness and suffering, which medicine, as a metaphysical certainty, is incapable of ever eliminating completely. Such feelings can lead too easily to the writing of a lethal prescription as a solution to problems that are, in reality, as much the physician's as they are the patient's.

Another source can be physician fatigue in the face of the demands of caring for those who suffer from chronic, progressive, eventually fatal conditions. 'Compassion fatigue' and burnout are common in physicians, especially those who work with populations of patients whose conditions are incurable, such as many cancers and some psychiatric conditions. Care for such patients is hard work. Given his or her role, the physician often cannot consciously acknowledge his own wish to be freed from the tedious, unrewarding task of caring for such persons, yet will often harbour unconscious wishes for the patient's death as an escape from this laborious task. According to countertransference theory, legalization of PAS would provide a socially sanctioned route for such an escape. Caregiver fatigue can readily be re-cast as a patient's right to die, and patients will readily introject the external cues from the physician that urge their election of this 'right'.

Physicians' acquiescence to requests for assisted suicide might also be as much an effort to work out personal and familial issues as an effort to help the patient. The plight of the patient might bring to the subconscious mind the agonizing death of a parent. The patient's passing expression of desire for death might evoke subconscious thoughts of the suicide of a sibling. The physician may never have come fully to terms with these deaths in his or her own life and might reach for the prescription pad as the solution to the patient's predicament when, in reality, he or she is really trying to kill off painful memories.

The power imbalance in the patient–physician relationship makes these countertransference issues especially troubling. And when the physician is formally given lethal power over the patient, those who understand the dynamics of countertransference believe we ought to pause.

Assisted Suicide, Ethics, and the Dynamics of the Patient–Physician Relationship

For the past 2,500 years, Western medicine has been guided by broadly Hippocratic principles that establish the minimum conditions necessary for the patient to entrust his or her vulnerable body and psyche to the physician. These conditions are set forth in the Oath sworn by the physician, establishing the safety of this fragile interpersonal space. At minimum, the physician swears to any and all patients a few simple but absolute, basic, almost animalistically primitive things: 'I will not use you for sex. I will not kill you. Please understand that this means you will be safe under my care. You can trust me'. It is precisely one of these primitive conditions of trust that the legalization of PAS would seem to threaten.

Surveys do not reveal that the general public reports that they think they would have less trust in physicians were PAS to be legalized (Hall et al. 2005), but surveys of the attitudes of the general public reveal nothing about the true psychodynamics of the patient–physician relationship in its privacy and intimacy.

The ethical perspective of Emmanuel Levinas can cast an important light on discussions of PAS once one begins thinking about this practice as an event that occurs, by definition, in the context of the patient–physician relationship. Levinas argues that before the Face of the Other, the ethically aware person is compelled to attend to the cry of the primordial imperative of all ethical responsibility, 'Do not kill me' (Levinas 1985). There is a strongly Levinasian character to an understanding of the prohibition on physicians killing patients as part of the establishment of the primitive conditions of trust necessary for a healing relationship. The encounter between patient and physician, rather than being an exception to this imperative, would seem to represent the most extreme circumstance in which this cry from the Other would issue as the foundational moral primitive. If there is to be such a thing as medical ethics, the physician must be compelled to see in the patient the Face of the radically Other. In almost no other human encounter is the primordial ethical situation envisioned by Levinas more clearly evoked than when a physician stands before a patient – the secure standing before the vulnerable, the strong before the weak, the young before the old, the possessor of arcane knowledge before the ignorant, the well before the sick. The Face of the patient, nude and vulnerable, *is* the physician's call to be ethical. From a Levinasian perspective, to let go of this imperative would be to undermine the meaning of anything that could be called medical ethics.

Degnin (1997) has attempted to make a Levinasian argument for at least some cases of PAS, arguing that the Face of the patient demands both nonviolence and the caring attention of the physician, so that in at least some cases a refusal to acquiesce to the patient's request to be killed would itself be an act of violence. Yet it seems that Degnin's interpretation does violence to Levinas in coming to this conclusion, undermining the very heart of the imperative of ethical responsibility. The moral imperative at the heart of the patient-physician relationship must be ɔnger than 'I will not kill you ... unless you want me to.' This is ꞁecially because the absolutely free will of the patient that Degnin presupposes as the basis for this exception is a philosophical abstraction with little basis in lived reality. A subtler understanding of the clinical encounter would recognize the fragility of the will of the sick person in the face of the life-threatening illness that is said to justify PAS in the first place, and the power imbalance inherent in the patient–physician relationship. The fact that all PAS laws require physician concurrence that the suicide is rational, justified, and medically indicated means that the act is never a purely autonomous choice of the patient but a request that must be vetted by the powerful physician, sanctioned as medically indicated, and enacted by a formal prescription. In this setting, the countertransferences of physicians, as described earlier, loom large. What might appear even to the patient to be a pure expression of his or her own free will may well be nothing more than an acquiescence to the will of the physician. It is precisely such a possibility that makes ethics necessary and constitutes the sense of this Hippocratic and Levinasian boundary condition: 'Do not kill me'.

Those Who Are Left Behind

It is often averred that rational suicide is a private, self-regarding act. It is argued that attempts to regulate physician assistance in suicide represent an unwarranted intrusion of state authority over and against individual liberty because, if it is desired by the patient, suicide does not harm the patient, and since it has no impact on others, rational suicide harms no one. Emerging data suggest otherwise.

It is well known that suicides have a major impact on surviving family members (Cerel et al. 2008; Tal Young et al. 2012). Recognizing this impact and regarding suicide as an act of interpersonal communication, even revenge, renowned liaison psychiatrist Edwin Cassem regularly used to ask patients contemplating suicide, 'In whose closet do you intend to leave your skeleton?' That is to say, suicide always has long-lasting effects on those who are left behind, and the person contemplating suicide is at least subconsciously aware of this fact and intends such a lasting harm. Surprisingly, however, little research has been conducted regarding the impact of PAS on family members. Ganzini et al. (2009) reported no difference in mental health outcomes for families of patients who requested lethal prescriptions under the Oregon Death With Dignity Act compared with families of other dying patients, but the study has multiple limitations: they sampled only those who requested PAS, not those who carried it out, they did not assess for PTSD, and the sample size was small and probably subject to referral bias. By contrast, a more recent Swiss study showed that 20 per cent of family members who witness the assisted suicides of their loved ones develop symptoms of PTSD (Wagner et al. 2012).

The impact of legalized assisted suicide, however, may extend far beyond the circle of the suicide's intimates. Suicide contagion is a well-recognized phenomenon (Cheng et al. 2014). Suicide contagion refers to the increase in suicide that accompanies publicity about suicide. For example, after the publicity that surrounds the suicide of a well-known figure, or public reports of an unusual method of suicide, or even some popular fictionalized cases of suicide, there are spikes in the rate of suicide in the general population and increases in the number of cases of suicide 'copying' the publicized mechanism. This has been demonstrated to occur with assisted suicide. There are data showing a social contagion effect of PAS. For example, Marzuk et al. (1993; 1994) showed spikes in suicide by drug overdose and asphyxiation in the general population after the publication of the Hemlock Society's Derek Humphry's how-to manual for suicide called *Final Exit* (Humphry 1991), which explicitly described these methods.

More recently, Jones and Paton (2015) have demonstrated increased rates of suicide among the general public in those states in the United States that have legalized PAS relative to those states that have not. Mechanisms for this phenomenon remain unclear, but they include a social contagion effect due to general publicity about suicide, social 'normalization' of suicide through its legalization or vaguer (but perhaps more powerful) social networking effects (Kheriaty 2015).

Thus, it seems fair to say that legalized PAS has a number of negative effects on other persons that are rarely noted in public debates, which often characterize legalization as a way to permit private choice about a purely self-regarding act.

The Psychological Influence of Social Environment

The social environment into which legalized assisted suicide is being introduced also exerts subtle but powerful pressures on both clinicians and patients that are often inadequately accounted for in public debates about the propriety of this policy. These include the obsessions of the Western world with youth, beauty, independence, and control. The loss of any of these makes one socially undesirable and can lead to thoughts of worthlessness. Such thoughts set the stage for suicide.

One of these social pressures is also the pressure to contain health care costs. The United States does not guarantee health care to its citizens and has the world's largest free market in health care delivery and insurance. In the face of continual innovation and a rate of health care inflation that has, for decades, outpaced the overall rate of inflation in the US economy, insurers are being pressed by both the government and private employers to control health care expenditures. Case reports have surfaced, for instance, describing insurers alerting patients to their right to PAS while denying them medically indicated but expensive new treatments (Karlamangla 2015).

Since it is physicians who order the tests and treatments, pressure to control health care costs is most often transferred directly to physicians. In recent decades, physicians everywhere in the developed world, but especially in the United States, are repeatedly being reminded of the need to practice frugal medicine, and to do their part to rein in the spiralling costs of health care. My colleagues and I (Sulmasy et al. 1998) have shown that the stronger the tendency of a US physician to practice in a frugal manner, the more likely it is that this physician would practice assisted suicide (adjusted odds ratio = 6.4). This association, while very strong, does not prove a cause-and-effect relationship. It may not be the case that frugal physicians choose to assist with suicide as a means to conserve resources. It could be that those who think it rational to conserve resources are simply also more likely to think it rational to assist with suicide. Nonetheless, given the countertransference concerns described in this chapter, this association is troubling. The confluence of these rationales suggests a sort of broad approach to medicine as an instrument of social utility, such that it is simply 'rational' to conclude that worthless medical interventions ought not to be pursued and that those who have come to judge their lives as worthless ought to be aided in ending their worthless lives. Physicians are under increasing pressure not only to pursue 'value-based medicine', but simultaneously to attend to patient preferences and to demonstrate patient satisfaction with the care they give. All of these domains are being measured and physician incomes are being tied to these measures through the US version of a financing strategy often called 'Pay for Performance' (McKethan and Jha 2014). Given such external pressures and the confluence of rationales for cost-containment and PAS, assisted suicide would simply become the only rational choice, achieving all these goals simultaneously, satisfying those who prefer it, while simultaneously decreasing health care costs. A physician's 'value based' rationale for suggesting PAS, subconscious encouragement of PAS, and acquiescence to the request for PAS can thus be represented to the patient and to the payers, through the mechanisms of countertransference, as simply the 'right choice' for the patient, even were the patient inclined to hesitate.

Some have suggested that studies showing that the wealthy are more likely than the poor to commit suicide with the assistance of a physician, provides evidence that there is no influence of cost-control pressure on the practice of PAS (Coombs-Lee 2014, Battin et al. 2007). Such reasoning, however, is fallacious. First, the poor are not the only persons who can be vulnerable (Krag 2014). The wealthy use health insurance and consume common resources when they are sick. Wealthy, independent, white males are vulnerable in the sense that whatever threatens this privileged status can be perceived as a severe threat to their identities. They operate in social circles in which the 'dismissive' personality type described earlier is normative. As long as the social elite remain fixated on being in control, wealthy and powerful persons can be offered the appearance of control in the form of PAS, which achieves the cost savings sought by a utilitarian society without appearing exploitative. Second, data show that groups traditionally considered vulnerable, such as the poor, African Americans, and the elderly are less likely to be interested in PAS (Emanuel et al. 2000; Koenig et al. 1996). Their absolute numbers will therefore be small in any study reporting on those who have requested or carried out PAS. Under such conditions, the statistical power to detect financial pressure on this group will be very low. Absence of such evidence should not be taken as evidence of the absence of the effect.

Psychiatric Illness as an Indication for Physician-Assisted Death

In the United States, psychiatric illness is not, as yet, a legally recognized indication for physician assistance with suicide. Legislation in the states of California, Oregon, Vermont, and Washington require that patients receiving lethal prescriptions suffer from a terminal *physical* condition and that they not suffer from any mental condition that would interfere with the capacity to choose suicide rationally.

How long such a restriction will last is unknown. Increasingly, arguments are being mounted that such a limitation unfairly restricts the rights of the mentally ill and represents a bias, privileging the physically ill with access to permanent release from their suffering while condemning the mentally ill to prolonged psychiatric pain which, in justice, ought to be treated as equally worthy of relief (Schuklenk and van de Vathorst 2015; Varelius 2015; Wijsbek 2012; Hewitt 2010; Berghmans et al. 2013).

In the Netherlands and in Belgium, practice is already outpacing such theorizing. In the Netherlands, while the law is silent with respect to psychiatric indications, patients are required to have intact decision-making capacity in order to request euthanasia. Yet they need only to demonstrate 'unbearable suffering' with no prospect of improvement in order to be eligible. In a famous legal case regarding Dr Boudewijn Chabot's euthanizing of a very unhappy patient with no specific psychiatric diagnosis, the Dutch Supreme Court ruled in 1994 that, while Dr Chabot was guilty of not following protocols, his patient's mental suffering met the criteria of law and he was not punished (Wijsbek 2012). This was widely viewed as permitting a psychiatric indication for euthanasia (Berghmans et al. 2013). Data are scant on how often psychiatric illness is the only indication for euthanasia in the Netherlands, but, while not unusual, it appears to account for much less than 1 per cent of all cases of Dutch euthanasia (Groenewoud et al. 2004; Snijdewind et al. 2015). Physician support for psychiatric euthanasia is not as widespread as is physician support for euthanasia for patients suffering from physical conditions. Only 34 per cent of Dutch physicians report believing that psychiatric indications alone would ever lead them to participate in euthanasia, and only 27 per cent would ever do so solely for 'tiredness of living' as the sole indication (Bolt et al. 2015). Nonetheless, Pols and Oak (2013) report that psychiatrists are under increasing pressure from the public to acquiesce to requests for euthanasia for purely psychiatric indications. Raijmakers et al. (2015) report that being 'tired of living,' in absence of serious physical or even psychiatric disease, would be acceptable as an indication for their own euthanasia by 21 per cent of Dutch people.

In Belgium, legislation explicitly allows euthanasia for psychiatric indications (Thienpont et al. 2015). In 2011, 3.5 per cent of cases of euthanasia were performed solely for psychiatric indications (Deschepper et al. 2014). As in the Netherlands, pressure on physicians to comply with requests based on psychiatric symptoms has been intense. The legal standards are vague, requiring that the patient suffer (1) 'unbearable mental suffering due to a mental disease', (2) that the situation be 'untreatable', and (3) that the physician exercise 'due care' in evaluating the request (Deschepper et al. 2014). Thus, almost any chronic psychiatric state in which residual symptoms persist despite treatment can be considered eligible. Diagnoses for those making the request under the rubric of mental suffering have included depression, schizophrenia, anorexia, borderline personality disorder, chronic fatigue syndrome, and somatization disorder (Thienpont et al. 2015). Three-quarters have been women. Half of these requests were granted, although some patients withdrew their requests, and others committed suicide before euthanasia could be carried out. Many of these euthanasias were carried out by the evaluating psychiatrists themselves. Four of the patients studied by Thienpont et al. (2015), whose requests were refused by the evaluating psychiatrists, went on to commit suicide without medical assistance. These suicides were described as 'dramatic', although further details were not disclosed out of confidentiality concerns.

While it is not (yet) a widespread practice in the United States, there is no principled reason that has been offered to justify PAS for patients with somatic illnesses that could not be applied equally to patients with psychiatric illnesses. Indeed, in most jurisdictions where PAS or euthanasia are legal, these practices are applied on the basis of mental suffering not only of physical suffering or terminal illness. This is the status quo in the Netherlands, Luxembourg, Belgium, Switzerland, and, since 2015, also in Canada. It seems wrong to classify suffering occasioned by psychiatric illness as less worthy than suffering occasioned by somatic illness. Since suffering is a subjective notion, its intensity cannot be challenged by an objective standard. If it is respect for patient autonomy that justifies acceding to a request, then it must be acknowledged that most patients with psychiatric illnesses retain autonomy, have decisional capacity, and ought not to be excluded from access to any treatment, including PAS, on the supposition that psychiatric illness routinely diminishes autonomy.

Moreover, it is not clear that decisional capacity is the critical issue. Once one has acknowledged that it is discriminatory to exclude patients with somatic illnesses who have diminished decisional capacity (such as patients with stroke or dementia) from access to PAS and/or euthanasia, then it must be deemed equally discriminatory to exclude patients with diminished decisional capacity from access to PAS and/or euthanasia. In the Netherlands and Belgium, euthanasia for patients who lack decisional capacity but who, it is assumed, would want it ('euthanasia without a specific request') has become a common occurrence (van der Heide, et al. 2007; Pereira 2011; Chambaere et al., 2015a). Why not euthanasia without explicit consent for someone with refractory schizophrenia so severe that he or she is deemed lacking in decisional capacity, so long as a family member is willing to say that the patient has 'suffered enough'?

The Power to Kill

By the same token, however, whatever can be said to be worrisome about PAS for the mentally ill only sharpens what can be said to be worrisome about PAS for patients suffering from any medical condition. All PAS and euthanasia happens in the context of a patient–physician relationship. That relationship is quiet, subtle, and private; alive with deep psychodynamic resonances that are often unnoticed or overlooked; and extremely fragile. Aesculapian power, the power of the white coat, is a very real phenomenon that clinicians, the profession, and society need to circumscribe vigilantly, channelling that power towards medicine's most beneficent ends. Legalized PAS and euthanasia remove an essential check on that power, granting the physician absolute power over life and death.

Of course, medical power needs to be checked at the other extreme as well. Physicians ought not overestimate the power of medical technology and ought not to treat patients past the point of any real hope of biomedical benefit. Establishing this limit on medical power has been perhaps the chief achievement of the last 50 years of the bioethics movement. The traditional distinction between killing and allowing to die has thus served this important function – it checks medial hubris by permitting clinicians to cease their ministrations when the patient is overwhelmed by disease, yet also keeps Aesculapian power in check by not granting physicians the authority to kill directly. This distinction makes an absolute statement of the limits of medical power, creates a context of trust in which the patient can be assured of safety in his or her vulnerability and thus placed in the optimal situation for healing, while maintaining a healthy respect for the ambiguity of the line between life and death.

Propelled by the powerful (but often invisible) currents of countertransference, empathy for the chronically ill (whether physically or mentally) can become an ironically lethal force. The message that may be communicated, even if never directly spoken, can be, 'I understand how deeply you are suffering. I'd think about killing myself too if I were in your shoes.' The traditional Hippocratic ban on physician assistance with suicide and euthanasia is meant to keep such a message from ever becoming explicit. Legalized assisted suicide and/or euthanasia makes this message direct, real, and actionable. That seems dangerous, especially to the mentally ill.

The pressure to conform to the views of peers is so great that prevailing social mores are often introjected and re-interpreted by the subject as his or her own autonomous preferences. This can clearly happen in the setting of legalized PAS, in a society in which celebrities say on TV, 'If I ever get that way please shoot me', and polls show the vast majority of persons supporting legalized PAS or euthanasia. Legalization flips the default switch, psychologically, for those who suffer from chronic, disabling, and eventually lethal conditions. For most of the history of Western medicine they have had to argue that their time has come and that their life-prolonging treatments ought to be withheld or withdrawn. With the legalization of PAS, however, the default question becomes, 'Why have you not yet availed yourself of the opportunity to rid yourself (and us) of the burdens of your condition by requesting PAS?' And so the patient asks, 'Doctor, would you give me the pills so I can end it all now?' Since the words come out of the mouth of the patient the request may seem autonomous, but it well may be, in reality, merely the introjection of the disdain in which the patient is held by a community that fears its own suffering and wants to eliminate reminders of that possibility from the environment. The physician accedes to the request and, on the surface, all seems well. Yet an ominous fracture in the moral bedrock of society has taken place deep beneath that tranquil surface. The stage is set for the further moral tremblors that await a society that ultimately chooses death over suffering, no matter what the cost in human dignity, freedom, truth, solidarity, or justice.

Conclusion

In this chapter, I have reviewed the existing literature on the psychiatric aspects of legalized assisted suicide with an eye towards the United States, but have considered sources from other nations as well. Each psychiatric dimension reviewed raised questions about the propriety of legalized PAS. First, most terminally ill patients who think about assisted suicide are depressed, but diagnosing depression in this setting is difficult and very few patients who make the request are evaluated by psychiatrists. Second, while neurological or psychiatric illnesses do not always take away patient decisional capacity, it seems to be the case that to be severe enough to 'warrant' assisted suicide, the patient would probably need to suffer from an incapacitating form of neurological or psychiatric disease. This means that PAS will generally need to be administered in advance of any lack of capacity, raising questions about how many patients would have changed their minds, or would never actually have developed disease severe enough to meet the threshold for justifying PAS. Third, physical symptoms are rarely the reason patients seek PAS. Patients who follow through on PAS, at least in the United States, appear to have a distinct personality type, characterized by a need for control and a dismissive attitude towards other persons. They represent only about 0.5 per cent of the US population. Questions can be raised about 'normalizing' this personality type, and about whether risks to the other 99.5 per cent of the population justify acceding to wishes of this small minority. Fourth, PAS has a distinct negative impact on physicians that has been underappreciated. It can be questioned whether the fact that this negative impact attenuates with repetition of the act is actually a good thing. Fifth, the impact of legalized PAS on the patient–physician relationship has not been studied in depth. The well-recognized phenomenon of countertransference, by which the physician's subconscious motives and issues can become powerful and unrecognized influences on the patient's decisions, looms large in this setting. Physicians may actually wish, subconsciously, to be rid of their patients, and this can be introjected by the patient and expressed as his or her own apparently autonomous wish. Such tendencies might be exaggerated and find further self-justification in an atmosphere of increasing pressure on physicians to control health care costs. Sixth, collateral effects of assisted suicide have also been understudied, but preliminary data show evidence of PTSD in family members and a social contagion effect of increased suicide in the wider population. Seventh, psychiatric illness itself has become a justifiable indication for PAS, and there seems no principled way of preventing such a development on the basis of all the standard justifications for legalizing PAS for those suffering from somatic illnesses.

Finally, it should be noted that the traditional Hippocratic ban on physicians killing patients makes sense from the perspective of the psychodynamics of the patient–physician relationship. The preconditions of trust that constitute the safety of the interpersonal space in which the patient can expose his or her vulnerability to the physician in order to be healed would seem to include, at a minimum, that the physician pledge to the patient, 'I will not kill you'. Deviations from this boundary condition, one that has traditionally circumscribed the patient–physician relationship, might well have wider implications for social morality than is commonly thought.

PART II

Euthanasia and End-of-Life Care

4

Assisted Dying

The Current Situation in Flanders: Euthanasia Embedded in Palliative Care

PAUL VANDEN BERGHE, ARSÈNE MULLIE,
MARC DESMET AND GERT HUYSMANS

In 2002, three laws concerning the end of life were almost simultaneously passed by the Belgian parliament: a law decriminalising euthanasia, a law affirming the right to palliative care for all and a law concerning the rights of patients in general. At that time, a substantial part of the Belgian palliative care community, like the Belgian healthcare community in general, was very reticent to become involved in euthanasia, for different reasons.

One of them was the radical nature of the act of euthanasia (defined in Belgian law as 'the intentional termination of the life of another person at his/her request'[1]), which is completely at odds with everything healthcare professionals are usually taught. Another reason was the widespread opinion that optimal palliative care, starting with a thorough clarification of the patient's request for help to end their life, would eliminate the need for euthanasia.

Ten years later, in Flanders (the northern, Dutch-speaking part of Belgium), and to a lesser extent in the rest of the country,[2] the caring practice of 'euthanasia accompaniment' (euthanasiebegeleiding) is part of the daily work of palliative care professionals, who support the treating doctor and team in all aspects of the patient's request, while only very

---

This was originally published in the European Journal of Palliative Care as Vanden Berghe et al. 2013. It is reproduced here with the reference system used throughout the present volume, but with the text otherwise unchanged. It is followed by a Postscript composed for this volume.
[1] Full text of the 2002 Belgian law on euthanasia (in Dutch and in French).
[2] This chapter is mostly about Flanders, the Dutch-speaking, northern region of Belgium. The developments it describes partly apply to the rest of the country as well: certainly to the Brussels region, but probably not yet to the same extent to Wallonia, the French-speaking, southern region.

occasionally carrying out euthanasia themselves. This 'euthanasia accompaniment' includes clarification of the request, communication with the family, consideration of other possibilities, medical and other assistance if euthanasia is performed and support of the team afterwards. It takes place with full respect for each professional's personal choice regarding their involvement.

How did this major shift happen and what questions does it raise?

Opening Up to Euthanasia

Leaving Presuppositions Behind

This shift in mindsets and attitudes was induced by different experiences. In some cases, palliative care professionals were finding that patients' responses to palliative care interventions were poor and that euthanasia effectively appeared to bring a 'good death'. In other cases, palliative care professionals were declining patients' requests for euthanasia and subsequently finding themselves confronted with a situation where patients nevertheless received euthanasia, but from an external medical practitioner. Even if this was done following state-of-the-art guidelines and good practice, the fact that it happened outside the context of the regular and familiar care team (treating physician, family nurse, etc.), sometimes without the knowledge of the family, made those palliative care professionals realise that it was not optimal care. For them, the change to a more positive engagement, first as witnesses only, was clearly a 'lesser evil'. In a large number of cases, they witnessed euthanasia that was being correctly administered from a medical point of view, after thorough clarification of the patient's request and adequate communication, and that had good results. Whether or not all palliative possibilities had been exhausted, the patient was relieved and grateful that their final days did not have to last any longer. This convinced those professionals that euthanasia could be part of genuinely good care.

Moreover, since the key reasons for euthanasia requests appeared to be a desire to be in control, fear of dependency and existential despair, euthanasia no longer seemed a failure of, or antagonistic to, palliative care, but something that could be served by it.

These different experiences led to the growing involvement of palliative care professionals and teams in the accompaniment of euthanasia. In the name of continuity of care, they chose not to abandon patients asking for euthanasia by referring them to external practitioners, outside the familiar care environment, but to continue to provide them with all the necessary support.

An Evolution Supported at all Levels

Through this growing involvement, what is and should be the natural stance gradually became clearer: for the sake of good care, transferring a palliative patient requesting euthanasia outside their familiar care environment is never the best option. This stance was actively supported from the beginning by the *Federatie Palliatieve Zorg Vlaanderen* (Federation of Palliative Care Flanders [FPCF]) in numerous ways: through team consultation, guided group supervision of the different professionals involved in palliative care (doctors, nurses, psychologists, social workers, etc.) and education on how palliative care could open up to euthanasia. This happened at all levels, within care organisations but also within regional network members of the FPCF.

In 2003, under the direction of its Steering Group for Ethics (with Professor Bert Broeckaert from the University of Leuven as ethical advisor), the FPCF published a reference text on how to deal with euthanasia and other forms of medically assisted dying (FPCF 2003). In 2006, it published a framework document on treatment decisions in advanced disease (FPCF 2006).

In 2011, a reference document on palliative care and euthanasia (FPCF 2011) was unanimously accepted by the Federation's Board of Directors. It both confirmed and supported the evolution of the past decade. This document states that the complexity of a number of difficult-to-treat symptoms and end-of-life issues often exceeds the competence of primary caregivers. In such cases, the advice of the palliative team, which is particularly knowledgeable in crucial domains (physical suffering that is difficult to relieve, unrecognised depression, guilt issues, pressure from the family, loss of meaning etc.) has an important added value. Specialist palliative care advice is particularly recommended when it comes to inform patients who ask for euthanasia about the palliative possibilities, as required by the Belgian law on euthanasia. In this way, both patient and physician can be sure that there is really 'no other reasonable solution' to relieve the intolerable suffering – which again is a requirement of the law (see Box 1).

This reference document further states that palliative care teams, with their multidisciplinary character, possess the highest standards of

---

BOX 1 MAIN REQUIREMENTS OF THE BELGIAN LAW ON EUTHANASIA

According to the Belgian law on euthanasia passed on 28 May 2002, the major legal requirements for performing euthanasia are:

- Repeated and consistent request from an adult patient who is competent (that is, who has full mental capacity), made under no external pressure and in writing (or expressed in a written advance directive in the case of a patient in an irreversible state of unconsciousness).
- Persistent and intolerable suffering, physical and/or mental.
- Caused by an irreversible medical condition (accident or disease).
- If patient not expected to die within foreseeable future, two independent colleagues must be consulted and a moratorium of one month must be respected between the patient's written request and the administration of euthanasia.
- Patient duly informed of their condition, life expectancy and other therapeutic options, including those offered by palliative care.
- Patient and doctor reaching the conclusion that there is no other reasonable solution.
- Discussion of the request by the doctor with significant others, if patient wishes so.
- Euthanasia carried out by a doctor after consultation with the nursing team and one competent and independent colleague; the doctor has to be present until the patient's death.
- Case reported to the Belgian Federal Euthanasia Control and Evaluation Committee.

---

palliative care skills (including communication skills) and thus are well qualified to practice end-of-life care and also provide euthanasia accompaniment both in a careful (regarding the legal conditions) and caring way. These palliative care teams act as secondary teams: they do not take over the patient's care but support the familiar primary healthcare professionals, who are thus trained, looked after and strengthened.

Where Are We Today?

Today, one in two non-sudden deaths in Flanders occurs with the support of specialist palliative care professionals (FPCF 2012), whether within mobile home care teams, hospital support teams (which are available in every hospital), hospital palliative care units (there are 29 in the region totalling 209 beds) or through 'reference persons for palliative care' in homes for the elderly.

In 2011, 1,133 cases of euthanasia were reported to the Belgian Federal Euthanasia Control and Evaluation Committee. Unofficial figures show 1,430 cases in 2012 and 445 in the first quarter of 2013. In 2011, 918 of the 1,133 cases were registered in Dutch, which amounts to about 1 per cent of all deaths in Flanders (FCECE 2012). If the 2007 estimated number of unreported cases is taken into account (Smets et al. 2010), this figure comes to 1.9 per cent.

No data are yet available on the provision and extent of specialist palliative support in the reported – and unreported – cases of euthanasia. However, we can safely say that, during the past few years, all palliative care teams in home care and hospital settings in Flanders have been providing support in the care of people requesting euthanasia. Some hospitals are more restrictive than others, imposing additional conditions on the practice of euthanasia, such as obligatory intervention by the palliative care team.

According to the WHO definition of palliative care (WHO 2016), palliative care should not intend to hasten death. Therefore, euthanasia cannot be part of palliative care. However, we think that euthanasia and palliative care can occasionally be considered together when caring for one and the same patient. This does not necessarily mean that we systematically perform euthanasia when a patient requests it. Only a small number of requests eventually lead to actual euthanasia.

Palliative Care not Harmed but Strengthened

Euthanasia was introduced in Belgium in a generally cautious way, and this certainly has something to do with the fact that palliative care, initiated in the 1980s by volunteers, was already well developed before 2002 (Chambaere et al. 2011b, KCE 2009). Belgian palliative care had a head start over euthanasia practice, which remained exceptional in the country (by contrast, in the Netherlands, the law authorising physician-assisted dying and euthanasia that came into effect in 2002 (Leget 2013) decriminalised an already existing euthanasia practice). In 2010, Belgium took joint fourth place worldwide on the quality of death index of the Economist Intelligence Unit (FEPZ 2008). This provided a favourable context for palliative care professionals to support patients asking for euthanasia in the most careful and caring way.

After ten years of experience, an intermediate conclusion is that some of the consequences of the introduction of euthanasia initially feared by its advocates or opponents did not materialise. Palliative care did not obstruct or delay the performance of euthanasia. Conversely, it can also be safely stated that palliative care was not harmed by the introduction of euthanasia, but on the contrary was forced to develop further.

The overall feeling is that end-of-life care in general has substantially improved. Healthcare professionals and patients alike are more knowledgeable on end-of-life care; they are better able to distinguish between the six or seven broad choices that can be made regarding end-of-life care (FPCF 2006); the demands of patients are better acknowledged; and professionals are more aware of what they are doing. It is the experience of many of us that the developments seen in the last ten years have resulted in more professional end-of-life care that better responds to patients' wishes. End-of-life care is certainly not perfect yet, but this has more to do with the huge workload and lack of staff (notably nurses) to cope with increasing demand. Standards of care are rising – obviously a good thing – partly because of the influence of palliative care, which in a way has become a victim of its own success (professional caregivers are significantly overburdened).

There is no indication of an alarming increase in the number of euthanasia cases or of significant misuse of any medically assisted end-of-life decision (such as alleviation of pain, palliative sedation, assisted dying without request etc.). On the contrary, the decriminalisation of euthanasia has stimulated more thorough communication around end-of-life care, starting with advance care planning, between patients and their close relatives, but also between patients/relatives and professional caregivers. This communication is happening at the micro level of the individual, the intermediate level of institutions and organisations and the macro level of public policy (including around financial and ethical issues). Patients have the right to consent to or refuse a treatment, at any moment, including at the end of life, as well as the right to request euthanasia (which is not the same thing as the right to euthanasia, which does not exist in Belgium).

Our experience indicates that the provision of care at the end of life results in the greatest satisfaction when patients' families, proxies and informal caregivers are involved as partners in the process. In Flanders this is commonly called 'autonomy in relationship' (*autonomie in verbondenheid*): close relatives do not obstruct the expression of the patient's autonomy, but their involvement can help the patient clarify his/her own wishes and achieve their realisation in the most comprehensive way.

A True Ethical Labour

This article should not suggest that any of these matters are taken lightly, let alone trivialised. In all communication, special attention is given not to convey the implicit message that a palliative care professional is only a true professional if they can 'go the full way' in matters of euthanasia, whether as a physician, nurse, psychologist, social worker, spiritual caregiver or any other member of the palliative care team. The law states that no healthcare professional can be forced to be involved in the act of euthanasia. Every professional has the right to set their own ethical limits. What is expected of them is that they indicate these limits clearly, forthrightly and, above all, in a timely manner. From our experience, it is actually recommended that critical voices remain present in the team as it advances in the decision-making process.

It must be stressed that, in the course of these recent evolutions, the palliative care community of Belgium has been – and still is – carrying out a profound ethical labour. The situation described and views expressed in this article are the result of an intensive reflection, not only by ethicists, but first and most importantly by every single professional in Belgian palliative care, including on personal presuppositions, convictions, pace and outcomes, carried out at the level of the individual, teams and organisations involved.

Issues and Concerns

Yet, despite the favourable context and the constant engagement of numerous healthcare professionals and organisations, there are issues and concerns, which can be described as insidious side-effects of the introduction of euthanasia in the general landscape of care in Belgium. There are three major threats – that of legalism and proceduralism, of euthanasia following its own course and of instrumentalisation – all of which are at odds with the spirit of (palliative) care.

Legalism and Proceduralism

All (medical) care practice occurs against a general legal background, but the fact that there is a law for that one single intervention, euthanasia, has undoubtedly increased the trend towards proceduralism and legalism in end-of-life care. The regulation of euthanasia by a law articulating precise conditions and procedures provides not only society, but also healthcare professionals, with some reassurance that it is correctly performed. When (and only when) all legal conditions are met, euthanasia does not equate to murder, but to a legal life-ending act. The danger of legalism emerges when people think that meeting those legal conditions is in itself a sufficient condition for good care.

This problem does not only occur with legal requirements, or in end-of-life care, but also with all kinds of tools (e.g. guidelines and care pathways), and in all healthcare domains. What is specific in the case of euthanasia is that some professionals start perceiving all other end-of-life interventions, which are not specifically subject to a legal framework, as not being legal. This erroneous view can be more or less explicit, but when it affects end-of-life care practice, it raises the threshold for interventions other than euthanasia – such as withdrawing or withholding treatment, refusal of treatment, intensification of symptom control or palliative sedation – which are no less necessary, have their own indications and occur far more often.

Conversely, some professionals may be tempted to avoid euthanasia and steer care towards other end-of-life interventions precisely because there is no specific legal framework regulating them (no formal procedure, no legal conditions, no obligation to declare them), and therefore no risk of questions being raised, or even prosecution being conducted by a body such as the Federal Euthanasia Control and Evaluation Committee. It should be clear to professionals that all end-of-life interventions have their own indications and are not interchangeable.

This trend has given rise to repeated calls for legislating and/or introducing the compulsory registration of end-of-life interventions that, unlike euthanasia, are strictly medical acts: first palliative sedation, but by extension all types of end-of-life interventions. The assumption is that this would directly improve the quality of care. This is peculiar compared with other fields of healthcare, where it is commonly accepted that quality is not enhanced by legislation, which entails major risks such as loss of flexibility, inaccessibility of certain interventions and an overload of resource-consuming administrative work.

Euthanasia Following Its Own Course

Beyond this tendency to want to regulate a broader range of end-of-life interventions, there are also loud calls for an extension of the law on euthanasia to cover other population groups, such as minors, people with advanced dementia and those who are 'tired of living'. There may well be good reasons, and possibly sometimes even majority support among the general public, for such an extension – including among palliative care professionals themselves. There is no indication of an increase in the number of reported cases of euthanasia performed for indications other than those legally accepted. However, these loud calls cannot be missed. Since 2002, over 20 proposals to change the law and extend the conditions under which euthanasia can be performed have been introduced – so far none have brought about a change in the law. At the time of writing, new proposals are expected to be examined by the Belgian Senate in October 2013.

The rationale behind such an extension follows a certain logic. Pointing to forms of suffering other than those covered by the current law that could be terminated by euthanasia, those advocating its extension denounce the existing criteria as arbitrary.

- Age – why euthanasia only from the age of 18, and not 17½ or 15?
- Full mental competence at the moment of the request – what about patients who made a written advance directive for euthanasia when they still had full mental capacity (for example, in the event of dementia), no longer have it, but are not irreversibly unconscious (an irreversibly unconscious patient being the only case in which an advance directive is considered valid)?
- Disease or accident – what about those who are simply 'tired of living'?
- Irreversibility – what about patients who may have a chance of cure if they accept further treatment, but decline it?
- Intolerable suffering – how can you distinguish between present suffering, which might be tolerable, and expected suffering, the expectation in itself becoming a source of intolerable suffering?

Relieving suffering at the end of life being one of the primary concerns of palliative care, these questions must be taken seriously and debated in a society that is in constant evolution. However, for the FPCF – an organisation that believes palliative care should be part of regular healthcare provision – the medical grounds of suffering should be paramount.

Given the radical nature of euthanasia – where suffering is 'solved' by terminating the life of the sufferer – it can never be a first resort. To avoid the risk of euthanasia being administered for improper reasons, extending it to further populations groups should only be considered if basic palliative care is fully provided to these groups. The force with which its advocates demand an extension of the law provides, in practice, a good incentive for improving the care given to these groups, which is a positive side-effect – just as greater interest in end-of-life care was a positive side-effect of legalising euthanasia. However, there is an indication that euthanasia, once the barrier of legalisation is passed, tends to develop a dynamic of its own and extend beyond the agreed restrictions, in spite of earlier explicit reassurances that this would not happen – in Belgium, such reassurances were given when the 2002 law was being debated.

The effort to extend the law on euthanasia, like the effort to legalise euthanasia in the first place, is not exclusive to Belgium but is on the agenda of many movements worldwide, which often enjoy strong public support. In Flanders, one such organisation, LEIF (*Levens Einde Informatie Forum* – a Forum for End-of-Life Information), was set up in 2003 to provide information and training to physicians who give advice in case of euthanasia. An equivalent, Forum EOL (Forum End-Of-Life), was later created in Wallonia, the southern, French-speaking part of Belgium.

It should be stressed that LEIF has played a major role in favour of patient emancipation and empowerment, which is resulting in better end-of-life care. However, the organisation's outspoken promotion of the autonomy of the individual person – expressed, for example, by its claim to the right of radical self-determination – has made its philosophical viewpoint far removed from mainstream health- and end-of-life care. This restricts collaboration with the established representative organisations of healthcare professionals, in particular palliative care ones. This in turn leads to the risk of a 'twin-track policy' in end-of-life care, characterised by little genuine dialogue between each side and a separation between euthanasia and regular care, in spite of what is often good bedside collaboration between the professionals belonging to organisations supporting euthanasia and those working in organised, regular palliative care (several of whom belong to both groups) (FPCF 2008).

Instrumentalisation

Often, the endeavour to extend the law on euthanasia is not only an expression of genuine concern about suffering, but also a manifestation of the tendency to deal instrumentally with death. End-of-life interventions such as euthanasia are seen as an instrument to end a process of disease (or old age) that is demanding and difficult to bear, instead of letting it follow its course. Although euthanasia can make a good death possible under certain conditions, its legal introduction has set, or at least amplified, this trend towards instrumentalisation. Healthcare professionals note that family members and proxies tend, much more than before, to consider the dying process as undignified, useless and meaningless, even if it happens peacefully, comfortably and with professional support. Requests made by family members for fast and active interventions from healthcare professionals regarding elderly parents are often very coercive, with little nuance or subtlety. While the mediatisation of end-of-life issues has had many positive side-effects, including the growing awareness that one can express one's own end-of-life care preferences, this trend is without doubt a negative one.

Euthanasia Embedded in Palliative Care

The three major concerns described above tend to disconnect euthanasia from (palliative) care and thus threaten optimal end-of-life care. The problem is not euthanasia as such, but rather its dissociation from the context of (palliative) care. The antagonism is no longer between euthanasia on one hand and palliative care on the other, but between euthanasia outside and euthanasia inside the realm of (palliative) care.

Every patient at the end of life has the freedom to call on palliative care or not. In a common position paper, the three Belgian palliative care federations (the FPCF, the *Fédération Wallonne des Soins Palliatifs* and the *Fédération Pluraliste Bruxelloise de Soins Palliatifs et Continus*) insisted that they 'respect the choice of patients who want euthanasia' and 'place them in the centre of the process'.[3] They further stated that 'patients must be able to freely and autonomously call upon one or more practitioners of their choice. For one patient, this will be their GP or the specialist in charge of their incurable disease. A second patient will also have recourse to the palliative team that has supported them since they learned about the incurable nature of their disease. A third patient will prefer to call upon a practitioner who is a member of an association such as LEIF or EOL.' This implies a clear rejection of the so-called palliative filter; that is, the obligation that all palliative care possibilities have been examined and exhausted before a patient can receive euthanasia – which is not a requirement of the current Belgian law on euthanasia.

---

[3] Common position paper of the three Belgian palliative care federations, 2010 (unpublished).

While sharing this point of view, the FPCF also affirms its own vision that high-quality palliative care must offer continuity of care, up to and including euthanasia accompaniment, and at the same time respect the freedom of conscience of each individual professional. In our view, palliative care can guarantee that euthanasia requests will be dealt with in a careful and caring way.

The above-mentioned threats do not change the fundamental commitment of the FPCF to participate in the debate and work towards solutions in the face of new medical or societal challenges. The FPCF does not claim to have a monopoly on good care, but affirms its preference for a model of care where euthanasia requests are addressed with an offer – not an obligation – of expert palliative care by the multidisciplinary team. We have learned through experience, including mistakes, that this is in the best interest of patients as well as their families and friends.

Postscript: Death as Disruption or Disruptive Dying? Some Further Reflections Since 2013

PAUL VANDEN BERGHE, MARC DESMET AND GERT HUYSMANS

Introduction

In our contribution of 2013, we presented a critical but balanced view on the implementation of euthanasia in the healthcare landscape in Flanders/ Belgium since its depenalisation in 2002: how euthanasia is embedded in palliative care. We do not have a negative a priori stance towards euthanasia. But while we pointed to several positive aspects of the introduction of euthanasia, we also expressed some major points of concern. Already in 2013, we stated that the trajectory since its introduction in 2002 was developing at a remarkable speed. But is it still going that fast? And if so: what tendencies can we discern? Were we too critical, or rather too naïve?

Our answer consists of four lines of argumentation: figures, facts, experiences and – in the guise of a conclusion – some reflections/ interpretations of a more philosophical character.

Figures

We restrict ourselves to some of the more striking numbers. In recent research, Chambaere et al. (2015a) conclude that 4.6 per cent of all deaths in 2013 could be qualified as death by euthanasia. Due to a broad interpretation of euthanasia this number may be overstated. But taken together with new figures as reported by the Federal Euthanasia Control and Evaluation Committee – 1432 in 2012, 1807 in 2013, 1928 in 2014 and 2022 in 2015 (FCECE, Sixth report 2014, Seventh report 2016), it is clear that the proportion of death by euthanasia in the total number of deaths since 2013 is still growing and is not plateauing yet.

Moreover, the study by Chambaere et al. showed that 73.3 per cent of all euthanasia deaths were accompanied by some form of palliative care in the disease trajectory. This was only surprising to outsiders or sceptics. It certainly confirms our experience that euthanasia is more than ever embedded in palliative care. Fifteen years after the unsuccessful efforts of the palliative care movement to have this accompaniment included, expressly, as a prerequisite in the law on euthanasia, the so-called palliative filter, it seems that it has become a reality in everyday practice.[4]

Another figure: a recent publication by Thienpont et al. (2015) states that from a sample of 100 psychiatric patients with a request of euthanasia, followed between October 2007 and December 2011, 48 of the euthanasia requests were accepted and 35 were carried out.

And a last figure: in the 13 years since its introduction, and as the first and sole case in more than 12,500 reported euthanasia deaths, (FCECE, Seventh report 2016) one case of euthanasia was reported to the public prosecutor in October 2015 by the Federal Euthanasia Control and Evaluation Committee. And this only after its public revelation through a documentary by an Australian broadcasting company. An 85-year-old woman received euthanasia (in fact physician assisted suicide) on the indication of a so-called reactive depression less than three months after the death of her daughter.

Facts

In our 2013 article, we described the tendency to broaden the law on euthanasia to other target groups and other indications. In 2014, a bill was passed, making euthanasia possible for minors under certain stricter conditions. In September 2016, however, the first case was reported to the

---

[4] The aim of palliative care is not to reach 100 per cent of euthanasia cases, since not all euthanasia candidates are strictly speaking also palliative patients. The more euthanasia evolves further in the direction of assisted suicide, without medical indication, the less palliative care will be relevant to these patients.

committee, and almost immediately leaked to the press (in spite of the wish for discretion of the parents). Similar political efforts are being made to broaden the indications for euthanasia for persons suffering from dementia and other neurological conditions after they lose their full mental capacities (not only before they lose them, as is already possible now). For the application of euthanasia in this population, the reticence among caregivers is substantial.[5] The general public, however, feels little or no doubt about the expansion of euthanasia to people suffering from dementia and other neurological conditions, out of fear they might suffer from these conditions themselves one day. Finally, euthanasia for patients suffering from psychiatric conditions, or for people tired with life,[6] is no longer exceptional.

Parallel with these political efforts to enlarge the indications for euthanasia, the same forces plead louder than ever for a registration of all cases of palliative sedation, similar to the registration of euthanasia. It is true that knowledge and good practice in relation to palliative sedation is not sufficiently distributed among all concerned physicians or settings. However, it is very likely that a requirement to register all cases of palliative sedation could hinder the proper use of what is a normal medical practice and could ultimately lead to a worsening of pain and symptom control. The plea for the registration of palliative sedation cases clearly fits in the disparagement of palliative sedation as an ineffective intervention (that is only called legitimate under severe monitoring in a hospital intensive care setting), and always suspected to serve as a substitute for euthanasia. At the same time, the activity of the Federal Euthanasia Control and Evaluation Commission, with its pseudo-democratic composition, is not serious and rather symbolic, as observers of all tendencies agree, including several academics. At the same time, academics have denounced the fact that the data are not made accessible for scientific research and that there is little funding for qualitative research into euthanasia.[7] This is without considering the problem that

---

[5] And the reticence increases the more they are specialised in the disease or population: see Bolt et al. 2015.

[6] Following a number of cases reported in the press, of couples both requesting euthanasia (one partner terminally ill, the second out of fear of being left behind, in grief and/or tired of living) were the occasion for a parliamentary question to the national minister of health, already in 2011, who passed the question to the Belgian Federal Advisory Committee on Bioethics for further advice.

[7] Ezekiel J. Emanuel points to the fact that there are no data from Belgium on problems or complications with euthanasia or PAS (Emanuel et al. 2016, p. 86).

a physician will be unlikely to report to the Commission that he or she performed euthanasia in a way that was contrary to the legal conditions. It has been argued that the development of palliative care did not suffer from the depenalisation of euthanasia (Bernheim et al. 2008). It is true that with a substantial budget rise, in the years just after 2002, the palliative care sector in Belgium was brought up to a level and quality that was one of the best in Europe. However, palliative care expenditures have virtually stagnated – at least since 2008 – and therefore do not keep pace with the increasing number of euthanasia deaths, of which the majority is part of the work of the palliative care teams. (FEPZ 2008, FEPZ 2014) One could expect the budget for palliative care to evolve according to the rising budget for health care in general, considering the growing elderly population. However, we experience the opposite. There is also no substantial funding for research into better care for people tired with life or for specialist 'palliative' care for psychiatric patients for which there are no therapeutic options left ('crustative care'). Many palliative caregivers and teams, in all settings, are overburdened, overworked and demotivated by this lack of recognition.

These facts, described above, in one way or another, all relate to the fact that the polarisation in the end-of-life landscape in Flanders/Belgium is still not resolved. There is clearly a contrast between the practice which does not polarise, and the public debate which is almost always polarised. With some pro-euthanasia movements, fruitful dialogue is certainly possible. But the leading Belgian pro-euthanasia organisation actively avoids all dialogue and constitute a movement which, for many years, has entrenched itself in a self-chosen isolation. From there it cherishes its 'unique selling position' (and its 'life insurance') against organised palliative care in Flanders/Belgium. This movement holds that palliative care should not interfere with euthanasia requests of their patients, for fear – and effectively the allegation – that this will hinder the unimpeded performance of euthanasia.[8] Interestingly, with this position, it has also

---

[8] FCECE, Second Report, 2006, repeated in subsequent reports: 'obligations légales-Comme le rapport précédent l'avait relevé, la commission constate que les médecins ont eu fréquemment recours à des consultations supplémentaires de spécialistes en plus des obligations légales (391 médecins et 274 équipes palliatives). La commission considère le fait comme témoignant de la rigueur et du sérieux avec lesquels les médecins déclarants ont agi. *Certains membres estiment cependant qu'il convient de veiller à ce que des consultations médicales supplémentaires n'aboutissent en fait à créer des conditions non prévues par la loi au détriment du respect de la volonté du patient*' (emphasis added).

become an ally of all those voices within palliative care in Europe who defend the same antagonism between palliative care and euthanasia (Radbruch et al. 2015). It goes without saying that this polarisation jeopardises the further development of palliative care in Belgium, including support of patients who are considering euthanasia. This again became obvious on the topic of palliative sedation, mentioned above.

Experiences

First and foremost: euthanasia is perceived in the majority of cases as a 'good death', or at least the death patients wanted for themselves, which is not quite the same. The termination of a life, on the request of an incurable patient who is suffering unbearably, has been exempt from prosecution in Belgium, but it remains killing. It constitutes the transgression of a line one normally does not transgress. This is the reason why it still falls under the penal code, and is not subject to prosecution only when certain conditions are fulfilled. There is no evidence (but also little research conducted) to show that it complicates the process of bereavement for families and relatives, and some indication of the opposite.[9] The sheer possibility of euthanasia, even when it is not performed, the 'euthanasia talk' (Norwood 2009, p. 293) seems to be a reassurance and a comfort to patients facing the end of their lives. It is our everyday experience that dialogue with patients on the options of palliative care in many cases starts with a discussion on euthanasia, or is able to continue once they know that, in their case and with their condition, euthanasia is a valid option. In order to avoid all misunderstanding, and very painful conflicts in the final stages of life, caregivers have learned to pick up hints or suggestions on euthanasia by the patient and to discuss this in a timely fashion, i.e. in advance, with the patient (and if possible with family and next of kin).

This brings us to the practice of advance care planning (ACP). In our 2013 article we mentioned how euthanasia works as a powerful catalyst for better communication on end-of-life issues. In 2015, 22,406 declaration forms of ACP were registered at the municipal services and a multiple number were written by civilians (in good health). These documents, however, constitute an illusionary guarantee and appear often to be of poor value when they are consulted at the relevant moment. In the

---

[9] See discussion by Sulmasy in this volume.

last stage of a disease, when the crucial decisions are to be made about providing or foregoing further treatment, people very often push their limits to a point they would never have imagined in healthy times, and far beyond the point they have fixed in an earlier written form. In the worst case scenarios, these 'papers' emerge, through the next of kin, in the very last stages of the dying process. The patient him- or herself cannot be questioned anymore and the family refers to the anticipatory declaration on euthanasia 'in case of irreversible coma' to claim euthanasia. This may occur even when in fact a terminal coma, as a normal part of the dying process, has set in in the last days or hours. Intended for chronic coma or Permanent Vegetative States, this was not the scope the lawgiver had in mind for such anticipatory declarations. However, it is extremely difficult and painful to have to explain this to a family in distress.

Much painful misunderstanding is caused, at least in part, by a climate and a discourse of autonomy and euthanasia promotion whereby euthanasia is presented as a right or entitlement. The general public has come to believe that they have a right to euthanasia, rather than a right to request euthanasia. Some high profile euthanasia cases reported in the media in recent years, on or over the edge of the law, have nourished this idea. We think of the twins who were blind and feared becoming deaf, or of the transgender person whose surgery did not turn out as expected, or of the couples of which one was terminally ill and the other tired of life. The same is true for a few cases brought to court. To this adds the common experience that 'you can get your euthanasia anyway', if you only seek out enough physicians or hospitals or contact the right one from the beginning. It is very discouraging for physicians or hospitals if, for example, a chronic psychiatric patient with a euthanasia request, for whom they foresee/started a careful trajectory of up to one and a half years of caring investigation into the possible treatment or alleviation of his or her suffering, is able to obtain euthanasia elsewhere in less than three weeks. In this way, patients – often the most vulnerable ones – disappear from the therapeutic trajectory, in favour of the euthanasia 'fast lane'.

Belgian caregivers would therefore welcome guidelines – a 'state of the Art' approach – about those aspects of euthanasia that shape the daily practice, but that are not written in laws or robust scientific research. How can one counter this radical divergence of what should be optimal care? How can one avoid opening the gates to euthanasia too widely out of fear that the patient will, otherwise, take matters into his or her own hands? How can one support the caregiver who, out of large-heartedness, barely can resist any request from patient and/or family? What is meant by 'if the patient is not expected to die *within the foreseeable future*'? How far can a nurse be involved in the preparatory acts and the act of euthanasia itself? Can the euthanasia be performed if the patient loses his or her full mental capacity after the completion of the preparatory acts, including the planning of the euthanasia, but before the actual perform-ance? This could be discussed within, for example, the several associ-ations of physicians or by the Belgian Federal Advisory Committee on Bioethics, but the polarisation mentioned in this section has undermined all attempts so far.

The support of guidelines would even be more welcomed for those more complex non-terminal situations, which are rarely urgent: why not agree on a procedure of *an a priori consultation*, with all parties con-cerned: the patient, if possible, his or her next of kin, a multidisciplinary team of familiar caregivers and independent experts, instead of the current a posteriori reporting and registration? Unfortunately, in the meantime, in the words of Paul Feyerabend (1975): 'anything goes'.

Interpretation: Disruptive Dying

The rapid widespread introduction of euthanasia in Belgium has without doubt brought about a much higher readiness to discuss end-of-life preferences. This, however, is not in itself an indication that the taboo on death and dying is lifted, and that a greater acceptance of finitude has grown. Nor that greater attention is given to social pain or spiritual/ existential suffering, the care of which is still in its infancy. That Belgium is European leader in hospital admissions in the last month of life and that 16 per cent of Belgian cancer patients receive chemotherapy in their final month (Bekelman et al. 2016), reveals that therapeutic futility remains a major problem. In this light, euthanasia could be rather a continuation of this (therapeutic) obstinacy, an instrumentalisation and a medicalisation till the very end-of-life. When 'nothing more can be done', we can – impatient with death – still perform the last and final act, euthanasia as the cure for a dying process that is too slow. Backed by the idealisation of euthanasia in popular media, celebrating oversimplified autonomy, this constitutes a new social framing of death by euthanasia as the new dying: timely, properly scheduled, highly economic, without ambiguity or uncertainties. The tragic we love on stage or in film because it elevates us in a cathartic way, thus evaporates from our own human existence. Euthanasia becomes the victory of postmodern man on suffering at the end of life. The question remains: 'Which is prior: unbearable suffering for which euthanasia is the ultimate solution? Or does the suffering become unbearable because, henceforth, there is such a way-out as euthanasia?' Could it be that, in the long term, unbridled euthanasia thus enhances the suffering it pretends to relieve? It would then overshadow the profoundly beneficent effects of the laws of 2002, on patients' rights, palliative care and also euthanasia. It would then undermine the possibility of an untroubled and serene way of dying, well attended by skillful palliative care, be it with or without euthanasia.

5

The Practice of Continuous Sedation at the End of Life in Belgium

How Does it Compare to UK Practice, and is it Being Used as a Form of Euthanasia?

SIGRID STERCKX AND KASPER RAUS

Introduction

How people die has changed significantly throughout history and we now live in a time where more people die as a result of chronic disease (e.g., Cohen et al. 2007; Chambaere et al. 2011a). Surveys show that for Belgium, for example, in 2007 only 32 per cent of all deaths could be labelled as sudden (Bilsen et al. 2009), meaning that almost two-thirds of patients had a protracted dying trajectory. The latter is often accompanied by at least some degree of physical or psychological suffering (e.g., Steindal et al. 2011). Palliative care is devoted to battling end-of-life suffering, but at times physical and/or psychological suffering can be so severe that more far-reaching medical decisions are considered. One such decision is continuous sedation at the end of life. What exactly constitutes continuous sedation at the end of life is up for debate as many different terms are used to refer to the practice (e.g. continuous sedation, palliative sedation, terminal sedation, proportionate sedation, etc.) and there is no single agreed label or definition (Jones 2013a).[1] Despite these differences in definition, the practice can be roughly described as involving lowering a patient's consciousness to relieve suffering until he or she passes away. Various types of sedation can be distinguished, as sedation can be either light (the patient still retains some degree of consciousness) or deep (all conscious experience is taken away). Moreover, sedation

[1] As to the label, we prefer 'continuous sedation at the end of life', as we will explain below. Throughout this chapter, when using the term 'continuous sedation' we mean 'continuous sedation at the end of life', i.e., we do not refer to other contexts in which the practice is used, such as intensive care medicine.

need not always be continuous and is sometimes given intermittently (e.g., sedation during the night or respite sedation).

Studies from Belgium, the Netherlands and the United Kingdom suggest that continuous sedation is highly prevalent. In Belgium in 2013, it occurred in 12 per cent of all deaths (Chambaere et al. 2015a),[2] while in the United Kingdom in 2007–2008 the frequency of continuous sedation reached 16.5 per cent of all deaths (Seale 2009a).[3] Although these numbers are sometimes questioned and different incidences have been reported (e.g., Claessens et al. 2008), all studies indicate that continuous sedation is a highly common practice; much more common than euthanasia in both Belgium and the Netherlands.

The practice of continuous sedation is often discussed in relation to euthanasia, another far-reaching end-of-life practice and one that aims to take away suffering by ending a patient's life. Whereas euthanasia is often seen as ethically problematic, continuous sedation, by contrast, is sometimes claimed to be less ethically controversial (see ten Have and Welie 2014 who give an overview of what they label the 'dominant view'). Various reasons are commonly given for this. First, it is often claimed that whereas euthanasia clearly shortens life, continuous sedation (when used properly) does not (e.g., De Graeff and Dean 2007). Various studies indeed suggest that continuous sedation has little or no life-shortening effect (e.g., Morita et al. 2001; Sykes and Thorns 2003). However, the manner in which the presence or absence of a life-shortening effect should be measured is debatable. Bruinsma et al. (2014) compared two approaches to measuring a potential life-shortening effect of continuous sedation: a direct one (i.e., asking physicians to estimate the possible life-shortening effect) and an indirect one (i.e., subtracting the duration of the sedation from the life-expectancy at the time sedation was initiated). The study found significant discrepancy between these two approaches, with the direct approach resulting in higher estimates of possible life-shortening effects. Second, various commentators argue that even if continuous sedation would have a life shortening effect, this is not

---

[2] By way of comparison, in the same year (2007) in Belgium, euthanasia accounted for 1.9 per cent of all deaths (Bilsen et al. 2009). In the most recent year for which the prevalence of medical end-of-life practices has been studied, 2013, the prevalence of euthanasia had markedly increased, to 4.6 per cent of all deaths, whereas the prevalence of continuous sedation had decreased, to 12 per cent of all deaths. (Chambaere et al. 2015a).

[3] For the Netherlands in 2010 the incidence was 12.3 per cent (Onwuteaka-Philipsen et al. 2012). In the same year (2010) in the Netherlands, 2.8 per cent of all deaths resulted from euthanasia (Onwuteaka-Philipsen et al. 2012).

generally the primary intention, but merely an unwanted side-effect (e.g., Boyle 2004). This supposedly distinguishes continuous sedation from euthanasia where ending the patient's life *is* an undeniable intention. Commentators advocating this argument thus justify the practice by reference to the so-called Doctrine of Double Effect. Third, continuous sedation is often portrayed as providing a 'natural death' in which the patient dies in his or her sleep as a result of the underlying disease (e.g., Tännsjö 2004a).

Various guidelines have been drafted that support this conception of continuous sedation as an acceptable medical practice. A Dutch national guideline issued by the Royal Dutch Medical Association (KNMG) (2009) submits that continuous sedation is an acceptable end-of-life decision when it is used for refractory suffering and on patients with a life expectancy of less than two weeks (to avoid potential life-shortening effects). Examples of other guidelines are a Flemish guideline (Broeckaert et al. 2010), a guideline drafted by the European Association for Palliative Care (EAPC) (Cherny and Radbruch 2009) and the recently revised guideline issued by the Norwegian Medical Association (Førde et al. 2015).

Despite these publications that claim that continuous sedation is fairly uncontroversial, a considerable number of commentators remain critical of the practice (e.g., van Delden 2007; Jansssens et al. 2012; Battin 2013; Holm 2013). In earlier work we have critiqued many of the common ways in which continuous sedation is portrayed as a non-controversial practice. First, we have argued that death after continuous deep sedation is not natural, but is in fact highly medicalized as it involves keeping a patient in an artificially maintained state of complete unconsciousness. Moreover, even if it were natural, this would not automatically make the practice less ethically controversial as the issue of 'naturalness' is irrelevant to the question whether or not the practice is ethically acceptable (Raus et al. 2012). Many things that are natural are actually bad (e.g., an earthquake), whereas many things that are unnatural are good (e.g., various medicines). Second, justifying continuous sedation by referring to the Doctrine of Double Effect is problematic (Raus et al. 2013). Further, although continuous sedation is often said to be administered proportionally to the severity of symptoms, the degree to which patients are *actually* sedated is rarely monitored. If there is monitoring, it is not clear whether the most commonly used techniques, i.e., clinical observation and/or sedation scales, are suited adequately to measure the consciousness of sedated patients at the end of life. It can therefore not be reliably ascertained that sedated patients at the end of life are indeed unconscious and free of physical and psychological suffering (Raus et al. 2014). In short, it is far from obvious that continuous sedation is a preferable alternative to euthanasia or physician-assisted suicide (Raus et al. 2011). Many commentators see sedation as potentially more problematic than euthanasia, as sedation might be used as a backdoor to euthanasia (e.g., Battin 2008). Indeed, the practice has even been labelled as 'slow euthanasia' (Billings and Block 1996) or 'euthanasia in disguise' (Tännsjö 2004b). In any case, it is clear that some versions of the practice do not differ from euthanasia in ethically significant ways (Holm 2013). Of course, whether that renders these versions of continuous sedation ethically unacceptable is a different question, which we do not address here.

For this chapter, we want to look at the ways in which continuous sedation at the end of life is performed and perceived by physicians and nurses in Belgium and the United Kingdom. Research suggests that the way continuous sedation is performed or perceived varies between these countries (Anquinet et al. 2012), and we will focus on the main differences between the UK and the Belgian practice. Next, we will address the issue of whether continuous sedation is in effect used as a form of euthanasia in Belgium, as a focus group study we carried out earlier suggests that the line dividing both practices can become blurred (Anquinet et al. 2013).

Methods

In order to address the above-mentioned questions, we will rely on the literature as well as on the results of an international interview study with which we were involved (the UNBIASED study). We will only give a short summary of the methods here, as the protocol for this study has been published elsewhere (Seymour et al. 2011). The UNBIASED study concerns an interview study with Belgian, Dutch and UK nurses, physicians and relatives who had recently been involved in the care of a sedated patient or loved one.

Inclusion

For this study physicians who were willing to participate were asked to identify cases of continuous sedation at the end of life in which they were involved. A case was eligible for inclusion if it concerned a person over the age of 18 with a cancer diagnosis who had received sedative medication causing a decreased awareness in order to relieve suffering and these medications had been given up to the patient's death. In order to obtain a maximal variety of cases, we included cases from the home care setting, the normal hospital setting and the specialist palliative care setting.[4] The inclusion period ran from January 2011 to May 2012.

Interviews

When cases that fit the inclusion criteria were signalled to the researchers by the physician, an interview was conducted with that physician as soon as possible (to avoid recall bias). Wherever possible, interviews were also conducted with the most involved nurse and the most involved relative in order to obtain three different perspectives on the same case. This resulted in interviews with 57 physicians (17 UK; 22 NL; 18 BE), 73 nurses (25 UK; 28 NL; 20 BE) and 34 relatives (8 UK; 13 NL; 13 BE) who were involved in a total of 84 cases (22 UK; 35 NL; 27 BE).[5] All interviews were semi-structured and were guided by an aide-memoire that was the same for all three countries. The interviews were audio recorded and transcribed verbatim, thereby removing all identifiable data.

Analysis

The basis for analysis were the written interview transcripts. The method used was a constant comparative analysis whereby open coding was used in a first stage. Later on, these codes were grouped together in larger categories, which led to the development of a coding tree. Coding was always independently checked by a minimum of three researchers and findings were always discussed and debated by the entire team. The software that was used for this analysis was NVivo 10.

Some Differences between the Belgian and the UK Practice of Continuous Sedation

This chapter will not present *all* the differences between the UK and Belgian practice of continuous sedation at the end of life, but focuses on

---

[4] For the Netherlands and the United Kingdom this concerned hospices, while for Belgium this refers to palliative care wards in hospitals.

[5] The reason why only 57 physicians were interviewed for a total of 84 cases was that some physicians were interviewed on multiple cases, though never more than three, to maintain a diversity of perspectives.

some, which we believe are highly relevant, namely: (1) a difference in labelling; (2) a different attitude towards 'proportionality' and (3) a different perspective on what the intentions are, or can be, of a physician or nurse performing continuous sedation at the end of life.

Labelling

As mentioned in the introduction, there is little agreement on which term should be used to label the practice of continuous sedation. An article by de Graeff and Dean (2007), for example, mentions nine different terms used in the literature, and these do not include the label we use in this chapter, viz. 'continuous sedation at the end of life'. Moreover, these different terms should not be taken to always cover the same practices. In fact, the terms 'palliative sedation' or 'continuous sedation' (or alternative terms) often refer to a wide array of different practices ranging from intermittent light sedation to continuous deep sedation. Jones (2013a) has drafted a manifold definition aimed at including all different types of sedation, and the only way to do this was by including as many as 17 elements in the definition, which implies that the definition covers a total of 129,140,136 different variations of sedation.

Which term one chooses to label the practice is not a neutral choice. 'Terminal sedation' has been criticized by some as suggesting that the practice is related to 'terminating' a patient's life (Morita et al. 2002), while 'palliative sedation' has been criticized as being overly euphemistic and implicitly justifying the practice as being part of regular palliative care (van Delden 2007). Some of the fascinating differences in language use and the impact thereof on ethical reasoning have been discussed in detail by Seale et al. (2015).

As regards the use of labels, an interesting difference can be noted between Belgian and UK physicians and nurses. In our interview study, most Belgian physicians and nurses clearly identified the practice and labelled it as 'palliative sedation', both in their communication amongst each other and in their communications with patients and families. The practice was also almost always considered as a practice in its own right, and Belgian respondents were frequently able to say exactly when the sedation was initiated. This was often preceded by a goodbye moment where loved ones said their goodbyes to the patient. For many deep sedations, it was explicitly stated beforehand that the goal was for the patient not to wake up again, but rather to keep him or her sedated until he or she passed away. An example of such a case is given by a Belgian nurse discussing a patient who had recently received continuous sedation until death:

> He was ready to go, he was finished, he was physically finished. He had been able to say goodbye to everyone properly ... all the children came, grandchildren, great-grandchildren, all of them ... It took him a week to get up the courage to do it ... And on the day the sedation started, he again said goodbye to the children and grandchildren ... he had had enough ... and the doctor then gave [midazolam], and he fell asleep very quickly. And we immediately attached the pump and he went to sleep and he didn't wake up again.
>
> (Belgium, home care nurse, case T11)

For UK physicians and nurses this was very different. For example, unlike the Belgian respondents, no UK physician or nurse used the label 'palliative sedation'. Instead, although they sometimes used the term 'sedation', even that term was often not mentioned at all and physicians and nurses instead used terms such as 'symptom control' and 'easing of suffering' as explained by a UK nurse:

> I don't usually use the word 'sedation', I use the term 'make him more comfortable and settled'.
>
> (United Kingdom, hospital nurse, case 3)

Also, while Belgian respondents recognized 'palliative sedation' as a distinct medical decision, taken at a particular moment in time, and often recorded as such in the medical file, many UK respondents described sedation as the result of a gradual process of continuing care. The aim was often said to be to relieve distress and to achieve comfort, but as time goes on, UK respondents said, this might require the use of sedatives in sufficiently high doses to make patients unconscious. A good example is a UK hospice physician discussing how he explains the use of sedative medications to the patient or his or her relatives:

> It's about trying to relieve distress and relieve symptoms at end of life and I often have an open discussion with either patients or relatives to say, 'We're using sedative medicine ...' – so I will use that term – '... we're using sedative medicines to help relieve distress or make you feel more relaxed, but, you know, what comes with sedative medicines is that you might feel more sleepy. But my aim is not to shorten your life or to knock you out, to make you feel sleepy. We want to titrate that medicine; we want to increase that medicine slowly to the level whereby your symptoms are relieved but you're not knocked out, but we can't always achieve that'.
>
> (United Kingdom, Hospice physician, case L1)

Proportionality

All guidelines on sedation at the end of life (as well as most commentators in the literature) stress that continuous or palliative sedation should be administered 'proportionately' to the severity of symptoms (e.g., KNMG 2009; Cherny and Radbruch 2009). For less severe suffering, an intermittent or light sedation might suffice, while more severe suffering may require higher doses of sedatives and sometimes even complete unconsciousness of the patients. This is said to distinguish continuous sedation from euthanasia, as in the latter case the dosage of drugs used is not proportionate to the symptoms but is given with the aim of ending the life of the patient.

However, although all guidelines emphasize the need for proportionality, it has been argued that in fact proportionality is rarely measured (Raus et al. 2014). The most commonly used techniques for determining the 'right' level of sedation are clinical observations and sedation scales. However, these methods might not be error-proof, making it at least possible that some patients who are believed to be sedated proportionately are in fact (semi-)conscious and experiencing suffering. Certain simple and non-invasive techniques exist for measuring consciousness, yet, surprisingly in our view, these are not used in clinical practice or in research involving patients who are continuously sedated at the end of life. Indeed, research is urgently needed to substantiate claims regarding the proportionality of sedation at the end of life.

Moreover, research from the Netherlands suggests that medical professionals sometimes take very different approaches to how to achieve proportionality (Swart et al. 2012). For some physicians this means starting with a low dose and carefully increasing this dose when the physician deems this to be necessary, whereas other physicians stress the importance of starting with a higher dose to make sure the patient is not experiencing suffering.

In our interview study we also noted a clear difference in how physicians from Belgium and physicians from the United Kingdom approached the issue of proportionality. UK physicians strongly emphasized the importance of always sedating proportionately, which they interpreted as starting with the lowest possible dose and then increasing or decreasing the dose when deemed necessary. In some cases, high dosages were reported to be used for patients whose suffering could no longer be otherwise controlled, but these cases were said to be rare and, according to our UK respondents, higher doses were never given right from the start. In cases where physicians and nurses had needed to administer higher doses of sedative drugs, they often reported feeling uncomfortable about this. A UK hospice physician, for example, explained:

> For other patients you can sometimes feel a little bit more uncomfortable when they're not responding to your initial doses of medicines and you need to be escalating those doses, and certainly I've been involved in patients where you're using much bigger doses, and you are managing to relieve their distress. It's very uncommon that you can't relieve someone's distress, but the doses that you're having to use sometimes make you feel a little bit uncomfortable.

(United Kingdom, Hospice physician, case L1)

Belgian respondents also claimed that they titrated in response to the patient's symptoms, but they generally appeared to be less worried about giving higher doses of drugs when needed. At times it was an explicit goal to sedate a patient deeply from the start and this was communicated as such to the patients and the families.

> Normally the idea is that when we sedate, [the patients] are really properly asleep. Because for the family it is often confusing if they fall asleep and then wake up . . . For palliative sedation I prefer to have them fully sedated.

(Belgium, physician on oncology ward, case O16)

When asked whether patients sometimes wake up when continuously sedated, a Belgian physician said:

> No, that's not the goal of palliative sedation. We make sure they are really sedated, otherwise I don't think it's a palliative sedation. I truly think that they have to be calm and unconscious. Otherwise you are not giving enough, I think.

(Belgium, physician on oncology ward, case O18)

Intention

A final difference we would like to highlight here between the UK practice and the Belgian practice of continuous sedation is related to the intention with which physicians and nurses say the practice is performed. Most guidelines specify that the primary intention of continuous sedation at the end of life should be to relieve physical suffering, which is further demonstrated by the guidelines that no more sedatives should be given than is necessary to relieve suffering. Should there be any negative effects of sedation (e.g., shortening of life), then these are claimed to be merely a side-effect and therefore less, or even not, ethically problematic. This 'double-effect' type of reasoning represents the most commonly used ethical justification for continuous sedation at the end of life and is supposed to distinguish the practice from euthanasia, whereby ending life *is* the main intention. However, as mentioned earlier, although dominant in the debate, this ethical justification of sedation is questionable (see, for example, Raus et al. 2014).

Nevertheless, this 'double-effect' type of reasoning, according to which the intention of continuous sedation is to relieve symptoms and not to kill, and any shortening of life is an unintended side-effect, was used very frequently by both UK and Belgian respondents. UK physicians and nurses were especially adamant in stressing that they never had the intention to shorten a patient's life. Some UK respondents even denied an intention to sedate and merely stated an intention to relieve suffering. For example, one UK general practitioner, reporting on the drugs used for sedation, said:

> the drugs were very definitely to try and control her pain and as a secondary result of that, they were sedating her.
>
> (United Kingdom, general practitioner, case GPROT 2)

Many UK respondents expressed a fear of *being perceived* to shorten life. While they claimed to be certain that sedation had not shortened life, they were at times very concerned about how their actions would be perceived and judged by others. One nurse expressed such concerns as follows:

> If I was to give, I don't know, 20mgs midazolam might have been what he needed, and then he died 20 minutes later what does that say to the family? How do you justify that? In a Court of Law would that be accepted?
>
> (United Kingdom, nurse on oncology ward, case O1)

Belgian physicians mostly denied an intention to hasten death and used the same type of 'double-effect' reasoning. Often, however, the possibility of life shortening with continuous sedation was more openly acknowledged and seen as less of an issue than for UK physicians and nurses. Belgian physicians and nurses seemed less afraid of being perceived to shorten life. One general practitioner reported being religious and unwilling to perform euthanasia, but at the same time said he felt very comfortable about continuous sedation:

> Well, [when administering sedation] I don't stop the natural process, and if my act would then somewhat shorten it [the patient's life], I have no issue living with that.
>
> (Belgium, general practitioner, case T4)

Moreover, even though this was exceptional, some Belgian physicians and nurses openly admitted to having had a clear intention to shorten life when using continuous sedation. One physician on an oncology ward reported on exceptional cases and stated:

> We just systematically drive up the dose. We don't just instantly give them a bolus so that they pass away because that would really be active euthanasia, but you could almost call it passive euthanasia. It's just driving up the dose further and further and at a certain point the doses are high enough for them to pass away. Yes, we sometimes do this.

(Belgium, physician on oncology ward, case O16)

This is in accordance with findings from other studies performed in Belgium. We know, for example, that some physicians in Belgium performing continuous sedation indicate that they had an intention to shorten life. In 2007, for example, physicians reported a co-intention in 13 per cent of cases and a primary intention in 4 per cent of all sedation cases (Chambaere et al. 2010; Papavasiliou et al. 2014). A study among Belgian nurses in 2007 indicated that in the most recent case of continuous deep sedation in which they were involved, they perceived a partial intention to hasten death in 48 per cent of cases and an explicit intention in 28 per cent of cases (Inghelbrecht et al. 2011). Though this evaluation of intention may be incorrect, it at least shows a perception that hastening death is or can be an intention when performing continuous sedation at the end of life. Such an intention to shorten life was rarely reported by UK respondents.

Continuous Sedation at the End of Life and Euthanasia

As mentioned earlier, considerable debate exists on whether continuous sedation at the end of life differs from euthanasia, or is actually a different way to perform euthanasia (e.g., Billings and Block 1996; ten Have and Welie 2014). Focus group research has shown that, for Belgian nurses and physicians, the line between euthanasia and continuous sedation can become blurred (Anquinet et al. 2013). From our interview study it appears that, in Belgium, while the practice of continuous sedation is often very different from euthanasia, sometimes it can also resemble euthanasia. There are various possible reasons for this potential resemblance. First, for continuous sedation, as for euthanasia, there is often an 'official' goodbye moment where patients say goodbye to their loved ones. Second, patients are sometimes sedated deeply from the start without any intention to wake them up again, implying that continuous sedation often marks the end of a patient's conscious life. Third, some physicians report a clear intention to shorten life when administering continuous sedation.

Some of our Belgian respondents explicitly considered continuous sedation an alternative to euthanasia. They described four ways in which sedation can be an alternative to euthanasia.

Continuous Sedation as a Compromise between the Patient and His or Her Loved Ones

Respondents reported some cases where the patient's loved ones did not agree with his or her decisions. Sometimes, for example, a patient preferred euthanasia, but the family had a hard time accepting this. Sedation can then become an alternative that is acceptable for both the patient and the family. A Belgian physician reports:

> What we regularly see is that for patients who choose euthanasia, the family has a really hard time accepting this so [the patient] ends up saying: 'okay then do palliative sedation instead'.
>
> (Belgium, home care physician, case T24)

Euthanasia Is Not in Line with the Values of the Physician or the Institution

Even though euthanasia is allowed in Belgium (provided all the due care criteria specified in the law are met), physicians can, of course, always conscientiously object to being involved in euthanasia. Some respondents explained that some care institutions are hesitant to allow euthanasia to be performed within their walls. Continuous sedation, on the other hand, was mostly reported as acceptable to all, and could therefore at times provide a way to relieve the suffering of patients while respecting the ethical values of the individual physician and/or the care institution. In one case, for example, a Belgian physician discussed a case in which a patient wanted euthanasia, but this was not possible in the nursing home where the patient resided. The physician discussed this with the patient:

> And then I just said to him, the only option that fits the values of the care centre is sedation and they made absolutely no problem of that.
>
> (Belgium, General practitioner, case T21)

Practical Reasons

In rare cases, continuous sedation was initiated for practical reasons. One example concerned a case in which a patient wanted euthanasia quickly, but the responsible physician did not feel comfortable organizing it in a very short time span. The physician explained that she wanted to prepare for euthanasia instead of rushing into it, so sedation was initiated, the patient eventually passed away and euthanasia was never performed.

> We don't do euthanasia in weekends. We always plan this and want to prepare ourselves ... so I said: 'I propose to do palliative sedation, starting tomorrow'.
>
> (Belgium, palliative care physician, case P23)

Choice for the Patient to Make

Some physicians and nurses expressed the view that whether a patient receives euthanasia or continuous sedation should be determined by the patient himself or herself according to his or her own preferences. These respondents tended to stress the importance of autonomy and of adequately informing patients and then letting them choose what they prefer. For example, a Belgian physician provided the following explanation for why continuous sedation was performed in a certain case:

> It was a completely self-chosen trajectory and we knew where we were heading. It only depended on how the patient would evolve and her making a decision: 'I want to go to euthanasia or I want to get palliative sedation'. And I had adequately informed her about that and she made a conscious choice.
>
> (Belgium, General practitioner, case T11)

Concluding Remarks

Continuous sedation at the end of life covers a wide variety of practices and can mean different things in different care settings and countries. In our study, physicians and nurses reported very different kinds of cases. When commentators or clinical professionals use the same term to refer to significantly different practices without making this explicit, significant confusion can arise.

In this chapter we have focused on some of the differences between the practice and perception of continuous sedation in the United Kingdom and Belgium. In our view, the three most relevant differences are the following: (1) a difference in the terminology and labels used by Belgian versus UK physicians and nurses; (2) a different approach to proportionality and (3) a different view on the intentions of physicians and nurses when using continuous sedation.

Taking account of these differences is an important prerequisite for having a proper ethical debate on the practice of continuous sedation at the end of life. For example, the terminology used to refer to the practice is generally portrayed as descriptive but is actually often value-laden. Referring to sedation as 'making him more comfortable and settled' could be seen as using a euphemistic label that can serve to justify the practice, for making a patient comfortable is clearly a commendable and ethically justified practice.[6] However, it might obscure some of the relevant features of continuous sedation at the end of life. Second, the different approach to proportionality is crucial from an ethical perspective, as the practice of continuous sedation is often justified by referring to the principle of proportionality. Usually, it is claimed that no more sedation is given than is needed to provide comfort or symptom relief. However, although proportionality serves as one of the main justifications for sedation in the international literature, there are different ways to interpret proportionality, as our study confirms. Moreover, as mentioned earlier, proportionality is usually assumed, but rarely measured in practice. Third, perhaps the most common justification of continuous sedation at the end of life is the Doctrine of Double Effect, which relies heavily on intentions. It is clear from our study that clinical professionals in the United Kingdom and Belgium often have a very different perspective on the intention that is at work when performing continuous sedation. If one intends to relieve suffering and causes unconsciousness as a side-effect (as was claimed in the UK interviews), a double effect type reasoning might apply. However, if one intends to sedate to full unconsciousness or has an intention to shorten life, the application of the Doctrine of Double Effect becomes problematic (see also Raus et al. 2013).

In short, continuous sedation might refer to different sets of practices in the United Kingdom and Belgium. This is highly relevant, since different sets of sedation practices may raise different ethical concerns.

Obviously, there are some important limitations to the analysis presented here that we are aware of and that need to be mentioned. First, we

---

[6] Euphemistic labelling is one of the techniques of moral disengagement identified by Bandura (2002).

only focused on the differences in practice and perception, which may create a distorted picture. Many important similarities exist between the United Kingdom and Belgium as regards the practice of continuous sedation, so this chapter should not be read as implying that the practice of sedation is unrecognizably different in the United Kingdom and Belgium.

Second, for Belgium, cases of continuous sedation were identified and supplied by physicians using a questionnaire. Hence the cases that were included in the study might reflect a bias. It is therefore possible that some of the differences between the United Kingdom and Belgium relate to the difference in cases we were supplied with rather than to actual differences in clinical practice. However, physicians were not asked to provide us with cases of 'continuous sedation' since, as shown above, this term may mean different things for different physicians. Rather, physicians were asked to report cases that met certain well-defined criteria, thereby limiting potential inclusion bias.

Third, our study is qualitative in nature and hence not generalizable to *all* physicians and nurses. Nevertheless, we believe to have highlighted important views and experiences that resonate with the findings of others.

We believe our study represents a valuable addition to the available (empirical and theoretical) research on continuous sedation at the end of life. It shows, for example, that labelling, proportionality and intention are not just the subject of theoretical concerns, but also highly important practical issues that occur on a daily basis in the clinical practice of many physicians and nurses. Moreover, our study demonstrates that investigating daily clinical practices and experiences can shine a light on things that are overlooked or denied in some theoretical reflections. For example, while all guidelines on continuous sedation at the end of life (including the Flemish guideline, Broeckaert et al. 2010) stress that continuous sedation is strictly different from euthanasia, our study shows that in practice sedation *can* strongly resemble euthanasia in some cases. Clearly, there is still a long way to go towards a more open, evidence-based and intellectually honest debate about continuous sedation and about medical end-of-life practices in general.

6

2002-2016: Fourteen Years of Euthanasia in Belgium

First-Line Observations by an Oncologist

BENOIT BEUSELINCK

Introduction

Since 2002, Belgium has been one of the very few countries in the world in which physicians can perform euthanasia. This is possible if the patient is an adult or emancipated minor who is competent and aware at the time of the request, and provided that the patient is in a hopeless state of constant and unbearable physical or mental suffering that cannot be alleviated and is the result of a serious and incurable disorder caused by an accident or illness. This law permits euthanasia in cases of physical suffering in terminally ill patients, but also in cases of mental suffering and in non-terminally ill patients.

Development of the law was motivated by two major reasons. The most important one was the possibility to end a patient's life if he or she was suffering from severe, difficult to control, physical symptoms such as refractory pain, suffocation or terminal anxiety.[1] We could call this euthanasia for physical reasons occurring mostly in the terminal phase of a disease. For some promoters of the law, respect for autonomy was another important reason. They claimed that one should be able to decide when to die as the ultimate liberty: not only for severe physical suffering in the terminal stage of a disease, but also for non-life-threatening diseases with controllable physical symptoms. These would include psychiatric disorders such as depression, or merely because a life does not make any sense anymore (even without any underlying disease, for instance, in case of isolation or a lack of meaning in life) or even

---

[1] Terminal anxiety is a medical condition occurring in the last 24 to 48 hours of life. It is due to the decline of vital functions with confusion and restlessness.

because of a fear of future physical decline. In the latter cases, mental suffering and not physical suffering is emphasised. This mental suffering is certainly more difficult to define in an objective way compared to physical pain, suffocation or terminal anxiety. Moreover, several promoters of the law claimed that all suffering, including physical suffering, is reducible to mental suffering and that this mental suffering is a subjective phenomenon (FCECE 2014, p. 55; Distelmans 2013a).[2]

Since the law was introduced, the number of patients reported to be undergoing euthanasia has steadily increased reaching 2,022 in 2015 and a total number of 12,726 patients since 2002 with an increase in the number, and generally also the proportion, of euthanasia cases on non-terminally ill patients: 299 patients in 2015, i.e., 15 per cent of cases (FCECE 2016, p. 5), versus 49 patients in 2008, 7 per cent of cases (FCECE 2010, p. 8). Euthanasia is now applied, for instance, in presence of the first symptoms of chronic diseases such as Alzheimer's, in patients suffering depression and in older persons suffering poly-pathology such as the combination of two or more complaints such as urinary incontinence, osteoporosis and blindness.

Before 2002, it was possible to have theoretical concerns about euthanasia and anticipate practical problems. Fourteen years later, we can observe how the Belgian law on euthanasia is applied and whether the theoretical and practical concerns that some expressed before the approval of the law were justified. In a way, Belgium became a kind of real-life experiment. In a society in which an empirical approach is the most trusted, an observation of the evolution in Belgium seems to be warranted for other countries that are preparing laws on euthanasia and other end-of-life practices.

The aim of this chapter is to report the impact of the law on euthanasia on the daily life of an oncologist. As cancer was in 2013 the underlying disease in 73 per cent of Belgian euthanasia cases (FCECE 2014, p. 55), and still in 2015 represented 68 per cent of such deaths (FCECE 2016, p. 5), oncologists are among the doctors that are the most exposed to euthanasia requests. I will compare my personal experiences as an oncologist with data published in scientific journals or reported by mass media.

[2] Wim Distelmans, president of the Federal Commission for Control and Evaluation of Euthanasia: 'The reports of the federal commission euthanasia show that in most cases (of approved demands of euthanasia) some form of psychological suffering is mentioned: loss of independence, dependence on others, unworthiness. Although his cancer pain is perfectly controlled, the patient may suffer unbearable loss of independence. Consequently, all suffering can eventually be reduced to psychic suffering'.

Medical Profession in Danger

For doctors, euthanasia is not an easy practice. Although several cases of euthanasia have been presented in the Belgian mass media as a 'warm family gathering' and a 'nice happening with champagne' (Matton 2014), euthanasia is certainly not a party for the doctor. Stevens reported that many doctors from the Netherlands and Oregon, who have taken part in euthanasia or assisted suicide, suffer emotional and psychological distress. They were obliged to put aside a fundamental value of medicine. They felt that taking part in euthanasia contradicts their commitment to the treatment of the sick and the protection of the integrity of each human being. They are also affected by the sudden effect of their act and can suffer from the pressure of their patients requiring euthanasia (Stevens 2006). This research confirms what I have seen among my Belgian colleagues, several of whom have reported that they no longer want to perform euthanasia because it has been a difficult experience. Other doctors reported that they could not get used to euthanasia even though they were increasingly taking part in such practices.

In a recent study, Chambaere et al. reported an increase in the number of euthanasia requests from 3.5 to 6.0 per cent of deaths between 2007 and 2013. The proportion of granted requests increased from 56.3 to 76.8 per cent (Chambaere et al. 2015a). This study confirms what is being noticed in daily clinical practice, that patients are increasingly asking for euthanasia. After only fourteen years of practice and thanks in large part to the promotion of euthanasia in the mass media, euthanasia is rapidly becoming *a normal way of dying* (the so-called normalisation of euthanasia). This increasing demand is a burden for doctors who have recently been complaining in the media that they were too often called to perform euthanasia. This is because other doctors do not want to take part in such procedures (Beel 2013a) or that the number of euthanasia cases they were expected to perform had become too high – a situation with which they could no longer cope (De Paepe 2012). End-of-life discussions take a lot of time in a busy day. If several patients ask for euthanasia on the same day, this will have an impact on the level of health care that can be provided for the other patients scheduled for that day who need all the attention of their oncologist.

The request for euthanasia often occurs even in very early stages of the patient's disease. There is an increased fear of suffering and, in some cases, even a lack of interest or motivation to be treated. Sometimes, at the very first consultation in oncology the patient can already be asking for euthanasia, without taking into account other therapeutic options. This is challenging for oncologists, because their first objective is to treat patients in the best way they can and to prolong their lives in good conditions. An oncologist is involved in clinical research and tries to find new effective therapies from a hopeful perspective. His or her core business is to cure and to care. Suddenly, he or she is asked to end the life of his or her patient in whom a malignant disease has just been diagnosed.

The shift from euthanasia for physical suffering towards euthanasia for reasons in part, or sometimes even completely beyond, physical suffering is an additional burden for doctors. When patients no longer believe that their lives are worth living, this compels doctors to become the judge of autonomy questions and of existential/mental suffering while seeking to resolve these problems through the administration of death. It is possible to recognise why doctors became involved in physical suffering. However, in cases of euthanasia for existential or mental reasons, the doctor is acting outside his or her proper role and competence, both in relation to the indications, and in relation to the proposed solution. Recently, Dr Marc Cosyns, one of the promoters of euthanasia in Belgium, said in an interview: 'Today, some of the persons who ask for euthanasia are not really patients. They should rather be helped with a law that foresees assisted suicide. And maybe it should not be doctors who decide what to do with their demand. Maybe social helpers could do this' (Beel 2013b). This is a clear recognition that euthanasia is no longer a purely medical affair, if indeed it ever was.

The law on euthanasia is also putting the doctor's autonomy in danger. The 2002 law foresaw the possibility that a doctor might refuse euthanasia by expressing a conscientious objection. In 2013, legal proposals were seriously considered that would have obliged doctors to refer their patients to a colleague to perform the euthanasia. Moreover, there has been increasing pressure to make euthanasia available in all health care institutions, including Catholic hospitals, nursing homes and palliative care centres. This is striking because, for the promoters of euthanasia, respect for autonomy is the most important value. In fact, only the autonomy of the patient seems to be important. The autonomy of doctors and institutions is not promoted or even protected. The pressure on doctors also increases due to communication with slogans. If euthanasia is defined as 'dying with dignity', doctors who do not perform euthanasia are implicitly labelled as inhumane.

Euthanasia can also damage the relationship of trust and dialogue between doctors and those among their patients who are now afraid to go to the hospital because they might have their lives ended without their request (Foley and Hendin 2002). In my clinical practice, I have witnessed more than once how family members were afraid that the doctors would apply euthanasia to their sick relative without their agreement or even without notification.

Palliative Care in Danger

In my opinion, the acceptance of euthanasia has induced a growing confusion about what constitutes the essence of palliative care, which was initially developed for terminally ill patients suffering from end-of-life symptoms. The aim of palliative care is to offer 'all that we can do, when there is nothing anymore to do'. It is the 'care beyond the cure' and 'adding life to days and not days to life'. Palliative care services have the experience to take care of all aspects of wellbeing (physical, social, mental and spiritual) in terminally ill patients. The World Health Organisation has repeatedly stressed that palliative care is not compatible with euthanasia (Sepulveda et al. 2002; Pereira et al. 2008a). Over the last ten years, several studies have consistently shown that the majority of medical doctors, and in particular doctors involved in palliative care, is opposed to physician-assisted suicide and euthanasia (Finley et al. 2005; Bittel et al. 2002; McCormack et al. 2011; Seale 2009b).

Nevertheless, when the promoters of the Belgian law launched euthanasia as a controversial way to end a patient's life, they had to face the very good reputation of palliative care services. In order to increase the acceptance rate of euthanasia, they decided to introduce euthanasia as one of the possible end-of-life decisions to be taken in palliative care units. As a consequence, palliative care units are in danger of losing their initial objective and specificity. Several articles have been published in recent years exploring the difficulties of palliative care workers when physician-assisted suicide is introduced to their hospitals or palliative care services (Harvath et al. 2006; Volker 2001; Pereira et al. 2008b).

As a result of this confusion, some patients have lost their trust in palliative care services and refuse to be transferred to them out of fear that they would undergo euthanasia. For example, I can cite the case of an 85-year-old man suffering prostate carcinoma, who was admitted to the ward. He was a widower, and had been for several years, had no children and lived alone. Each day he went to the cemetery to visit his wife's tomb and then to the restaurant, because he was unable to cook a warm meal. He had reached the stage of castration-resistant prostate

carcinoma and the next treatment option was chemotherapy. Nevertheless, the patient was frail and suffered severe renal insufficiency. Chemotherapy was a clinical challenge in this patient. He agreed that providing
supportive care would be the best we could offer him. Given his age and
the fact that he was living alone, without children, we were thinking that
he was an ideal candidate for a hospice. However, this patient refused to
be transferred to the hospice because 'in the hospice they would oblige
him to accept euthanasia, which he did not want to undergo'.

Moreover, in the first proposals of the Belgian law, a palliative
filter was foreseen. This meant that when a euthanasia request was
received, the possibilities of palliative care should first be considered.
However, this proposal was not retained in the final legislation. As a
consequence, in Belgium, a palliative consultation is only undertaken
in around 40 per cent of euthanasia cases. This percentage has remained
stable over the years (FCECE 2010, p. 9). It should also be noted
that Raphael Cohen-Almagor reported that the palliative filter does not
work well in Belgium. One of the reasons is the limited knowledge of
the possibilities of palliative medicine among doctors and the lack of
demands for information from the patient and their relatives (Cohen-
Almagor 2009b).

Palliative care units are even at risk of becoming 'houses of euthanasia', which is the opposite of what they were meant to be. As doctors
are often reluctant to perform euthanasia, they may try to transfer their
patients who request euthanasia to the palliative care unit, thinking that
the doctors in that unit are used to deal with end-of-life issues. Consequently, doctors working in palliative care units will, unfortunately,
have to euthanise patients who have been referred specifically for this.
As a result of this evolution, some palliative care units have decided no
longer to admit patients if they have an active euthanasia request to
prevent their palliative care units from becoming the executing unit of
all demands of euthanasia in their hospital. This would have been an
impossible burden for nurses, social workers and doctors at the hospices since it is in complete contradiction with their initial desire
to administer genuine palliative care to terminally ill patients. Some
Belgian palliative care units, that have opened their doors to patients
requesting euthanasia, have seen nurses and social workers leaving the
unit because they were disappointed that they could no longer offer
palliative care to their patients in an appropriate way. They were upset
that their function was reduced to preparing patients and their families
for lethal injections.

Patients' Lives in Danger

In terms of survival, the difference between euthanasia and palliative sedation in a terminally ill patient suffering end-of-life symptoms such as severe pain, asphyxia and terminal anxiety, may not be relevant. However, if euthanasia is approved for non-terminally ill patients, a patients' life can be shortened by several years.

In a considerable number of cases, the natural evolution of a disease is difficult to foresee. I have witnessed the case of a 70-year-old patient admitted to a cardiac intensive care unit because of a cardiomyopathy with a remaining left ventricular ejection fraction of only 10 per cent. The normal value should be 55–65 per cent. The patient was suffering from severe dyspnoea and peripheral oedema as the consequence of the cardiac disease. There was no available treatment for the underlying cardiac disease and no improvement of her situation was obtained with support-ive care such as with diuretics. She became a bed-to-chair patient. As a consequence of her discouragement and the lack of therapeutic options, the patient asked for euthanasia. The cardiologists agreed with this deci-sion as they considered the disease to be severe without any chance of improvement. The palliative support care team was consulted and was uncomfortable with the request for euthanasia. Finally, the patient accepted genuine palliative care and was admitted to the palliative care unit. After several weeks in the palliative care unit, her cardiac function improved and after three months she was discharged. She recovered, returned home and since then, comes to greet us occasionally.

Similarly, not all the doctors are aware of the therapeutic possibilities in a given oncologic disease. Patients can now die several years early due to false diagnosis and lack of adequate treatment.

The percentage of patients dying from euthanasia is very variable from one hospital to another. This does not depend on the pathologies being treated at these hospitals, but rather on the ethical opinions of the doctors concerning euthanasia, as well as on the institutional ethics policy on euthanasia that is approved by the ethics committee and the management of the health care institution. An approval for euthanasia will also depend on the second doctor who will be consulted (Cohen-Almagor 2009b). If a doctor is convinced that euthanasia should take place, he or she will be inclined to consult a colleague who is likely to agree. It is important to note that the law foresees a second opinion, but that the law does not indicate who should be consulted and whether this second opinion is compulsory.

Finally, the demand for euthanasia will depend on how individuals face illness and what meaning they can give to their lives despite the disease. Most of our patients (some 80–90 per cent) can find a meaning in their lives, even if they are suffering from cancer. Some of them want to live until the wedding of their child, foreseen in some months. Others want to see the birth of their first grandchild. Others want to take some holidays. Only a minority of patients cannot find a reason to live despite the disease. Depressed and isolated patients are the most at risk. Precisely, as one of the characteristics of depression is a wish to die, this is the symptom that should be treated.

The thoughts of a person in relation to his or her health or on future disease can change during his or her lifetime. When persons are healthy, they may fear illness and disability. This can lead to the completion of an advance directive. But when the illness occurs, they find that they are still happy to be alive and will face disease in another way. However, if ever individuals go through a phase of acute medical problems, and a resuscitation is required, the advance directive can have severe consequences.

A colleague neurologist reported the frequent situation of persons suffering a cerebrovascular accident. Some make an end-of-life declaration stating that they want euthanasia or that they refuse treatments if ever they have a cerebral haemorrhage. Nevertheless, his experience is that patients who survive a cerebrovascular accident, even if they can suffer consequences and even if they will have a long re-adaptation treatment, are still 'happy to be alive'. They learn to live under new circumstances. But what should the doctor do when a patient is unconscious and comes to the emergency department with a cerebrovascular accident if he or she has an advance directive indicating that he or she wants euthanasia?

Finally, laws are necessary for the protection of the vulnerable. Old and weak persons have to be protected because in a society there will always be individuals who try to enrich themselves putting other persons at risk. Therefore, clear rules such as the prohibition of intentional killing are necessary. A colleague reported that he witnessed a case of a false declaration written by the son of a patient asking for euthanasia. Similarly, on a website created to focus on the difficulties resulting from the law on euthanasia, one case of euthanasia was reported for economic reasons by the director of a nursing home. A grandmother was worried about the high costs of her journey in the nursing home and, to please her granddaughter, she agreed to undergo euthanasia (Lievens 2013).

Families in Danger

The Belgian law on euthanasia states that relatives can be informed about the patient's demand for euthanasia if this is the patient's wish. This lack of a requirement to inform the family is causing serious problems. The two first and ongoing court trials have been launched by the children of patients who underwent euthanasia without their family being informed (Mortier 2013; Waterfield 2015; Aviv 2015). The principle of respect for autonomy has become more important than the principle of relational connectedness or solidarity. In my experience, I witnessed several difficult situations in which a depressed patient asked for euthanasia, but the husband wanted to take care of the patient and accompany her through her therapeutic journey, which was a useful therapy. For a spouse, it can be very difficult and sad to see the partner accept euthanasia while he or she is opposed and convinced that there are alternative solutions.

Although in 2002, it was said that euthanasia would only apply for adults, in 2014, the law was extended to competent children of any age, if the euthanasia request was approved by the parents. Nevertheless, some commentators are already proposing that euthanasia on children should be permitted without the approval of the parents. This is a surprising fact given the responsibility that parents have for their children until the age of 18 years. Nevertheless, the president of the Federal Commission for Control and Evaluation of Euthanasia, Dr. Wim Distelmans stated that 'the approval of the parents will make everything more difficult' (Beel and Sioen 2013). If the parents' approval were not necessary, a 14-year-old girl with anorexia nervosa, a disease which often induces a strong desire to die, would be able to accept euthanasia, even if her parents were opposed and wanted to find a treatment.

The mourning process is not always easy in cases of euthanasia. Often families report that all has been so quick and that there was not enough time to spend with the patient. The last days the family can spend with a dying person are very important, because they can be the opportunity for reconciliation and the expression of the last signs of affection. In my experience, when family members are encouraged to consider these last moments as the last opportunity to grow in love, they are often very grateful afterwards. It can be a healing process for families to spend some days with a dying relative.

Moreover, the decision whether or not to accept euthanasia can cause an additional stress for families at a moment when they are already suffering. It is painful to see several children around their parent's bed debating whether he or she should undergo euthanasia. It is also painful to see the struggle of patients who are hesitating over whether or not they should request euthanasia.

Solidarity in Danger

When an illness occurs in a family, this can be an occasion to rediscover solidarity. The last phase of a person's life can become the unique moment of reconciliation between persons who have been separated by difficulties in life. In many cases, men and women who have been married for a long time and in whose life monotony has grown, can rediscover how love can come into action through the care given to an ill partner. Palliative care workers help patients and their relatives cope with the disease taking care also of the psychological and social aspects of dealing with a life-threatening disease. In the course of palliative care, family members can – even through sometimes dramatic situations – rediscover the joy and peace of taking care of one another.

But strikingly, patients are often requesting euthanasia in order to not be a burden for their family. In a study on 83 patients who requested physician assisted suicide in Oregon, frequent underlying reasons were concerns about being a burden and not wanting to be cared for by others (Ganzini et al. 2008b). I learned to deal with this situation, as illustrated by the following case. A 72-year-old woman was asking for euthanasia. She had been suffering metastatic breast cancer for several years and was now receiving an ineffective systemic therapy. She wanted euthanasia because transfers to the hospital for the therapy became too difficult and because she did not want to be a burden for her daughter, who also had to work and care for her family. We went to see the patient. We agreed that her therapy, although well tolerated, was a burden, because it was not very effective while obliging her to come every three weeks to the hospital. We agreed to stop the therapy and to go for best supportive care at home. But she did not want to be a burden for her daughter. I asked her if – during her life – she took care of some sick people. She said that she took care of her father during the last three years of his life and then – when he died – of her mother who was ill for one year before dying. 'Was this a burden for you to take care of your parents?' 'Oh, no, doctor, not at all, I was very happy to do so'. Before I could tell her that she would not be a burden for her daughter, the daughter took the feet of the patient and started crying, asking her mother whether 'she could please take care of her in the coming months'.

Alternative Solutions

In our General Medical Oncology Department, requests for euthanasia are rare. We believe that this is due to our policy on communication and our avoidance of therapeutic obstinacy.

During the course of a malignant disease, we have a policy of maintaining an open dialogue about the prognosis of the disease and the chances for definitive treatment of prolonged remission. The course of a disease depends on its aggressiveness and on the efficacy of the therapy. Both factors are explained by molecular mechanisms which are largely undiscovered. As a consequence, we can only estimate the chances of cure or remission. Usually we can say the disease cannot be cured, but that several therapies are available and that long-lasting responses are possible. Our aim is to inform the patient in a realistic way, avoiding a too positive or too negative communication. Moreover, new therapies are being developed and could change the perspective of some diseases in the coming years.

This realistic communication is not the case everywhere. It is not rare that doctors and even medical oncologists are uncomfortable with the announcement of incurability. As a consequence, they will present the situation in an over-optimistic way. And when the patient is becoming weaker because of progressive disease and a lack of response to the therapy, some doctors will announce a new therapy rather than admit that the patient is entering into a palliative situation. This unrealistic communication will lead to therapeutic obstinacy and causes tensions because, on the one hand, the patient has access to all the information on the Internet and, on the other hand, he or she feels in his or her body that there is a lack of coherence between the doctor's words and his or her health situation. Moreover, the doctor will not have informed his or her patient at the right time of the possibilities of palliative care. The patient will become increasingly exhausted suffering from side effects of his or her inefficient therapy. This physical and mental stress will easily lead to a desire for euthanasia, because the patient can no longer endure the situation. Hence, it is important to avoid therapeutic obstinacy.

Patients should also know that the dying process is usually smooth even if there are exceptions. Several conditions like renal or hepatic insufficiency or brain herniation can lead to an irreversible coma. It is important to alleviate the fear of suffering and dying. Diane Meier, a professor of geriatrics at Mount Sinai School of Medicine in New York, states that 'the movement to legalize assisted suicide is driven by the "worried well", by people who are terrified of the unknown and want to take back control' (Aviv 2015).

It is also necessary to avoid therapeutic obstinacy in treating complications. 'A pneumonia is an old men's best friend' is a famous sentence.
When age is progressing or when a disease is weakening a person, we all
know that this person will die. At that moment, the occurrence of
pneumonia or a complication can be a relief for the patient. Doctors
should not feel obliged to treat each complication, because if each is
treated when possible, many complications will remain that are a lot
more difficult to treat. What is the sense of treating a patient with kidney
or liver dysfunction due to obstructions of the urinary or biliary tract
with a stent, if that patient will not die from a renal or hepatic coma in
the first days, but from bone pain or epilepsy in the following weeks?
A patient has the right to refuse any therapy for the underlying disease or
any therapy for any occurring complication.

The introduction of euthanasia and its large scale promotion has
certainly led to a decrease in importance of the taboo of death. Patients
are now less afraid to hear that they would eventually die from their
disease and they will themselves begin to discuss a fatal issue with their
doctor. Thus, it will become easier to talk about the relative efficacy of
therapy and about death that will come ineluctably. This will also be the
opportunity to address the fear of suffering. It will be the occasion to tell
them that usually patients die smoothly and that most symptoms can be
controlled with palliative care.

Although in most cases, the process of dying is quite smooth, some
patients can suffer at the end of their lives from physical pain and
suffocation as well as anxiety. When these symptoms can no longer be
controlled, palliative sedation can be initiated. In a study on 266 patients
admitted to 8 palliative care units in Belgium, 7.5 per cent received
palliative sedation. This study revealed that palliative sedation is only
administered in exceptional cases where refractory suffering is evident
and for those patients who are close to the end of their lives (Claessens
et al. 2011). The survey of Chambaere et al. reported a rate of use of
continuous deep sedation until death of 12.0 per cent in 2013 in the
Dutch-speaking part of Belgium (Chambaere et al. 2015a).

Some promoters of the law on euthanasia stated that there is a grey
zone between adequate palliative care, with the possibility to shorten life
as a side effect of symptom control, and euthanasia, which could be
dangerous for doctors if euthanasia were not legal. They also said
that euthanasia was already administered in an illegal way. Therefore,
a regulation on euthanasia was sought. Instead, it may be preferable to
advise a country to make a law on good palliative care including a

paragraph stating that doctors who would involuntarily shorten a palliative patients' life will not be pursued as long as they were trying to control the symptoms. In that case, the legal prescriptions would be in agreement with the principle of double effect.[3] Moreover, the legalisation of euthanasia in Belgium did not resolve the problem of the grey zone. A significant proportion of cases of euthanasia is still not declared: 27 per cent in Flanders and 42 per cent in Wallonia (Cohen et al. 2012), which means 792 cases in 2013. Finally, based on the results of a survey, Papavasiliou et al. reported that in Belgium, continuous deep sedation until death was initiated without consent or request of either the patient or the family in 27.9 per cent of the cases reported by medical specialists (Papavasiliou et al. 2014).

Conclusion

Since the introduction of a law on euthanasia in Belgium, in 2002, a considerable proportion of doctors are experiencing serious difficulties. An important value of our society, the unconditional respect of human life, has been overruled. As a consequence, the legalisation of euthanasia has put a burden on doctors, families, palliative care services and has put in danger the patient's own life. Together with several colleagues, we believe that the law on euthanasia has created more problems and difficulties than solutions. It is not the core business of doctors to answer the existential questions of their patients and fellow human beings and even less if the answer is the administration of death. It is the core business of doctors to offer genuine palliative care and to alleviate the physical suffering of a patient while taking care for the mental, social and spiritual aspects of his or her suffering. It is my personal opinion that a law on euthanasia is not necessary but, rather, is a threat to the genuine practice of medicine.

---

[3] The principle of double effect is advocated for evaluating the permissibility of acting when one's otherwise legitimate act (for instance, relieving a terminally ill patient's pain) may also cause an effect one would normally be obliged to avoid (sedation and a slightly shortened life). The principle of double effect states that an action having foreseen harmful effects practically inseparable from the good effect is justifiable if the following conditions are fulfilled. The nature of the act is itself good, or at least morally neutral. The agent intends the good effect and not the bad either as a means to the good or as an end itself. Finally, the good effect outweighs the bad effect in circumstances sufficiently grave to justify causing the bad effect and the agent exercises due diligence to minimise the harm.

7

'A Last Act of Grace'?

Organ Donation and Euthanasia in Belgium

TREVOR STAMMERS

Introduction

Since the very first successful kidney transplant in 1954 (Merrill et al. 1958), organ transplantation has become one of the great success stories of modern medicine. It is highly cost-effective (Machnicki et al. 2006) and with many of its technical and immunological challenges largely overcome,[1] the primary limiting factor preventing more patients benefiting from transplantation is the shortage of organs.

Belgium is one of eight countries[2] collaborating together as Eurotransplant,[3] an organization that aims to 'ensure an optimal use of available donor organs'[4] between member states. There were 14,928 patients on the Eurotransplant organ-transplant waiting list as of 1st January 2015, with only 7,194 transplants from deceased donors having taken place during the preceding year and 1,299 patients dying whilst still waiting.[5]

The total number of patients on the transplant waiting list in Belgium at the start of 2015 was 1,248 (of whom 821 were awaiting a kidney), with 819 deceased donor transplants taking place and 80 patients on the list dying during 2014.[6] In terms of the total number of transplants (from deceased and living donors) carried out per million population, Belgium (82.6 in 2014) is in the top three Eurotransplant countries after Austria (92.5 in 2014) and Croatia (83.1 in 2014).

---

[1] Rejection (Kim et al. 2014) and thrombosis (Harraz et al. 2014) however do still present ongoing challenges.
[2] The others are Austria, Croatia, Germany, Hungary, Luxembourg, the Netherlands and Slovenia.
[3] www.eurotransplant.org (access 24 October 2016).
[4] www.eurotransplant.org/cms/index.php?page=about_brief (access 24 October 2016).
[5] www.eurotransplant.org/cms/index.php?page=home (access 24 October 2016).
[6] http://statistics.eurotransplant.org/ (access 24 October 2016).

As well as being highly successful, transplantation has also been one of the most universally accepted of modern medical advances. Such ethical issues as do arise, as with those considered in this chapter, are to do with the sourcing of organs rather than on the practice of transplantation *per se* which is endorsed in principle at least, by all the major world faiths (Oliver et al. 2011).[7]

It is not surprising then that the default mode of many clinicians and ethicists, when considering any means to enlarge the pool of donors is to ask 'Why not?' rather than 'Why?' After all *'Careless Thought Costs Lives'*, as the title of a recent book advocating (*inter alia*) payment for organs, presumed consent and abandoning the dead donor rule bluntly puts it (Radcliffe Richards 2013).

Organ donation following euthanasia (hereafter ODfE) has been practiced in Belgium for quite some time. More recently euthanasia by vital organ removal has been suggested as an improvement over ODfE for maximizing both the number and quality of organs for transplantation. This latter procedure (which at the time of writing remains entirely hypothetical and is not currently practiced) has been dubbed variously organ donation euthanasia (ODE) by Wilkinson and Savulescu (2012) and euthanasia by removal of vital organs (RVO) by Coons and Levin (2011). I will refer to it here as euthanasia by removal of vital organs (ERVO) to clearly distinguish it from the already established current practice of ODfE. As Wilkinson and Savulescu observe, inasmuch as both of these options 'conflict with ethical norms governing transplantation to varying degrees, the cost of preserving those norms will be the death or ongoing morbidity of many individuals' (2012, p. 33). A utilitarian ethical analysis will always tend to gravitate towards expanding the pool of donors from whom organs can be taken.

The *Belgian Act on Euthanasia* and Organ Donation

In October 2001, the Belgian Senate passed the proposal of a report approved by a Senate commission to legalize euthanasia. This resulted in the *Belgian Act on Euthanasia* of May 28th 2002. This Act was amended on 13 February 2014 to legalize euthanasia by lethal injection for children with no lower age limit. There are a number of elements of both the original 2002 Act and the 2014 amendment which are especially

---

[7] Though some minority groups, notably Jehovah's Witnesses, do not support it in principle.

relevant with respect to organ donation. Section 3.1 of the 2002 Act states that (*inter alia*) euthanasia may be carried out on his or her request if

> the adult or emancipated minor patient is in a medically futile condition of constant and unbearable physical or mental suffering that cannot be alleviated, and that results from a serious and incurable disorder caused by illness or accident.

This means that the patient does not have to be terminally ill and indeed may be in perfect physical health, since mental illness and suffering are specified as being sufficient grounds in themselves for euthanasia to be legally carried out. This increases the pool of potential organ donors amongst euthanasia cases considerably as many terminally ill patients, including most of those with malignant disease would not be suitable as organ donors because of the risk of transplanting cancerous cells to the recipient. The documented rise in euthanasia for 'neuropsychiatric' conditions (including depression) from 6 reported cases in 2004 to 63 in 2015 and the increase in percentage of euthanasia for non-cancer patients from 6 per cent to 32 per cent of the total of reported cases in the same years, both imply an increase in the potential ODfE donor pool (FCECE 2006, FCECE 2016).

If the donor organs are taken from children and adolescents, this would be even better for organ quality and in addition expands the availability of organs for transplants for sick children. Section 3.1 of the 2014 amended Act also now permits euthanasia when

> the minor with the capacity of discernment is in a medically futile condition of constant and unbearable physical suffering that cannot be alleviated and that will result in death in the short term, and that results from a serious and incurable disorder caused by illness or accident.

This clause, however, imposes three additional restrictions for minors – the child must have 'the capacity of discernment', he or she must have a terminal illness, and mental suffering is excluded as sufficient criterion. In practice, this is likely to restrict greatly the pool of children who would be suitable to be organ donors following euthanasia. Furthermore, section 3.2.7 states the euthanizing doctor must, 'when the patient is an unemancipated minor, consult, in addition, a child psychiatrist or a psychologist, and inform him about the reasons for this consultation.'

However, this is only for the purposes of written certification of the child's capacity of discernment. The second specialist is *not* required to offer an independent opinion on whether they consider euthanasia appropriate in the specific case.

In addition, the wording of the Act only specifies that the *legal representatives* of the child have to *agree with the request of the minor*. The child's parents are not specifically mentioned at all.

Section 3.1 also specifies that for euthanasia to be legal, 'the request is voluntary, well-considered and repeated, and is not the result of any external pressure'.

This criterion applies equally to both adults and children and it should be noted that the legality of organ donation after euthanasia may constitute an external pressure *in itself* and one to which children are especially vulnerable. Children with capacity of discernment may, never the less, not be competent to evaluate the conflicting motivations and emotions surrounding the possibility of saving the lives of others by their own death. The ethics and practicalities of separating the request for euthanasia from consent to organ donation are fraught with complexity in adults let alone in children whose decision only has to meet with the agreement of their legal representatives who sometimes will not be their parents but representatives of the State.

One final relevant point to note about the text of the *Belgian Act on Euthanasia* is that there is no requirement in the reporting on individual cases of euthanasia to specify if organs for transplant were taken from the deceased. Hence information on this practice is absent from official reports on euthanasia in Belgium.

Impact of the *Belgian Act on Euthanasia* on Organ Transplantation

Since the introduction of the Act, the number of cases of euthanasia has risen sharply. A recent analysis (Chambaere et al. 2015a) of records of almost 4,000 doctors in Flanders (the northern, Dutch-speaking part of Belgium) showed that one in twenty people died by euthanasia in 2013. The percentage of euthanasia deaths increased from 1.9 per cent of all deaths in 2007 to 4.6 per cent of all deaths in 2013. The authors state that 'the overall increase relates to increases in both the number of requests (from 3.5 to 6.0 per cent of deaths) and the proportion of requests granted (from 56.3 to 76.8 per cent of requests made)' (2015a, p. 1179).

Though many of these cases will be in patients with advanced malignant disease, not all of them will be and as the numbers of cases with organs suitable for transplantation rise, the utilitarian moral pressure for not letting these organs 'go to waste' inevitably rises in parallel. This is well-illustrated by Dr David Shaw, a bioethicist at the University of Basel who, in a recent interview (Wurz 2014), stated in response to a question about using organs from physician-assisted suicide (PAS) cases in Switzerland:

> This is a situation where you have people who want to die, you know when they're going to die, and many of them are probably registered organ donors. So it's also more respectful to the people to let them do this final kind of parting gift to humanity. The trouble when you have an idea like this is that some people might get a hold of it and say, 'These crazy ethicists. They want to kill everyone and take their organs out.' Not the case at all. I'm just saying, people are dying because we don't have enough organs.

While I am sure it is the case that Dr Shaw does not want to 'kill everyone', it is equally true that he is not *just* saying that people are dying because of organ shortages. He is actively advocating that the organs of at least registered donors should be taken from PAS cases and is also on record that he does not consider the family should have any right of veto where donors have clearly stated their wishes in advance (Shaw 2012).

Detry et al. from the University of Liege, describe the case of a 44-year-old woman with locked-in syndrome who, the day before her euthanasia in 2007, 'expressed her will of after-death organ donation' (Detry et al. 2008, p. 915). Her liver and kidneys were removed and transplanted and one year later all three recipients where 'enjoying normal graft function'. The authors conclude that the case 'demonstrates that organ harvesting after euthanasia may be considered and accepted from ethical, legal, and practical viewpoints in countries where euthanasia is legally accepted' (2008, p. 915). It is important to note they offer no moral argument for its acceptance but rather assume and assert acceptance of such surgery as the inevitable consequence of its effectiveness.

Eurotransplant has been accepting organ donations from euthanasia cases since 2007 (Detry et al. 2008; Ysebaert et al. 2009) and in 2011, a team from the thoracic surgery department at the University Hospitals, Leuven (Van Raemdonck et al. 2011) favoured the suggestion that euthanasia donors should have their own classification code - Controlled DCD (Donor after Circulatory Death) Category 5, added to the four existing categories of DCDs identified in the 1995 Maastricht classification[8]

---

[8] In the latest version (version 4.1, 16 February 2015) of the Eurotransplant Manual however it specifically states in chapter 9, The Donor that 'DCD after euthanasia is reported as DCD III and documented as euthanasia'. www.eurotransplant.org/cms/mediaobject.php?file=Chapter9_thedonor29.pdf (access 24 October 2016).

(Koostra et al. 1995). The reason they advanced for this new category is that, though euthanasia donors resemble Maastricht Category 3 donors (awaiting cardiac arrest in a non-brain-dead patient), in that their organs will inevitably undergo a period of warm ischemia following death, most euthanasia donors will not be on life support on a ventilator (indeed if they were, euthanasia would almost always not be necessary). The mode of death by lethal injection in euthanasia is completely different from (and more certain than) the hypoxic cardiac arrest following ventilator switch-off. This means that with even greater control of the process of death, the state of the organs can be optimized for transplantation with even greater precision. It was therefore considered important to classify them in a different Maastricht Category so that, over time, the anticipated better survival rates and lower morbidity from organs from euthanasia cases could be confirmed or refuted.

At the 21st European Conference on General Thoracic Surgery in Birmingham, United Kingdom in 2013, a Belgian team reported that six (12.8 per cent) of their patients undergoing lung transplants from controlled DCDs, received their organs from Category 5 donors between January 2007 and December 2012 (Van Raemdonck et al. 2013). At five years post-op, only one of the six recipients had died (three months after surgery from an unrelated cardiac problem). The authors concluded 'Immediate post-transplant graft function and long term outcome in recipients was excellent. *More euthanasia donors are to be expected with more public awareness*' (Italics mine). It is not clear if this greater public awareness is expected to increase the number of offers to donate organs from a steady state of euthanasia requests or if the authors expect that the total numbers of requests for euthanasia might also increase.

The Procedure of Organ Donation following Euthanasia (ODfE)

The most detailed account to date of the actual mechanism and procedure of organ donation after euthanasia (Van Raemdonck et al. 2011) is interesting. The transplant team stress their 'independence' from both the physicians granting the euthanasia request and the 'three independent physicians as required by Belgian law for every organ donor' (2011, p. 41) who pronounce and certify the donor's death. The nature of these other physicians' 'independence' is not specified but presumably only extends to their not working on the same team. It does not seem practicable that they would all have to come in from other hospitals.

An ambivalence in the Van Raemdonck paper raises further concerns. The authors state, 'Only patients suffering from a debilitating benign disease such as a neurological or muscular disorder are considered suitable for donation' (2011, p. 45). This is probably specified to make clear that most patients with malignant disease would not be suitable donors. However what is not spelled out is that though three of the four cases they describe, fall into the 'only' suitable categories they mention, the remaining one is stated to have been euthanized at the age of 52 for an unspecified *mental* illness.

Whether then euthanasia is requested for mental or physical illness, a few hours before being carried out, the donors had a central venous line inserted in a room adjacent to the operating theatre. They were then heparinized 'immediately before a cocktail of drugs was given' (Van Raemdonck et al. 2011) by the euthanasing doctor. What the 'cocktail' consisted of is not specified in the paper. This is curious since lethal injections may have a variety of toxic effects which may be of no importance if euthanasia is the only aim. Drugs given to stop the heart in euthanasia are usually intended to stop it beating forever; with hearts to be used for transplantation, this would however be counter-productive. This is a principal reason why currently, hearts from cases of euthanasia, are *not* suitable for transplant. Written details of the precise lethal injection protocol in Belgium prior to organ donation are remarkably elusive, though it is likely to parallel the Dutch protocol for euthanasia (KNMG/KNMP 2012).

Immediately after certification of cardiopulmonary death, the donor was moved into the operating theatre, intubated, shaved, cleaned, disinfected and draped and a sterno-laparotomy performed. The abdominal aorta was cannulated to enable a rapid flush cooling of the abdominal organs to preserve the liver and kidneys. The pleural cavities were then opened and topical cooling of the lungs initiated with ice cold saline. The lungs were then prepared for explantation and removed before being transported to the recipient hospital.

The Ethics of Organ Donation following Euthanasia

One of the features that has undoubtedly facilitated the increase in organ donation worldwide has been the element of altruism involved and the freedom from coercion. This is perhaps why in discussing ODfE, Cohen-Almagor states that it might also, along with other categories of donation, be viewed as a 'last act of grace' (2013, p. 517)

In 2008, the Ethics Committee of Eurostransplant passed six recommendations on organ donation after euthanasia (Eurotransplant 2008) which state:

1. Euthanasia has to be an accepted procedure in the legal framework of the donor country.
2. The euthanasia procedure and the determination of death after the euthanasia procedure have to be in line with national law and national practices.
3. The euthanasia procedure itself and the explantation should follow a clear protocol.
4. The euthanasia procedure and the organ retrieval as well as the organ allocation should be kept as separate as possible.
5. All donors have to be reported to Eurotransplant (ET), the allocation should follow the NHBD (non-heart beating donor) allocation rules in the recipient's country.
6. Organs from donors after a euthanasia procedure shall only be allocated to patients registered on the waiting list for organ transplantation in ET, and within ET, in countries that accept the transplantation of this type of donor organ. In addition the possibility to indicate the acceptance of organs from donors after a euthanasia procedure should be added to the center- and patient-specific donor profiles in ENIS (Eurotransplant Network Information System).

Apart from listing these criteria, the only other two ethical concerns emphasized by the Leuven transplant team are (1) organ donation should not be discussed with (and presumably not raised by) the physician intending on performing euthanasia until after the 'request for euthanasia is granted according to law' and (2) the request for and execution of euthanasia should be clearly separate from the organ procurement in order 'to exclude any conflict of interest between the donor and the recipient and between the teams involved' (Van Raemdonck et al. 2011, p. 45).

The separation between granting the request for euthanasia and the discussion of organ donation in this way may, however, be much more difficult in practice than in theory. First, it is completely contrary to the increasing trend of raising the possibility of organ donation at as early a stage as possible in most other situations where such donation can be foreseen. In the first reported case of donation after euthanasia (Detry et al. 2008, p. 915) it is stated that the patient only raised her intention of organ donation the day before her planned euthanasia.

Whilst this would indeed indicate, in this case, a clear temporal separation between the two intentions, it does raise questions about why the desire to donate suddenly arose only 24 hours before death and a possibly indecent haste to make the necessary donation arrangements rather than postponing the euthanasia for a day or two.

However, at the other end of the time spectrum from last minute decisions, a dossier from the European Institute of Bioethics, *Euthanasia in Belgium: 10 Years On* questions a new practice of accompanying a request for euthanasia with a form for organ donation to be filled out by the patient. 'To what extent does this possibility risk weighing on the decision taken by a patient who believes that his or her existence is worthless? Does the patient still meet the conditions required by the law – i.e., without any external pressure – in order to formulate a request for euthanasia, when he/she is invited at the same time to agree to organ donation?' (de Diesbach et al. 2012, p. 7).

As well as the timing of discussion about organ donation, there is also the question of who first raises the issue. In the 2011 report of Van Raemdonck et al., almost a quarter of their lung donors after cardiac death from 2007–2009 were from euthanasia donors whereas reported euthanasia cases only accounted for 0.49 per cent of deaths in 2007. Drawing attention to this striking disparity, Cohen Almagor comments:

> More research needs to be conducted as to who raised the issue of organ transplantation. Is it the patient or someone else? If not the patient, questions need to be raised regarding the motives for raising the issue with the patient ... The concern is that patients might be motivated to consider euthanasia for the purpose of organ procurement and that the planning of the death procedure might be against the wishes of the patient, against her best interests, premature and possibly for profit. Adequate checks need to be squarely in place to ascertain that such abuse does not happen.
>
> (2013, pp. 517–518)

The language used by the authors of a recent paper supporting organ acquisition after euthanasia shows that such abuse could easily happen when they affirm that euthanasia, as in the Detry case (2008), would 'make organ donation possible for some patients who would not otherwise be able to donate. In an extreme case, they might choose to undergo euthanasia *at least partly to ensure their organs could be donated*' (Wilkinson and Savulescu 2012, p. 42). The ease with which one can move from euthanasia *followed* by organ donation to euthanasia (at least in part) *for* organ donation could not be clearer.

As we have seen, the numbers of reported cases of ODfE in Belgium are very small so far and even if the rising trend for euthanasia continues at its current rate from 1.9 per cent of deaths in 2007 to 4.6 per cent in 2013 (Chambaere et al. 2015a, p. 1179), they are likely to remain low, since as already noted 'the majority of patients requesting euthanasia do not fulfil the criteria for organ donation because of terminal cancer' (Van Raemdonck et al. 2011, p. 45). However the numbers of suitable donors could be much larger and hence many more lives saved by their organs, if both the mode and scope of euthanasia for organ donation were to change. It is such future possibilities that will now be considered as Belgium is well-placed to be the first country to change its euthanasia Act to incorporate them, just as readily as it has already amended it to permit euthanasia of children.

Euthanasia by Removal of Vital Organs (ERVO)

In their paper quoted earlier, Wilkinson and Savulescu propose that since all methods used so far to increase the number of organs donated, whether changes to consent arrangements or improvements to optimize the donation infrastructure within hospitals and nations as well as internationally, have failed to relieve the shortage, a more radical alternative is needed. As the centrepiece of seven specific *Options for increasing the number and quality of organs from LSW[9] donors,*[10] they advocate the use of cardiac and neuro-euthanasia followed by organ donation, and ERVO as 'rational improvement(s) over current practice regarding *withdrawal of life support*' (2012, p. 32; italics mine).

Though Wilkinson and Savulescu note that 'organ donation after cardiac euthanasia has been described in a patient[11] in Belgium' (2012, p. 42), they immediately recognize that this would lead to a lower overall total of available organs than is possible from a heart-beating donor. They therefore proposed what they term neuro-euthanasia in which (after general anaesthesia *if* there were 'concerns about possible discomfort to the patient' (2012, p. 42)) bilateral catheter occlusion of the internal carotid and vertebral arteries would be carried out to cause brain death while life support was continued to preserve the other vital organs. Though the number of organs

---

[9] Life Support Withdrawal (LSW).
[10] The other four are changes to consent processes, organ donation prior to natural death, non-brain ante-mortem ECMO (Extracorporeal Membrane Oxygenation) and reducing the asystolic period prior to cardiac death.
[11] The case described by Detry et al. (2008, p. 915).

(and specifically hearts) suitable for donation from neuro-euthanasia would be likely greater than from cardiac euthanasia, brain death can also compromise organ function and quality. For this reason, they prefer ERVO[12] over neuro-euthanasia as a means of maximizing organ availability as well as pointing out that in those countries that already permit euthanasia, it is unlikely that neuro-euthanasia would be widely undertaken when ERVO serves the purpose of organ optimization far better.

The logic of Wilkinson and Savulescu's argument appears irrefutable from a utilitarian perspective. Since it is both permissible a) to withdraw life support from a patient in whom further treatment is considered futile and b) to remove their organs after they have died, why they then ask 'should surgeons have to wait until the patient has died as a result of withdrawal of advanced life support or even simple life prolonging medical treatment?' (2012, p. 41).

Far better, they suggest, both from the point of view of organ optimization and less suffering for the patient, to carry out euthanasia by anaesthetizing and removing the requisite organs including the lung and heart *to cause* death. A win-win scenario they claim, since no one dies 'who would not otherwise have died' (Wilkinson and Savulescu 2012, p. 41) and more organs can be taken in total, as even the heart can be used and there will be less ischaemic time before all organs are removed. Furthermore patients and their relatives could rest assured that their organs would actually be more likely to be transplanted rather than in donation after circulatory death (DCD) cases following withdrawal of life support, when many patients do 'not die sufficiently quickly ... for organ retrieval' (Wilkinson and Savulescu 2012, p. 41).

These claims, however, ignore the fact that we will *all* die 'otherwise', if we are not given ERVO; it is not only the mode of death which is affected but the *timing* of death. The fact that the life is being ended earlier than would otherwise be the case with withdrawal of life support, should at least be acknowledged, even if its importance ethically or practically is disputed.

Furthermore, the assumption is made that if relatives are fully informed about what is being proposed, they will be reassured. Trust in medicine is crucial; without it, relatives may be concerned that they agreed to the hastening of the death of their loved one for the sake of acquisition of their organs. One needs time to process such decisions and when a match for the

---

[12] Though they refer to this as organ donation euthanasia (ODE), I have used the term ERVO (euthanasia by removal of vital organs) following Coons and Levin's terminology to avoid confusion with ODfE.

organs is found, the recipients' need could easily trump making time available to the donor's relatives to decide in an unpressured environment. It would only take one case where relatives instead of feeling relieved were left feeling litigious, to severely damage trust in the whole transplant system.[13]

It is important to note that what Wilkinson and Savulescu are advocating is ERVO not just for terminally ill patients or patients capable of giving consent to euthanasia but also for patients who are 'permanently unconscious, for example those in a permanent vegetative state, or anencephalic infants . . . whose organs can be removed because they have no prospect of regaining consciousness and continued life cannot benefit them' (2012, p. 40). They cite with approval Rachels' (1986, p. 24) famous assertion about such cases that 'while their biological life continues their biographical life has ended'.

Wilkinson and Savulescu's coup de grace is their suggestion that 'although most arguments for euthanasia are distinguished from questions of organ donation, it may be that the benefits of donation, for the individual and for others, provide the *strongest case* for euthanasia' (2012, p. 41). Though this may well be a perfectly acceptable argument for those who favour both euthanasia and organ donation, for any who do not support the former and *all* who are contemplating the latter, it is a very disturbing suggestion that having one's life taken by euthanasia is of benefit to the individual providing the organs.

In spite of the serious issues just raised, there is considerable utilitarian moral pressure to accept ERVO for life support withdrawal cases since its utilitarian benefits are undeniably impressive. Wilkinson and Savulescu (2012, p. 41) calculate that its introduction in the United Kingdom would potentially result in up to another 2,201 organs per year becoming available from an extra 655 heart-beating donors,[14] thus totally eliminating the current UK organ shortage with organs to spare. They note, however, that this would depend on the consent rate for donation, but of course if organ 'conscription', which they also suggest (2012, pp. 44–45), were introduced, such consent would not matter anyway.

The practice of ERVO is not going to be introduced in the near future in the United Kingdom, since both euthanasia and physician-assisted suicide

---

[13] There are precedents of analogous situations in, e.g., Japan (Toshiro 1989), Singapore (Berger 2007) and Brazil (Csillag 1998).

[14] They assume a yield of 3.9 organs per heart-beating donor and consent rates 'similar to current levels in the UK' (Wilkinson and Savulescu 2012, p. 47).

are currently illegal there. If however we consider the most recent analysis of modes of death in Belgium (Chambaere et al. 2015a), we find that whilst euthanasia accounted for 4.6 per cent of deaths in 2013, withholding or withdrawing life supporting treatment (called life-prolonging treatment in the table in the paper) accounted for 17.2 per cent of the 6,188 deaths in the sample. With a total of all deaths of 61,621 in 2013, this would increase the number of potential candidates for ERVO in Belgium to around 10,600 per annum – though not all of those would be suitable to be donors and not all of those who are suitable would consent.

Wilkinson and Savulescu acknowledge that ERVO clearly conflicts with the dead donor rule (DDR) as well as the principle of not killing and it also could conflict with both patient and family autonomy (2012, p. 39). Nevertheless, they justify ERVO on the grounds that it results in a Pareto improvement (i.e., at least one person is better off and no one is worse off) because 'more lives are able to be saved by harvesting functioning organs' (2012, p. 41) with ERVO.

Coons and Levin (2011, p. 237) are quite explicit in their view that the DDR is not justified 'either in principle or in practice' in the first place. The DDR 'states that organ donation must not kill the donor; thus, the donor must first be declared dead' (Bernat 2013, p. 1289) but Coons and Levin claim there is a broad class of cases in which it is not only morally acceptable but sometimes 'perhaps *obligatory* to procure vital organs from living individuals' (2011, p. 237 Italics mine).

Execution by Lethal Injection and Euthanasia by Removal of Vital Organs

Though Coons and Levin state they 'take no stand on the permissibility of either voluntary active euthanasia (VAE) or capital punishment (CP)' (2011, p. 238) they admit that CP is 'less clear' and consider it at greater length. They express their particular concern that using ERVO 'to execute will require that a *doctor* kills: if the executions were carried out by some other method, no doctor need be implicated in the killing. Arguably policies that allow doctors to participate in executions threaten professional values and may indirectly alarm or threaten the public' (2011, p. 238; italics theirs).

What they mean of course is that using ERVO to carry out executions will require that a doctor *executes* rather than kills. They seem not to recognize that doctors kill, whether carrying out executions or ERVO. Therefore policies that allow doctors to participate in euthanasia may also threaten professional values and may indirectly alarm or threaten the public as well. Any ethical boundaries that they seek to draw between the participation of doctors in executions and euthanasia *with regard to voluntary consent to use of organs after death* seem to be very tenuous as there are far more similarities between the two procedures than there are differences. They themselves even acknowledge that 'execution by lethal injection mirrors euthanasia in the Netherlands and often uses the same drug combinations', a fact confirmed by a more recent discussion on why doctors should not act as executioners – 'Thiopental followed by pancuronium forms the basis of today's Dutch euthanasia protocol, pancuronium having been introduced because prolonged death and writhing with thiopental alone distressed families' (Dyer 2014). As outlined earlier, the Belgian euthanasia protocol is very similar to the Dutch[15] and a widely reported case in Belgium has recently drawn into focus some striking ethical dilemmas and disconnects concerning euthanasia, CP and subsequent organ donation.

Frank van Den Bleeken, having already served 30 years of a life sentence for murder and serial rape, requested that his life be ended by euthanasia on the grounds of 'unbearable psychological anguish' (Bacchi 2014), a request which is completely understandable in view of the treatment of sex offenders by other inmates in prison, quite apart from any other considerations. Since mental suffering is a valid reason for euthanasia in Belgium, the Belgian justice minister, Koen Geens, eventually granted his request and euthanasia was scheduled for 11 January 2015.

However, the week before the planned euthanasia, Geens declared that he would instead allow Mr Van Den Bleeken to be transferred to a psychiatric treatment facility in the Netherlands – a request previously denied to Van Den Bleeken until he was facing euthanasia. The doctor who was to carry out euthanasia then withdrew for 'confidential personal reasons'. Van Den Bleeken's lawyer stated 'it is always the doctor who must decide in all conscience. His freedom of conscience must be respected' (RTBF 2015). However, this does not resolve the problem of some 15 other Belgian prisoners who are reported also to have requested euthanasia. Such a possibility prompts profound ethical questions for a country which, though it abolished the death penalty in 1996, is carrying out euthanasia in rapidly increasing numbers.

Again and again in the context of state execution of prisoners, ethicists who oppose the death penalty but are either open to, or advocates of,

---

[15] Though differences in the law and practice between the two countries have been outlined by Nys (see Chapter 1 of this book) and Smets et al. 2009.

legalized euthanasia, find themselves in a difficult place when trying to justify the moral inconsistency between these two positions. For example Gerald Dworkin states:

> I believe it is incontrovertible that there is sufficient explicit text, whether in specific oaths taken by physicians or in the principles adopted by the medical community or in the code literature, to ensure that participation in lethal injections by physicians would be contrary to their professional code of ethics.
>
> (Dworkin 2002, p. 183)

and

> At this point I cannot think of a plausible non ad-hoc set of principles to support the following three judgements: euthanasia is under certain conditions legitimate; it is illegitimate for doctors to participate in lethal injection even if the prisoner has a choice about his mode of execution; and organ donation surgery[16] is sometimes permissible.
>
> (Dworkin 2003a, p. 214)

Silver likewise considers that

> We can fruitfully compare the autonomous choice of the condemned prisoner for lethal injection to the autonomous choice of the terminally ill patient for physician assisted suicide. As far as autonomy is concerned, there is no reason to think that the patient's choice in the manner of her death is more significant than the choice of the condemned prisoner over the manner of his death.
>
> (Silver 2003, p. 207)

Varelius (2007) believes that he has found a way out of the impasse both Dworkin and Silver find themselves in, by formulating a principle that would permit both organ donation surgery and euthanasia and yet make a doctor's participation in execution by lethal injection impermissible even if the method is the prisoner's choice. He states his principle as follows:

> (T)he proper ends of medicine are to use medical skills and training to maintain or improve the condition of the persons affected, subject to their autonomous consent and causing minimal possible harm.
>
> (Varelius 2007, p.145)

This principle differs from a similar principle proposed by Silver (2003, p.209) in its significant extension from an individual person (whether

---

[16] The reason that organ *donation* surgery is specified is that short-term harm (and possibly longer term) is done to the donor for the sole benefit of others and not the actual donor.

patient or prisoner) to relevant others, such as the recipients of organs removed from the terminated individual. In his argument as to why he believes this rules out execution by lethal injection even by autonomous choice by the prisoner, Varelius simply asserts that such execution 'would not be a minimally harmful way of serving the prisoner's medical interests'. In the Van den Bleeken case however, the prisoner claims that it would be. Moreover he is not under a state-imposed death sentence but is choosing death for himself rather than continue his 'unbearable psychological suffering' in prison.

Varelius does actually acknowledge that his principle, by introducing other parties in to the moral equation, opens the way for execution by lethal injection to be permissible when the execution would be the minimally harmful way of serving the interests of those other parties. He appears to be unaware of the full logical implications of his argument however when he further insists:

> In such a case, in addition to being given the lethal injection, the prisoner would also have to consent to being used to serve the medical interests of third parties and the physician would have to administer the injection with the intention of helping others, not of punishing the prisoner. Consequently, a physician's giving this kind of lethal injection would not I think count as execution.

> (Varelius 2007, p. 146)

On this premise, then, the death penalty is not an execution if the prisoner consents to donate their organs afterwards and the executing physician need not trouble his conscience that he is doing anything other than serving the proper goals of medicine.

One can easily see where this might lead if the treatment Mr Van den Bleeken receives in the Netherlands does not relieve his unbearable suffering. Should this be the case, and his subsequent renewed requests for euthanasia continue to be denied on the grounds that it is not the minimally harmful way of serving *his* interests, all he has to do is to consent to organ donation after death in order to make the moral argument for acceding to his request irrefutable according to Varelius. Furthermore, Savulescu and Wilkinson's claim, considered earlier, that 'the benefits of donation, for the individual and for others, provide the *strongest case* for euthanasia' (2012, p. 41; italics theirs) would seem to imply that those same benefits would also provide the strongest case for the death penalty, were both the lethal injection and the subsequent organ donation to be carried out with the prisoner's consent.

Organ Donation and Euthanasia in Belgium: Future Trends

Belgium legalized euthanasia in 2002 and the first reported case of success-ful organ transplantation using organs acquired following euthanasia was carried out in 2007 (Detry et al. 2008). Since then, the total number of such transplants reported have remained in single figures and the actual numbers suitable for organ transplantation are likely to remain low.

In contrast, Wilkinson and Savulescu have estimated that the imple-mentation of ERVO for those having life support withdrawn, would com-pletely eliminate the organ shortage in the United Kingdom. There is little doubt that it would do the same in Belgium and, since euthanasia is already legal there, the utilitarian pressure to introduce ERVO is sure to increase.

Eurotransplant (2008) are on record on their website for the condem-nation of the acquisition of organs from prisoners in China:

> The commercial exploitation of organs from executed prisoners is con-sidered a breach of human rights and is an unacceptable practice. Aware of the burden of human suffering that flows from the worldwide shortage of ethically acceptable organs, any act that risks calling the practice of transplantation into disrepute is to be regretted.

It is worth asking whether similar acts risk transplantation being brought into disrepute in Belgium. In view of the suggested moral obligation to use the organs of those requesting euthanasia (Wilkinson and Savulescu 2012), if as reported there are fifteen Belgian prisoners currently request-ing euthanasia, how long will it be before another such request is granted, as it was originally for Van den Bleeken? Is there then not a moral obligation to seek consent at least for ODfE in such cases? Indeed, if Varelius were correct, that such consent more or less makes euthanasia obligatory and it does not even constitute execution in these circum-stances, then surely ODfE or even ERVO for prisoners would seem the inevitable consequence of current practice.

It would of course be the ultimate irony if a country which no doubt prides itself (rightly in my view) on abolishing the death penalty as an inhumane practice, ended up having reintroduced it (at least for prisoners requesting it) to relieve the organ shortage. Then again, though it would be couched in different language, is not organ donation after euthanasia as performed in Belgium since 2007 already effectively equivalent to this? There appears to be a very thin line between a 'last act of grace' and a final act of desecration.

PART III

Euthanasia and Particular Vulnerable Groups

8

A Life Worth Living?

Disabled People and Euthanasia in Belgium

KEVIN FITZPATRICK AND DAVID ALBERT JONES

A Letter from a Philosopher

The aim of this chapter is to reflect on the relationship of disability to the practice of euthanasia as this is performed in Belgium. A lens for this reflection is provided by comments made by the American philosopher Rush Rhees (Rhees 1999, pp. 109–127, Fitzpatrick 2013). Rhees is useful for several reasons. A student of Wittgenstein, he was a subtle and interesting thinker in his own right. His remarks on euthanasia, though brief, are densely packed with deep considerations of the matter, which are not usually evident in the current debate. Euthanasia was a subject about which Rhees was conflicted and indeed regarded it as '[not] really a good subject for public debate' (Rhees 1999, p. 109). This caution prevented him from overestimating the weight of conventional arguments for or against the practice and from short-circuiting the discussion one way or the other.[1]

As deeper discussions must, Rhees considers carefully some of the most challenging cases. Our focus here on the case in which 'there is no hope of recovery – or none of recovering a life such as may have made sense before the illness' (Rhees 1999, p. 112). This is an example of the so-called hard cases frequently invoked by those campaigning for legalising euthanasia or assisted suicide, where these are not already legal.

The primary author of this chapter is Kevin Fitzpatrick who provided most of the material it contains. Ill-health prevented him from completing a polished draft and, with his prior agreement, David Albert Jones took on the task of finishing the chapter. Kevin Fitzpatrick died of cancer on 14 January 2016 (Campbell 2016). This volume is dedicated to his memory.

[1] Rhees is also chosen as he was supervisor to Kevin Fitzpatrick and helped form his own philosophical thinking, but more so because Rhees seems to offer insight on the vexed question of euthanasia.

133

These cases are sometimes presented as a kind of 'proof'. However, such cases and the idea they may 'justify' anything, have been so badly stretched out of shape, and certainly from the way Rhees used the example he gave, as to bear little resemblance to their natural uses. We need to get back to 'rough ground' (Wittgenstein 1958, § 107), that is, to the cases in the original context and our unreflective descriptions of them, before they were put to use in a politico-legal argument.

What Rhees thought, and how he expressed himself, are in some ways problematic, but trying to understand why, and what he was hoping to explain, is potentially revealing; more so, because misunderstandings of the kind of point he was making are deeply embedded in the modern debate, as is evident in the practice of jurisdictions such as Belgium. So, clearing up those confusions will be vital to achieving some clarity about where the contemporary debate goes wrong.

Rhees presents the following example:

> suppose the case of someone whose death can be only a matter of weeks, and whose suffering is bringing with it a degeneration of character and mind; so that the person is no longer himself, and is sure to become less and less so. He is becoming what he would have had a horror of becoming – a far greater horror than he would have had of pain and suffering.
>
> (Rhees 1999, p. 113)

It might seem that horror of mental decline and disability on the one hand, and pain and suffering on the other, are being presented here as constituents of the seriousness of the consideration of euthanasia. This is not what Rhees himself is doing, for he is offering an example, not more at this point, but it is certainly what others seek to do. The idea that such cases provide obvious justification for euthanasia is prevalent in several countries, not least in Belgium, as will be illustrated below.

The 'Hard Case'

While Rhees was not convinced of the arguments presented in favour of euthanasia, neither was he convinced that euthanasia could be ruled out by appeal to general or universal principles. 'My argument is that you cannot condemn euthanasia on general principles which are meant to hold for all circumstances whatever' (Rhees 1999, p. 113).

Rhees was sceptical of universal systems of morality of the kind proposed by Immanuel Kant or attributed to Thomas Aquinas. This is not to imply that euthanasia is morally justified in some circumstances.

Rhee's point, to the extent that it is valid,[2] applies equally to the system of Jeremy Bentham, or to contemporary appeals to autonomy, or to the 'four principles' of Beauchamp and Childress (2001, pp. 138–139) whether they are invoked in favour of or against the moral permissibility of euthanasia. Rhees doubted that such rules, generalities or universal considerations were sufficient to judge the morality of individual cases and their circumstances.

Legislation, on the other hand, simply is a system of rules and the question is precisely whether there should be a rule in this area, and if so what form this rule should take. On this question, Rhees was clear that a robust legal prohibition of euthanasia was vital to make someone pause before taking the life of another:

> anyone who does practise [euthanasia] should know he is breaking the law and that he is liable to grave penalties. This will probably [sic] keep him from sanctioning it lightly.

> (Rhees 1999, p. 111)

Keeping euthanasia illegal will not prevent euthanasia from occurring, but should at least prevent it becoming trivial or routine. If faced with the threat of legal penalties then 'doctors will agree to it only when the case seems to them very strong' (Rhees 1999, p. 110). Rhees died in 1989, after the founding of assisted suicide organisations in Switzerland in 1982 and the effective legal toleration of euthanasia in the Netherlands in 1984, but before the effects of these changes were evident, and long before any country had passed legislation to decriminalise euthanasia. Since 2002, the practice in Belgium (as elsewhere) has demonstrated that so far from applying only to a few 'hard cases', euthanasia is being extended to cases that few would recognise as 'very strong'.

This has been illustrated recently by a number of very high profile cases reported in the media, perhaps most striking that of a young woman of 24 who has had a depression for a number of years and has now been approved for euthanasia, though this has not been performed at the time of writing.[3] This is but one of a growing number of cases in

---

[2] Rhees here is overly sceptical but our point is simply that such considerations cut both ways, they weaken (utilitarian or autonomy-based) arguments in favour of euthanasia just as much as they weaken (virtue or natural law) arguments against.

[3] See Buchanan 2015. The story of 'Laura' first appeared in Belgian *De Morgen News* on 19 July 2015 (Maas 2015b). On 10 November 2015, the *Economist* released a video interview with 'Emily' and her psychiatrist, Lieve Thienpont. The video is presented as

Belgium in which euthanasia has been approved for people with mental health conditions who are not otherwise physically ill or disabled, and who are not terminally ill (see FCECE, Sixth Report 2014, Seventh Report 2016; Thienpont et al. 2015).

Without looking any further at this point into the circumstances of Laura's case, these circumstances are far from the archetypal 'hard case' most commonly presented in favour of euthanasia. It is true that euthanasia for mental suffering alone was already covered in the Euthanasia Act 2002. Nevertheless, the 'hard cases' that helped carry public and medical opinion in favour of the act were more like the case that Rhees describes, and the practice of euthanasia in the first few years was overwhelmingly dominated by serious physical disease, and especially cancer. Over the years there has been a steady increase in euthanasia for non-terminal disease and for mental suffering, an increase not only in absolute numbers but as a proportion of all euthanasia cases.[4]

Despite such extensions of the practice, the appeal to the 'hard case', of the kind that Rhees outlines, has an enduring significance in the euthanasia debate, even in Belgium. This can be illustrated by the recent extension of the law in Belgium to minors. So controversial was this legal move that, for minors, the law is restricted to cases of children 'in a medically futile condition of constant and unbearable *physical suffering* that cannot be alleviated and that will *result in death in a short term*, and that results from a serious and incurable disorder caused by illness or accident' (Belgian Act on Euthanasia 28 May 2002 as amended 13 February 2014, chapter II, section 3 §1, see Appendix I, emphasis added). Here not only is appeal to the 'hard case' evident, but the law attempts to limit euthanasia in minors to this case. However, such legal safeguards in the case of minors only serve to emphasise the lack of similar limits in the case of adults.

The continuing extension from 'very strong' cases to those in which the case is, at best, extremely thin and at worst, a travesty of the serious considerations of the most difficult cases, is akin to the misapplication of a discrete subset to a whole set in mathematics. In that misapplication,

---

an apologia for euthanasia in the circumstances of youthful depression, though happily it ends without Emily taking the lethal dose.

[4] See respective FCECE reports. The Seventh Report 2016 is the first not to see a substantial increase. See also chapters by Montero and by Jones in this volume. The present chapter is concerned not with the analysis of such statistical trends but, rather, with the effective rationale of euthanasia as practiced in Belgium and the relation of this rationale to fear of disability.

Rhees' point about generality is lost; but so too is much else. The failure to 'keep to those lines' and the increasing drift in Belgium towards euthanasia for people who are not terminally ill destroys the seriousness in the example Rhees gives; at the same time, it misuses that sense of seriousness to claim a 'higher' moral ground for supporting euthanasia. It is a strange reversal.

Pain and the Criterion of 'Unbearable Suffering'

The example that Rhees gives, juxtaposes the fear of 'becoming what he would have had a horror of becoming' with the fear of 'pain and suffering' (Rhees 1999, p. 113). The former is said to be 'a far greater horror' than the latter. Such a judgement may well underestimate the burden of chronic pain, and certainly underestimates the possibility of living well with disability. It should also be noted that Rhees is not, by his example, seeking to justify a more general distinction between pain and 'physical suffering', on the one hand, and psychological, existential or 'mental suffering', on the other.

The concept of 'pain' is already philosophically tricky, the notion of a somehow separable 'mental suffering' is even more problematic. Some pains related to obvious physical damage as detected by sensors and communicated by nerves to the brain, but not all 'physical' pain is of this kind (an obvious exception is 'phantom limb' pain). Furthermore, the experience of pain due to physical disease or injury will both be influenced by, and influence, the personal and social environment and the person's mental state. Similarly, people often describe extreme psychological pressure, frustration, anxiety or humiliation as 'painful' experiences. There is a family of concepts here which relate to experiences from which one recoils, and which may be so unpleasant they overwhelm the psyche and make it hard or impossible to function. While the distinction between 'physical pain' and 'mental suffering' may be useful for some purposes, one should be cautious about how far this distinction can be maintained, especially in the context of legislation.

The Belgian legislation requires that suffering whether physical suffering (in the case of minors) or also mental suffering (for adults and 'emancipated minors') is 'unbearable' (*insupportable/ondraaglijk*). This word also deserves close inspection. What makes pain or suffering 'unbearable'? Or to ask the question another way – what is it to 'bear' pain?

To bear means to carry as when one carries a burden. What is unbearable can no longer be carried as an animal may no longer be able to shoulder a burden and walk with it. Implicit in the idea of 'bearing' pain is the idea that it is a burden that is somehow voluntary and could be removed. This concept is like the idea of 'intolerable' suffering. What is tolerated can exist without interference. Bearing suffering has a further connotation of action despite suffering, of carrying on, of walking or *living with* a burden. The connotation is that there is a good in carrying on despite the burden. There is, implicitly, a reason to live with it.

Logically speaking, it may seem that someone cannot 'bear the unbearable' (a phrase famously used by Emperor Hirohito to encourage the Japanese to endure the humiliation of surrender). However, people do speak like this, as they also say, 'I cannot bear it!' even when there is no obvious means to change the situation and they are 'bearing' it. Here the phrase should perhaps be understood more as expressing a wish to be rid of the experience, that is, as an *expression* of distress, not a *description* of it (see Wittgenstein 1958, p. 244). It makes perfect sense for someone to say that they experienced 'unbearable' pain, meaning for example pain that was overwhelming, during which the person could not think or act, without thinking precisely how the burden could be lifted.

There is a problem, then, with regarding 'unbearable' as a description of a kind of suffering, and hence a problem with regarding 'unbearable suffering' as a criterion for euthanasia. It is not simply that different people can bear different *amounts* of suffering; there is a deeper problem with the whole language of 'bearing' suffering. The language is used in different ways. It can be used simply to express the fact of distress and need not 'point' (internally, as it were) to a certain level of distress. It also depends on what the person means as 'bearing', and on what 'intervention' is imagined, if any, as the relief of that burden. For example, 'unbearable toothache' might drive a reluctant person to visit the dentist or take time off work, but to call this pain 'unbearable' is not to say the person would contemplate suicide, at least this would not be the usual connotation. It might be said that the context of euthanasia anchors the phrase 'unbearable suffering' so that it is unambiguous, because this language relates clear alternatives (living with the suffering or dying by euthanasia). However, the phrase will be unambiguous only if 'unbearable suffering' means no more or less than, 'euthanasia appears preferable' but in this case how does the word 'unbearable' add anything to the fact that a person has requested euthanasia to alleviate their suffering?

The fundamental problem in seeking to use 'unbearable suffering' as a criterion is that 'this concept is considered to be subjective, dependent on personal values, and that it must be determined in the first place by the patient' (Thienpont et al. 2015, p. 7). The idea of a (legal) criterion which is necessarily subjective is akin to the idea that pain itself is private and is understood by the criterion of ostensive definition. Wittgenstein famously remarked that if pain were regarded as something private and subjective which only I had access to, as only I might be able to look inside a secret box, then this private thing could play no part in language (Wittgenstein 1958, § 293). The same holds with the idea that unbearable suffering is a criterion but that is subjective and determined by the patient. Despite sounding like a serious restriction, it is no restriction at all, it 'cancels out' for if the only criterion for being unbearable is that a person seeks euthanasia rather than wish to continue to live, then every request will fulfil this 'criterion'. The problem is not then simply that 'the concept of "unbearable suffering" has not yet been defined adequately, and that views on this concept are in a state of flux' (Thienpont et al. 2015, p. 7), though this is problem enough for a concept that is supposed to be a key criterion in the law. The deeper problem is that it is a mistake to regard 'unbearable suffering' as a kind of description which *could* function as a criterion. If interpreted in this way it will give the impression of seriousness while in practice excluding virtually nothing (one must say 'virtually' nothing as there may be further considerations that exclude someone, for example, who is so confused as to be unclear of the meaning of his or her words).

This digression about suffering has illustrated the difficulties in distinguishing between 'pain and suffering' and the fear of 'becoming what he would have had a horror of becoming' (Rhees 1999, p. 113). It may be that some practical distinctions can be made between 'physical pain' having a clear basis in injury or disease and 'mental suffering' related to the burden of, or fear of, disability. However, it does not follow that euthanasia could in practice be confined to the former. Indeed, it seems that, in the case of physical pain, euthanasia is less likely to be the only means to alleviate the suffering, as it is more likely that some alternative could be found, in the last resort by continuous deep sedation. The problem of mental suffering may be much harder to address and, according to Rhees, is also what people fear more. This may be so even for people who live with physical suffering. What is more frightening may be the visceral fear of 'degeneration of character and mind' (Rhees 1999, p. 113). Rhees is right not to flinch from this description because it helps disclose why euthanasia is in fact centrally concerned with the *horror of becoming disabled*.

This is evident in the debate in Belgium. During a public debate in Brussels, Prof Etienne Vermeersch, a senior adviser to the Belgian government, asserted that Belgium's euthanasia law, in operation since 2002, was specifically designed for disabled people. He declared that it was obvious 'a man with no arms and no legs' should want to die and it was 'his life's work' to make that possible for any disabled person, legally and practically.[5]

The Visceral 'Horror' of Becoming Disabled

Rhees takes as his example a 'degeneration of character and mind' such that 'the person is no longer himself, and is sure to become less and less so'. This is the object of his 'horror'. The description of a 'person' being 'no longer himself' should not be over-interpreted. There is a school of bioethics within which moral status is determined by 'personhood' and in which a 'person' is defined by relation to 'self-consciousness coupled with fairly rudimentary intelligence as the most important features' (Harris 1995, p. 8), that is to say, 'in terms of characteristics which may come and go and which are a matter of degree' (Anscombe 2005, p. 267). Rhees was writing before this bioethical doctrine was developed, but such attempts to define 'personhood' represent exactly the appeal to universal concepts or principles that Rhees opposed in moral philosophy. Rhees, in contrast, invokes the common ordinary use of this language, as when we say that someone is 'not himself today'. To be oneself, in this sense, is to be able to act according to an established character and within a coherent narrative or set of narratives. It is this ability that may be eroded by disease and that may provoke horror: horror at the prospect of an erosion of the self. People commonly fear loss of self-control and of a sense of self, the loss of so much that is valuable to oneself. Such fear is readily understandable, and might be described as 'visceral'. It runs deep.

Visceral reactions are in a sense 'natural', that is, spontaneous; the way a piece of music can move us, or a terrible fear of the dark that can be paralysing. A dread of becoming like someone else we see 'suffering' can lead us to the all-too-readily available conclusion that such a life is not, cannot be, worth living, for us, for them. Our 'visceral' reactions to devastating loss through injury or illness, whether from birth or later in life, are core to this debate.

It is not only our own individual feelings of grief to our own personal loss that we must consider, but also the reactions of others to such loss.

---

[5] Stated during a debate at the Goethe Institute Brussels 13 November 2013 at which Kevin Fitzpatrick was present.

Consider, for example, how most of us react instantaneously to someone with severe facial disfigurement. Such immediate reactions can be natural and, we may say, understandable; in one sense therefore, we are not responsible, cannot be blamed for having them. It is what we go on to do because of those feelings that needs to be questioned: the feelings do not themselves validate our behaviours in response to them.

If we do not recognise, acknowledge, these visceral reactions, if we are ashamed of them, feel guilty or suppress them, they are more likely to surface in less favourable treatment of disabled people. We are more likely to choose such euphemisms to describe their impairments, or their deaths, to avoid embarrassment, or to escape deeper questions and self-reflection about our feelings and the reactions to which they give rise.

In direct contrast, Rhees once gave an example of a saint who was capable of embracing people with leprosy, something which horrified others around him. In lesser mortals to do such a thing might require someone to really struggle to mask their feelings, overcome their visceral fear or disgust, to do what no others could contemplate doing. Rai Gaita cites a similar example from Primo Levi. Levi describes the reaction of his companion, Charles, to a young Dutch boy, Lakmaker who had dysentery. Despite the foul smell, the distasteful cleaning required, the terrible danger of disease and despite the prospect of liberation from the concentration camp in a few days' time, Charles, treated the boy with the 'tenderness of a mother' (Gaita 2004, p. xvi, citing Levi 1969). There is the force of what Charles and the saint did; they are such powerful examples precisely because of that force. There is perhaps a danger here of an insincere kind of piety in the telling of such stories, a soft-focus romanticising that covers over the details that might provoke disgust. There is also a danger of condescension: of the professional condescending to care for the patient out of pity. In this regard, it is salutary to note that, at least in the case if the Flemish missionary,[6] St Damien De Veuster, his efforts led to him contracting and dying from leprosy, and his reaching out was not only an affirming emotional encounter but also an expression of practical solidarity. He was concerned, for example, with how to improve the social conditions of those living with leprosy.

What is crucial here is how we respond to the visceral reactions we have, not suppressing these reactions but neither allowing our reactions

---

[6] The saint that Rhees had in mind may well have been St Francis of Assisi, as this is a well-known story about the popular saint, but in the context of the current book it is fitting that a missionary from Flanders provides a still clearer example, see Eynikel 1999.

to prevent us from seeking a mature understanding of 'what it is to live like them'. This can be achieved only by listening to and being with those who have experienced disability or disfigurement. The reaction of horror unchecked by the experience of others, represents a kind of moral isolation (one might say a 'moral solipsism').

It would be foolish to deny that becoming, for example, quadriplegic or blind or confused can be devastating, as are other consequences of trauma or disease. But the estimation of what it is like to live with a particular disability is not always accurate. One telling result of a survey conducted by a doctor, Ian Basnett, who himself became quadriplegic, is instructive: Only 25 per cent of Accident and Emergency doctors could envisage themselves living with quadriplegia; In contrast 90 per cent of quadriplegics say they are happy to be alive (Basnett 2001). What happens when we arrive there, so to speak, can be very different from how we imagine things in advance: projection gives way to another fundamental need, to first survive, and then accommodation, adaptation and so on can be experienced. Incontinence may remain an embarrassment but it is not the end of the world.

This is not to deny that disabled people are prey to these same visceral reactions. Why should they not be? Is that not the whole point – disabled people are people like any others? They too are open to error if they proceed to attempt to justify what cannot be justified, if their visceral reactions drive them to lose self-respect and succumb to discriminatory behaviours, even fatally self-harming ones.

Disabled people may reflect the views of the populations in which we live. It is therefore understandable that some believe that they should be allowed to die by euthanasia or to have someone else assist them to die by suicide. We can respect their views and understand their fear of a painful death or of not wishing to be a burden on others. However, assisted suicide and euthanasia are not acts that affect just the individuals involved, their families and associates: they threaten the lives of other disabled people if only by apparently legitimising the false notion that disabled people generally will (or should) want to die for reasons of their disability.

An important point here is that all human beings, regardless of disability, have a shared range of feelings, reactions, emotions and, amongst other things, a shared language as well as a shared way of living – that is what is meant by 'a human life'. It is the denial of that 'sharedness' in human life and living, which is crucial to understand in relation to discrimination against people with disability.

An illustrative example of visceral fear of disability by people who are already disabled comes again from Belgium, that of Mark and Eddy Verbessem. They were deaf twins aged forty-five, who were so afraid of also going blind that they decided to die by euthanasia (Peace 2013). Though they had coped very well with their disability, helping one another and living independently, they had a horror of further disability. It is instructive to tease out the true object of their fear. According to their brother, Dirk Verbessem, they were 'terrified of ending up in an institution' (Tomlinson 2013). Neither twin was in physical pain, nor terminally ill, what was 'unbearable' here was not current burden of disability but was fear of the future. They were afraid of being required to 'exist' in an institution and give up living independently, perhaps even being separated. Such a fear is not confined to Belgian disabled people. It is not a medical condition, it is not terminal and it raises the issue of how far their fears could have been addressed by adequate social support – had that been available.

A leading advocate and practitioner of euthanasia in Belgium has readily acknowledged that euthanasia is being used to address issues such as social isolation and lack of support.

'We at the commission are confronted more and more with patients who are tired of dealing with a sum of small ailments—they are what we call "tired of life".' Although their suffering derives from social concerns as well as from medical ones, Distelmans said that he still considers their pain to be incurable. 'If you ask for euthanasia because you are alone, and you are alone because you don't have family to take care of you, we cannot create family'.

(Aviv 2015)

We have seen that even the 'very strong' case that Rhees describes appears strong because of a visceral reaction to dependency and loss. This is a reaction that needs to be acknowledged but does not itself provide justification for euthanasia. There is always a second question of how best to respond. What is shown in the case of Mark and Eddy Verbessem, and in the words of Distelmans, is just how far it is possible to travel from the 'very strong' case. Their fear and Distelmans' open admission show how euthanasia can become a practical means to address a lack of social support for people living with disability. Death is trivialised. Like 'stepping off a bus' (Caldwell 2014 quoting Fitzpatrick), it is regarded in a 'profane' manner as a mere remedy, and an easy one at that. Such an attitude completely misses the critical matter that is the death of any human being. Simultaneously, it fails disabled people by leaving them with little choice but euthanasia. To rest with the statement that 'we cannot create family' is to fail to even ask how else the challenge of supporting people could be met.

It is important, for those opposed to euthanasia, to find a way to address honestly the thorny issue of those individual hard cases which call for recognition, but which also carry implications for others. Accepting the real force of the point that Rhees articulated, and a force sometimes both visceral and natural, need not and should not be converted into a *raison d'être* for undermining the status or protection of those with such disabilities.

The Moral Elevation of Euthanasia for Disability

What is evident in the story of Mark and Eddy Verbessem is that they were driven to seek euthanasia out of fear of the future. This is not exemplary of choice but of lack of choice. The same could be said more generally in relation to the concept of 'unbearable suffering'. Both horror at what might lie in the future and desperation over present suffering or with a situation that seems unmanageable and overwhelming seem to leave a person without options. This conclusion is expressed succinctly by the 24-year-old 'Laura': 'Death feels to me not as a choice. If I had a choice, I would choose a bearable life, but I have done everything and that was unsuccessful' (Buchanan 2015).

It is noteworthy how far such statements are from the language of autonomy, choice or empowerment that is often presented as the fundamental justification for euthanasia and physician assisted suicide. The case which is regarded as most serious, the 'hard case', is precisely where the person feels he or she has no choice. In contrast, an appeal by someone who has reached the calm decision, perhaps under the influence of stoic philosophy, that he or she had fulfilled what was necessary for a complete life and now wished to have assistance with suicide, has much less moral force. There are such cases and there are jurisdictions in which people could be provided with assistance in suicide on this basis (very likely in Switzerland), and this example is not far from the category of 'tired of life' which is even now being discussed in Belgium. However, the moral claim on others to aid in these cases seems very weak. It seems, ironically, that it is when people are least autonomous and most 'driven' that the urgency of their cries moves us most. These considerations show how close the 'serious' motivation for euthanasia is to that for suicide, and this in turn raises the question of how far euthanasia can be distinguished morally from the encouragement of (unassisted) suicide.

If someone says, 'I despair of my life and my future, and I want to die, now, I want to kill myself or have someone help me to do so', and that is, say, a man in his thirties, healthy, wealthy, with good job, beautiful loving family, 'everything going for him' so to speak, our imagined first response is to support him, help him out of despair, verify and treat any depression, succour him to a different perspective on his life, its value.

If someone with Spinal Muscular Atrophy[7] says 'I despair of my life and my future' why is the (supposedly) humane response to put a 'legitimising' white-sleeved (medical professional) arm around her shoulder and say 'Well, after all these years, you have done enough. We all understand why you, or anybody in your situation, should want to die. We would, in your place. Look how it will ease your family's pain and burden. So yes, we will do everything we can to speed your death'?

Is it not morally reprehensible to say to the disabled person intending suicide or requesting euthanasia 'Of course. We understand. We will help'? From the perspective of disabled persons, it is thus a mistake to elevate euthanasia deaths or acts of physician assisted suicide to a different moral plane from suicide *per se*. The differences that do come into consideration are not such that they elevate the former to a moral imperative of any kind. There is a false but pervading sense that a euthanasia death is of a different moral kind to a suicide; indeed, that euthanasia must be treated as 'morally obvious and irrefutably desirable' to meet an individual's wish to die. It fulfils the ideal of a desirable death. Non-assisted suicide is treated very differently.

This is an important but barely discussed aspect of this debate: the connection between suicide *per se*, and physician assisted suicide or euthanasia. The discussion so far has shown that the 'horror' of which Rhees speaks of is not crucially different in kind from the considerations which drive someone to unassisted suicide – the horror of becoming, or having become, what one has a horror of, through loss of money, status, power or control.

Lieve Thienpont, in her apologia for the euthanising of suicidal psychiatric patients argues that euthanasia is a preferable alternative to

---

[7] As Baroness Jane Campbell, the longest survivor in Britain with SMA, has pointed out, the proposed legislation puts her 'in the waiting room' so that one day when she is feeling low what would stop any doctor from responding to her request to die? (House of Lords debate, Hansard 17 July 2014).

unassisted suicide (Thienpont et al. 2015, p. 7). It is noticeable that in her description of a sequence of such deaths she described them all as 'euthanasia' yet elsewhere she expresses her preference for the patient to self-administer the lethal dose, to demonstrate that it is his or her 'own act of will' (Thienpont 2015, p. 188). However, in Belgian law, euthanasia is defined as 'the ending of life by someone other than the person at the person's request' (Belgian Act on Euthanasia, 28 May 2002, chapter I section 2). Self-administration of a lethal dose provided by a physician is not euthanasia but is physician assisted suicide. There is a deliberate attempt in Thienpont's account to avoid the language of assisted *suicide*. Such avoidance is characteristic of what may be called the 'special moral elevation' of euthanasia and physician assisted suicide for disability and the denial of any commonality between these practices and unassisted suicide.

It has been argued in this chapter that the visceral reactions that seem to justify euthanasia in the 'hard case' are essentially expressions of fear of living with disability and dependence, and thus are impossible to disentangle for broader attitudes to the worthwhileness of a life with serious disability. Euthanasia is thus a respectable form of medicalised suicide for disabled people that has falsely been elevated as a moral ideal.

The Absence of the Disabled Voice from the Belgian Debate

Another striking absence from the Belgian debate, in contrast to other jurisdictions, is the public voice of disabled people. In the United Kingdom, the United States, Australia and New Zealand, proposals to legalise assisted suicide or euthanasia have been greeted with mobilisation of opposition amongst disabled people organisations (DPOs), disabled individuals and some organisations providing services for disabled people.[8]

---

[8] Organisations opposed to euthanasia Include American Disabled for Attendant Programs Today (ADAPT), Association of Programs for Rural Independent Living (APRIL), Autistic Self Advocacy Network (ASAN), Boston Center for Independent Living, Cambridge Commission for Persons with Disabilities, Disability Policy Consortium, Disability Rights Education and Defense Fund (DREDF), Justice For All (JFA), Metro West Center for Independent Living, National Council on Disability (NCD), National Council on Independent Living (NCIL), National Spinal Cord Injury Association, Not Dead Yet (NDY), Not Dead Yet Aotearoa, Not Dead Yet UK, Disability Rights UK, Scope, UK Disabled Person's Council and Disabled People Against Cuts, among others. Disability

General terms give rise to confusion: 'disabled people' are not a homogenous group nor is there truly a single 'disabled voice'. There is nothing surprising if not all disabled people oppose euthanasia, since divergences of opinion also occur in 'the disabled community' where the use of the definite article is itself misleading. There are disabled people who not only support the legalisation of euthanasia or physician assisted suicide but who wish it to be available for themselves. Nevertheless, the lived experience of disabled people has become a potent source of social criticism about how euthanasia/ assisted suicide laws may stem from and may reinforce prejudice against them, solely on the grounds of their disability. Perhaps archetypal of this distinctive voice within the debate is the American organisation *Not Dead Yet*, linking in its message a rejection of euthanasia or assisted suicide with a call for greater support to help disabled people live their lives to the full.

Belgium, in contrast, does not seem to have experienced any organised opposition to legalising euthanasia from disabled people. The question then arises, is this because there is widespread support for the law amongst disabled people, or is the disability perspective simply absent from the debate?

One of the authors of this chapter, an advocate for disabled people for many years, attempted to identify disabled 'leaders' in Belgium, searching for DPOs particularly those which had raised any voice, whether in opposition or support for their legislation. He was unable to find any. There appears to be no record of Belgian 'disabled voices' explicit in either Belgian parliamentary debates or in any mainstream media, anywhere, inside or outside of Belgium.

In 2014, the Belgian senate discussed extending the euthanasia law to children of any age, which it then passed into law. A search for the word *'gehandicapt'* in the transcript of this discussion reveals no reference to disability matters, no reference to the voices of disabled people, either in opposition or in defence of euthanasia, or this extension of Belgian euthanasia law to children. In the report from the Belgian senate discussion in 2001, there are some references to *'gehandicapt'* but, according to Dr Tom Mortier, 'these are more about "mentally disabled" people because the discussion was about "self-determination" in 2001 . . . I don't know of any "disabled voice" in the newspapers or the media [and] I don't think there were any public consultations before the votes'

---

rights activists and academics opposed to euthanasia include Carol Gill (2010), Alison Davis (2004), Christopher Newell (2006) and Kevin Fitzpatrick (see Campbell 2016).

(personal correspondence). That is, no public consultation at all, never mind amongst disabled people. Professor Wim Lemmens concurred, 'To my knowledge, not much has been done to involve disabled people in this debate, here in Belgium'.[9]

Ironically, the euthanasia lobby is right in its insistence that dependency (and thus disability) is a key issue in this debate. They are however much mistaken, as are some newly disabled people in their grief, when they ignore what disabled people have learned about interdependency and how to achieve independent living. Certainly, this is dependent on environmental adaptation (though most far less expensive than generally portrayed), and financial support (also far less than generally counted) but, because these supports are so often lacking, it is principally dependent on human support. That humanity includes whether the attending doctor, at a critical juncture in conversation about 'what the future holds' sucks in his or her breath, or hesitates. Patients notoriously go wrong in trying to second-guess their doctors' true feelings and reactions; doctors find it notoriously difficult in not revealing those true feelings.[10]

The Challenge of Finding Life Worth Living

The public debate and the practice of euthanasia occur within the larger context of the place of disabled people within society and the attitudes to disability prevalent within society. In this regard, it is noteworthy that Belgium has been severely condemned several times by *the Comité Européen de Droits Sociaux*, for its lack of support for disabled people, the most recent in 2013.

> evidence [showed] ... a lack of effective access to social and medical assistance, social services and housing; a violation of the right to independence, social integration and participation in the life of the community; a lack of social, legal and economic protection against poverty and social exclusion; and discrimination.
>
> (Equal Rights Trust 2013, pp. 1–2)

Belgium's failure to provide adequate independent living support for disabled people is reflective of the same attitude to disability already implicit in the Euthanasia Act 2002 and is sometimes revealed overtly in comments by euthanasia advocates. The increasing provision of

---

[9] Personal correspondence, from Lemmens to Fitzpatrick.
[10] On this process of 'countertransference' see Chapter 3 in the present volume.

euthanasia and the inadequate provision of social support thus feed one another in a vicious cycle in which disabled people experience less rather than more choice. 'If I had a choice, I would choose a bearable life' (Buchanan 2015).

What helps most people to accommodate their new life as a disabled person, or cope with a further disability, and come to find value in life, is the sense that there are things worth living for in this different, adjusted life – love, marriage, family, work, friends, theatre, socialising, spectator sports and all the pursuits which enrich human lives, disabled or not. The right kind of medical and social support is crucial to arriving at a different perspective of living with a disability. It is understanding this that helps those devastated by loss through becoming disabled to accommodate their new lives (as most disabled people must – the rest being born disabled).

Therefore, the absence of availability of independent living support in Belgium is critical, and the reversal of this is perhaps the prerequisite to finding a strong disabled voice within the Belgian debate on euthanasia. It is a question of empowerment. When this kind of support is all but absent, the view that a 'disabled life is not worth living' takes root more easily. This in turn leads to the marginalising of the very perspective that should be key to the debate. Euthanasia, therefore, is not only about how to manage our instinctive 'horror' at physical or mental decline; instead and much more importantly, 'it is about the kind of society we want to live in'.[11]

[11] A comment made by Baroness Helena Kennedy QC during the debate hosted by the Southbank Centre at their 'Festival for the Living' 30 January 2012 on assisted suicide at which Kevin Fitzpatrick was present as a fellow speaker.

9

Euthanasia in Patients with Intolerable Suffering Due to an Irremediable Psychiatric Illness

A Psychiatric Perspective

JORIS VANDENBERGHE

Maybe someone who is balancing on the threshold between life and death might need someone who says: I don't want you to go.

Introduction

The Belgian euthanasia legislation created a radically new situation for physicians and psychiatrists specifically. They are confronted with patients suffering from a psychiatric illness requesting euthanasia. This chapter explores this reality from a psychiatrist's point of view. The legal possibility of euthanasia is in sharp contrast with the way psychiatrists usually deal with suicidal patients: preventing suicide with a combination of protective measures and treatment options. We have a vast array of protective measures that have been proven effective: establishing a therapeutic alliance with the patient, giving hope, removing weapons and other possible lethal means, crisis plans, treatment of the underlying psychiatric illness, family involvement, surveillance, hospitalisation, exceptionally even the use of coercion. Sometimes, the suicidal thoughts and plans are judged to be a well-considered, deliberate choice and not a symptom of the psychiatric illness, as reflected in the term 'rational suicide' (Hewitt 2013, Ho 2014, Wittwer 2013). Then psychiatrists might refrain from using coercion and focus on voluntary measures to reach the patient and try to prevent suicide. But ending the life of a patient or helping the patient to die at his or her well-considerate, deliberate request, as the Belgian legislation allows since 2002 under specific conditions, is utterly different.

In Belgium, as in the Netherlands, euthanasia is legally possible for patients with intolerable physical and/or mental suffering resulting from an incurable medical condition with no prospect of alleviation (the Belgian law regarding euthanasia, 2002). Psychiatric illnesses are not excluded and can legally qualify after an explicit, deliberate, well-considered and repeated request. If the condition is not terminal, as is the case with psychiatric illnesses, the law demands extra conditions and precautions as there must be an interval of at least a month between the written euthanasia request and the actual euthanasia, and there must be an additional independent evaluation by a physician (in the case of a psychiatric illness: a psychiatrist).

This is the legal context in Belgium. After ample debate, the Belgian legislator deliberately chose not to exclude psychiatric illness in the euthanasia law, but rather to provide extra conditions for all non-terminal conditions. In the same year, legislation regarding patient rights (2002) was also passed and the same logic was followed: in order to promote patient emancipation and empowerment and to avoid stigma and discrimination, all patients are given the same rights, patients with a psychiatric illness and others alike, regardless of their pathology.

Euthanasia, according to the Belgian law, means ending the life of a patient through the administration of lethal medication by a physician at the patient's explicit request. Physician-assisted suicide is the self-administration by the patient of lethal medication prescribed and/or delivered by a physician. However, if in the latter case this medication is taken under the same legal conditions and precautions as for eutha-nasia and in the presence of a physician, the Belgian National Order of Physicians (ANCBNOP 2003) as well as the Federal Control and Evaluation Committee on Euthanasia (FCECE First Report 2004, p. 24) consider it to be equivalent to euthanasia. Despite those two rulings, from a judicial point of view, the practice of physician-assisted suicide is still somewhat controversial because Belgian law explicitly defines the scope of the law, euthanasia, as ending one's life *by someone else than the person him- or herself*, at his or her explicit request. Nevertheless, some of the registered cases of euthanasia are in fact cases of physician-assisted suicide. Because patients who are suffering from a psychiatric illness are usually still physically able to take the drug themselves, and because helping to die is ethically and emotionally very different from ending a patient's life, physicians – and often patients alike – may prefer this type of physician-assisted suicide. With a group of academics of Leuven University, we argued to settle this contradiction between the law and these two rulings by changing the euthanasia legislation to include physician-assisted suicide under the same strict legal criteria as euthanasia, as is the case in the Netherlands (Vandenberghe 2013, pp. 46–7). In this chapter we use the term euthanasia as a shorthand for 'euthanasia and/or physician-assisted suicide under the same legal conditions and precautions as for euthanasia and in the presence of a physician'.

Scope of This Chapter

This chapter will not discuss the ethical aspects of euthanasia in general, nor will it explore in depth the fundamental discussion whether a separate judicial framework is needed for patients suffering intolerably from a psychiatric illness, or whether they should be judicially excluded from the possibility of euthanasia, as pleaded for by a group of Belgian academics and clinicians (Bazan et al. 2015). This is a broader discussion, touching on the value and validity of the medical model in psychiatry and of psychiatric nosology. A psychiatric illness is always a matter of brain and mind, of disturbances in biology and intrinsically interwoven disturbances in meaning and relationships with others, in being in the world. A euthanasia request and the reactions it encounters do not influence for instance a progressive cancer. However, it might influence the course of a psychiatric illness, and for some this is reason enough to refrain from opening up the possibility of euthanasia in psychiatric conditions. From a psychotherapeutic perspective, giving hope is funda-mental in severe and chronic psychiatric illness. Some will argue that this perspective is utterly incompatible with the possibility of euthanasia. Some will fundamentally oppose euthanasia in psychiatric illnesses due to their unpredictable course, since recovery has been reported in severe and chronic cases, even after decades. Others might call this therapeutic relentlessness. Some argue that a patient suffering from a psychiatric illness is never sufficiently competent to decide on his or her own death, and that such a patient uttering a death wish is always a vulnerable patient in need of protection. Another argument against euthanasia in psychiatric conditions is that the possibility of euthanasia might under-mine societal efforts to combat suicide and suicidal feelings. It might also lead to an implicit pressure on, or a message to, patients that choosing death is what society expects when they become dependent, in need of care and no longer productive. Those and other arguments will not be explored in depth.

Then what is the scope of this chapter? We focus on the psychiatrist's perspective on euthanasia in patients with a psychiatric illness exclud-ing neuropsychiatric conditions as dementia, since this is quite a different discussion that is dealt with elsewhere. The psychiatrist's perspective presented in this chapter is based on insights and evidence from clinical psychiatry complemented with my personal point of view and my own clinical experience in this field. Our starting point is a democratic vote for legislation allowing euthanasia in patients with intolerable suffering due to a serious and incurable psychiatric illness with no therapeutic perspective nor prospect of alleviation. Based on this legislation, physicians and psychiatrists specifically are confronted with patients suffering from a psychiatric illness requesting euthanasia. As the law provides, every physician is free to inform the patient that they have personal or moral objections, and that they are willing to talk about the patient's feelings and thoughts, but are not prepared to play a role in a euthanasia evaluation or procedure. But if a psychiatrist is prepared to play a role in a euthanasia evaluation or procedure within this legal framework, what are the caveats and pitfalls? From a professional psychiatric and ethical perspective, do these pitfalls imply the need for extra criteria and precautions? What is, from a clinical psychiatric perspective, the cautious and careful way to proceed while interpreting and applying the legal framework in the context of a psychiatric condition?

The Motives of a Psychiatrist Who Is Prepared to Play a Role in a Euthanasia Evaluation or Procedure for Some Patients, Can Differ

For some, it is a matter of absolute principle. They believe that all patients alike have a right to choose when and how to die, and they advocate patient autonomy, empowerment and emancipation. They are convinced that a patient with a psychiatric illness can be sufficiently competent to decide on his or her own death. They argue against stigma, discrimination and any differentiation made in dealing with patients with a psychiatric illness on the one hand, and patients with a 'physical illness' on the other hand. They plea that psychiatry should recognise its therapeutic limits and recognise that there are situations where treatments, interventions or psychotherapy are very limited in their ability to alleviate suffering.

For others – and I consider myself as part of this group – dealing with a euthanasia request is a more prudential decision, e.g. the determination to avoid the euthanasia request being dealt with by other physicians with insufficient reluctance and insufficient focus on life and on treatment options; or the conviction that the patient would be worse off (e.g. the possibility of or the fear for unassisted suicide) if the euthanasia request is not dealt with; or the conviction that the exploration process of a euthanasia request is paradoxically the only way left to help the patient to continue living. In other words, they hope that dealing with the euthanasia request might prove to be therapeutic. Indeed, some patients describe this process as helpful in fighting suicidal feelings. Some patients testify that the possibility of euthanasia being made concrete is the one thing that helps them to continue living: the knowledge of an escape route, an emergency exit being prepared, alleviates their suffering and makes life more bearable. A large subgroup of patients requesting euthanasia for psychiatric suffering – and in some psychiatrists' experience, a large majority – finally do not choose euthanasia but choose to continue living. The assumption that is made by these psychiatrists is that a euthanasia request is always more than what it is at face value: the wish to die and the request for help to die. As a request or question, it is also a social interaction, a way of reaching out, of getting in touch, of sharing thoughts and feelings, of connecting with the outside world. It is fundamentally different in many ways from a person isolating himself or herself and preparing or committing suicide on his or her own. A patient requesting euthanasia makes an appointment, interacts with a physician, continues living while doing so, gets out there in the world connecting and collaborating with others. Maybe asking for help to die is broader than just that. Maybe dealing with the euthanasia request in a cautious way is sometimes the only way to broaden the request for help and to offer help to live.

Those are some of the possible *conscious* motives of a psychiatrist who is prepared to play a role in a euthanasia evaluation or procedure for some patients. Some unconscious motives and interferences are dealt with further in this chapter, when discussing transference and countertransference.

Facts and Figures

The Belgian practice of euthanasia in patients with intolerable mental suffering primarily due to an irremediable psychiatric illness is not well documented (Vandenberghe 2011). The reports of the Federal Control and Evaluation Committee on Euthanasia do not offer details and use broad categories as 'neuropsychiatric (or neuropsychological) illnesses' which also include dementia, 'other illnesses' and 'several illnesses'.

Focusing on the most recent years with the most reliable registration and reporting (2006–13; an 8 year period), in 180 (2.3 per cent) of the 7,775 registered cases of euthanasia in Belgium, the diagnosis was a non-terminal neuropsychiatric illness. In the same period, in 314 (4.0 per cent) of the 7,775 registered cases of euthanasia in Belgium, only mental and no physical suffering was reported. Figures are rising: of these 180 and 314 cases, 101 (56.1 per cent) and 178 (56.7 per cent) respectively date from the last 2 years (2012–13) of this 8 year period (FCECE Third Report 2008; Fourth Report 2010; Fifth Report 2012 and Sixth Report 2014). Wim Distelmans, the president of the Federal Control and Evaluation Committee on Euthanasia confirmed that in the two year period 2013–14 around 100 cases of euthanasia were registered for psychiatric reasons (Carpentier and Antonissen 2015). The number of euthanasia *requests* by patients with a psychiatric illness is much higher but not registered. A report documenting 100 euthanasia requests primarily due to an irremediable psychiatric illness describes that 35 of these 100 patients died from euthanasia, with the evaluation process still ongoing for some of the others (Thienpont et al. 2015). Interestingly, a substantial percentage of the patients requesting euthanasia choose to continue living, often after having gone through the whole evaluation process and after acceptance of their request. They report that this procedure and the possibility of euthanasia helped them to hold on, to fight their suicidal thoughts and feelings and to regain their orientation towards life.

Discussion of Four Problems that Arise Specifically or More Poignantly in a Euthanasia Request by a Patient with a Psychiatric Illness

We focus on four problems: decision-making capacity, the irremediable nature of the illness, the implicit meanings and interpersonal dynamics underlying the request and the effects of the evaluation process proper on what is evaluated (Vandenberghe 2012 and 2013). Of course more than four problems arise, e.g. the evaluation of the unbearable nature of the suffering (van Tol et al. 2010) and the evaluation of the causality (is the suffering caused by the illness?), which is problematic particularly in psychiatric illnesses where meaning, emotions and social interactions are impacted in a complex interwoven manner by the illness as well as by life events, coping style and character.

Decision-Making Capacity: Is the Euthanasia Request
a Deliberate, Well-Considered Choice?

A death wish, or a wish to stop living (like this), underlies a euthanasia request. Psychiatrists are familiar with patients who have a death wish. It is usually a symptom in depression and other psychiatric illnesses; it can result in suicidal thoughts and behaviours and often requires protective measures as discussed earlier. If a euthanasia request is based on a death wish that is a symptom, it will of course not be seen as well-considerate because the patient is thought to have strongly impaired decision-making capacity regarding matters of life and death due to his or her depression. Such a death wish is part of the clinical picture of depression and disappears as the depression remits. Depression and the hopelessness that goes with it emotionally and cognitively skews and biases the way one sees oneself, one's future, one's past and the world. So the question is: can a patient with a psychiatric illness have sufficient decision-making capacity to request euthanasia in a well-considerate way, as an existential choice and not as a symptom?

Decision-making capacity is conceptualised as a specific capacity, i.e. regarding a specific decision, e.g. the decision to request euthanasia and choose death. Decision-making capacity is evaluated clinically by examining whether a patient is able to understand, weigh and reason with all relevant information: the nature of the situation, the different options and the consequences of his or her decision. It is not merely a cognitive capacity, but requires integrating emotions and values in a consistent way with intact reality testing regarding the decision at hand (Palmer and Harmell 2016; Vellinga and Vandenberghe 2010). In the context of a euthanasia request, it requires careful, repeated and thorough clinical assessment by an experienced psychiatrist. This assessment can be systematised by a validated instrument or tool. Most research is done on the 'MacArthur Competence Assessment Tools for Clinical Research and for Treatment', but none of the available instruments is validated for use in the context of a euthanasia request (Appelbaum and Grisso 2001; Dunn et al. 2006).

In an acute depression, a death wish can never be a well-considered choice. But if a depression becomes chronic, despite adequate and multiple treatments, a new situation arises. From the understanding of and insight in his or her condition and illness, some patients might be capable of balancing his or her (quality of) life, suffering, perspective and (lack of) therapeutic options in a well-considered and realistic way. In his or her evaluation, the psychiatrist has to weigh this deliberate choice against the influences of the depression on the decision-making process. In my opinion and clinical experience, a patient with a psychiatric illness – be it depression or other – can sometimes be capable of formulating a considerate, deliberate and competent death wish and euthanasia request. Evaluation of decision-making capacity in this context, however, is difficult and requires high standards and carefully articulated justifications (Kim and Lemmens 2016). This aligns with the discussion on 'rational suicide', as mentioned earlier (Hewitt 2013; Ho 2014; Wittwer 2013). In the debate on rational suicide, the approximately 10 per cent of the suicides where no psychiatric illness was present is often mentioned (Isometsä 2001). But also in the presence of a chronic psychiatric illness, a suicide might be 'rational' and a death wish well-considered and deliberate, as described above. In conclusion, elucidating the specific decision-making capacity in the context of a euthanasia request is difficult and requires time, specific expertise and repeated careful evaluation.

The Irremediable Nature of the Illness: When Is a Psychiatric Illness Incurable, Treatment Resistant and *Without Therapeutic Perspective nor Prospect of Alleviation?*

While the intolerable suffering is subjective in nature, the irremediable nature of the illness is a more objective criterion, not determined by the appreciation of the patient but by a formal psychiatric assessment. A psychiatric illness is not progressive and degenerative. As a rule, its evolution and the patient's prognosis is uncertain. Future partial recovery and relief – spontaneous or after treatment or life changing events – can often not be excluded, even not in personality disorders. In the only published sample of 100 patients, personality disorders constitute – together with depression – the most frequent diagnosis in Belgian euthanasia requests for psychiatric reasons (Thienpont et al. 2015). Personality disorders were once thought to be the psychiatric disorders least subject to spontaneous or therapeutic change, as they were considered to be structurally imbedded in one's personality. However, recent empirical findings show partial but significant recovery in a majority of patients with personality disorders, through therapy or even over the course of time without therapy (reviewed in Biskin 2015). Social and relational functioning – a major source of distress and suffering in personality disorders – often remains impaired, but prognosis in terms of symptomatic improvement and broader psychosocial functioning is much more beneficial than was thought previously. Unfortunately, we have no empirically supported parameters to predict in which patients improvement will occur, making it very hard to predict the course and evaluate the irremediable nature of the illness. Of course possible alleviation of the suffering in the long run does not imply that the suffering here and now can be alleviated.

In the Dutch guideline for physician-assisted suicide in patients with psychiatric illnesses, the irremediable nature of the illness is operationalised as the lack of a reasonable treatment perspective. For a treatment perspective to be reasonable, it must offer a real prospect of improvement, it must be possible to administer the treatment within a reasonable period of time and there must be a reasonable balance between the expected treatment results and the burden of treatment (e.g. side effects) for the patient (Tholen et al. 2009). In other words, all evidence-based therapies that offer a reasonable treatment perspective have to be tried for an illness to be considered as irremediable. Availability and accessibility of the therapy and willingness of the patient are important prerequisites. In this way, the euthanasia debate touches on the societal debate on insufficient financing for mental health care, stigma, lack of reimbursement for psychotherapy, waiting lists and other thresholds to care. The Dutch guideline states that refusal of a treatment with such a reasonable perspective in principle implies that the illness cannot be considered to be irremediable and that euthanasia (or physician-assisted suicide) is not an option (Tholen et al. 2009).

The Implicit Meanings and Interpersonal Dynamics Underlying the Euthanasia Request

A third challenge is distinguishing the face value of a euthanasia request from the implicit meanings and interpersonal dynamics underlying the request. A euthanasia request has an explicit, face value content, but also an underlying implicit content. Is there a question behind the question? A patient asking for euthanasia may at the same time – consciously or unconsciously – express an appeal to hold on, a deep wish that someone will say: I don't want you to go, I don't want to let you go, I care for you. A patient asking for euthanasia might want to convey the message that he or she cannot hold on anymore and might need others to bear with him or her. He or she might want to convey the gravity of his or her pain and suffering, the despair he or she is feeling. He or she might want to induce feelings in the clinician to whom he or she addresses the euthanasia request. A sincere euthanasia request can at the same time be a cry for help, posing a difficult challenge for the clinician to carefully balance the duty of care and the importance of patient autonomy (Gillett and Chamberlain 2013). An additional complicating factor is that clinicians sometimes have to endure intense pressure from their patients, e.g. when a high suicide risk is present (Deschepper et al. 2014).

All this obviously relates to the interpersonal dynamics between the patient and other parties, including the clinicians addressed and other caregivers. Implicit meanings and interpersonal dynamics can be coloured by psychopathological processes: a psychiatric illness is not a mere neurophysiological disturbance, but affects people in their perception, feelings, thoughts, judgement, search for meaning and social interactions. Furthermore, the encounter between patient and physician is shaped by past experiences and relationships. The feelings this elicits in patients are called transference and offer important material in psychotherapy to recognise and change habitual patterns of interaction. The feelings the patient induces in the physician are called countertransference (e.g. frustration, sympathy, feelings of despair or powerlessness). For a physician, feelings of countertransference challenge him or her to conserve a professional, open, engaged and attuned attitude, actively listening while continuously finding a balance between distance and proximity.

Implicit meanings, transference and countertransference influence a euthanasia request and the reactions to it. Therefore it is crucial – as is also stated in the Dutch guideline – to elucidate these meanings and the interpersonal dynamics carefully with sufficient psychotherapeutic expertise and external perspective, e.g., in peer consultation, intervision or supervision (Tholen et al. 2009).

The Evaluation Process of a Euthanasia Request Might Interfere
with What Is Evaluated: The (Course of) the Psychiatric Illness,
the Patient's Death Wish and Attitude

The evaluation of a euthanasia request requires a long process and is not just a detached and neutral observation and application of a checklist of criteria. It is inevitably an intervention in its own right, which might influence (the course of) the psychiatric illness, the patient's death wish and attitude. It might work both ways. On the one hand, the focus on death and on the patient's death wish, on the unbearable suffering, on the irremediable illness and on the lack of perspective, risks undermining hope and an orientation towards life, both of which are crucial to safeguard the chance for partial recovery (Berghmans et al. 2013). In this way, the evaluation process of a euthanasia request might induce a self-fulfilling prophecy, negatively influencing the course of the illness and impairing recovery. On the other hand, the evaluation process might influence the course of the illness and the death wish for the better. Patients often are relieved that their death wish and euthanasia request is heard and taken seriously and this might help them to regain partial control over their illness, reduce suffering and/or the influence it has on their daily life (Callebert et al. 2012). Paradoxically, the knowledge that euthanasia might be a possibility often helps patients to fight their suicidal thoughts and feelings. In some, it might prevent a horrible and painful suicide (attempt) that can also be painful, traumatising or dangerous for others. Exploring and evaluating a euthanasia request, no matter what the outcome will be, might help to overcome the often unbeneficial polarisation: the patients wants to die and the caregivers do everything they can to convince him or her to continue living, or actively prevent him or her (sometimes even using coercion) from attempting suicide. In this polarisation, the positions risk drifting further apart, as the patient does not feel understood and is compelled to convince the caregivers of the seriousness of his or her death wish.

Dealing with a Euthanasia Request from a Patient Suffering from a Psychiatric Illness: Towards Standards of Care and Professional Guidelines?

The complexity of a euthanasia request, the dynamics involved, and the problems and pitfalls discussed in the previous sections call for extra precautions from a professional and ethical perspective, beyond the legal framework. These precautions should be made clear to the patient in a transparent way, early in the process, in an empathic and supportive way and with the understanding that this is not an easy message for the patient.

A Dual-Track Approach

To avoid narrowing down all options to a choice to die, to guarantee that all efforts are made to alleviate the suffering, and to honour the fact that a large subgroup of patients requesting euthanasia finally choose to continue living, a dual-track approach is needed. Parallel with the 'euthanasia track', the process of exploring and evaluating the euthanasia request, another track focused on therapy and recovery is crucial which often means the continuation or expansion of care that was already there (Callebert 2014). We will call it the 'recovery track'. 'Recovery' is used in its specific meaning, described as the user-based definition by Schrank and Slade (2007) and others: a process of personal growth and development, regaining control and establishing a personally fulfilling, meaningful life and a positive sense of identity despite the psychiatric illness and its impact. It focusses on meaning, connection and strengths ('empowerment') rather than deficits, symptoms and functioning, in a process of personal discovery of how to live (and how to live well), even with enduring symptoms and vulnerabilities. It is described as a deeply personal, unique process of changing one's attitudes, values, feelings, goals, skills and/or roles, developing new meaning and purpose as one grows beyond the impact of mental illness (Anthony 1993). Recovery and society based care, away from psychiatric institutions, form the basis of mental health care reform worldwide. Key elements are hope, adjustment of the environment (e.g. work and housing), redefining expectations, refocusing and regaining control by developing a meaningful life despite symptoms and limitations. Therefore, from a recovery perspective, irremediable is an obsolete or at least relative term.

Continuing or restarting this 'recovery track' parallel with the 'euthanasia track' needs to be a condition for starting a euthanasia track. This can be realised in different ways. A hospitalised patient for instance can consult and frequently see a psychiatrist that is not part of the hospital unit team, exploring and evaluating his or her euthanasia request, while the recovery- and/or treatment oriented approach is continued. An outpatient can combine ambulatory care with consulting a psychiatrist or team regarding his or her euthanasia request. Transparency, consultation and cross-talk between the teams of both tracks is crucial.

An Exploration and Evaluation Process Requiring Ample Time and Contact

An exploration and evaluation of a euthanasia request demands time and frequent contact and consultation, no matter how long the previous treatment process of a patient has been. In the context of a euthanasia request, other work needs to be done than in this past treatment process. Also for the patient, it is a new situation where meanings and experiences can shift and where other things are at stake. As a lot of complex issues have to be dealt with and as things can shift due to the exploration itself, exploring and evaluating a euthanasia request of a patient suffering from a psychiatric condition requires a process and not just an evaluation moment. Although each number is somehow arbitrary in this context, where every situation and patient is different, an exploration and evaluation process of at least one year and with at least ten contacts with one of the psychiatrists involved in the euthanasia request, seems a reasonable minimal standard given the complexity and number of elements that need to be explored and evaluated. Is the diagnosis correct and complete? Has any – somatic or psychiatric – comorbidity been missed that can be the starting point for other treatments or interventions? Has every reasonable treatment option or intervention to alleviate the suffering been tried? Were these treatments and interventions done in a professional, judicious and state-of-the-art way? Has the scope been broadened to a recovery-based approach, including psychotherapy, adjusting one's life circumstances with social interventions (housing, welfare, work, other kinds of assistance)? Is the patient competent to choose death, or is the death wish a symptom of the psychiatric illness? Is the patient's choice deliberate and well-considered? Have all explicit or implicit pressures that the patient might experience, been explored and dealt with? Is the request to be taken at face value, or is there a hidden hope or question behind the request? Is transference influencing the patient's request? Is the judgement of the psychiatrist blurred by countertransference? Has all ambivalence in the patient's death wish been explored? In the process, have all opportunities to redirect the patient towards life been taken? Has the potential therapeutic value of the recognition and the exploration of the euthanasia request been fully used and explored? Is the timing of an eventual euthanasia been thoroughly and repeatedly discussed, including the possibility of delaying the decision or the euthanasia? Have all other end of life decisions been discussed (palliative care, DNR-code, living will)? Has the patient prepared for death in all the ways he or she wants (will and other practical arrangements, funeral, saying goodbye, involving others, goodbye letters or messages, 'bucket list', legacy)? Is the patient given ample chance to change his or her mind?

All these questions, one by one, are complex requiring time, sensitivity and experience to elucidate. In my experience, one year with ten consultations is an absolute minimum to guide the patient through these themes in a thorough and careful way. It is a process of evaluation, promoting autonomy and well balanced decision-making and making sure all options are explored to reduce suffering or to make suffering more bearable. Only then ending suffering by ending life truly is a last resort.

A Formal Evaluation of the More Objective Legal Criteria:
The Psychiatric Illness Is an Incurable and Irremediable
Medical Condition; There Is no Reasonable Therapeutic
Perspective nor Prospect of Alleviation of the Suffering

The intolerable suffering is the legal criterion that is subjective in nature,
giving weight to the patient's appreciation of his or her own suffering.
More objectively, the law states that the suffering has to have a medical
foundation (the consequence of a medical condition, psychiatric or other),
and that this condition is not only incurable, but also irremediable: there is
no reasonable therapeutic perspective nor prospect of alleviation of the
suffering. The medical terms used are refractory, treatment resistant or
intractable, although one could argue that irremediable has an even stronger
connotation. We will call this the legal 'irremediable medical condition'
or 'lack of medical prospect' criterion. It should be noted that this does not
relate to the lack of prospect or perspective subjectively experienced by the
patient. Quite differently, it is an objective medical evaluation based on
the diagnosis, the patient file and history and all previous treatments: have
all well-established evidence-based treatments and interventions (in the
broadest sense) been tried in order to conclude that no reasonable treatment
or intervention can be offered to potentially relieve or alleviate the suffering?
This is a question that requires a clinical answer based on clinical knowledge
and scientific research, as is offered in the scientific evidence regarding
treatment effectivity and in evidence-based diagnosis-specific treatment
guidelines. This legal 'irremediable medical condition' criterion is not
subordinate to the patient's autonomy and repeated and well-considered
wish, nor to the patient's intolerable suffering. All those criteria, including
the 'irremediable medical condition' criterion, are in juxtaposition and
are cumulative: from a legal perspective, each and every one of them needs
to be fulfilled in order to make euthanasia a legal option.

Operationalising the 'irremediable medical condition' criterion can be
informed by considering the procedure followed in invasive and/or
experimental treatments. For deep brain stimulation (DBS) for instance,
strict criteria are applied to judge whether a patient qualifies (Nuttin et al.
2014). For DBS, electrodes are inserted in the brain to selectively stimu-
late certain target brain areas in order to relieve symptoms in severe
intractable psychiatric illnesses. Strict diagnosis-specific inclusion and
exclusion criteria are used for duration, chronicity and the treatment-
refractory nature of the illness. Only after positive advice of a multidisciplinary committee, including experts in the illness, experts in DBS

and an ethicist, confirming for example that all evidence-based treatments are tried, DBS becomes an option.[1]

Inserting electrodes in someone's brain sure is an invasive procedure, albeit reversible. But is not ending one's life much more 'invasive' and above all irreversible? Then should not the criteria for euthanasia be at least as stringent than the criteria for invasive treatments? Operationalised diagnosis-specific criteria for the 'irremediable medical condition' criterion can of course not be included in the law, but should be devised by a panel including experts in every specific diagnosis. In the Netherlands, a guideline has been developed for physician-assisted suicide in patients with psychiatric illnesses (Tholen et al. 2009). This guideline states that 'any therapeutic option for a particular condition must meet the following three requirements: (1) it must offer a real prospect of improvement, (2) it must be possible to administer adequate treatment within a reasonable period of time and (3) there must be a

---

[1] For refractory depression for instance, these are some of the inclusion criteria:

(a) Major depressive disorder, severe, unipolar type, diagnosed by Structured Clinical Interview for DSM-IV (SCID-IV), judged to be of disabling severity.
(b) 24-item Hamilton Depression Rating Scale (HDRS) score of at least 25.
(c) Global Assessment of Function (GAF) score of 45 or less.
(d) A recurrent (>4 episodes) or chronic (episode duration >2 years) course and a minimum of 5 years since the onset of the first depressive episode. Major impairment in functioning or potentially severe medical outcomes (repeated hospitalisations, serious suicidal ideation or a history of previous suicide attempts or other self-injurious behaviour).
(e) Failure to respond to:
   (1) adequate trials (>6 weeks at the maximum recommended or tolerated dose) of primary antidepressants from at least 3 different classes AND;
   (2) adequate trials (>4 weeks at the usually recommended or maximum tolerated dose) of augmentation/combination of a primary antidepressant using at least 2 different augmenting/combination agents (lithium, T3, stimulants, neuroleptics, anticonvulsants, buspirone or a second primary antidepressant) AND;
   (3) an adequate trial of electroconvulsive therapy (ECT) (>6 bilateral treatments) AND;
   (4) an adequate trial of individual psychotherapy (>20 sessions with an experienced psychotherapist), AND;
   (5) adequate relapse prevention by antidepressant medication or maintenance ECT

. . .

(k) Candidates may have undertaken additional trials of potentially beneficial novel combinations of medication and psychotherapy, or they may have undertaken trials of novel interventions lacking definitive evidence of efficacy in severe depression (e.g., light therapy, herbal therapy, transcranial magnetic stimulation, vagal nerve stimulation).

For another indication for DBS, refractory obsessive-compulsive disorder (OCD), another set of criteria was developed based on the evidence and guidelines in OCD. (Nuttin et al. 2014)

reasonable balance between the expected treatment results and the burden of treatment consequences for the patient'.

Not every psychiatric disorder is dealt with in this guideline in the light of the 'lack of medical prospect' criterion, but for treatment-resistant major depressive disorder, the Dutch guideline gives a list of all psychotherapies, classes of antidepressants and other drugs that should have been tried while clearly stating that electroconvulsive therapy (ECT) should also have been tried. Moreover, according to this guideline, the legal requirement is not fulfilled if the patient refuses a biological treatment like ECT, ruling out the possibility of euthanasia.

This sure is not the case now in Belgium. Not all patients who died through euthanasia for serious intractable depression, have gone through all treatments listed under (e) 'failure to respond to' in the DBS-criteria[3], a list that for good reasons includes ECT. In the article 'The Death Treatment' in The New Yorker (Aviv 2015), the Flemish psychiatrist Lieve Thienpont is mentioned. She is very active in the field of euthanasia and psychiatry and is the first author of the previously quoted study reporting on 100 patients requesting euthanasia (Thienpont et al. 2015). The following quote was obtained from the New Yorker article:

> Before approving a euthanasia request, she does not require patients to try procedures that they think are invasive. Godelieva [a patient whose euthanasia process is described in the New Yorker article] had never had electroconvulsive therapy, though it is effective for about half of patients with depression. 'Sometimes it really is too late' Thienpont told me. 'If the patient's energy is gone, then it is not humane to say, "Well, maybe if you go to a hospital that specializes in your problem for two more years it will help". I think we have to respect when people say, "No – that is enough".'

I disagree: If there is a reasonable therapeutic option left, the humane thing to do is to use the euthanasia request and the legal requirements to reorient the patient to a recovery track, while at the same time exploring the death wish and euthanasia request. Especially in the domain of psychiatric illnesses with their unpredictable course and evolution, even more so in a recovery approach, the interpretation of the legal requirements should be strict, as in the Dutch guideline. If not, we end up in the perplexing situation that it is easier for a patient to qualify for euthanasia than for a treatment for treatment-resistant major depressive disorder as in the case of DBS, where a committee of specialists evaluates on the basis of strict criteria including of course a trial of ECT. The study of Kim et al. (2016) reveals that the Dutch euthanasia practices involving patients with a psychiatric illness do not necessarily correspond with the Dutch guideline and can be criticised as well.

Other media reports on patients with a psychiatric illness who died through euthanasia are at least as worrisome. The Flemish TV news programme Terzake ('*Euthanasie voor ondraaglijk psychisch lijden*' 2016) reported on a euthanasia only a few months after the formal request was made. During the evaluation of the euthanasia request, a new diagnosis of autism spectrum disorder (ASD) was made. ASD describes a range of mild to severe neurodevelopmental disorders characterised by social deficits and communication difficulties, stereotyped or repetitive behaviours and interests, sensory issues and in some cases, cognitive delays. Two months after this new diagnosis, the patient died through euthanasia. How can the 'irremediable medical condition' criterion be fulfilled if the necessary time has not been taken to explore the therapeutic options arising from this new diagnosis? Even apart from the therapeutic options, a patient and his or her family need to be given time after a new diagnosis to be informed and educated about the diagnosis and its implications, and to adjust, accept and cope. A diagnosis can, if given time, lead to a personal framework to understand one's own condition and troubles, to seek contact with peers, to adjust one's expectations and way of life and to refocus on strengths and personal meaning despite the diagnosis. In my experience, patients who received a late (as an adult) diagnosis of ASD often go through a transformative process if given time. The diagnosis, psycho-education, therapy and peer contact can help them reach a point where they feel relieved and revived, finally making sense of what they could not grasp about themselves and their problems before the diagnosis of ASD.

We can conclude that the Belgian euthanasia law distinguishes between the subjective dimension of intolerable physical and/or mental suffering on the one hand, and the more objective medical requirement on the other hand: the suffering is due to an incurable and irremediable medical condition with no therapeutic perspective nor prospect of alleviation. Given the unpredictable course of psychiatric illnesses, it is very hard to meet this legal requirement if interpreted with scientific rigour, and luckily so.

Not Only Post-Factum, But Also Prior Review of Euthanasia Requests Based on Unbearable Mental Suffering Because of a Psychiatric Illness

Given the diverging interpretations and lack of systematic evaluation of the 'irremediable medical condition' criterion in current euthanasia practice in Belgium, as is illustrated in the above examples, we question whether this evaluation can be left to the few physicians (amongst whom is at least one psychiatrist according to the law) involved in evaluating a euthanasia request. What is needed, surely, is a committee review based on diagnosis-specific standards and criteria, before euthanasia is performed in cases of unbearable mental suffering because of a psychiatric illness. Inspired by the example of DBS evaluation, a multidisciplinary, inter-university and pluralist committee composed of lay people and experts in the specific diagnosis, end of life and euthanasia experts, ethicists and academics from different universities and ideological backgrounds is needed.

The current post-factum case review by the Federal Evaluation and Review Committee is insufficient for the complex cases of euthanasia requests for mental suffering from a psychiatric illness. Unlike the large majority of euthanasia cases in Belgium where the patient is in a terminal stage of the illness, there is time to seek prior review in cases of mental suffering, when patients have a mean life expectancy of years and even decades. Moreover, there is no structural representation of psychiatric expertise in the Federal Evaluation and Review Committee.

This suggestion is of course a requirement beyond the current legal framework. Nowadays, some academic centres already use a kind of prior review in collaboration with their local medical ethics committee. A professional guideline could promote the practice of prior review, but only a change of the euthanasia legislation, specifically for euthanasia for unbearable mental suffering because of a psychiatric illness, could guarantee that this becomes standard practice. As euthanasia is irreversibly about life and death and every avoidable euthanasia is one too many, we urge that there be a legal requirement of prior review in these euthanasia requests.

Involving all the Necessary Specific Expertise in Evaluating the Euthanasia Request

Exploring and evaluating a euthanasia request is one of the most difficult tasks a psychiatrist encounters. Specific expertise is needed in evaluating the patient's decision-making capacity or competence regarding his or her own death. Expertise in end of life issues and euthanasia is paramount, from a clinical, judicial, ethical and professional deontological perspective. Psychotherapeutic expertise is crucial for the evaluation of the layers of meaning in a euthanasia request and for elucidating the influence of transference and countertransference. System and family therapy expertise is often needed to deal with the patient's family and other third parties. Diagnostic expertise is needed to validate whether earlier diagnostics were accurate and complete. And last but not least, specific expertise in the psychiatric illness at stake in that individual patient requesting euthanasia, is essential. A thorough scientific knowledge and specific clinical experience is needed to judge whether all reasonable treatments and interventions have been tried to reduce or alleviate the mental suffering and whether there truly is no medical prospect. If, for instance, a patient is requesting euthanasia for unbearable suffering due to an incurable and refractory bipolar disorder, a psychiatrist specialised in bipolar disorder is needed to judge whether there are any reasonable therapeutic options left, based on the patient history, the case file, the anamnesis and the mental, physical and technical examinations and investigations.

Those different fields of expertise can only be realised by a collaboration of a team of psychiatrists, in a different composition for each patient with a euthanasia request. For a patient with schizophrenia, a different kind of expertise is needed than for a patient with an eating disorder. In order to realise a careful, thorough, conscientious and ethically founded practice in exploring and evaluating a euthanasia request, the different expertise needing to be present and documented in the team of the 'evaluation track' or in the committee that reviews the request before euthanasia can be performed.

Communication, Exchange and Consultation with all Caregivers and Evaluators Involved

Euthanasia may never be a matter of collecting separate 'positive advices' to get permission so that euthanasia is granted. An exchange, dialogue and discussion amongst all professionals, caregivers (the 'recovery track') as well as evaluators (the 'euthanasia track') is part of the evaluation process. A review meeting of an evaluation committee as described above can offer the opportunity – often an additional opportunity after earlier exchanges – to hear all parties (possibly including the patient) and perspectives involved and discuss the euthanasia request. Currently, a negative evaluation, i.e., the consulted physician judges that the legal criteria for euthanasia are not fulfilled, is sometimes reason to ask another physician for an evaluation, sometimes until two positive evaluations are gathered. If in the process a negative evaluation was given by a physician (psychiatrist or other) who was consulted, this evaluation should be made available to the committee and be discussed.

Involvement of Family and/or Important Third Parties

The Belgian euthanasia law allows for the involvement of family and others during the euthanasia request evaluation process, if the patient gives permission and only with those persons the patient allows. From a legal perspective, euthanasia is essentially an autonomous decision and family or friends' involvement is not mandatory. From a clinical and ethical perspective, not involving family and /or the patient's significant others is problematic. In psychiatry, we focus on autonomy-in-connection, and as clinicians we work with a person embedded in a social context in connection with others. Furthermore, psychiatric illnesses are intrinsically about interaction, connection, communication and (loss of) meaning derived from relations with others. Not involving the patient's significant others implies missing out opportunities to restore connection, belonging, communication and meaning. In my experience, the involvement of family members and/or significant others in the euthanasia request evaluation process is the single most recovery promoting intervention, even with the capacity of averting the euthanasia and redirecting the patient's focus on life. Pronouncing and exploring one's suffering and death wish with significant others has the capacity to change the suffering and the death wish. It often initiates a fundamental change in relations and in the way people relate to each other, with reactions and far reaching ramifications that change the patient's reality, often for the better. Letting go of a strict autonomy-based approach and broadening to a contextual or system-based approach, can be therapeutic and can improve the prognosis of a psychiatric illness.

And if eventually the process leads to euthanasia despite all efforts for recovery, the family members and significant others have had the opportunity to also go through a process instead of being struck unprepared by the news of the loss of a family member or friend by euthanasia. The traumatic impact of such a loss is described poignantly in the New Yorker article we mentioned earlier[3]. If a euthanasia is meant to be 'a good death' as the etymology of the word promises, a good farewell should be part of it.

Involvement of family and/or important others cannot be legally required from a patient requesting euthanasia. However, the Belgian euthanasia law allows a physician to attach additional conditions to his or her active involvement in a euthanasia. If clearly stated to the patient well at the beginning of the evaluation process, it is possible for a physician to tell the patient that involvement of family and/or important others in the process is necessary for him or her to be involved in the euthanasia. Who exactly are involved and what is discussed with them, is of course to be determined in shared decision making. And if the patient refuses, he or she can of course not be forced, but then the physician is free to say that he or she cannot engage in a euthanasia request evaluation process if that condition is not met. In my experience, this is often a difficult message for patients, but if given time with a careful and caring approach, it makes sense to them and was never a reason to go looking for another physician to deal with their euthanasia request. I have seen patients re-establish contact with their parents after years or even decades of distance, more than once fundamentally changing the suffering, death wish or psychiatric illness. Or to quote a patient who testified in a Belgian newspaper: 'Looking back, I can only be contented that the psychiatrist insisted on inviting my parents to join me for a consultation. It re-established contact and no matter how limited, that is really valuable' (Van De Perre and Daenen 2016).

Conclusion

Euthanasia in patients with intolerable mental suffering due to a serious, incurable and irremediable psychiatric illness is only possible in a few countries worldwide. It is highly controversial and raises difficult ethical and clinical issues. In this chapter, the possibility of euthanasia in patients with a psychiatric illness is not rejected completely and a priori, but a plea is made for openness to hear and explore a euthanasia request, using it to start a process that is directed towards life and death, with sufficient reluctance to act on the request. The current differences in the Belgian euthanasia practice are reasons enough to raise the bar for applying extra precautions. The Belgian euthanasia legislation has facilitated the dialogue between patients and psychiatrists on their death wish and suicidal feelings, although patients are still not always heard by their psychiatrists. Nevertheless, it has been argued here that the law has not implemented sufficient checks and balances to promote reluctance to act on a patient's death wish. It allows for a careful and ethically founded practice of euthanasia of patients with a psychiatric illness, but does not offer sufficient guarantees for it. A conscientious, careful and ethically founded practice is only realised if the physicians, hospitals and institutions involved apply standards, conditions and precautions above and beyond the legal requirements. As discussed, these extra standards, conditions and precautions imply, for instance:

- a close collaboration with the institutional clinical ethics committee, which reviews and discusses each case in advance;
- a sufficiently long and thorough evaluation process with ample and frequent contacts between the physicians, as well as other professionals involved, and the patient;
- a careful consideration of the patient's context;
- the strict use of scientifically based standards to determine whether the legal criterion of a lack of medical perspective has been met, guaranteeing that every reasonable treatment option or intervention to alleviate the suffering has been tried according to the state of the art;
- involvement of the family and/or important third parties;
- consultation and discussion amongst all physicians and caregivers involved;
- an imperative two-track approach, always combining the 'euthanasia track' with a parallel 'recovery track' with ongoing orientation towards life during the process;
- specific expertise in all aspects of the evaluation (expertise in the evaluation of decision-making capacity, expertise in the evaluation of diagnosis and of the therapeutic options for the specific condition that leads to the unbearable suffering, psychotherapeutic expertise for the evaluation of the layers of meaning in a euthanasia request and of the influence of transference and countertransference);
- a committee-based multidisciplinary evaluation before euthanasia can be performed, instead of the current system of post-factum review. The main reason for having only a post-factum evaluation (i.e. urgency) does not apply if the patient is not terminally ill, and even has a mean life expectancy of years or decades, as is the case in patients suffering from a psychiatric illness.

Without these standards, conditions and precautions above and beyond the legal conditions, an ethically founded practice is not possible, leading to dramatic and avoidable deaths through euthanasia, and traumatic loss for the next of kin. Fourteen years of Belgian experience and accumulating evidence from national and international media and scientific reports suggest that some of the euthanasia requests and actual euthanasia cases are processed without sufficient regard for these extra-legal but ethically and professionally imperative conditions and precautions. It remains to be discussed whether these extra-legal standards should be realised by professional guidelines or by a revised, more extensive and strict legal framework for euthanasia in patients suffering from a psychiatric condition, incorporating these standards and conditions. Although an excellent guideline (Tholen et al. 2009) is available in the Netherlands since 2004 (revised in 2009 and currently under revision), the current Dutch practice as examined by Kim et al. (2016; Appelbaum 2016), suggests that a guideline might not be sufficient.

To conclude, the debate on euthanasia cannot be seen separately from the societal context: stigma; health care policy and financing and availability and accessibility of mental health care, including palliative care specifically for patients with a severe and irremediable psychiatric illness. As a society, we have an ethical duty to care. Therefore, as a society, we urgently have to invest in mental health, in mental health awareness (as part of global health) and literacy and to ensure allocation of sufficient financial resources for an accessible, recovery-oriented mental health care embedded in society. Often, but not always, this might prevent patients coming to a point where a euthanasia request is formulated.

10

Euthanasia in Children

Keep Asking the Right Questions

STEFAAN VAN GOOL AND JAN DE LEPELEIRE

Introduction

Belgian legislation to legalize euthanasia for minors was passed on 28 February 2014, and consists of one page, one half in Dutch and the other half in French (*Belgisch Staatsblad* 2014). The law amends the law of 28 May 2002. The term 'adult who has the legal capacity' ('*handelingsbekwaam*') is amended to 'minor who has the capacity to judge' ('*oordeelsbekwaam*'), meaning having full ability to judge the situation and the full weight of the request for and consequences of euthanasia. Of note, the law does not use the term 'decision-making capacity' ('*beslissingsbekwaam*') or capacity for discernment ('*onderscheidingsbekwaam*'). The minor should be conscious at the time of request and he or she should sign the written request. A paediatric psychiatrist or psychologist should evaluate the ability of the child to make his or her judgement. The legal representatives should also sign their agreement. The amendment restricts euthanasia to minors with terminal physical (not psychiatric) diseases. Of note, there is no downward age restriction, which contrasts with the legal situation in the Netherlands where a lower age limit is fixed at the age of 12.

Discussions and debates during the drafting of the amendment were held in the Senate, which is the appropriate place for ethical discussion within the Belgian parliament (the Belgian Senate). On 20 February and 6 March 2013, academic experts from the field were heard, amongst them a director of an intensive care unit, a director from a paediatric clinic, a haemato-oncologist and a director of a neonatology service, besides experts from ethics committees, from law and from the field of children's rights.

A further hearing on legal issues was held on 23 March 2013. Hearings on general issues related to the law were held on 4 and 15 May 2013, followed by internal parliamentary discussions on 12 and 26 June, 17 July and 9 and 16 October 2013. A final series of internal discussions took place on 6, 19 and 27 November 2013. Of note, the input of a paediatric psychiatrist as expert was invited once on 8 November 2013. This expert pointed to the loyalty of the minor to the surrounding careproviders, such as the parents, family members, guardians and friends, ending in a sort of 'syndrome of the sponge': the minor will sense suffering and will aim to release his or her surrounding from it. This can trigger the euthanasia request. The expert next pointed to the side effects from a strict procedure during the request and further questioned the expertise of an external consultant to judge in an objective way a concrete situation that is in the first place very subjective, and held a plea to consider the psychologist at this stage as being part of the caregiving surrounding. Finally, there are no solutions for the consequences for the minor and for those surrounding him or her if the external consultant makes a negative evaluation.

An open letter 'Euthanasia for children, now!' was published on 6 November 2013 in an important newspaper, signed by 16 paediatricians from all parts of Belgium (Vox Europe 2013).

Is There an Urgent Need to Have a Law on Euthanasia for Children?

First, one should look at some facts and figures. As the amendment stipulates, the restriction is placed for only those minors who have the capacity to judge their situation and who have a terminal disease. This excludes already a whole range of younger minors by restricting euthanasia to children who are most likely to be teenagers. Based on epidemiology data, it is estimated that more than 70 per cent of the children who die are aged below 1 year, and a further third of children who die between 1 and 15 years of age die in an acute setting because of external causes. This means that 20 per cent of severely chronically ill children aged below 15 years start a patient-oriented treatment trajectory because the fatality of the disease is expected sometime in future. From this group, a minority will ultimately obtain a capacity level to judge and evaluate their situation at a terminal stage (Kind en Gezin 2014; Van der Heyden 2012).

In the Netherlands, where the law regulates euthanasia for teenagers from the age of 12 years, only five cases were registered between 2002 and 2012, and four of them were related to children at the age of 16 or 17 years with only one 12 year old child being euthanized

(NOS 2014). In Belgium, the group of euthanized patients aged between 20 to 39 years consisted of 175 out of 7066 reported cases, or 2.5 per cent (FCECE 2014). In the Belgian reports of 2002–2003, 2004–2005 and 2006–2007 (FCECE 2004, FCECE 2006, FCECE 2008), only one, two and one patient of less than 20 years respectively are reported to have been euthanized. These four patients of 18 or 19 years old represent only 0.05 per cent of the total group of euthanized patients, demonstrating the extremely low prevalence, and the extremely low need for euthanasia in this age group below 20 years of age. Indeed, in 2012–2013, there were no reported cases of euthanasia in persons younger than 20 years of age. In September 2016, the media announced a first case of euthanasia of a 17 years old adolescent.

Nevertheless, in response to the demanding note 'Euthanasia for children, now!,' a short survey was performed using an existing email list for paediatric neuro-oncologists and an email list for paediatric oncologists involved in histiocytic disorders worldwide. Three questions were asked relating to the extent to which the paediatric oncologists perceive such an amendment to the law as being necessary. The questions were specifically focused on euthanasia of adolescents and predefined answers were provided with a score range from 1 to 4.

1. What is the status of a legal framework on euthanasia for adolescents in your country (there is no legal framework/ discussions to develop a legal framework are starting/ discussions to develop a legal framework are ongoing/ there is a legal framework).
2. If there is no legal framework, does the general community in your country feel a need to start discussions for developing a legal framework on euthanasia for adolescents (not at all/ some people feel a need/ most people feel a need/ everybody feels a need).
3. If there is no legal framework, do the paediatricians in your country feel a need to start discussions for developing a legal framework on euthanasia for adolescents (not at all/ some paediatricians feel a need/ most paediatricians feel a need/ all paediatricians feel a need).

Personal opinions and reactions were invited at the end of the questionnaire.

These questions were sent to 253 colleagues of whom 54 colleagues from 19 countries responded and 22 colleagues also provided personal comments.

The results reflect the fact that a legal framework for euthanasia in minors exists at that time only in the Netherlands (and Luxembourg).

There is no legal framework in Australia, Austria, Czech Republic, Denmark, France, Hungary, Ireland, Israel, Italy, Norway, Portugal, Slovenia, Spain, Sweden and the United Kingdom. In the United States, assisted suicide (but not euthanasia) is regulated at the state level. For Germany, one paediatrician believed that discussions had been initiated to develop a legal framework. The other German colleagues replied that there was no legal framework, and no initiative to develop one. In Austria, Czech Republic, Denmark, Hungary, Ireland, Israel, Italy, Norway, Portugal, Slovenia and Sweden paediatricians estimated that there was no felt need to develop a legal framework either in the general population or in their own professional category. In Australia, France, Germany, Spain, United Kingdom and United States, colleagues estimated that a minority of the general population and a minority of paediatricians feel a need to have some legal framework in place.

Several paediatricians provided personal comments. Outside two comments supporting at least a community-based and professional discussion on euthanasia for minors (e.g., 'In both cases the best available palliative care [by an internationally renowned specialist] did not help them sufficiently. With these patients I learned that we lie, when we say that we can assure a pain-free death'.), 20 out of 22 reflected opinions expressed against the development and implementation of a law for euthanasia in children. Although some comments reflected a principle statement ('I justifiably reject euthanasia and the destruction of life not worth living'.), most paediatricians pointed to well-developed palliative care programmes (e.g., 'With established professional palliative care available for everyone (especially for children and adolescents) euthanasia should be no option at all. Physicians should care for their patients not kill them'.) and large experiences on pain treatments currently available in all countries (e.g., 'I am not religious but I am completely against euthanasia particularly since it is easy nowadays to keep patients pain free and treat depression'). Because of that, paediatricians also noted the absolute rareness of a clinical situation in which a question for euthanasia would emerge (e.g.,'Given my more than 30-year experience in paediatric and a short time also adult oncology I do not remember a single patient who gave euthanasia consideration or asked whether this was possible if needed at some point'.). Two responses referred explicitly to religious arguments (e.g., 'I am absolutely convinced as human being, Christian (Roman Catholic), and physician that euthanasia should be no option neither for adults nor for adolescents, and I truly believe that good holistic palliative care is sufficient in nearly all "cases" to prevent any serious euthanasia discussion'.).

Two sources of bias must be kept in mind. First, colleagues who are opposed to euthanasia for minors or in general may have responded more than colleagues who are indifferent or rather in favour of developments of a law for euthanasia. Second, reflecting on euthanasia for minors in a country with no possibility for euthanasia at all, is different than in a country where the legal possibility for euthanasia has existed for more than ten years.

How Can an Expert Objectively Assess the Capacity to Judge in a Minor?

In the amendment to the law on 28 February 2014, the term 'legal capacity' was changed towards 'capacity to judge' because a minor cannot have full legal capacity by law itself. This was debated in the preparatory discussions in the Senate (Senate 2013). However, it is very difficult validly to assess 'capacity to judge' in minors.

The domain is very complex, as children usually still stand close to the 'alpha' of life, facing growth, development, future perspectives, and are now confronted with difficult questions around the 'omega'. A lot of actors and factors play a role which interact with each other. For each question for euthanasia from a minor, at least four groups of people are involved: the minor him- or herself, those who are responsible for care including the legal representatives, the medical team who provides the treatment and the external consultant being the paediatric psychiatrist or psychologist. Although individual autonomy in making the decision to request euthanasia is of major importance, this is always happening as an interaction between the minor and his or her surroundings.

Factors that should be considered are the chronologic age of the patient and the type of disease from which the patient is suffering, but also the level of personal development and the capacity to judge their own situation and requests. The diversity between minors in their pathway to adulthood is very large. Hence, even if one can consider normative developmental phases, one cannot apply them automatically to an individual case. Although the full capacity to judge the situation and the full weight and consequences of the request for euthanasia is to be considered as a task-specific term and hence strongly depending on the concrete thinking and experiences about disease, dying and death, one cannot neglect these global developmental phases for each individual case. The meaning of the concept of death emerges only at the age of about seven years. From the age of 12 years, one becomes aware of the universal mortality of all living things. The child realizes that everyone, including himself or herself, will eventually die (Eiser 1990). This means that the medical world must provide solutions for these patients when they reach a situation of incurable terminal or non-terminal disease and suffering that is difficult to address. These very difficult and emotional situations have triggered the debates of euthanasia, although these situations should be kept strictly separated from the term 'euthanasia'. Terms like 'medically accompanied death at terminal illness' and 'appropriate medical support at non-terminal illness' are used to define the correct and accepted medical behaviour for these patients (Nys 2013a).

For each minor, the capacity to judge is unique and not necessarily related to chronological age. Therefore, the assessment of capacity to judge should be done for each minor individually, considering these developmental phases in multiple domains.

With respect to personality development through the lifespan, Erikson (1968) defined eight stages of social-emotional development:

1/ Trust versus mistrust (hope),
2/ Autonomy versus shame (will),
3/ Initiative versus guilt (purpose),
4/ Industry versus inferiority (competency),
5/ Ego identity versus role confusion (fidelity),
6/ Intimacy versus isolation (love),
7/ Generativity versus stagnation (care) and
8/ Ego integrity versus despair (wisdom).

The fifth stage tapping into identity formation is situated between the ages 12 to 20 years and is very important in the development towards social-emotional maturity: who am I, how do I stand in my life, how do I interact with other people and with the community?

Recently, developmental psychologists even considered identity development as a process that continues long after the classical period of adolescence. Authors like Arnett initiated the term 'emerging adulthood', going from 18 to 25 years of age, which consists of a strong exploration of one's own identity (Arnett 2000). Reaching adulthood is indeed not only dependent on classical sociological criteria like marrying and having children, but on developing a mature identity, autonomy, etc. as well. In our community, young people study much longer, have many more choices and possibilities. Even in their early twenties, they perceive themselves as an adult in some domains but not in all, and they are further discovering and constructing their own identity.

With respect to cognitive development, Piaget (1971) defined four stages based on the cognitive operations that the growing-up minor is able to do:

1/ sensorimotor stage,
2/ preoperational stage,
3/ concrete operational stage and
4/ formal operational stage which starts from about 12 year of age.

In the last stage, the minors have the capacity for abstract, systematic thinking enabling them, when faced with a problem, to start with a hypothesis, deduce testable inferences and isolate and combine variables to see which inferences are confirmed. They can also evaluate logic of verbal statements without referring to real-world circumstances.

In relation to the question of euthanasia for minors, it seems that at least this last stage should be reached. While such a stage is usually reached around 12 years, in general cognitive operational behaviour this last stage continues to develop throughout adolescence. It is noted that some adolescents do not even reach this level by the end of adolescence. Moreover, this last stage is not like the stage of adult cognitive operational thinking, called postformal thinking, in which rationality and logic is present but in which also dealing with emotions and sensations is integrated to make fine-tuned context-dependent decisions.

The postformal thinking stage can be found back in the theory of moral development proposed by Kohlberg (1991). Three levels are defined:

1/ preconventional level when morality is externally controlled,
2/ conventional level when conformity to social rules are considered important and current social system is maintained to ensure positive relationships and societal order and
3/ postconventional or principled level moving the human beings beyond unquestioning support for their own society's rules and laws and defining morality in terms of abstract principles and values that apply to all situations and societies.

For answering to an authentic moral attitude, the individual should have the capacity to judge at the postformal and postconventional level for taking vital decisions, hence with attention to both reason and emotion and starting from his or her own values and convictions.

Even more complicated is the faith development to deal with existential questions from life to which suffering and dying belong. Faith is defined as an activity of trusting, committing and relating to the world based on a set of assumptions of how one is related to others and the world. Six developmental stages were proposed by Fowler and Dell (2006):

1/ primal or undifferentiated faith,
2/ intuitive-projective faith,
3/ mythic-literal faith (school children),
4/ synthetic-conventional faith (12 years to end of adolescence),
4/ individuative-reflective faith (mid-twenties to late thirties),
5/ conjunctive faith and
6/ universalizing faith or enlightenment.

The synthetic-conventional faith is characterized by conformity to religious authority and the development of a personal identity. Any conflicts with one's beliefs are ignored at this stage due to the fear of threat from inconsistencies.

Full capacity to judge for questions related to euthanasia implies therefore at least the individuative-reflective faith stage which even then holds some anxiety and struggle. At this stage, the individual is taking personal responsibility for his or her beliefs and feelings. As one can reflect on one's own beliefs, there is an openness to a new complexity of faith, but this also increases the awareness of conflicts in one's belief.

In summary, there is a large variability in the development between individuals. There are no standard routes to develop from child to adult and there is no fixed developmental speed. The minimal developmental levels reflecting full capacity to judge the situation and the full weight of the request for, and consequences of, euthanasia are rarely if ever reached during the teenage years.

The developmental phases in multiple domains are associated with obvious changes in the brain architecture, which extends the whole period of adolescence up to the third decade of life (Petanjek et al. 2011; Lebel and Beaulieu 2011) and involves changes in the large-scale organization of anatomical and functional networks (Raznahan et al. 2011). General developmental trajectories of the brain network organization have been discovered using advances in Brain Magnetic Resonance imaging for functional brain connectivity studies, particularly those examining intrinsic functional connectivity at rest (Ernst et al. 2015). Early adolescence is highlighted as a period of significant maturation of the brain's functional architecture (Sherman et al. 2014). From age 10 to 13 years, there is increased integration between the posterior cingulate cortex and the medial prefrontal cortex in the default mode network, increased segregation between the posterior cingulate cortex and the central executive network, increased connectivity between the dorsolateral prefrontal cortex and other central executive network nodes, as well as increased default mode network segregation. Analysis of cortical folding patterns shows an important modification of the cerebral cortex during late brain maturation which is related to cognitive development (Klein et al. 2014).

The asynchronous development of different neural systems like the left temporo-parietal junction, the right dorsolateral prefrontal cortex and the anterior medial prefrontal cortex are associated with changes in social cognition and behaviour (van den Bos et al. 2011). Sex differences in the way the cortex matures over times have been described with a higher rate of cortical thinning in females compared to males in the right temporal regions, the left temporo-parietal junction and the left orbito-frontal cortex (Mutlu et al. 2013). Once again, all these developmental changes are described at the level of groups of children/adolescents and can in no way be translated to an individual (ill) child.

The complexity of normative development is even more complicated when dealing with children with a serious disorder. Recent studies have focused on this domain. A large proportion of minors with chronic diseases like diabetes mellitus or congenital heart diseases have no particular problems during their social-emotional, moral and/or cognitive development (Seiffge-Krenke 1998; Luyckx et al. 2008; Rassart et al. 2013). They form the unexpected success story (Gortmaker et al. 1993) and reach a good functional stage within society despite facing some challenges related to treatment compliance and to continuous adaptations to treatment. However, in some instances the development to autonomy is hindered by physical diseases like spina bifida (Friedman et al. 2009). Some developmental aspects like behavioural autonomy may be slowed down. Such patients face more problems with respect to social integration and educational adjustment. These developmental challenges may affect their capacity to judge. For minors with more complex neurological diseases, differences in these multi-directional developmental routes might be even stronger.

Another issue is related to the minors with normal development but who face, at a certain time point, a life-threatening disease but with potential curative chances. There are no systematic studies available, at the moment, about how these children are affected at different developmental phases through the lifespan and how their personality and identity is potentially changed due to this experience. Moreover, some of them need permanent medical support after being treated or cured, while others still must fulfil preventive medical surveys. This large variety of outcomes should be considered when such a patient asks for euthanasia because of an illness.

One should remark that the concept of death in children experiencing a life-threatening illness develops differently than in healthy peers. Because of their experience with the illness, they develop an awareness of the seriousness of their condition, and therefore a sense of their own mortality. This has been observed at a time when children with leukaemia have been left completely uncertain about the nature of their illness. In an observational study, children from the age of four years expressed the awareness they had about the fatal nature of their illness, long before the general stage of dying awareness (Bluebond-Langner 1977). The gradual shift in consciousness context about disease and death is important for a good assessment of the fatally sick child. An extra challenge is that children usually do not talk about their thoughts and fears about death, as they tend to protect themselves. They avoid a confrontation with negative emotions in others that they would introduce themselves. The child needs to continue to see the parents, in particular, as being strong and supportive, and not to confront them with anxieties that would induce suffering and uncertainty (Van Veldhuizen et al. 1991).

The law foresees that an external consultant, a paediatric psychiatrist or psychologist, should assess the capacity to judge of a minor with a terminal disease and suffering from incurable pain, who asks for euthanasia. Already the contextual situation and the life history of the patient and care providers before the first contact with the consultant, makes this task very challenging. Nevertheless, the assessment of the legal capacity of an adult with a serious disorder to give informed consent for participation into a clinical trial has been studied, and some instruments have been developed to make this assessment in an objective way (Dunn et al. 2006). These instruments vary strongly, and do not take the contextual factors into consideration. For minors, however, there is no validated instrument available to assess the capacity to give informed consent for participation into a clinical trial, although attention has been paid to the need for such an instrument. In the Netherlands, such an instrument is under development at this moment (Hein et al. 2012). Neither for adults, nor for children, is there an instrument to assess the capacity to request euthanasia, be it legal capacity, capacity to judge, decision-making capacity or capacity for discernment. A valid assessment is, however, required.

Dealing with external influences

Studies exist that investigated minors in different situations, including medical situations, and the way capacity is reached to an acceptable level to participate in important decisions.

A proposal by Steinberg (2013a) is the so-called doctrine of the sevens: young children between 0 and 7 years of age, children between 7 and 14 years and adolescents above 14 years of age. There is a general acceptance in society today that minors above 14 years can already take decisions for themselves, like adults. Also for medical decisions, this general acceptance allows an atmosphere of trust and serenity between the adolescent and the physician to take medical decisions. Based on observations and analyses, it is proposed that minors who are older than 14 years of age generally can be termed 'mature minor' being able to take decisions in medical situations similar to persons older than 18 year, that is, adults with legal capacity.

Considering the complexity and the variability within the developmental phases as described above, it is clear that any acceptance of the capacity to judge by mature minors as being similar to adults is criticized by many participants in the debate (Partridge 2013). There is a body of evidence demonstrating the importance of effective parenting for the developmental phases of minors (Adaljarnardottir and Hafsteinsson 2001; Huver et al. 2007). There is a natural transfer of moral, social and existential values characteristic to the family in which the minor's life is formed and exists. In general, parenting induces determinations of decisional capacity given the benefits from parental involvement. This interaction between the minor and parents during development, and especially in a situation of severe and/or terminal illness, is unique and may not be crossed by law and procedures.

Also for giving informed consent in medicine, the capacity of the minor to completely understand medical terms and details is insufficient (Iltis 2013). Their appreciation and evaluation of decisions and consequences will differ from adults. This experience of uncertainty and eventual awareness of such weaknesses creates a situation of dependence by the minors on the strong and evident authority of their parents. Therefore, the external influences in taking very difficult decisions are usually very strong, and the autonomy for the decision-making process is diminished (Barina and Bishop 2013). Although interaction between the minor and surrounding care givers, be it their parents, family members, guardians and friends, is in most situations unique, serene, helpful and honest, it may not always be the case. Even in optimal situations, it might turn into the appearance of the 'syndrome of the sponge' where the minor will try to take responsibility and look for methods to alleviate in his or her surroundings the suffering for which he or she is the cause. Even worse are the situations where the minor loses (or is perceived to lose) an unconditional support from his or her surrounding caregivers, even via non-spoken signals. The minor might feel guilty of causing problems and conflicts to the ones he or she still loves. The right to request euthanasia might be perceived by the minor as a chance, even an obligation, to use this right. In this way, freedom and autonomy induce pressure to use freedom, which of course contradicts autonomy.

Overall, it is evident that the influence from those surrounding each child and adolescent is strong and cannot be neglected. Influence can exist through unspoken signals. Influences can exist over a long period of time and can cause imprinting, a rapid phase-sensitive learning that is independent of the consequences of behaviour. It is impossible to assess these influences in an objective way and to weigh them at the time when a minor requests euthanasia.

How Can One Deal with Impulsiveness in Decision-Making Processes?

Another major challenge to the concept of the mature minor is the notion of impulsiveness. Decision-making processes in teenagers are not as controlled as those of comparable adults. When teenagers take decisions, the limbic structures are generally activated, and there is yet much less control from the prefrontal cortical areas. These notions have been extensively demonstrated with brain-imaging studies (Schmithorst and Yuan 2010; Olesen et al. 2003; Vincent et al. 2008; Liston et al. 2006) which demonstrate the neurophysiological basis of the later steps of the neuropsychological developmental stages as described above. Wilhelms and Reyna noticed how minors were much more impulsive in taking decisions for medical situations as compared to adults (Wilhelms and Reyna 2013).

The impulsiveness in the decision-making processes and the supporting neurophysiological data are generally accepted in the community when it comes to court decisions about adolescents' criminal culpability in cases of serious crimes (Buchen 2012; Steinberg 2013b). All accept the assessment of higher risks and hence higher costs when it comes to providing insurance for driving a car to young adults between 18 and about 25 years of age.

Because of the same sense of impulsiveness, regulations by society have been put forward for issues. For example, since 1 January 2014, buying and possessing of alcohol in the Netherlands is limited to adults, being older than 18 years (Rijksoverheid 2014). These are all regulations to improve quality of life and safety for the community as well as for the minors themselves because we generally accept that a less controlled use might happen at younger age. Having these elements in mind, Cherry warns that the status of mature minors in relation to medical questions is a negation of scientific data as well as insights and forms, in fact, a serious danger to the minor (Cherry 2013).

Concluding Reflections

The Belgian legislation regulating euthanasia for minors restricts, very clearly, the conditions to be fulfilled before a minor can begin the procedure to request euthanasia. This means that the law does not cover all other challenging situations outside the restrictions, which should still be resolved with best optimal palliative treatment considerations. The law is focused on an extremely small group of potential candidates for euthanasia. For these rare cases, probing questions concerning the ability to take these kinds of decisions, sustained by important scientific literature as we developed in this chapter, are not answered at this moment. Therefore, we believe that the law should be evaluated as premature and potentially dangerous for some minors in particular situations.

The amended legislation does not consider reasons why adults may want euthanasia. Besides emerging symptoms of pain and suffering, there are other reasons, such as fear of loss of control, fear of loss of dignity and growing insights of becoming a burden to others. Therefore, adults might refuse intense palliative treatment and even full sedation during the last days of their life. Children and adolescents, however, lack the capacity to develop an over-arching conviction against life under appropriate symptom control by palliative treatment. With this law, however, they seem to be faced with 'taking their right' based upon a choice between danger of unbearable suffering, on the one hand, versus immediate death on the other.

The amended legislation does not prevent the strong need to further develop palliative care for children. Expert palliative treatment must be available for each child enabling him or her to come to the end of his or her life in a good way being at home surrounded by parents, family, friends, guardians, etc. Since the law of 18 March 2009, palliative care teams began to be licensed by the national health system. They belong to university hospitals, and consist of doctors and nurses with extensive experience. These teams can be asked for help by any physician caring for a child with any disorder in a palliative situation. With this interesting system, academic experience in palliative treatment is brought to each home for each child thereby providing specific knowledge and help to the local care giving team, such as the general practitioner, home nursing and physiotherapists. Moreover, materials and aids for the patient are provided by the palliative care teams to help and support the child and control symptoms at home. This way of acting has proven to be highly efficient and effective over the years. Therefore, there is a strong appreciation from patients, families as well as from the local care providers.

No piece of legislation can regulate each difficult situation. There will always be situations where the law does not bring a solution, and where the palliative care teams and the local care providers face a conflict between the fact 'outside the strict regulated framework, a doctor is not allowed to terminate life' and the principle that 'a doctor has to alleviate suffering'. In this case, one comes into a situation of exigency. Important elements to consider very carefully are the assessment of the suffering, the evaluation of all possible treatment options to alleviate this suffering and whether actively ending a life is the only potential solution. This confrontation with exigency should be clearly discussed with the patient, when possible, with the surrounding care providers, with the palliative teams and ideally with an external ad hoc committee or existing ethics committee. A procedure should be available so that the doctor facing such exigency can follow guidelines to document the situation. This will avoid situations of low exactitude that still exist today.

Finally, during the three years between the positive vote of the Belgian paediatric euthanasia and writing this text, two single cases have been reported. Is there a need for this law?

Acknowledgements

This work is a continuation of the METAFORUM working group at the University of Leuven (www.metaforum.be). In the METAFORUM, multidisciplinary scientific expertise has been put together to discuss and form an opinion on the extension of euthanasia in Belgian legislation: extension towards minors, extension towards patients with advanced dementia and extension towards patients with psychiatric disorders. Participants in the METAFORUM were: Bert Broeckaert, Chris

Gastmans, Manu Keirse, Johan Menten, Herman Nys, AntoonVande-
velde, JorisVandenberghe, Rik Vandenberghe and Stefaan Van Gool.
Chair of the METAFORUM was Jan De Lepeleire. We thank Koen
Luyckx, Patricia Bijttebier (School Psychology and Development in
Context) and Jurgen Lemiere (Paediatric Clinical Psychology, University
Hospital Leuven, Belgium) for their critical comments on previous drafts
of this chapter.

11

Euthanizing People Who Are 'Tired of Life'

RAPHAEL COHEN-ALMAGOR

Introduction

In Belgium and the Netherlands, a debate is developing about people who express a desire to end their lives although they do not suffer from an incurable, life-threatening disease. In 2000, a court in Haarlem in the Netherlands considered the case of 86-year-old Edward Brongersma who had expressed his wish to die to his general practitioner, Dr Philip Sutorius, claiming that death had 'forgotten' him. His friends and relatives were dead, and he experienced 'a pointless and empty existence' (Sheldon 2000). After repeated requests, Dr Sutorius euthanized his insisting patient and was then put on trial. The public prosecution recognized that Dr Sutorius fulfilled all the legal criteria but one: 'hopeless and unbearable suffering'. Therefore, the patient's request should have been refused. The court did not discipline Dr Sutorius, saying that the patient was obsessed with his 'physical decline' and 'hopeless existence' and therefore was suffering 'hopelessly and unbearably'. A spokesman for the Royal Dutch Medical Association reacted to the court judgement by saying that the definition of 'unbearable suffering' had been stretched too far and that 'what is new is that it goes beyond physical or psychiatric illness to include social decline' (Cohen-Almagor 2004). The then Justice Minister Benk Korthals said that being 'tired of life' is not sufficient reason for euthanasia (Sheldon 2000). Since then, the debate as to whether physicians should comply with euthanasia requests of people who are 'tired of life' has been widened and many people in Belgium and in The Netherlands are calling for the law to be expanded in order to include similar patients (Van Wijngaarden et al. 2014).

I am grateful to Chris Gastmans, David Albert Jones, Calum MacKellar, Bert Keizer and Sigrid Sterckx for their comments on a previous draft of this chapter.

The methodology of this research is based on a critical review of the literature supplemented by communications with leading scholars and practitioners. First, concerns are raised about euthanizing people who say that they are 'tired of life'. Some suggestions designed to improve the situation are offered. The Belgian legislators and medical establishment are invited to reflect and ponder over these proposals to prevent potential abuse.

People Who Are 'Tired of Living'

Studies have shown that age-related losses, inability to carry out daily activities, decreasing sociality, lack of valuable relations and companionship, low self-esteem, self-withdrawal that leads to depressive feelings, personal characteristics and beliefs are associated with euthanasia requests (Rurup et al. 2005a; Rurup et al. 2011; Van Wijngaarden et al. 2014, 2015). Elderly people face the diminution of their family and social circles as they withstand life hardships while their loved ones pass away. Sometimes they suffer a string of bereavements in succession. A Belgian study from 2013 showed that being tired of life was a relatively common reason for physicians to grant euthanasia requests. In declining order, the most important reasons were the patient's request (88.3 per cent), physical and/or mental suffering (87.1 per cent), no prospect of improvement (77.7 per cent), expected further suffering (48.3 per cent), low expected quality of life (45.1 per cent), loss of dignity (52.1 per cent), thinking that life should not be needlessly prolonged (30.7 per cent), being 'tired of life' (25.3 per cent), family's request (23.4 per cent), situation was unbearable for the family (13.8 per cent) and other reasons (0.4 per cent) (Dierickx et al. 2015). I have dealt with the problematic involvement of the family in decision-making processes at the end of life elsewhere (Cohen-Almagor 1996, 2011). Here I wish to focus attention on one controversial reason for euthanasia: being "tired of life". Such cases concern people who do not suffer from a physical or medically defined psychiatric disease yet they are unhappy with their lives and wish to terminate them. These cases are not unique to Belgium (Calman 2004; Pike 2010; Withnall 2014; Van Wijngaarden et al. 2014). They are, however, salient in Belgium and in The Netherlands because of their respective euthanasia laws and the slow process by which both societies are broadening the situations in which euthanasia can be considered, such as for mental suffering and children. Debates are taking place concerning people who are 'tired of

life', psychiatric patients and patients with dementia.[1] In the Netherlands, it is estimated that requests for euthanasia on the grounds of
being 'tired of life' are made approximately 400 times a year (Rurup
et al. 2005a). These requests pose a delicate moral dilemma that
deserves close consideration. According to the Dutch physicians, being
tired of living was one of the important reasons for the request for
euthanasia and assisted suicide in 14 per cent of patients suffering from
cancer (282/2056), 30 per cent of patients with another severe disease
(81/271) and for 74 per cent of patients who had no severe physical or
psychiatric disease (45/61) (Rurup et al. 2005a).

Euthanizing People Who Are 'Tired of Life'

The Oxford English Dictionary defines 'tired' as 'fatigued, wearied; also,
sick or weary of, impatient with' (2016a). People who are tired go to rest,
rejuvenate, collect themselves and return to their daily routine. People
who are 'tired of life' presumably do not wish to rejuvenate, collect
themselves and return to their daily routine.

In 2009, Amelie Van Esbeen asked her doctors for euthanasia after she
indicated that she had ceased appreciating her life. Her physicians did
not believe that she was suffering from a 'serious terminal illness' and
'constant and unbearable pain that cannot be relieved' as the law stipulates, hence they refused her request. The 93-year-old woman began a
hunger strike and after ten days a different physician helped her die.[2]
The controversial case re-launched the debate as to how life should end;
about quality of life, and whether such requests should be honoured.
Wim Distelmans, who heads the Belgian Federal Control and Evaluation
Commission for Euthanasia, said that euthanasia can only be performed
when there is a question of 'unbearable suffering' ('93-year-old Belgian
Woman on Hunger Strike' 2009; 'Belgian Woman Dead after Fighting for
Assisted Suicide' 2009; 'Amelie Van Esbeen est décédée par euthanasia'
2009; 'Belgian Euthanasia, Controversy Is Served Again' 2009; 'Belgian
Woman, 93, Gets the Help to Die that She Wanted' 2009). This sounds
like a restrictive view of euthanasia. But Distelmans maintained that

---

[1] For discussion, see Thienpont et al. 2015; Moonen et al. 2016; Claes et al. 2015; Cohen-
Almagor 2016.
[2] In her comments on an early draft of this paper (13 March 2011), professor Sterckx noted:
'This is a rogue doctor and this should be condemned and many have done so; but it is
only ONE case.'

older persons often suffer from many illnesses: poor sight, poor hearing, poor verbal skills and dependence on others:[3] 'Put together this could amount to unbearable suffering. I don't believe it's wrong to request euthanasia in such situations' ('93-year-old Belgian Woman on Hunger Strike' 2009).[4] Distelmans voiced his belief that the Belgian *Euthanasia Act* should be changed to enable seniors who are 'tired of life' to be able to request euthanasia ('93-year-old Belgian Woman on Hunger Strike' 2009).[5] But Distelmans' view is contested. Research has shown that a significant number of physicians interpret 'unbearable suffering' to require serious physical symptoms (Van Tol et al. 2010; Pasman et al. 2009; Bolt et al. 2015).

A 2015 study by Bolt et al. shows that 3 per cent of all euthanasia and physician-assisted suicide requests in the Netherlands are from people who are 'tired of life' and that only a minority of physicians find it conceivable that they would grant such a request. Bolt et al. (2015) think that legal arguments and moral objections deter most physicians from complying with such requests.

In 2014, a British woman who was neither terminally ill nor seriously handicapped but who had become fed up with the modern world of emails, TVs, computers and supermarket ready meals wished to end her life. As no physician in Britain would help her, she travelled to Switzerland where her wish was granted by the Dignitas assisted suicide clinic (Withnall 2014).[6]

Ethical Considerations

The raison d'être of medicine and health care is to relieve suffering, to assist patients in coping with their ailments, and to seek to treat or heal. Physicians are there to serve the best interests of their patients on matters that concern their health. Does terminating the lives of people (I refer to

---

[3] One referee noted the increasing number of euthanasia deaths for 'multiple pathologies' in Belgium. This may suggest increasing euthanasia not for terminal illness but for the many illnesses of old age. Some of them are conducted based on being 'tired of life'.

[4] Dr Keizer remarked on a draft of this paper that in the Netherlands there is also much pressure to outline a new law under which frail, tired, elderly persons can ask for an overdose.

[5] Professor Sterckx doubted that Distelmans said this and suggested to check with him whether the press release is accurate. I wrote to Distelmans but received no reply.

[6] See also 'Second British woman "tired of life" helped to die by Swiss suicide clinic aged 99' 2014.

them as 'people' not 'patients') who are 'tired of life' fall within this raison
d'être? I believe the following considerations should be included.

Autonomy

People have the right to control what happens to their bodies. The central
idea of autonomy is self-rule, or self-direction. Accordingly, the view is
that individuals should be left to govern their business without being
overwhelmingly subject to external forces. We are said to be free when
our acts are not dominated by external impediments, thus enabling us to
form judgement, to decide between alternatives and to act in accordance
with the action-commitments implied by our beliefs. Thus, autonomy
means that an informed, competent adult can refuse or accept treatments, drugs and surgeries according to his or her wishes.

The autonomy argument is weak because these people suffer, and
they are dependent on others. They may consider themselves to be
autonomous, self-determined people who make a rational choice to end
their lives but in effect their self-rule is impaired. They are vulnerable,
needy and depend on others, including their doctors. Thus, we are
considering a restricted sense of autonomy and deficient capacity for
self-rule.[7]

Furthermore, the issue is not denying individuals to exercise what they
perceive as their right. Granted that some people may believe that death
serves their best interest, but they do not commit suicide. They want
the physician to help them. Respecting the autonomy of the person
would require changing the scope of medicine and health care to include
providing aid-in-dying to people rather than to patients.

Neil Calman (2004) tells the heart-wrenching story of 'Sarah Brown-
stein' (this is a fictitious name), 92-year-old New Yorker lady of sound
mind who was 'tired of life' and asked his assistance to die. Sarah was
lonely. She had difficulties hearing and reading. She had difficulties
thinking. She felt unworthy, of no use to anyone, not even to herself.
She wanted the doctor to end her misery. At the same time, Sarah's
medical condition was stable. She lacked most signs of depression. She
was eating and sleeping well. She dressed up and put on make-up every
morning. She also obediently took her many medications. The doctor
could not come to her aid as Sarah requested; such act was against

---

[7] One referee noted that people who are tired of life do not always have a diminished
autonomy capacity.

New York law. He did tell Sarah that it was her right to end her life if she so chooses. As Sarah continued to insist, he finally told her she can stop taking all her medication. This was completely within her control. This way she could exercise her autonomy without compelling the physician to violate the law.

Nonmaleficence

'First, do no harm' is the bedrock of medical ethics, *sine qua non* that guides the work of all health care providers. In every situation, health care providers should avoid causing harm to their patients (Beauchamp and Childress 2013). Granted that some treatments may cause some harm thus the requirement is that the treatment should not be disproportionate to the benefits of treatment. We assume that people who are 'tired of life' are suffering. But is their suffering so unbearable that death is the solution? Even if there are situations in which some people suffer a lot because they are neglected and have no hope to improve their abysmal situation, enlarging the scope of medicine to end the life of such people may entail disproportionate harms.

Beneficence

The autonomy of the person is important. Not harming others is a professional value of medicine. Beneficence dictates that health providers contribute positively to the welfare of their patients. Beneficence connotes acts of kindness, charity, mercy and friendship (Beauchamp and Childress 2013). Health care providers should consider the benefits and risks of their decisions. They should act in a way that benefits the patient. They must strive to improve their patient's health, to do the most good for the patient in every situation. Granted that what is good for one patient may not be good for another, thus each situation should be considered individually. Those who are 'tired of life' are not interested in efforts to improve their health condition. But beneficence requires that physicians will exhaust all treatment options which do not impose disproportionate burden and which have not been refused by the patient. Beneficence requires to positively come to those people's aid. Whether kindness and mercy require ending the lives of those who are 'tired' of living is an open question but this conduct should always be the last resort.

Dignity

The term 'dignity' is derived from the Latin noun *dignitas*, which means: (a) worthiness, merit; (b) greatness, authority and (c) value, excellence. The noun is cognate with the adjective *dignus* (worthy), from the Sanskrit root *dic* and the Greek root *deik*, which have the sense of 'bringing to light', 'showing' or 'pointing out' (Lowental 1984; Bayertz 1996; Velleman 1999; Cohen-Almagor 2001).

When using the phrase 'death-with-dignity', we refer to the timing and setting of death, i.e., patients should be allowed, whenever possible, to choose the time and setting of their departure. With the help of medical professionals, patients should be able to control the process of dying, maintaining autonomy at the end of life, not being humiliated, perceiving themselves with honour. The concept of dignity refers to a worth or value that flows from an inner source. In this context, I wish to distinguish between *dignity as recognition* and *dignity as liability*.

Dignity as recognition is about us recognizing the inner spark of the soul that we all possess, the inherent quality of the person. It is not given from the outside but rather is intrinsic to the bearer of dignity. As Lawrence Ulrich (1999) notes, a painting may have value but it does not have dignity. The value is placed upon it by the members of the artistic community considering the skill of the artist and the aesthetic priorities of the community. The value does not derive from the painting itself. Persons, on the other hand, can be said to possess dignity as an inner source of worth. Inherent dignity should be recognized by oneself and also by others. If this were not the case, people would simply be the bearers of instrumental value like all other objects in the world. Instead, human beings are set apart and treated in special ways. Human beings are precious; their lives are appreciated and should be protected.[8]

Because the concept of dignity also relates to the inner self, it involves not only *objective* but also *subjective* notions. It is the source from which human rights are derived, and it also refers to one's own feelings about oneself. To have dignity means to look at oneself with self-respect, with some sort of satisfaction. It means to feel human, not degraded. A subjective concept of the self refers to how a person perceives his or

---

[8] Contra Peter Singer 1993, I am a 'speciesist'. I believe first of all in my own species, the human race. Contrary to Singer, I believe that the very birth of human life is morally significant, something of great importance. Contrary to Singer, I believe that it is only a humane and preferable inclination to think first about our fellow humans.

her life, achievements and place in the world. The subjective evaluation is affected by the individual's self-respect, relative to the abilities he or she believes he or she possesses relative to peers and surroundings.

I have argued that we all have a right to dignity (Cohen-Almagor 2001, 2013). *Dignity as liability* requires that we all respect persons *qua* persons. People deserve to be accorded a certain treatment from birth. We are endowed with dignity and have the right to be treated with dignity. While people cannot expect concern from fellow humans, we can expect respect from others.

More specifically and regarding the role of physicians, preserving dignity means helping patients to feel valuable. The preservation of one's dignity involves, inter alia, listening to the patients' complaints, helping patients cure their diseases or at least assisting them in controlling pain, responding to their distress and anxieties, making an effort to relieve them, demonstrating sensitivity to the physical indignities that occur in severe illnesses, making the patient sense that he or she is a human being and not an infant, a case study or worse, a body that occupies a bed and consumes resources. Maintaining the patients' dignity requires physicians as well as the patients' families to help the patients retain at least some of their self-respect. The aim is to secure dignified living in severe health conditions.

The subjective feeling of loss of dignity is a significant consideration for those who request euthanasia and assisted suicide in the Netherlands (Rurup et al. 2005b). People who are 'tired of living' come to believe death is their preferred option. They wait for death because they have nothing to live for. Patients who suffer from incurable deadly disease have little or no hope because present medicine cannot provide suitable answers. But people who 'are tired of life' are not in the same position. They do not suffer from such life-threatening diseases. There is some hope for them and they can regain self-worth and value.

My research in eight countries (Australia, Belgium, Canada, Israel, New Zealand, the Netherlands, United Kingdom, United States) has shown that most patients find some meaning in their lives even when they are severely impaired, bed-ridden, limited in movement and in constant need of help (Cohen-Almagor 2001, 2004). We are talking about a very small number of people who are 'tired of living' and who come to entertain the option of shortening their lives. Many of these people who are 'tired of living' were independent, active and energetic. They become in their own eyes dependent upon others. They reach the conclusion that their lives have become a burden to them and to people they love. They might lose their sense of humanity as well as ir self-respect, and this might lead them to lose interest in life and to _ oose death. The challenge is to make them resume the zeal for life. The challenge is to make them acknowledge the richness of life even when the alternatives presented before them are more restricted compared to what they used to have. Death awaits all of us. The medical profession should exhaust all avenues of helping those people, aiming to accommodate their needs and to refill the void in their lives before opting for euthanasia.

Compassion

But what about those people whom we cannot help? We have tried everything. Nothing helps. They suffer from some medical conditions that are not life-threatening. They may be old and lonely. We are unable to arrange sufficient company for them and to garner enough points of interest to make their lives worthy of living. Should we just ignore these people?

The virtue of compassion combines active regard for another's welfare with an emotional response of sympathy, tenderness and discomfort at the other's misfortune or suffering. It is expressed in acts of beneficence that aim to alleviate suffering. Indeed, the principles of respect for autonomy and beneficence, and the virtues of care and compassion offer solid reasons for recognizing the legitimacy of physician-assisted death (Beauchamp and Childress 2013).

Calman (2004) was unable to assist Sarah. As he advised her to stop taking her medication he reassured her that, should she become uncomfortable or filled with fluid from heart failure, he would prescribe a pain medication to take away the sensation of being out of breath, without treating her heart failure. He promised to come to see her any time day or night. Sarah followed his advice but continued living for a few more months, and became more agitated as death failed to visit her instantly. She was angry with her physician who felt deep remorse for his inability to help her as she wished. Calman (2004) concluded with the hope that when his own time will come, his physician will have a good understanding of palliative care and end-of-life options, will have the courage to act on his behalf, and that the legal situation will be such as to facilitate more merciful assistance at the end of life.

The issue of people who are 'tired of life' is a 'hard case'. The moral dilemma is real and significant. I can think of situations

in which strong-willed people who lost some of their capab
lonely and who are trapped in their own comparative r
their previous times of life when they were active, soc
they had led a meaningful life with significant others ᵀ
these people lost the zeal for life, do not see a way out ᵤ
and prefer death. We should help them to the best of our abiliᵤ
I think we should be very careful in providing a licence to physicians
to aid their dying. Such people, in such condition are exceptional.
The Belgian *Euthanasia Act* should not be expanded to cater for them.

Having said that, I believe medicine should try to help *all* people, not
only the majority of them. Thus, while I am against enlarging the scope
of the *Euthanasia Act* yet again (in 2014, the *Act* was amended to include
minors), I do recognize that exceptions can be made.

In the next section below, I will make some suggestions as to how to
accommodate exceptions. I oppose expanding the law yet again because
it is impossible to build a policy that will keep shifting as individual
situations present themselves. Furthermore, to honour death requests
because people are 'fed up with life' is a dangerous move. People who
experience mental, physical or existential tiredness and who request
death should receive proper psychological counselling, not lethal medication. They should receive recognition, a caring treatment, respect and
concern that could potentially renew their zeal for life. Judging from
experience, and observing the Belgian tendency to widen the circle of
eligibility of euthanasia beyond the 2002 *Euthanasia Act*, there is a
considerable danger that if being fed up with life becomes a legitimate
consideration for ending life, otherwise healthy people may want access
to euthanasia. These include, among others, those who have just been
separated from their spouses, married people who are grieving over the
death of their spouse and find it difficult to carry on, people who lost
their jobs or parents who have lost a child. Debate will ensue, pressure
will mount on Parliament, some legislatures and physicians will argue for
listening to such appeals and the permissive euthanasia culture in
Belgium might seriously entertain further expansion of the *Euthanasia
Act*. Society and end-of-life practitioners are better off refraining from
engagement with such requests.

Professional Integrity

All the above considerations directly relate to those who are 'tired of life'
and ask physician's aid-in-dying. However, I wish to highlight another

,nsideration that seems to be of important relevance. This consideration refers to the coherent integration of the moral characteristics of the field of medicine. It is about maintaining certain professional standards that are essential for maintaining trust between physicians and those who are dependent on them.

The relationships between physician and patient are not equal. The physician is usually situated in a power position above the patient. The physician has authority and a position to decide the fate of the patient. Thus, power should be exercised judicially and carefully. We know that power can be used and abused. While most physicians will use the power granted to them sensibly, some might either lack the necessary discretion or would not always act with utmost caution. Physicians should be the first to acknowledge this possibility. Therefore, it is in their best interests not to open the door to procedures that might increase the likelihood of abuse. Enlarging the scope of the law to include euthanasia for people who are 'tired of life' might pejoratively affect the integrity of the medical profession. This might 'rock the boat' and undermine trust between physicians and others. The sensible thing is to continue speaking about 'patients' than about 'people' at large.

Moral dilemmas are difficult to resolve. Often their solution is not perfect. Compromises are sought where we weigh each option's benefits and risks. Here the risks are too weighty. Medical professionals must set a certain level of risk that they are expected to assume. Beyond that level, decisions should be optional rather than obligatory. This 'level drawing' is difficult and it may be contested as societal norms are different from one country to another (for instance, Dutch and Belgian societal norms regarding euthanasia are different from the norms in Britain and in Israel). Societal and medical-professional norms are in flux and they do not always exist in harmony (in Britain, polls show that 82 per cent of the public back assisted dying but the British Medical Association opposes all forms of assisted dying),[9] and technology may introduce new standards. At present, medical-professional standards should not include euthanasia for people who are 'tired of life'. If physicians did terminate lives of people who are not suffering from a life-threatening disease, this would change the *raison d'être* of the profession and might endanger lives of many more elderly (or younger), vulnerable people who wish to live.

[9] See Gallagher and Roxby 2015; 'Assisted dying debate: The key questions' 2015; Walsh 2015.

The culture of medicine and the principle of beneficence *should not include death as a way for improving people's health.*

Suggestions for Improvement

The legal guidelines are there to protect and to provide control. The Van Esbeen case was used by euthanasia supporters in Belgium to undermine the guidelines and to enlarge the scope of euthanasia. This enthusiasm opens the door wider for abuse. A fine line distinguishes between ethical decisions regarding a specific case, and policy making. The law is not designed to tailor each scenario and incident. We have courts to decide on specific cases, whether they have standing and whether they are justified. However, courts are often slow and expensive. Thus, it is suggested to address this moral dilemma by putting in place specific regulations. The regulations would require the establishment of an ad hoc committee for each euthanasia request made by people who are 'tired of life'. The ad hoc committee would include three senior experts in the relevant fields of medicine that concern the 'tired of life' applicant. The committee should also include a lawyer and a public representative, possibly an ethicist. The ad hoc committee will consider all the aspects of the petition, meet with the applicant twice in a span of several weeks and decide whether an exception to the law should be made. This procedure of allowing exceptions rather than enlarging the law seems to be more sensible and signals that the role of medicine is still to heal. Only as a last recourse, after exhausting all other options, the autonomy of the person, beneficence, the dignity of the person, care or compassion may persuade physicians to provide aid-in-dying.

In September 2014, an elderly husband and wife from Brussels Francis, 89, and Anne, 86 revealed their plans to die by assisted suicide. Neither was terminally ill, but they feared loneliness if one died before the other. Francis said: 'We want to go together because we both fear for the future . . . It is as simple as this – we are afraid of what lies ahead' (Roberts 2014).[10]

Fearing for the future is natural. We all have some fears regarding the future. Fearing for the future in an old age is understandable. Old people are more vulnerable, less secure. They feel that their journey has come to

---

[10] One editor remarked: The issue of a double assisted suicide/euthanasia raises questions of coercion or influence. In the case of double suicides, it seems that, typically, it is the man who takes the lead. Where one has a terminal illness and the other does not (but is 'tired of life' – or afraid of bereavement) the question of influence is even more difficult.

an end, and that their lives matter less. Some of them lost their viability, their energy. Some feel their contribution to society and to their loved ones is diminished. But if they are provided with the assurance that their lives do matter, that people around them are still enjoying their company, that they are important to them, then they may reconsider their position. As most people wish to continue living, my assumption is that it is possible to rekindle the urge to live. What we need is to reassure old people that they are appreciated, and that it is time for payback: it is time for their loved ones to reward them for many years of caring that they gave for their family. If elderly people do not receive this kind of support from their family, then we should strive to grant them such support, making them feel valuable not vulnerable, precious not obsolete. With the supporting environment, the attraction of death would cease to exist.

I acknowledge that some people are feeling trapped in their present situation. They no longer see the candle that lights their lives. Life lost its meaning for them. They want a way out. Offering death as solace is relatively easy and far less demanding than investing in patients' time and resources. Such an investment is what we should opt for as warranted by humane and compassionate medicine that endorses the values of beneficence, justice, nonmaleficence and enabling patients to make reasoned informed choices (Beauchamp and Childress 2013). Death might then be only one of the available choices, and the very last act after carefully exhausting all other alternatives.

There is a need to involve palliative care consultants to treat people who find life too difficult to bear (Bernheim et al. 2008; Kuin et al. 2004; Cohen-Almagor 2002, 2004, 2015). Being 'tired of life' is not a disease. It is a mental state. It can be addressed with comprehensive care that seeks to improve the patient's mental, spiritual and physical condition. What is suggested is combined efforts of palliative care and involving the patient's loved ones in treatment. Palliative care means a holistic treatment that is designed to help individuals resume their will to live, helping them to rediscover meaning in life. Palliative care aims to relieve suffering and improve the quality of life through specific knowledge and skills, including communication skills; management of pain and other symptoms; psychosocial, spiritual and bereavement support; and coordination of an array of medical and social services (Morrison and Meier 2004; Sampson et al. 2014).[11] It is suggested that all general practitioners in Belgium should undergo such training.

---

[11] For further discussion, see Schenker and Arnold 2015; Leemans 2014.

Conclusion

More than a decade ago, the Dutch Supreme Court considered the 'tired of life' reasoning for euthanasia. The Netherlands has had long experience with the practice of euthanasia and in many respects paved the way for those who pushed for such legislation in Belgium. In a landmark decision, the Court ruled that physicians may not perform euthanasia or help with suicide unless the request comes from a patient suffering from a medically classifiable physical or psychiatric sickness or disorder. Merely being 'tired of life' cannot serve as a basis for physicians to grant euthanasia (Sheldon 2003).

The liberal state has an obligation to protect the vulnerable. Protecting the vulnerable means caring for them. The Belgians are researching the way their dying patients are being handled in a medical context. Their culture of self-searching is certainly necessary. This issue should be put on public agenda and open for debate, examining the pros and cons of every choice of conduct.

The Belgian *Euthanasia Act* was passed only in 2002, and the country is still in the early learning stages (Cohen-Almagor 2009a). We can hope that the Belgians learn from their experience and will devise ways to address the concerns. Having said that, looking at the short history of the euthanasia laws, policy and practice, in Belgium and in the Netherlands may lead us to think that there is something intoxicating about the practice that blinds the eyes of decision-makers, leading them to press forward towards further end-of-life practices without paying ample attention to caution. The scope of tolerance towards the practice of euthanasia is thereby enlarged so that yesterday's red light becomes obsolete today. As the restrictions are removed, practitioners and law-makers are already debating the next step and the additional groups to be included within the more liberal euthanasia policy. This is quite astonishing as human lives are at stake. What is required is a careful study, together with an accumulation of knowledge and data, addressing the above concerns, thereby learning from mistakes and attempting to correct them before rushing to introduce more liberal ways to euthanize people.

12

Euthanasia in Persons with Severe Dementia

CHRIS GASTMANS

Introduction

Global population ageing confronts us with a large variety of challenges (WHO 2015). The number of care dependent older people is expected to increase drastically from 101 million in 2010 to 277 million in 2050 (Alzheimer's Disease International 2013). The sharp rise in the ageing population, furthermore seems to be driving the emergence of the dementia epidemic (Prince et al. 2013; Sosa-Ortiz et al. 2012). Research predicts that the number of people with dementia will double every 20 years (Prince et al. 2013; Ferri et al. 2005). By 2050, 115.4 million people will live with dementia (Prince et al. 2013).

This demographic evolution has increased clinical interest in early diagnosis of dementia and even presymptomatic testing to determine one's risk for developing dementia. These developments were accompanied by advances in genomics, biomarkers, neuroimaging, and refinements in neuropsychology (Brodaty et al. 2011; Draper et al. 2010). Early diagnosis of dementia has some benefits, especially regarding the ability of patients to make autonomous decisions. Patients with dementia recognize early on what is happening, and they can foresee what lies in the future. This gives people the possibility of writing an advance directive while they still have the necessary capacities to do so. In this way, orientations for future care in case of incompetence can be provided (de Boer et al. 2010a). But these opportunities also bring challenges to these affected people. They must adjust emotionally to a condition that will result in loss of mental competence, and they must learn to deal with a complicated future perspective (Draper et al. 2010). Moreover, they must face a lot of uncertainties. The time of onset of symptoms and decline to a dependent state are inexact. Perhaps the most difficult prediction involves whether quality of life will be compromised by the development of dementia, at least during the early and middle stages (Draper et al. 2010).

The demographic as well as clinical evolutions regarding the prevalence, diagnosis, and treatment of dementia result in important new responsibilities for older people, in general, and people with dementia, in particular. How do they deal with the risk of being affected by dementia? What do they think about the quality of their life with dementia and about their subsequent end of life? What are their opinions about vulnerability and dignity in case of dementia? What arrangements do they want to make with their family about the care they will need when they become more dependent? What do they consider to be 'good care' and 'a good death' for persons with dementia? What do they consider to be their own responsibility in 'preparing for the future'? Do they want to write advance directives to plan their life and death after they become incompetent? What do they think about legal regulations regarding patients' rights, advance directives, euthanasia, as well as assisted suicide, and what do these legal frameworks mean for their own situation?

Given the fear of dementia, it is not surprising that in Belgium where euthanasia can only be conducted based on an actual request of a competent person, a growing number of persons with early-stage dementia worry that they will miss the transition to loss of competency. Although many people with a diagnosis of dementia want to postpone euthanasia as long as possible, they want to be sure that euthanasia will be conducted before they lose their competency. The death of the Belgian writer Hugo Claus in 2008 is one of the most mediatized cases of euthanasia in persons with early dementia. This case has certainly encouraged an increase of euthanasia cases in this patient category, although no data are available for Belgium.[1] These cases also provoke much debate about the assessment of competency to express an actual euthanasia request (Draper et al. 2010).

It is precisely the fear of persons with dementia to be euthanized too soon or of missing the opportunity and no longer being able to request euthanasia that provides the context within which older people might wish for an advance euthanasia directive. Although the public in Belgium expresses a positive attitude towards euthanasia in persons with severe dementia, as decreed in an advance euthanasia directive, it is currently not allowed by the Belgian Act on Euthanasia. However, bills have been put forward in the Belgian Parliament to extend the current Act on

---

[1] An indication for this increase is the rise of euthanasia in neuro-psychiatric cases, the category which includes Alzheimer disease (Chambaere et al. 2015a).

Euthanasia towards persons with dementia. By contrast, in the Netherlands, euthanasia in persons with severe dementia, as decreed in an
advance euthanasia directive, is allowed by law (Dutch Ministry of Justice
and Dutch Ministry of Health, Welfare and Sports 2001). The implementation of euthanasia in this patient population, however, is under
discussion (Kouwenhoven et al. 2015; Rurup et al. 2005c).

This chapter formulates critical arguments towards euthanasia in
persons with severe dementia, in which the persons' wishes are decreed
in an advance euthanasia directive. Euthanasia in persons with early-
stage or pre-dementia based on an actual euthanasia request falls outside
the scope of this chapter. First, we briefly outline some information about
dementia, end-of-life decisions in persons with dementia, attitudes
towards euthanasia in dementia, and experiences of the public regarding
old age and dementia. Second, we consider euthanasia for persons with
severe dementia from two major ethical approaches – principlism and
care ethics. A central topic that is used in this section to make our ethical
evaluation more concrete is that of advance euthanasia directives.

End-of-Life Care for Persons with Dementia

In what follows, we outline some relevant information on end-of-life care
for persons with dementia as well as on attitudes towards euthanasia in
persons with severe dementia.

Disorder-Oriented Diagnostics

In this chapter, dementia is used as a generic term to refer to a spectrum
of clinical syndromes. These syndromes are caused by various brain
disorders and are all characterized by combinations of multiple problems
in cognition, mood, or behaviour (American Psychiatric Association
2013). Up to now, the diagnosis of dementia, irrespective of aetiology,
is based on a complex spectrum of clinical inclusion and exclusion
criteria and on neuropsychological and radiologic results. In this
context, the reliability of dementia diagnoses ranges from 65 per cent
to 90 per cent in specialized clinical settings (Dutch Association of
Clinical Geriatrics 2005).

The exact duration of dementia is uncertain, due to the ambiguity
about when dementia begins. Very often, decline is apparent for years
before the diagnosis is made. About five years pass before a person needs
constant care; and death comes, on average, in about three years after this

(Mitchell et al. 2009). Prognostication in severe dementia is challenging and a barrier to providing end-of-life care. Hospice eligibility for dementia is largely based on the Functional Assessment Staging Scale (Mitchell 2007). Stage 7 is defined as having profound memory deficits, total functional dependence, no knowledge of recent or past events, no verbal communication, and no ability to ambulate. The duration of this stage ranges from days to months.

Care-Oriented Diagnostics

Besides diagnosing the disorder, determining the care needs of patients and assessing the burden on, and the capacity of, the informal care system is crucial. For persons suffering from dementia, long-lasting and intense care is an especially important consideration. Most people with dementia are cared for at home and are supported by informal caregivers and professional caregivers. Informal caregivers often assume their duties in good spirits and because of their commitment to the person suffering from dementia; however, sometimes the task of caregiving can become overwhelming (Papastavrou et al. 2007). Caregivers, on the one hand, face the physical burden of daily physical care, and on the other hand, they also face mental stress. The latter derives from several sources: grief over the loss of the person who was once their partner, father or mother; guilt for sometimes failing in some aspect of caregiving, losing one's temper or relinquishing care to a nursing home; shame because of the behaviour of the person with dementia; and social isolation. Even doubt about the course and the unpredictable nature of dementia symptoms can be a real burden.

End-of-Life Decisions in Persons with Dementia in Belgium

Treatment decisions at the end of life are common in contemporary clinical practice. Findings from postmortem questionnaires sent to physicians attending a representative sample of deaths in Flanders (between 1 June 2007 and 30 November 2007) and Brussels (between 1 June 2007 and 30 September 2007) reveal that at least one end-of-life decision was made in 50.7 per cent of deceased persons with dementia (Chambaere et al. 2015b). According to Bert Broeckaert et al. (2009), end-of-life decisions, in principle, can be grouped into three categories. The first group contains decisions whether to initiate or withhold, continue or withdraw curative or life-sustaining treatments, e.g. cardiopulmonary resuscitation, mechanical ventilation, antibiotic treatment, enteral tube feeding.[2] In this group, non-treatment decisions refer to 'withdrawing or withholding a curative or life-sustaining treatment, because in the given situation this treatment is deemed to be no longer meaningful or effective' (Broeckaert et al. 2009, pp. 30–32). In 2007, treatment was withheld and withdrawn in 28.5 per cent and 26.9 per cent of persons with dementia, respectively (Chambaere et al. 2015b).

The second group of treatment decisions according to the conceptual framework of Broeckaert et al. (2009) refers to decisions whether to alleviate pain and other symptoms with, for example, opioids, benzodiazepines, or barbiturates. In this group, the focus of the decisions shifts from a curative and life-sustaining approach to a palliative approach. Pain control refers to 'the intentional administration of analgesics and/or other drugs in dosages and combinations required to adequately relieve pain' (Broeckaert et al. 2009, pp. 32–33). In 2007, intensified alleviation of pain and or symptoms was performed in 37.3 per cent of persons with dementia (Chambaere et al. 2015b). A specific form of pain control is palliative sedation[3]: 'the intentional administration of sedative drugs in dosages and combinations required to reduce the consciousness of a terminal patient as much as necessary to adequately relieve one or more refractory symptoms' (Broeckaert 2002, p. 246). Unfortunately, no data about palliative sedation in persons with dementia are available in Flanders and Brussels.

The third group of treatment decisions at the end of life contains decisions whether to administer purposefully lethal medication. Voluntary euthanasia – the intentionally terminating the life of a patient by someone other than the patient, at this patient's request – did not occur in persons with dementia in Flanders and Brussels in 2007, although 1.3 per cent had made a formal euthanasia request (Chambaere et al. 2015b). Non-voluntary euthanasia[4] is the intentional termination of the life of a patient by someone other than the patient, not at this patient's request.

---

[2] A Cochrane review revealed that there is insufficient evidence to support that enteral tube feeding is beneficial in patients with advanced dementia. Data are lacking on the adverse effects of this intervention (Sampson et al. 2009).

[3] Although palliative sedation is mostly initiated to relieve physical suffering (pain), it is sometimes also initiated to relieve psychological distress.

[4] As Belgium follows the Dutch definition of euthanasia ('the intentionally terminating of life of a patient by someone other than the patient, at this patient's request'), intentional termination of life without request is not 'euthanasia' in the strict sense of this definition.

This illegal practice occurred in 2007 in 3.9 per cent of persons with dementia (Chambaere et al. 2015b).

Palliative Care in Persons with Dementia

The current scientific state of affairs suggests that persons with dementia typically do not suffer severely from the dementia itself. Rather, any severe suffering they may experience is more likely to be related to symptoms (e.g., trouble breathing, agitation, confusion, pain, fear) caused by other disorders. For example, pneumonia is the immediate precipitating cause of death in more than 50 per cent of cases (Chen et al. 2006). It is difficult to diagnose physical suffering in persons with dementia; therefore, it often remains undertreated (van der Steen 2010; Scherder et al. 2005).

Specific studies performed in hospices proved that applying a palliative care approach in the care of terminally ill patients with dementia contributes greatly to a dignified end of life, especially when caregivers apply adequate pain control and when they support the patient's close relatives and loved ones (Nuffield Council of Bioethics 2009; Mitchell et al. 2007). Even though hospice services benefit persons with severe dementia, most do not receive these services. Barriers to hospice enrolment include accurate prognostication, lack of recognition of dementia as a terminal condition, and accessibility of hospice services in nursing homes (van der Steen et al. 2014).

Attitudes Towards Euthanasia in Persons with Severe Dementia

Since the early 1990s, an intense social debate about euthanasia in persons with severe dementia has existed in the Netherlands. Research into the practice of euthanasia in persons with dementia reveals that from 1998 till 2012, about 4.3 per cent to 6.8 per cent of Dutch elderly (65–90 years old) have completed an advance euthanasia directive (Evans et al. 2015). The following types of elderly people were more likely to have an advance euthanasia directive: elderly who were single, elderly who did not adhere to a specific faith, elderly who did not trust their physician to carry out their end-of-life wishes, and elderly who suffered from a chronic disorder or who experienced functional restrictions (Rurup et al. 2006a).

Only a few cases of euthanasia in persons with dementia based on an advance euthanasia directive have been reported in the Netherlands

(Sheldon 2011). However, this does not necessarily mean that euthanasia in persons with dementia does not occur more regularly in the Netherlands. Twenty-nine per cent of Dutch physicians (general practitioners and nursing home physicians) stated that they have already treated a person with dementia who had an advance euthanasia directive (Rurup et al. 2005c). Three per cent of these physicians stated that they have performed euthanasia in a person with dementia based on an advance directive. Forty-four per cent stated that, although they have not performed euthanasia in these patients to date, they have not ruled out the possibility of performing euthanasia in the future. Fifty-four per cent of the physicians ruled out the possibility of performing euthanasia on persons with dementia in the future. The latter considered euthanasia in persons with dementia to be unacceptable. Furthermore, they did not view an advance euthanasia directive as a valid request. In more recent empirical studies, the negative attitudes of Dutch physicians towards euthanasia in advanced dementia were confirmed (Kouwenhoven et al. 2015; Kouwenhoven et al. 2013; de Boer et al. 2011; de Boer et al. 2010b). Crucial in the reticent attitudes of physicians appears to be the impossibility of patient-physician communication at the time of decision making as well as the impossibility to receive confirmation of the unbearableness of suffering.

The study of Rurup et al. (2006b) showed that, in the Netherlands, the patients' relatives often adopt a more tolerant attitude towards life-terminating behaviour in persons with dementia than nurses and physicians. Ninety per cent of relatives, 57 per cent of the nurses, and 16 per cent of physicians agreed with the statement that euthanasia based on an advance directive in persons with dementia is acceptable. However, in more recent studies, some relatives and members of the general public were found to be reluctant to adhere to advance euthanasia directives in case of dementia (Kouwenhoven et al. 2015; de Boer et al. 2011). A similar trend was reported in other countries (Tomlinson and Stott 2015). A qualitative interview study with dementia carers in the United Kingdom revealed that while there was a general acceptance of the right to die, the need for caution and careful deliberation was emphasized (Tomlinson et al. 2015). In Finland, 8 per cent of physicians are in favour of euthanasia in persons with severe dementia (Ryynänen et al. 2002). Studies in Australia, Canada, Finland, and the Netherlands report that approximately a third (or just under) of nurses support euthanasia in persons with severe dementia (Rurup et al. 2006b; Ryynänen et al. 2002; Armstrong-Esther et al. 1999; Kitchener and Jorm 1999). Studies in

Finland, the Netherlands, and United Kingdom examining general public attitudes towards euthanasia in severe dementia found that around 50 per cent were in favour (Williams et al. 2007; Ryynänen et al. 2002; van Holsteyn and Trappenburg 1998). Kouwenhoven et al. (2013) even reported 77 per cent of the Dutch sample in favour. No research results are reported concerning the attitudes towards euthanasia in persons with severe dementia in Belgium.

Psychosocial Experiences of the General Public

Today's generation of older people living in Western societies perceives the prospect of progressing dementia in their own way (Nuffield Council on Bioethics 2009). The mental suffering one experiences as one faces a progression towards dementia is influenced by the fear of having to be dependent on others, the fear of losing one's dignity, and the fear of being a burden.

Many healthy seniors take for granted their ability to arrange their lives according to their own desires and needs, with only minimal assistance from others. Autonomy as a social goal does not only mean that older people who lose the capacities to lead an autonomous life are rather perceived as a 'burden' than as human beings. It also entails that these people consider themselves to be 'less of a person', as people 'who count as nothing' (Agich 2003). Thus, older persons may view their situation as 'problematic' rather than ideal, if they involuntarily become dependent on others (Lloyd 2004).

Many older people often associate dignity with autonomy, independence and preserving one's intellectual powers (Woolhead et al. 2004). Some especially believe that the fear of losing one's intellectual capacity and the risk of being handed over to the will of others when one becomes incompetent are notable reasons for wanting to be euthanized in a timely way (Kouwenhoven et al. 2015; Hardwig 1997).

A growing number of seniors do not wish to become a burden to their relatives. They do not want to be reduced to people who are merely the object of other people's responsibility. For many older persons, the fear of becoming a burden to their relatives is greater than their fear of death (Dening et al. 2012; Pearlman et al. 1993). Financial matters do not represent the only aspect of burden; rather, older persons mainly fear that their relatives will have to pay a high emotional price when caring for them (McPherson et al. 2007).

Euthanasia in Persons with Severe Dementia: Ethical Approaches

Although, to our knowledge, no official ethical documents on euthanasia for patients with severe dementia exist, some philosophical ethical studies (Cohen-Almagor 2016; Cholbi 2015; Gastmans 2013; den Hartogh 2013; Nys 2013b; Johnstone 2013; Sharp 2012; Alvargonzalez 2012; Gastmans and De Lepeleire 2010; Draper et al. 2010; Gastmans and Denier 2010; Hertogh et al. 2007) have been conducted. The topic of advance euthanasia directives for patients with dementia enables us to present two influential ethical approaches to end-of-life care in persons with dementia; the principles-oriented autonomy approach that generally favours the use of advance euthanasia directives on the one hand, and the care-oriented relational approach that mostly criticizes advance euthanasia directives on the other hand.

Principles-Oriented Autonomy Approach

As already indicated in this chapter, many older people associate dignity with autonomy, independence, and preserving one's intellectual powers. Losing one's autonomy and cognitive capacities may be the reason for some to request euthanasia via an advance euthanasia directive in a timely way (den Hartogh 2013). These advance directives rely on the authority of the competent pre-dementia person (the 'then' self) to govern the welfare of the incompetent person with dementia (the 'now' self) (Draper et al. 2010; Dworkin 2003b; Dworkin 2006). Proponents of this 'precedent autonomy or critical interest' approach underline the stewardship responsibility of the 'then' self for the journey into forgetfulness (Dworkin 2006; Dworkin 2003b; Post 1995). Therefore, post-dementia decisions should be based on historical lifetime values and beliefs. De Boer et al. (2010a) clarify:

> The former decisions of a person with dementia, laid down in an advance directive, remain in force because the person now lacks the necessary capacity to exercise autonomy, and because the critical interests of the formerly competent person (the 'then' self) prevail over the actual preferences or experiences of the person who is now in a state of dementia (the 'now' self). The experiences of the demented person are not part of the autonomous decision-making.
>
> (de Boer et al. 2010a)

An important presupposition of this approach is that individuals are perfectly capable of determining their wishes concerning their end-of-life care individually as well as cognitively, and in such a way that advance directives unambiguously tell caregivers what to do. Persons are, in this approach, mainly considered as beings with thoughts, intelligence, reason, reflection, and consciousness (Hughes 2001). To facilitate the development of advance directives, decision aids are presented. These aids help people by providing neutral information about the dementia process, so that they can make an informed decision (Levi and Green 2010).

Respect for autonomy largely covers moral reasoning on advance euthanasia directives. Within the included literature, autonomy is mainly described as the right to self-determination and individual choice (den Hartogh 2013). Respect for autonomy is founded upon the ideal of the autonomous and rational agent. As an autonomous person, one is entitled to act in accordance with a freely self-chosen and informed plan. Within this anthropological viewpoint, advance euthanasia directives are instruments that enable the autonomous wishes of some people, concerning what they believe to be a dignified end of life, to be respected.

Care-Oriented Relational Approach

While the principle of respect for autonomy generally leads to an argument in favour of advance euthanasia directives, questions arise about its applicability to cases in which dementia patients are involved. Because dementia is marked by progressive deterioration, affecting both the memory and reasoning capabilities, dementia patients fall short of the ideal of the autonomous agent that grounds the principle of respect for autonomy (Nuffield Council on Bioethics 2009). Hence, according to the proponents of the care-oriented relational approach, ethical reflection on the end-of-life of persons with dementia should not start from the ideal of the autonomous and rational agent, but from the relational context in which dementia care practices are embedded.

By providing care, caregivers enter as persons into a relationship with a vulnerable fellow human being – a person with dementia – who needs care. However, it is not clear from the beginning what answer can be considered as the most adequate and appropriate answer to the care needs of a particular person with dementia. Finding the right answer is not the result of a general and abstract balancing of principles or of logical deduction, it is reached through a shared dialogical process of communication, interpretation, and understanding that takes place within the care relationship (Widdershoven and Berghmans 2001).

CHRIS GASTMANS

Based on this relational approach to dementia care, some clusters of problems that are associated with the use of advance euthanasia directives according to the above-mentioned autonomy approach have been formulated (Gastmans 2013; Gastmans and De Lepeleire 2010; Gastmans and Denier 2010; Hertogh 2009; Hertogh et al. 2007).

Interpretation

The first group of problems is related to the interpretation of a patient's wishes. As many authors have already pointed out, clearly expressing one's wishes and thoughts can be difficult. But also, interpreting the meaning of a patient's wishes is a difficult task for fellow human beings, such as family members and caregivers. A patient's wishes cannot be considered a given, whose contents can easily be deduced from an advance directive and which clarifies for all those involved what must be done for the patient throughout the consecutive stages of his or her care. What a patient would have wanted under specific circumstances needs to be constructed through fairly elaborated interpretative processes, based on what we know of his or her life, previous pronouncements (e.g., as reported in advance directives), and the patient's actual reactions to concrete proposals (Agich 2003). Even if persons with dementia might be incompetent, they still have the capacity to experience their life and the context wherein it is embedded (de Boer et al. 2010a). Hence, contemporary preferences, needs and desires, coupled with the present well-being of the person with dementia should be the main area for substituted decision making. This perspective on the relationship between the 'then' self who existed prior to the onset of dementia and the 'now' self who lives almost entirely in the present without any connection to the past, is known as the so-called experiential interest approach (Draper et al. 2010; Dresser 1995).[5]

Even if, as in advance euthanasia directives, the medical decision to be performed – euthanasia – is very clear, communication and interpretation is still needed. The specific difficulty resides in having to determine the moment when euthanasia should be performed. Suppose, for

---

[5] The distinction between the 'then self' and 'now self' should not be considered as a simple one and even not as a dichotomy. In general, one can say that both past and present views of the person with dementia should be considered. Whether one or the other perspective predominates might depend in part on the issue in focus, the danger of harm, as well as the basis behind prior decisions. This idea is extensively described by the Nuffield Council on Bioethics (2009).

instance, that a person with an early dementia diagnosis has been able to clearly state that he or she wants euthanasia from the moment that he or she no longer recognizes his or her child. This advance euthanasia directive is not self-executing. The physician should determine whether this person's actual situation does indeed match the circumstances specified by him or her in the advance directive calling for euthanasia to be performed. This is very difficult, for even carefully formulated specifications about the chosen moment of death require interpretation (Hertogh et al. 2007; Widdershoven and Berghmans 2001). For instance, how should one determine the act of recognition? There are many ways of recognizing a person. Where should the line be drawn (Widdershoven and Berghmans 2001)? The fact that it is almost impossible to determine the moment of death in such cases is especially due to the development stages of dementia itself. Patients suffering from severe dementia can still have good moments from time to time, no matter how diminished these may be (Gastmans and Denier 2010).

Future Forecasting

This brings us to the category of problems with future forecasting. They refer to the fact that a person's preferences and values can change[6]; to the fact that people's ability to constructively adapt to even the most severe debilities; and to the fact that previously communicated wishes may not reflect a change of heart (Hertogh 2009). The problem with a person suffering from dementia, however, is that it is impossible for that person to reconsider the decisions outlined in his or her advance euthanasia directive. The issue of irreversibility is much stronger in persons with dementia. It may be that the person with an advance euthanasia directive offers resistance when the action is performed. How is such resistance to be interpreted? Hence the dilemma faced by physicians and proxies: how to balance the actual preferences and experiences of the person with dementia against the patient's earlier opinions laid down in a now-forgotten advance directive (Gastmans and Denier 2010; de Boer et al. 2010a; Hertogh et al. 2007; Widdershoven and Berghmans 2001). Following the 'experiential interest approach', the well-being and interests

---

[6] For instance, person's preferences can change because of new developments in the treatment of dementia. New treatments can be developed which would be seen as acceptable to the person with dementia had he or she known about them at the time of writing the advance directive.

of the 'now' self are of moral significance, and the absolute primacy of precedent autonomy seems to be wrong (Post 1995). Goering clarifies:

> This does not mean that we should never make plans for our future-selves; rather, it means that we should take care to provide for flexibility in any advance directive, with the recognition that our values or priorities may change, and due to declining decisional capacities, those judgements may need to be made by others in conjunction with our future-selves, rather than solely and individually by our presently competent selves.
>
> (Goering 2007, p. 63)

Individual Versus Relational Autonomy

This brings us to another group of problems that is situated on the level of the patient's autonomy versus the patient being related to other people such as relatives, friends, and caregivers. It seems that, in the case of advance euthanasia directives, supporting the respect for autonomy principle is much more complicated. People's wishes and values are very often of a pre-reflexive and emotional kind. Without sufficient attention to emotions, feelings of grief or even resistance, within an ongoing, interpersonal face-to-face dialogue between the patient and other people (e.g., relatives, friends, caregivers), one risks entering a situation in which people can easily draft an advance euthanasia directive on their personal computer, while being in a state of panic or depression, or having little or unclear information about the course of dementia. In this case, advance euthanasia directives could even increase the vulnerability of the patient, as they do not reflect a well-informed wish of the patient (Gastmans and Denier 2010).

Finally, a patient's decision to write an advance euthanasia directive has important implications for all parties involved in the patient's care (Hertogh et al. 2007). The decision to perform euthanasia at a certain moment in time must be made by someone other (e.g. the physician) than the patient himself or herself. This can create dissensions between the parties involved. This clearly demonstrates the contradiction that is inher-ent to the autonomy approach when applied to advance euthanasia direct-ives in persons with dementia: To what extent can our fellow man be given the responsibility to ensure that our right of self-determination is respected?

Communication and Shared Understanding

All these critical remarks bring us to the basic problem that weakens the use of advance euthanasia directives: the lack of communication and shared understanding between the demented patient, on the one hand, and the caregivers, on the other hand. Margaret Battin (2007, p. 59) confirms:

> To end the life of a patient, even if fully legal, is not an easy process for a physician. We can assume it would be even more difficult when it is no longer possible for the physician to discuss the issue rationally with the patient and to have the patient's wish explicitly confirmed, and especially difficult when there is no evidence of current suffering other than the fact of having dementia disease.

This observation is confirmed by studies from the Netherlands where, despite the legal recognition of advance euthanasia directives for persons with dementia, euthanasia occurs rarely in this patient group (de Boer et al. 2011; de Boer et al. 2010b; Rurup et al. 2006a; Rurup et al. 2006b). The Dutch researchers concluded that:

> communication and interpretation are crucial in determining the circumstances as well as the exact moment of performing euthanasia and this cannot be captured in or replaced by advance euthanasia directives. This is precisely what seems to cause the fundamental problem of complying with advance euthanasia directives in cases of severe dementia.
>
> (de Boer et al. 2010b, p. 261)

According to Cees Hertogh (2009), conducting euthanasia in a person with severe dementia based on an advance euthanasia directive seems to be equivalent to attempting to operate in the dark. He refers to a fundamental vulnerability that physicians experience if the dialogical and interpretative aspects of end-of-life care are no longer present. This is precisely what becomes clear when caring for severely ill demented patients who are unable to discuss their euthanasia requests as formulated in advance euthanasia directives.

Given the above-mentioned difficulties that arise from advance euthanasia directives when conceptualized within a principles-oriented autonomy approach, some authors suggest a care-oriented relational approach to deal with advance euthanasia directives (de Boer et al. 2010a; Gastmans and Denier 2010; Hertogh et al. 2007). According to them, considering the dialogical and interpretative nature of ethical decision making should be a standard and indispensable element of good dementia care. As Moody says: 'The heart of the matter is not to be found in the legal instrument as much as in the process of communication and negotiation which leads up to the result' (Moody 1992, p. 92). In the care-oriented relational approach, the search for what is best for the patient should not solely focus on the patient's wishes as an isolated individual, but should always start with listening to the concerns expressed by the patient, his or her close relatives, his or her caregivers, etc., because they outline the rich relational context in which the person's care must take shape. Understanding persons implies an understanding of the relational stories in which they are embedded (Hughes 2001). Decision making is a process of sharing the decision between all people involved. There will never be a legal instrument or a simple paper process that provides an escape from this demanding process of communication and interpretation among parties to a decision. Therefore, these authors suggest that advance euthanasia directives have their uses, for example, to facilitate the ethical dialogue and the interpretation process among all people involved. However, such directives in fact cannot replace communication and interpretation (Tulsky 2005; Widdershoven and Berghmans 2001).

Conclusion

Ensuring a dignified end of life for persons with severe dementia is a subject that requires increasing attention from caregivers and from society, in general. In Belgium, there seems to be a public consensus that the legalization of advance euthanasia directives is to be considered a necessary step to be taken to improve the quality of end-of-life care for persons with severe dementia. This chapter showed that ensuring a dignified end of life for persons with dementia is not an isolated fact and is not only linked to the legalization of advance euthanasia directives. The view about whether to perform euthanasia in persons with severe dementia is linked to how we consider a good human life and a good death, and to what role autonomy and relational embeddedness play in people's lives. Furthermore, the decision about whether to perform euthanasia also fits in with the approach on end-of-life decision making. Principle-based and care-based approaches clearly suggest quite different ways to deal with end-of-life decisions in persons with severe dementia. Nevertheless, further ethical analysis is needed, so that simplistic answers are not provided to quite complex ethical issues.

PART IV

Euthanasia in Belgium

A Philosophical and Bioethical Discussion

13

Some Possible Consequences Arising from the Normalisation of Euthanasia in Belgium

CALUM MACKELLAR

Introduction

Since the legalisation of euthanasia, in Belgium, in 2002 it is now possible to examine whether developments in the normalisation of this practice are beginning to take place. In other words, it is possible to study whether euthanasia is becoming a more 'normal' occurrence in this country.

In this regard, it is acknowledged that what is 'normal' may lack any precise definition but the term may be used to mean what 'constitutes or conforms to a type or standard' (Oxford English Dictionary 2016b). That is, an object or quality or measure to which others should conform or against which others are judged. Alternatively, the concept of what is 'normal' can be characterised simply as what is 'regular' or 'usual' which represents something which 'commonly occurs' or be interpreted, in statistical terms, as being 'typical, ordinary, or conventional' (Oxford English Dictionary 2016b).

The tension between these two meanings gives rise to the naturalistic fallacy, the unwarranted move from the 'is' of mere frequency to the 'ought' of what is good or right. Nevertheless, while customs or conventions can be criticised, the existence of some social conventions and common attitudes is the presupposition for law and morality. The norms of a society are usually implicit in the actual practices of that society. It is for this reason that as practices become usual, meaning more frequent, they are increasingly accepted as normal, in the sense of conforming to a social standard. Such norms can be challenged but the more deeply rooted a practice becomes, the more it will carry the presumptive force of precedent or social approval.

With respect to human behaviour, it may be difficult to differentiate 'normal' from 'abnormal' because the distinction hinges on societal perceptions of the condition in question (Jackson 2001, p. 97). This also means that normality is not an all-encompassing permanent concept and may be viewed as '*an endless process of man's self-creation and his reshaping of the world*' (Syristová 2010).

From this perspective, the present study will restrict itself to examining developments in which euthanasia may be starting to be considered as normal in Belgium. It will do this without focusing on proposed theories about the way certain behaviours become normal. This will avoid the complex discussions relating to the validity of arguments concerning the causes of a societal behaviour such as 'slippery slopes' which have proved controversial.[1] This is not to say that slippery slope arguments are not plausible or valid. But the present discussion will seek to restrict itself to just observing the present existing, incontestable and verifiable situation while acknowledging that the normalisation of a procedure does not begin in a societal vacuum.[2]

In addition, the study will emphasise that what can be considered as normal in society is generally dependent on a significant number of factors which cannot just be considered independently from one another. These include, but are not restricted to, (1) the passing of time since the procedure was accepted, (2) the location of a state such as Belgium and the influence of its neighbouring countries and (3) an increasing number of persons accepting and accessing the procedure together with its eventual subsequent legalisation. What is normal also varies with societal expectations and norms though what may be perceived as the norm may not actually be the most common behaviour.

Normality and Timeframes

In considering the concept of normality, what may be considered as normal at one moment in time may be quite abnormal at another. For example, many elements in human behaviour have changed over the centuries and even decades. People no longer dress, speak or eat in

---

[1] Many commentators have defended the use of arguments, such as the slippery slope, in ethical analysis. For example: Volokh 2003; Keown 2002; Jones 2011; Lerner and Caplan 2015. Others, however, have raised questions relating to the relevance of such arguments such as: Burgess 1993; Lewis 2007; Enoch 2001; Catherwood 2006; Shariff 2012.

[2] For instance, it is very probable that discussions relating to the legalisation of euthanasia in Belgium began when societal values started to change including: (1) An increasing focus on individualism and personal autonomy amongst many members of society; (2) A reluctance to accept the existence of meaning in suffering which should, as a result, always be avoided at any cost; (3) A difficulty in understanding or accepting the inherent value, meaning and dignity of every human life which cannot be lost.

the same way as in the past. There is a continual evolution in time of normality. But, interestingly, for a behaviour to be considered as normal there is also a requirement that it remains established for a relatively prolonged period.

Thus, the fact that many years have now passed since the legalisation of euthanasia in Belgium, without any significant moves for the legislation to be repealed, makes it possible to accept that the procedure is becoming more normal and established in time. How this development is taking place will not, as indicated, be examined but is likely to involve very complex multi-factorial influences.

This acceptance of euthanasia over the years (Cohen et al. 2014) does, however, enable a more objective study to be considered in examining the factual and verifiable evolution of practice.

Normality and Location

Once more, what may be normal in one setting, such as in a certain country, may be considered very abnormal in another. For instance, people do not dress, speak or even eat in the same way in different parts of the world. Thus, what is considered as being normal will very much depend on the specific place or situation, including the geographical and cultural proximity of other communities.

This suggests that different countries do influence each other especially when they are neighbours or have similar traditions and communities. Neighbouring societies are, moreover, generally interested and curious about what is happening in their vicinity. This is probably what happened in the closely knit Benelux countries where euthanasia was first legalised in the Netherlands which was then followed by Belgium and finally by Luxembourg. The influence of the Netherlands in encouraging a euthanasia debate in Belgium, which eventually resulted in the legalisation of the practice, cannot be underestimated (Pereira 2011).

On the other hand, even though euthanasia may already be starting to be considered as normal in Belgium, the situation remains very different in several other European countries where it remains a very serious offence resulting in sentences which may include imprisonment.

Normality and Increasing Acceptance

Changes in the concept of what is understood to be normal may also depend on the number of people who begin to accept a new set of

s. Sometimes, this may represent a slow process in which adjust-
; in attitudes are only very gradual. In Belgium, for example,
ѵшсıal campaigns for the legalisation of euthanasia began as early as
1981 with the creation of the French speaking *Association belge pour le
droit de mourir dans la dignité* (Belgian Association for the Right to Die
with Dignity) followed by the formation in 1983 of its Flemish, Dutch-
speaking, counterpart entitled *Vereniging voor het recht op waardig
sterven* (Association for the Right to Die with Dignity) (Cohen-
Almagor 2009b).

These campaigns slowly began to influence the media as well as the
Belgian parliament with draft euthanasia legislation being submitted
as far back as 1984 (Broeckaert 2001). As a result, an active debate
developed in Belgian society including amongst academics and the official multidisciplinary *Comité Consultatif de Bioéthique* (Consultative
Committee on Bioethics) which was created to act as a focal point for
discussions and advice on bioethical matters (Cohen-Almagor 2009b).

Although euthanasia remained illegal at the time, being considered
under criminal law as intentionally causing the death of a person, there
were very few prosecutions and the practice was, to all intents and
purposes, tolerated in Belgium (Broeckaert 2001). Some reports indicated that even before euthanasia was decriminalised, a significant
number of deaths amongst the 10 million people living in Belgium could
actually be considered as 'informal' acts of euthanasia (Osborn 2001).
More specifically, a 1998 study which took place in Flanders, the Dutch-
speaking part of Belgium which includes about 60 per cent of the Belgian
population, stated that 1.3 per cent of all deaths in this region could be
considered as euthanasia or assisted suicide (Deliens et al. 2000).

This means that it was because several health care professionals deliberately ignored and broke Belgian law and were not prosecuted that
euthanasia legislation was apparently seen as necessary to make what
was already happening legal. The change ostensibly occurred as a kind of
'fait accompli' by several physicians before euthanasia had been decriminalised and without any appropriate consideration of the ethical reasons
behind the historical legal prohibitions nor of the possible future consequences that may arise. Such a development, however, is very concerning
because ignoring existing legislation in such a manner reflects a somewhat alarming and cavalier attitude towards the rule of law in a civilised
society.

Eventually, on the 20th of January 2001, and after the government
coalition had changed, a commission on euthanasia in Belgium's senate

voted to accept draft euthanasia legislation for adults an (Weber 2001). Following this, on the 25 October 2001, I house voted in favour of the proposed law by a maj(23 against, 2 abstentions and 2 senators who failed to re$

Amongst the general public, an opinion survey no 75 per cent of persons, responding to a questionnaire, wer in agreement with the legislation (Osborn 2001).

Finally, on the 16 May 2002, the Belgian lower house of parliament confirmed its support for the decriminalisation of euthanasia by 86 votes in favour and 51 against, with 10 abstentions (Griffiths et al. 2008, Cohen-Almagor 2004, p. 37).

Consequences Relating to Majority Votes on Legislation

The vote in favour of euthanasia in the Belgian parliament is significant because when the majority of members of the Belgian parliament, who represent the citizens of this country, began to accept that euthanasia should be legalised, this may also mean to some extent that it was starting to be considered as normal in society. Indeed, a democratic parliamentary vote is generally a good reflection of what many people in that country consider normal or want to consider normal.

As the Belgian sociologist, Kenneth Chambaere, indicates 'In Belgium, the fact that the majority supports euthanasia means that it has actually become part of our culture', adding: 'Ethical paradigms change over time. We've seen that throughout history' (quoted in Hamilton 2013). A majority vote in parliament is also a signal that there is now an official acceptance, on behalf of the state, that such procedures can take place without any fear of retribution.

Steady Increase in Numbers of Euthanasia Cases in Belgium

As already indicated (see chapters by Montero and Jones), an annual increase in the official number of persons accessing euthanasia in Belgium has been noted since the legalisation of euthanasia in Belgium in 2002.

This steady increase demonstrates, at least from the perspective of numbers, that the practice is 'increasingly considered as a valid option at the end of life in Belgium' (Chambaere et al. 2015a, p. 1180) and accepted as being more usual, and so more normal.

Horizon Scanning

Since the previous section indicates that several observed, undeniable and verifiable developments have taken place in Belgium, over several years, which have contributed to making euthanasia more acceptable, usual and normal, it is extremely unlikely that the present situation will suddenly just come to an end. Thus, it may be useful to now examine the way future developments may continue and how this can affect societal prospects. To do this, a horizon scanning exercise can be undertaken which has been defined by the United Kingdom Government in 2013 as: 'A systematic examination of information to identify potential threats, risks, emerging issues and opportunities' (UK Government Cabinet Office 2013). In other words, horizon scanning can be considered as an overall term for examining and considering future developments and consequences including the way in which emerging trends might potentially affect policy and practice.

This is important since in the same way as information about possible risks are provided to a patient before a medical intervention during the informed consent procedure, the same should also take place at a national level. This means that it is imperative that appropriate information about possible risks and advantages are provided to a society and its parliament before it can responsibly consent to legalise a certain procedure.

At this stage, however, it should be emphasised that what will be examined in the horizon scanning exercise are only potential prospects since it is impossible to predict the future with certainty or to demonstrate, rationally, that the following developments will happen. But this does not mean that what will be considered is very improbable and should be ignored. A responsible attitude demands that society and parliaments consider all possible developments, including how likely they are of occurring.

Possible Consequences of Normality

The Momentous Implications of the Legislation

Before trying to understand what possible risks and advantages may arise in the future because of developments in Belgium relating to euthanasia, it may be useful to return to what the Belgian parliament actually decided when it made its momentous decision to legalise the practice. Arguably, it was not just a decision to legalise what was already taking place or relating to the kind of safeguards to be implemented when considering the deliberate ending of a life. By far the most significant aspect was the acceptance, for the first time in Belgian history, that some lives may no longer have any value, worth and meaning and should be ended.[3] In this regard, John Keown, argues that the acceptance by a national parliament of a procedure, such as euthanasia, can only take place if it is 'grounded in the belief that some patients have lives which are no longer "worth living" and that they would be "better off dead"' (Keown 2014, p. 1).

This was the landmark decision that Belgium made concerning the way it now considers the value, worth and meaning of some human lives though many in Belgium may have been, or remain, unaware of this momentous change. It is on this basis and from this context, therefore, that the horizon scanning exercise must take place.

Having noted this radical change in how Belgium now considers the value of some human life, it is possible to try to consider likely advantages, threats and risks emerging from the legalisation of euthanasia in Belgium.

Possible Advantages Resulting from Legalising Euthanasia

There are certainly perceived advantages in legalising euthanasia especially in the way individuals may experience more freedom to make decisions at the end of their lives. For example, advocates of euthanasia suggest that individuals should be able to determine their own dignity and quality of life, unrestricted by the moral, cultural, religious or personal beliefs of others. Moreover, it has been proposed that persons who fear that they will lose their dignity during the final stages of a terminal illness should be able to 'die with dignity' before these stages occur.

Those supporting euthanasia also indicate that it would enable persons, who become terminally ill and find themselves in an unbearable situation, to avoid suffering a slow, drawn-out death. They suggest that nobody has the right to impose on the terminally ill and the dying an obligation to live out their lives when they, themselves, have persistently expressed the wish to die.

Advocates further argue that some persons' fear of disability and dependency should enable them to die through euthanasia, if they so

---

[3] It is indeed this message which American bioethicists William Reichel and Arthur J. Dyck (1989, p. 1322) have indicated may be the foundation of euthanasia movements.

wish, while they are still autonomous. In other words, individuals have the right to take decisions concerning their own life and death situations in accordance with their own values and beliefs. It is a question of freedom, autonomy and equality in the face of death.

But there are also several risks relating to the decriminalisation of euthanasia which cannot be ignored.

The State Cannot Control What Is Seen as Normal in Euthanasia

Interestingly, the normality of a procedure may be affected by its legalisation. This is because, for many individuals, what is perceived as legally possible may influence what they believe they can do and what is acceptable. For example, this idea was reflected by the Health and Sport Committee of the Scottish Parliament which indicated in 2015 that 'when law permits a practice, this is perceived as endorsement, and as society absorbs that endorsement, the general perception of the practice changes'. (Health and Sport Committee of the Scottish Parliament 2015, paragraph 275) In other words, the passing of legislation permitting a certain procedure may influence the manner in which this procedure is regarded which can then be the basis for further changes.

It has also been acknowledged that any piece of legislation cannot control all the different manners in which it may eventually be used. Because of the sheer number of different applications which arise in a large country, it is recognised that some legislation may eventually be pushed to its limit. As Paul Vanden Berghe et al., indicates 'there is an indication that euthanasia, once the barrier of legalisation is passed, tends to develop a dynamic of its own and extend beyond the agreed restrictions, in spite of earlier explicit reassurances that this would not happen – in Belgium, such reassurances were given when the 2002 law was being debated' (Vanden Berghe et al. 2013, p. 271)[4].

Similarly, Etienne Montero, explains that when 'precedents' and 'exceptions' exist they usually tend to expand the law (Montero 2013, p. 75) while concluding: 'The Belgian experience teaches that once euthanasia is permitted, it is very difficult to maintain a strict interpretation of the fixed legal conditions. By interpreting in different ways indications for euthanasia, they continue to diversify despite the initial

---

[4] This important article, by the Director, President, Honorary President and Ethics Committee Chair of the Federation of Palliative Care Flanders, is reproduced in chapter 4 of the present volume with a new postscript.

SOME POSSIBLE CONSEQUENCES OF EUTHANASIA IN BELGIUM 22

declarations and intentions of the legislator' (Montero 2013, p. 128, translated by C. MacKellar).

Extension of the Qualifying Conditions for Euthanasia

Legislation often comes under pressure because once a procedure begins to be considered as normal there then seems to be a tendency for procedures, only slightly different from the original one, to also be included in what should be considered as normal. This usually takes place, amongst several other possible explanations which will not be examined, through a reasoning process whereby it is demonstrated that the new procedures do not differ, in any significant or meaningful manner, to the ones that have previously been accepted and legalised by society.

With respect to euthanasia in Belgium this has already been observed, over the past years, in that special cases have been presented demanding, through reasoned arguments based on notions such as justice and equality, that they be considered in the same manner as what has already been accepted by society.

Since it is likely that the very basis for accepting euthanasia came as a response to what was (1) unbearable suffering and (2) a support for autonomy, several consequences may arise. These include the suggestion that when any individual's suffering becomes unacceptable or his or her autonomy is threatened, euthanasia may be a reasonable solution. If this is refused, it would be for society and the government to give appropriate reasons for allowing euthanasia in one set of circumstances but not in another.

To some extent, there is a certain rationale to this continuous extension of qualifying conditions for euthanasia (Volokh 2003). If one set of applications are accepted as new, compelling reasons for change become more reasonable through the process of acclimatisation, whereby individuals adjusts to a gradual change in their social environment. Through such a process, previous applications may be seen to become more acceptable and normal. A form of desensitisation may be taking place whereby a procedure may no longer be seen as contentious since it is now in a new social setting (Den Hartogh 2009). As indicated by American legal academic, Eugene Volokh, '[E]very decision changes the political, economic and psychological conditions under which future decisions are made' (quoted in Shariff 2012, p. 143).

Keown, illustrates this reasoning by presenting two imaginary identical twin patients who are both affected by the same terminal illness and suffering to the same extent though one is mentally competent while the other is not. If the one who is competent is given access to euthanasia because he can make a responsible decision and is experiencing unbearable suffering, it would be difficult to build a strong case opposing the extension of euthanasia to the second twin. This is because even though he does not have the mental capacity to make the decision, he would be suffering unbearably in a similar manner to the first twin (Keown 2002, p. 78).

On the basis of this reasoning, Keown concludes that while legislation may be drafted seeking to limit euthanasia upon request by individuals experiencing unbearable suffering, the justification for euthanasia, when taken to its logical conclusion, would also become reasonable for individuals who do not have the capacity to request euthanasia and to those experiencing less severe forms of suffering (Keown 2002, p. 80). In other words, it is through acclimatisation to the procedures and based on reasoned arguments relating to new applications that an extension of qualifying conditions for euthanasia may take place.

Relating to the possible extension of qualifying conditions for euthanasia, it is also useful to look at what has verifiably happened in the Netherlands since the proximity of this country is certain to have some influence on any future developments. In this respect, concern has been expressed by Canadian palliative care expert, José Pereira, while commenting on the verifiable developments that have taken place over the years in this country. He indicates:

> In 30 years, the Netherlands has moved from euthanasia of people who are terminally ill, to euthanasia of those who are chronically ill; from euthanasia for physical illness, to euthanasia for mental illness; from euthanasia for mental illness, to euthanasia for psychological distress or mental suffering—and now to euthanasia simply if a person is over the age of 70 and 'tired of living'. Dutch euthanasia protocols have also moved from conscious patients providing explicit consent, to unconscious patients unable to provide consent.
>
> (Pereira 2011, p. 43)

Pereira goes on to explain that it is now considered a form of discrimination to deny euthanasia in the Netherlands to persons with any form of disorder because it is unfair that persons who are suffering, but not dying, are forced to suffer longer than those who are terminally ill. Even non-voluntary euthanasia in the Netherlands is now being presented as a social duty of the state on the basis of the ethical principle of beneficence (Pereira 2011).

Because of a similar manner of reasoning, many proposals to cha
the law have been introduced in the Belgian parliament with the aim
extending the qualifying conditions under which euthanasia can ι
performed (Schamps and Overstaeten 2009). Each time, there is a certain
logical reasoning, based on notions such as equality and justice, behind
the proposals highlighting, for example, forms of suffering which were
not included in the original euthanasia legislation.

In this way, those supporting an extension of the 2002 euthanasia
legislation have already denounced the arbitrariness of some of its criteria
including the requirement (Vanden Berghe et al. 2013, pp. 270–271):

- For only irreversible (as opposed to reversible) unconsciousness to be
  determined in a patient before his or her advance directive on euthanasia becomes valid.
- That a disorder should exist because of a disease or accident excluding
  those who are simply aged or tired of living.
- For intolerable suffering to exist while excluding those who only expect
  this suffering to be present in the future.

Further changes to the law have also been suggested in 2011 by physician,
Wim Distelmans, the chairman, at the time, of the Belgian Federal
Committee on Euthanasia, including (Distelmans 2011a):

- The five-year validity limit for advance directives should be removed.
- Physicians who oppose euthanasia should be compelled to refer
  patients to colleagues who are willing to help with the procedure.
- Legislation should be clarified to include assisted suicide.
- The euthanasia of persons with dementia should be made possible if
  they have an advance directive stating that this would be their
  preference.
- No lower age limit for euthanasia should exist (which has since been
  decriminalised in 2014).

This means that it is very likely that an extension of the qualifying
conditions will continue to be considered in Belgium.

Euthanasia Becoming a Human Right

In Belgium, the nearest relatives representing the patient are increasingly
describing the dying process as 'undignified, useless and meaningless'
(Vanden Berghe et al. 2013, p. 271) even if the death takes place peacefully, without suffering and with appropriate expert support. Moreover,

there is a growing trend for nearest relatives to insist, sometimes even forcefully, that health care professionals should provide fast and active interventions for the ending of life of an elderly parent (VandenBerghe et al. 2013, p. 271). As such, there seems to be a growing sense of entitlement or even a perceived right to euthanasia amongst certain members of society and the media (Montero 2013, pp. 91–96).

In addition, because of the extension of the qualifying conditions to children and those persons who are increasingly losing their cognitive faculties, an imperceptible change may be taking place in Belgium from a 'right to end one's life' to a 'right to end the life of another'. This is because it is impossible for persons with very limited cognitive abilities to ever be able to appropriately consent to euthanasia (Montero 2013, pp. 86–91).

As Keown emphasises: 'Once the law abandons its historic, bright-line prohibition on intentionally ending the lives of patients, or on intentionally helping them to end their own lives, it invites arbitrary and discriminatory judgments about which patients would be "better off dead"' (Keown 2014, p. 1).

Montero explains that, in Belgium, euthanasia has imperceptibly developed into the perceived most humane and dignified answer to a situation of suffering. As the threshold of acceptable sickness and suffering diminishes, euthanasia has become unexceptional (Montero 2013: 62) and is no longer seen as an ethical transgression. As a result, it has started to be considered as belonging to the full set of practices that should be available in palliative care (Vanden Berghe et al. 2013, p. 267; Montero 2013, p. 94).

Further Increase in Numbers

As the numbers of persons accessing euthanasia in Belgium are continuing to experience a strong increase, it is unlikely that a levelling off of those agreeing to the procedure will be taking place soon. This means that the magnitude of individuals ending their lives in this way is likely to be far greater than originally suggested when first decriminalised.

Interestingly, a feedback system may also be taking place in that the perceived normality of a procedure may serve to further increase acceptance. This would reflect the statement of Montero that 'once you accept the principle of euthanasia ... It becomes more and more normal' (quoted in Hamilton 2013). This is an observation on experience rather than a logical demonstration, but it provides a *prima facie* indication that further rises in numbers, and further increases in the social acceptability of the practice, could reasonably be expected.

Impact of Euthanasia on Suicide

It remains very difficult to predict how the acceptance and legalisation of euthanasia will affect the way society considers suicide. But Belgium has a suicide rate that is well above the European average (indeed the highest in Western Europe) and while the suicide rate in Belgium decreased in the period 1995 to 2010, this reduction was smaller than the average decrease across Europe (OECD 2012).

Research has also shown that individuals living in countries with high suicide rates are generally more supportive of the idea of taking one's life than individuals from countries with relatively low suicide rates (Stack and Kposowa 2008). This may mean that, in some circumstances, it might be possible for suicidal individuals to begin to believe that they are entitled to euthanasia to end their lives.

If this happened, however, it would completely change the way a society considers any form of suicide. Instead of seeing such a prospect as a desperate situation which society should seek to prevent, it may begin to accept that all autonomous and rational persons have a right to end their lives, if they so wish and for any reason. For example, the American psychiatrist, Herbert Hendin, indicates: '"Normalizing" suicide as a medical option lays the groundwork for a society that turns euthanasia into a "cure" for suicidal depression' (Hendin 1995, p. 193).

A Possible Return to a Prohibition of Euthanasia in Belgium

Finally, it is possible to ask whether it would ever be possible for Belgium to return to a position where euthanasia is prohibited. This is because cultural changes do occur and it is possible that a practice that is accepted (or tolerated) is later rejected by popular opinion, for example after a scandal. Yet for this to happen would require a 'sea change' and a movement in the opposite direction, and there are no signs of this at present in Belgium.

It would also depend on the future values of Belgian society. In the same way as personal autonomy and the avoidance of suffering were some of the most important priorities when Belgium legalised euthanasia in 2002, another set of priorities would have to come to the fore if Belgium is to return to its previous position. In this regard, whether a belief in the inherent and equal dignity, value and worth of all human beings may be able bring back a prohibition on euthanasia is an open question.

But if Belgium eventually does return to its pre-2002 position, this may encourage other countries not to implement any legislation in this area.

Conclusion

Euthanasia is no longer presented in Belgium as an exceptional and ultimate solution for extreme situations (Montero 2013, p. 94). Instead, it is beginning to be a procedure which can be characterised as relatively normal. This is because, amongst other factors, (1) euthanasia is starting to be established in Belgian society with no attempts to repeal its 2002 legalisation, (2) Belgian's close neighbours have legalised the practice and (3) a strong increase in numbers accessing the procedure every year is occurring which will eventually make eutha-nasia quite common.

These factual and verifiable past developments in the acceptance and normalisation of euthanasia, as well as the extension of qualifying condi-tions, confirm some of the grave concerns expressed by opponents to euthanasia when it was first legalised in Belgium. In addition, these developments make it more likely that further changes will happen in Belgium strengthening the place of the procedure in society.

This may occur, for example, because social influences may develop encouraging many to give in to the prevalent views of a society (Bridgens 2009). In other words, people may access euthanasia just because they believe it is what is expected. Furthermore, peer pressures or other social influences, such as the fear of being considered by others or society as a burden, cannot be dismissed. As Montero indicates 'I am persuaded that there are vulnerable people who think today, "I must request euthanasia. I represent a burden for my loved ones. I am contributing nothing to society any more"'. He adds: 'What is presented at first as a right is going to become a kind of obligation' (quoted in Hamilton 2013).

In this context, a sustained opposition by a minority of Belgian individuals to euthanasia and its normalisation will undoubtedly con-tinue. Whether the 2002 law could ever be reversed cannot be predicted but this resistance could serve, if nothing else, to bear witness and record

for history the reality that some sections of Belgian society st
disagree with the direction in which their country is travelling.⁵

Of course, future developments in euthanasia are not logically inevi..
able but real risks exist and should not be ignored. No national community can ever take the moral high ground by affirming, either because of
its geography or history, that it is immune from possible abuse or
impervious to moral attrition. Such an attitude would reflect a significant
lack of humility and sense of reality!

The 1983 Nobel Prize winner for Literature, English novelist William
Golding, captured the collective moral erosion of a group of schoolboys
marooned on a desert island in his book 'Lord of the Flies'. They begin as
upper-middle-class civilised Englishmen but end up losing any restraint
and killing those who do not belong to their group. Golding's master-
piece, which was published in 1954, was written as an illustration of the
fragility of civilised society. It was also a warning to those who believe
they have a naturally kind, robust and decent society which cannot
eventually descend into barbarity if it loses its moral foundations. (Crawford 2002)

It is, therefore, important to be very careful when crossing the bright-
line acknowledging that a life may not be worth living. At first, it may
only be expressed as a subtle shift in emphasis in the basic attitudes of
physicians concerning those with very severe illnesses that cannot be
addressed. But this may then gradually expand to categories that were
never envisaged when first accepted (Alexander 1949).

Looking at the state of the 1949 culture of American medicine, the
American physician, Leo Alexander, warned concerning patients who
could no longer be treated that:

> In an increasingly utilitarian society these patients are being looked down
> upon with increasing definiteness as unwanted ballast. A certain amount of
> rather open contempt for the people who cannot be rehabilitated with present
> knowledge has developed. This is probably due to a good deal of unconscious
> hostility, because these people for whom there seem to be no effective
> remedies, have become a threat to newly acquired delusions of omnipotence.
>
> (Alexander 1949, p. 45)

In his conclusion, Alexander warned that there was a certain kind
of inevitable progression to the disappearance of civilised behaviour.

⁵ For example, concerns relating to the normalisation of euthanasia in Belgium have been
expressed by Professor Xavier Dijon see: Dijon 2016.

This begins by recognising the pragmatic use of scientific developments, it then continues by discarding traditional values in its pride of what can be achieved but always ends in a moral and ethical wasteland (Alexander 1949). Society then becomes a wilderness where the value of some human lives are increasingly considered as being of poor or even substandard quality – where it is possible to grade the worth of every human life to reflect its degree of usefulness and meaning.

To protect humanity from the risks of such a dystopia, a compassionate society must reject euthanasia while learning to accept that all human life has an inherent, equal and immeasurable meaning, value and worth in an environment that reflects its unconditional and equal acceptance of the suffering as well as the happy person. It will then continue to uphold and protect the important inherent equal dignity and value of all human beings – no matter how young or old, able or disabled, sick or healthy, close to or far from death they are – accepting them for who they are and suffering or rejoicing with them in compassion and care.

14

Euthanasia and Assisted Suicide in Belgium

Bringing an End to Interminable Discussion

DAVID ALBERT JONES

What the student is in consequence generally confronted with, and this has little to do with the particular intentions of his or her particular teachers, is an apparent inconclusiveness in all argument outside the natural sciences, an inconclusiveness which seems to abandon him or her to his or her prerational preferences.

Alasdair MacIntyre (1988, p. 400)

Framing the Modern Debate

This paper examines the use of empirical data in the debate over the legalisation of euthanasia and/or assisted suicide. Beginning with the historical roots of the modern debate, it asks why appeal to empirical data has failed to resolve, or even lessen, political disagreement. Seeking a way to combine ethical presuppositions and empirical data, the paper focuses on data from one jurisdiction (Belgium). These data will be examined from three divergent ethical frames: Hippocratic, utilitarian and libertarian frames in the hope of moving towards convergence on practical conclusions notwithstanding the divergent ethical starting points.

The first attempts in the modern era to develop legal provisions which would permit assisted suicide or mercy killing were put forward in the early twentieth century, especially but not only in the United States of America and in the United Kingdom. From the beginning the aim was to relieve the suffering associated with terminal illness and chronic conditions, but this was intertwined with a concern that some lives were not only a burden to those who possessed them, but were also a burden to society. Such eugenic concerns are evident in the writings of Glanville Williams, especially his 1957 work *The Sanctity of Life and the Criminal Law*. Here Williams sought to overturn the view that, in his words, 'it is our duty to regard all human life as sacred, however disabled or worthless or even repellent the individual may be' (Williams 1957, p. 19). In contrast Glanville Williams argued that allowing disabled children to be born and to live was a 'horrible evil' (Williams 1957, p. 234) and one to be avoided by sterilisation,[1] abortion[2] or, if necessary, infanticide.[3]

The concern to avoid sustaining 'disabled or worthless or even repellent' lives provides the context for the proposal of Williams that 'the law might well exempt from punishment the unselfish abetment of suicide and the unselfish homicide upon request' (Williams 1957, p. 310). Indeed, in some circumstances Williams regarded the case for acquiescing to requests to hasten death as so strong that he could see no possible rational argument against allowing this. He therefore claimed that the prohibition could only be understood as the vestige of the religious prejudices of a previous age: 'euthanasia can be condemned only according to religious opinion' (Williams 1957, p. 312).

In response to this book Yale Kamisar, then associate professor of law at Minnesota wrote a substantial paper entitled, 'Some Non-Religious Views against Proposed "Mercy Killing" Legislation' (Kamisar 1958). Kamisar described himself as 'a non-Catholic and self-styled liberal' (Kamisar 1958, p. 974) and his objections where not based on religious doctrine nor on a principled objection to killing per se. His primary concern was that legalisation of voluntary euthanasia or assisted suicide would lead to pressure being put on vulnerable people to end their lives and that it would lead to the incompetent being killed without their prior consent. In other words, once the door was opened to voluntary euthanasia then this would inevitably lead to the acceptance of other practices which are widely recognised as abuses. He called the basis of this form of argument the 'wedge principle' but it would later come to be called the 'slippery slope'.

---

[1] 'The obvious social importance of preventing the birth of children who are congenitally deaf, blind, paralysed, deformed, feeble minded, mentally diseased or subject to other serious hereditary afflictions, and the inadequacy of contraception for this purpose, has naturally given rise to the proposal to use sterilisation of the unfit as a means of racial improvement ... by keeping alive mentally and physically ill-equipped children, we are opposing natural selection' (Williams 1957, pp. 80–81).

[2] 'To allow the breeding of defectives is a horrible evil, far worse than any that may be found in abortion' (Williams 1957, p. 234).

[3] 'Regarded in this spirit, an eugenic killing by a mother, exactly paralleled by the bitch that kills her mis-shapen puppies, cannot confidently be pronounced immoral' (Williams 1957, p.20).

It would be no exaggeration to say that Glanville Williams's book and Yale Kamisar's rebuttal together provided the frame within which the international debate over euthanasia and assisted suicide has been conducted over more than half a century (Grubb 1998; Steinbock 2005; Keown and Jones 2008; Jones 2011). Following Williams, advocates of a change in the law have continued to appeal to the duty to relieve suffering, and have continued to caricature their opponents as exclusively religious. Following Kamisar, the dominant political argument against changing the law has been based on some form of slippery slope.

There have been other developments within this frame. For example, advocates have increasingly appealed to autonomy or freedom to choose, reflecting in part the shift in social attitudes in the 1960s and also perhaps hoping to invoke language that has proved politically successful in the abortion debate (though on the problematic elision of euthanasia and the abortion debate see Jones 2013b; Spindelman 1996; George 2007). In a further shift, especially in the last 25 years, the principles of autonomy and the alleviation of suffering have often been expressed in terms of human dignity[4]: the dignity of a chosen death and the indignity of suffering and dependence. At the same time, there have been developments in the self-understanding of those opposing euthanasia and assisted suicide. Their views have been reshaped by the perspective of the disability-rights movement and by the emergence of palliative care as a respected medical discipline. Arguments against euthanasia have also appealed to dignity, the equal dignity of individuals with disability and the dignity of the dying person, and of his or her family, as the focus of hospice care. The appeal to 'dignity'/ 'indignity' by both sides of the argument has led to some to recommend that the terms be avoided (Schuklenk et al. 2011), though they remain a feature of the contemporary debate and are perhaps implicit already in Glanville Williams's description of 'disabled or worthless or even repellent' lives (Williams 1957, p. 19).

There have thus been developments on both sides of the argument over euthanasia and assisted suicide. Nevertheless, 'the basic arguments for and against have not really changed since the issue was debated by Glanville Williams and Yale Kamisar nearly 50 years ago' (Steinbock

---

[4] For example Cohen-Almagor 2001, but further examples could easily be provided. The popularity of this language is evident in the name of the Oregon Death with Dignity Act 1997, in the name of the Swiss assisted suicide organisation *Dignitas* (1998) and in the change of name of the Voluntary Euthanasia Society to Dignity in Dying (2005).

05, p. 235). Advocates have primarily emphasised present suffering, pponents have primarily warned of future dangers.

The structure of the debate between Williams and Kamisar presupposed a consequentialist framework (Steinbock 2005), based on the predicted benefits to those seeking assisted suicide or euthanasia, weighed against the predicted risks of harm to them or to others. However, during the first 30 years of the debate neither side could provide convincing evidence to persuade the other of its assessment of the prospective benefits and risks. In the absence of any example of a contemporary society that had legalised euthanasia or assisted suicide, it was difficult to quantify the likelihood and potential scope for abuse. Arguments from the ostensibly benign euthanasia practices of ancient Greece (Dowbiggin 2005, pp. 7–10, though for a contrasting view see Papadimitriou et al. 2007) or from the more recent abuses in Nazi Germany (Boer 2007, p. 535 citing Gorsuch 2006, p. 43) both begged the question, as they presupposed that the situation in those societies was comparable in the relevant aspects. Anyone not already convinced of the ethical-political conclusion would not be convinced of the pertinence of such historical examples.

It is therefore unsurprising that from the 1950s to the 1980s the debate seemed irresolvable and interminable with little advance on the arguments set out by Williams and Kamisar. However, from the mid-1980s the situation began to change in that several countries decriminalised, legalised or regulated assisted suicide or euthanasia. As evidence from these jurisdictions was gathered and collated the debate took on a new form. Rather than arguing counterfactually about what might or might not happen, protagonists could now examine what had or had not happened. Those countries that permitted euthanasia or assisted suicide constituted a series of 'natural experiments' which became the new locus of the empirical arguments for or against a change in the law.

Emerging Evidence

Assisting suicide, where this is not done for selfish motives, has been legal in Switzerland since 1942. However, it was not until the establishment of organisations such as EXIT (in 1982) and *Dignitas* (in 1998) that this law became the basis for a system of assisted suicide for people who were chronically sick or elderly and tired of life. EXIT and *Dignitas* kept their own records but for many years these data were not audited by government or by independent academic or professional bodies. It was only in

2003 that the government began to collect such data (Steck et al. 2014) and only in 2012 that the first official report on assisted suicide was produced by the Swiss government (FSO 2012).

In the Netherlands a report by the Royal Dutch Medical Association in 1984 (Lagerwey 1988) and a subsequent judgement by the Dutch Supreme Court later that year (Driesse et al. 1988) allowed doctors to perform euthanasia without fear of legal sanction. In 1990, the government established the Remmelink Committee to monitor euthanasia and other end-of-life practices in the Netherlands. The Committee produced a report, examining data from 1990 (van der Maas et al. 1991). The same methodology was followed in a subsequent study into practice in 1995 (van der Wal and van der Maas 1996; van der Maas 1996) and a third study into practice around the time of the passing of the Euthanasia Act 2001 (van der Heide et al. 2007). It was exposition and interpretation of these studies which launched the new empirical phase in the debate over assisted suicide and euthanasia.

The third jurisdiction to legalise assisted suicide was the US state of Oregon.[5] From its first full year of operation in 1998, the Oregon Death with Dignity Act has been subject to annual government reports. These detail not only the numbers dying by physician assisted suicide, but the number of prescriptions given, the reasons for the request, whether the patient underwent psychiatric evaluation and a variety of other data. These reports soon joined the Remmelink reports as the locus of academic debate over euthanasia.

In 2002, Belgium became the fourth jurisdiction to legalise or decriminalise some form of medically assisted suicide or euthanasia. The law was similar, though not identical, to that passed in the Netherlands the previous year. The Belgium Act stipulated that a Federal Committee on Oversight and Enforcement be established and report every two years. Furthermore, in addition to these official data there has been a considerable amount of empirical research into end-of-life decisions conducted by academics, especially but not only relating to practices in Flanders (for example Chambaere et al. 2011b). Indeed, large scale academic research on end-of-life practices in Belgium preceded the passing of the law on euthanasia (in particular, Deliens et al. 2000). A literature search

---

[5] Of laws still in force, Oregon was the third. It was preceded by the Northern Territories *Rights of the Terminally Ill Act 1995* but that law was repealed after nine months and only four assisted suicides, all assisted by the same physician. The population of the Northern Territories at that time was approximately 180,000.

using PubMed identified over 300 papers co-authored by Luc Deliens on some aspect of end-of-life practice in Belgium. This research has allowed comparison of practice before and after the legislation and, in this respect at least, is potentially more illuminating than data from the Netherlands or Oregon. Another feature that makes Belgium of particular interest is the rapid increase in the prevalence of euthanasia in that country, such that it has now overtaken the Netherlands as having the highest rate of assisted death in the world (Chambaere et al. 2015a; Dierickx et al. 2015). For a variety of reasons, then, Belgium provides a particularly rich source of empirical data for reflection on euthanasia and other related end-of-life practices.

With more than a decade of official Belgian data augmenting substantially the empirical evidence from the Netherlands and Oregon, in addition to cumulative data from academic researchers in universities in those and other countries, it would seem that the debate initiated by Williams and Kamisar should now be able to be resolved by appeal to evidence.[6] At the very least there should be signs of convergence on a consensus among researchers as to what is implied by the available evidence to date. Instead, the increase in data has given rise to an increasingly acrimonious debate as to how these data are to be interpreted.

Dances with Data

The publication of the first Remmelink report in 1991 generated a number of commentaries (Gunning 1991; Fenigsen 1991; Ten Have and Welie 1992; Keown 1992; Nowak 1992; Pollard 1992; See also Keown 1995; Keown 2002), many of these critical of the end-of-life practices that were described in the report. A statistic which raised concern was that 1,000 patients had died because of Life-terminating Acts Without Explicit Request of the patient (LAWER: the term 'non-voluntary euthanasia' is not used in the Netherlands or Belgium because euthanasia is there defined as taking the life of another at the latter's expressed request,

---

[6] At the end of 2015 there were approximately 50 million people living within jurisdictions that permit assisted suicide or euthanasia. These were concentrated in three regions: the Low Countries, Switzerland and four states in the North of the United States (three of which border Canada). In order of size, by millions estimated as of 2014: Netherlands 16.8, Belgium 11.2, Switzerland 8.08, Washington 7.06, Oregon 3.97, Montana 1.02, Vermont 0.6 and Luxembourg 0.54, total 49.27 million. To date most empirical research has concentrated on the Netherlands, Oregon, Belgium and to a lesser extent, on Switzerland.

hence a different term is needed for unrequested acts of mercy killing). One common form of slippery slope argument in relation to euthanasia rests on the claim that the acceptance of voluntary euthanasia leads (logically and/or empirically) to acceptance of non-voluntary euthanasia (Keown 2002; Jones 2011), that is, death by LAWER. This prediction seemed to be confirmed by the Remmelink report. Defenders of euthanasia pointed out, however, that the presence of significant numbers of deaths by LAWER in the Netherlands did not show that there was, or had been, any slippery slope. To test this, it would be necessary to know whether this type of action had occurred more frequently in the Netherlands since 1984, when euthanasia had effectively been decriminalised (van Delden et al. 1993). Frustrated by what they considered misrepresentation, reordering and misinterpretation of the Remmelink data, and unwarranted accusations on this basis, Johannes van Delden and colleagues complained that what was needed on this topic was 'an open debate in order to improve the moral quality of decision making' but what was happening was mere 'dances with data' (Van Delden et al. 1993, p. 329).

The suggestion that deaths by LAWER in the Netherlands might be unrelated to the legalisation of euthanasia received some support from research conducted later by Luc Deliens and others in Belgium. The Belgian data indicated that the proportion of deaths by LAWER in Belgium in 1998, where euthanasia had not been legalised, was higher than that reported in the Netherlands where euthanasia had been legalised (Deliens et al. 2000). This point was further strengthened when the figure for death by LAWER in Belgium was lower in 2007 than it had been in 1998, prior to the introduction of euthanasia there (Chambaere et al. 2011a) and when it was shown to have declined in the Netherlands in the second Remmelink report (van der Maas 1996).

One problem with these seemingly reassuring data is the implicit assumption that the rate of reporting of death by LAWER remains constant over time. It may be, however, that the reaction against the revelation of such practices in the Remmelink report led not, or not only, to a change in practice but also to a tendency to re-envisage or re-describe actions. It should be noted that what is being measured directly in this research is not observed action but is self-reported action. Another factor that needs to be considered is the possibility that a decline in deaths by LAWER may be accompanied by the adoption of more ambiguous means to the same end, such as the use of medication for pain and symptom control, with the aim of shortening life but without the request of the patient. There is some evidence of such a shift in relation to the increasing use of sedation at the end of life in the Netherlands (Murray et al. 2008) and in Belgium (Rys et al. 2014), but again, the interpretation of this practice is ambiguous as will be discussed further below.

A debate over the meaning of the data is also present in relation to the most prominent of statistics, the headline figure for the gross number of deaths by euthanasia or by assisted suicide. The continual rise of euthanasia in Belgium is sometimes presented, implicitly or explicitly, as evidence of a slippery slope. In response, advocates of the practice often claim that the numbers of these deaths remain small as a percentage of annual mortality. For example, in Belgium the number of reported cases of euthanasia more than doubled between 2010 and 2015, from 953 to 2,022 respectively (FCECE 2016). This increase of 112 per cent in five years seems like a worryingly steep rise, but the latter figure still only represents 1.8 per cent of all deaths in Belgium which seems like a reassuringly small figure.

It is instructive to compare this move with the way in which figures for unregulated non-assisted suicide are reported. In that case researchers would not seek to minimise the significance of these deaths by saying they represented only a small percentage of total mortality. A clear difference is that, with unregulated suicide, it is widely held that 'every single life lost to suicide is one too many' (WHO 2014, p. 2), in which case an increase is necessarily a matter of concern. In contrast, there is no consensus in relation to euthanasia as to what would be the 'right' number of annual deaths (or even how to identify such a number). It would even be possible to argue, though few do so explicitly, that in relation to death by euthanasia or physician assisted suicide, 'An increase in the suicide rate may be, in a certain light, a welcome development, not something to be feared' (Brassington 2014).

There is therefore no objective measure against which an increase in the number of deaths by euthanasia (or by physician assisted suicide) could be categorised as modest or excessive, small or large, reassuring or worrying or even 'welcome'. The political or moral significance of the numbers seems not to be a characteristic of the data themselves but something measured by the observer, and different observers seem to have radically different measures of significance. Different commentators on the Belgian data on euthanasia seem like children each in turn looking down a deep dark well and each seeing at the bottom only the reflection of his or her own face.

The Retreat from the Empirical and the Priority
of Ethical Principles

After 25 years of the empirical debate over assisted suicide and euthanasia it is tempting to conclude that the seeming interminability of these
arguments reflects some underlying issue of principle, some flaw in the
way the question is framed. This flaw may, for example, be thought
expressive of the 'apparent inconclusiveness of all argument outside the
natural sciences' (MacIntyre 1988, p. 400). Matters of public policy may
be informed by factual judgements but they are essentially practical
judgements and so depend also on divergent preferences or rival visions
of the good. The attempt to resolve disagreement only by appeal to
empirical evidence will therefore always founder on unstated differences
of belief or principle.

On the assumption that such empirical debates are interminable, some
advocates of euthanasia have seen in the call for 'more evidence' a
disingenuous strategy of indefinite delay, a tactic resorted to by people
who have lost the argument about the ethical principles. Thus, Malcolm
Parker argues:

> What Capron lamented regarding the role of empirical evidence is neces-
> sarily the case. Empirical research becomes relevant only after the debates
> of principle have occurred ... According to those who wish to defer the
> euthanasia question prior to more data becoming available, the data
> would be interminably used to urge the view that requests for assisted
> dying are always potentially more than they appear, and as such they fuel
> a strategic opposition to the legalisation of euthanasia.
>
> (Parker 2005, p. 533)

In a similar vein, Andrew Batavia maintains that 'public policy relies
primarily and fundamentally on values. Although empirical data may
inform a policy debate, it cannot resolve it. The value central to those of
us who support a right to assisted suicide is autonomy' (Batavia 2000,
p. 557 replying to Gill 2000; see also Gill 2010).

What is curious here is that, whereas the debate over assisted suicide
and euthanasia is sometimes construed as a matter of pragmatic advocates, arguing from social realities, and absolutist opponents, arguing
from a priori principles, these two examples show that it is as common
for proponents to argue based on a priori principles (especially the
principle of autonomy) and for opponents to argue on the basis of
social consequences. Nor should either side assume that because each
understands the public policy questions in relation to ethical principles,

that empirical questions are irrelevant to them. It is rather that the empirical realities remain important, but they are understood differently, according to different concerns which are informed by different ethical principles.

Parker seems correct, for example, in his assertion that 'if you believe that killing is always wrong, you should have no interest in investigating the conditions under which euthanasia might be acceptable, since there simply are no such conditions' (Parker 2005, p. 535). However, it does not follow that if someone believes that (medical) killing is wrong then he or she should have 'no interest in investigating' how best to reflect this ethical principle in public policy or in investigating the consequences of legalising euthanasia or assisted suicide in jurisdictions where this has occurred. It is an empirical question whether people are better protected from intentional non-voluntary ending of life by the prohibition of euthanasia of all forms, or by the legalisation of voluntary euthanasia. Similarly, it is an empirical question whether euthanasia could safely be permitted as an exception for difficult cases, without affecting medical practice more generally, or whether it would have wider and possibly adverse consequences. If the legalisation of euthanasia were shown to prevent abuse, and if this practice could be circumscribed as an exception without adversely affecting medicine or other aspects of society, then to this extent the evidence would provide a reason for legally tolerating the practice, even for someone who remained opposed to it in principle.

A further problem in seeking to combine matters of principle and empirical evidence is that the view that someone takes of the principles frequently influences his or her expectations about the consequences. For example, someone who opposes suicide in principle will tend to think that legalising physician assisted suicide will have adverse consequences. Similarly, someone who conceives of suicide as a right will tend to think that legalisation will help protect against abuse. This is illustrated well by Batavia who states that, 'Those of us who support a right to assisted suicide believe that abuses, to the extent they are now occurring behind closed doors, are less likely to continue once assisted suicide is legalised and appropriately regulated' (Batavia 2000, p. 558). There is no reason to doubt Batavia's claim that supporters of a 'right to assisted suicide' are inclined to believe that legalisation would render abuse 'less likely'. However, whether abuse is in fact less frequent after a change in the law is not determined by whether people had *believed* it would be 'less likely'. The occurrence of abuse is an empirical phenomenon that is, in principle, open to independent investigation.

Authors such as Parker and Batavia have helpfully called attention to the irreducible place of principle in public policy discussion, and to the way in which discussion and interpretation of empirical evidence can mask differences of principle. Nevertheless, if requests for further evidence are potentially endless, and it is not reasonable to expect everyone to agree on the interpretation of the data before setting policy, the same can be said of principles. It is simply begging the question to dismiss rival moral and philosophical traditions, as though the argument had been decided and modern society was now based on a single shared philosophy. Indeed, the very basis of liberalism, which is arguably the current dominant philosophy in modern Western democracies, presupposes the enduring presence of different moral and philosophical views which are more or less tolerated. If anything, experience shows that arguments about principles are more intractable, more difficult to resolve, than are matters of empirical evidence and its interpretation. It is hardly a promising tactic to suggest that assessment of evidence be delayed until 'after the debates of principle have occurred' (Parker 2005, p. 533), when the principles are no less contested than the evidence, and no less prone to interminable disagreement.

The fact of such ongoing disagreement does not demonstrate that there is no truth of the matter, that ethical principles are irrational or that ethical statements are no more than expressions of feeling or intuition. What this disagreement shows is only that ethical arguments about issues need to be understood in relation to larger ethical traditions which, at least to a certain extent, offer rival conceptions of justice and of practical rationality. In relation to concrete questions such as the legal prohibition or decriminalisation of assisted suicide or euthanasia, questions over the interpretation of empirical evidence and questions of ethical principle thus arise not sequentially but simultaneously. Each distinct moral tradition must confront the empirical evidence and weigh the evidence according to the concerns and priorities of that tradition. There is merit then in considering the same evidence from more than one perspective to assess whether, with due acknowledgement of the reality of moral disagreement on principles, it is nevertheless possible to come to agreement on some practical conclusions.

Acknowledging that traditions are not hermetically sealed, and that there are also different schools of thought within traditions, it is nevertheless possible to distinguish broad traditions of moral thinking that remain influential in the modern world and highly pertinent to the issue of euthanasia. The following sections will consider the empirical evidence on euthanasia practice in Belgium from the perspective of three such rival traditions: Hippocratic, utilitarian and libertarian.

Euthanasia in Belgium: a Hippocratic Perspective

The ancient doctors' oath and other ethical writings ascribed to Hippocrates have found a receptive readership among Jews, Christians and Muslims, and this has facilitated their transmission within European culture.[7] Nevertheless, this approach to ethics does not presuppose a particular religious framework, indeed the modern restatement of the oath, the Geneva Declaration, makes no reference to God or the gods (Jones 2006). This restatement remains enormously influential as a touchstone of ethical medicine, notwithstanding that a range of alternative approaches to biomedical ethics exists.

The Hippocratic tradition understands medicine as the use of knowledge and skill in the service of life and health. The goods of life and health are not the only or the highest goods but they are the focus of the art of medicine. There is no duty on a doctor always to extend life, for medicines will often impose burdens, but the Hippocratic doctor will not deliberately seek the death of his or her patient and therefore will not assist suicide or perform euthanasia (Pellegrino 2001; Kass 2002; Jones 2007).

The change in the law in Belgium in 2002 clearly represents a departure from the Hippocratic understanding of medical ethics. Belgian law now permits a doctor deliberately to end the life of his or her patient. From a Hippocratic medical perspective, the interesting empirical question is whether Belgium shows that euthanasia can constitute an exception, which might perhaps be tolerated, without adversely affecting the practice of medicine more generally. This question could also be framed in the opposite way, by asking whether euthanasia in Belgium had had far reaching effects on health care, eroding the ethical distinctions through which medicine is properly understood.

From this perspective, the rise of up to 1,803 official euthanasia cases in Belgium in 2013 is clearly of concern, as it shows that the practice is no longer viewed as an exception but is 'increasingly considered as a valid option at the end of life in Belgium' (Chambaere et al. 2015a, p. 1180). Furthermore, research in Flanders published in March 2015 shows that

---

[7] Jones 1924 is still of great value and includes ancient Christian and Muslim versions of the oath. On Jewish reception see Kass1985. See also Cameron1991 and Jones 2003.

this official figure significantly underestimates cases of euthanasia. Chambaere and colleagues (Chambaere et al. 2015a) found that euthanasia represent 4.6 per cent of deaths (approximately 2,835 deaths in Flanders whereas the government figure based on reporting is 1454 deaths). Thus in 2013 only half (51.2 per cent) of euthanasia cases were reported. Furthermore, in addition to these euthanasia figures (reported plus unreported) an estimated 1.7 per cent of deaths in Flanders are by LAWER.

When researchers first noticed a rise in cases of continuous deep sedation until death in the Netherlands, the question was immediately raised as to whether this might also sometimes be a form of covert euthanasia (Murray et al. 2008). This has now been confirmed in the case of practice in Flanders. Research conducted in 2007 showed that, at that time, doctors intended or co-intended to shorten life in 17 per cent of such cases (Papavasiliou et al. 2014, table 4, combining the data for GPs and medical specialists). Another study, also using data from 2007, puts this figure between 10 per cent and 19 per cent (Anquinet et al. 2012). In comparison, doctors in the United Kingdom (in the same study) intend or co-intend death in between 1 per cent and 3 per cent of cases of end-of-life sedation. The Netherlands, in the same study, lies somewhere in between (3 per cent–8 per cent). Other qualitative research has shown clear differences in the rationale and practice of end-of-life sedation in the three countries, with the Belgian practice of continuous sedation at times resembling euthanasia, certainly more so than the UK practice, again with the Netherlands someway in between (see Chapter 5 by Sterckx and Raus in this volume).

From 2007 to 2013, there was a modest decrease in the rate of continuous deep sedation until death in Flanders, but it remains at 12 per cent of all deaths. If 17 per cent of these involved the intent to shorten life, then continuous sedation with the intention to end life would represents 2 per cent of all deaths. The administration of drugs with the intention of shortening life would then account for more than 8 per cent of deaths in Flanders (or >4,930 deaths in Flanders in 2013). This is without discussion of the vexed and much more subtle question of withdrawal of treatment with explicit intent to shorten life.

In these categories it is difficult to estimate the equivalent figures for Wallonia. It is known that the pattern of end-of-life practice differs between Flemish and French parts of Belgium, with the French speaking part having lower rates of reported euthanasia, higher rates of sedation, unknown rates of underreporting and with data gathering being less centralised and generating far less academic research. From official data, it is nevertheless clear that rates of reported euthanasia in Wallonia are increasing year on year and the dearth of research on other end-of-life practices in that region, such as the use of sedation, is not reassuring.

Overall, having accepted the intentional hastening of death in the case of euthanasia (as defined in the 2002 Act), doctors in Belgium are also allowing the same intention to shape their decision making and medical practice in other areas. Indeed, such intentions are not only present in practice but are even proposed in some professional declarations, for example, a 2014 statement paper by members of the Belgian Society of Intensive Care Medicine:

> This statement paper ... is not about giving analgesics or sedative agents to combat pain or agitation, nor about the so-called double effect, wherein analgesics given to alleviate pain may have the adverse effect of shortening the dying process. The discussion here is about the administration of sedative agents with the direct intention of shortening the process of terminal palliative care in patients with no prospect of a meaningful recovery ... we explain our belief in the concept that shortening the dying process by administering sedatives *beyond what is needed for patient comfort* can be not only acceptable but in many cases desirable.
>
> (Vincent et al. 2014, p. 174, emphasis added)

The practice of euthanasia in Belgium is thus not simply an exceptional practice that has left medicine unaffected, but has become increasingly common while having a much wider effect on the practice and rationale of medical interventions, not least in the use of sedation.

From a Hippocratic perspective, the close association of palliative care and euthanasia provision in Belgium is also deeply problematic. It is not that the law has inhibited the development of palliative care in Belgium, there is no evidence of such inhibition, but it has had an impact on the aims and thus the ethos of this practice. It has stripped palliative care of that security provided by a space within which a form of medicine is practised that 'intends neither to hasten nor to postpone death' (WHO 2016).

The Belgian model of palliative care and euthanasia going 'hand in hand' may appear to advocates to represent a culture with 'a high degree of tolerance and compromise' (Bernheim et al. 2014, p. 524) but it neither tolerates nor compromises with Hippocratic medical practice. It is possible for a doctor, as an individual, to conscientiously object to euthanasia, and currently they can refuse to refer patients for euthanasia, though this is under threat.[8] Nevertheless, Belgian law has not permitted any hospital or palliative care unit to maintain or protect a distinctively Hippocratic ethos in the practice of medicine. In order to be law-abiding these institutions must 'de facto become pluralistic' (Bernheim et al. 2014, p. 524). There is thus no 'safe place' (as it were) where patients can choose to go, in Belgium, where euthanasia may not be practised.[9]

Euthanasia in Belgium: A Utilitarian Perspective

Utilitarianism is an intellectual tradition which construes ethical reasoning as a species of calculation and which defines the right rule or action as that which leads to 'the greatest happiness of the greatest number' (Bentham 1977; Shackleton 1972). This tradition has been invoked both in favour and against the legalisation of euthanasia. For example, in favour is Glanville Williams, who is less systematic than a classical utilitarian, but who in his approach follows the 'utilitarian philosophy' of embracing 'the lesser evil' (Williams 1957, p. 200) in order to avoid a greater evil. This approach allows some actions, including euthanasia, to be 'justified by necessity' (Williams 1957, p. 322). Against euthanasia is Yale Kamisar, who is also overt in appealing to 'utilitarian ethics' (Kamisar1958, p. 974, n. 21) as the basis of his argument.

From a utilitarian perspective, the legalisation of euthanasia is justified if it leads to a net increase in the amount of happiness in the whole population. The prima facie justification for euthanasia, from this per-spective, is that it prevents suffering in the person who seeks euthanasia, and this is true whether suffering is understood in relation, for example,

---

[8] Bernheim asserts (without citing any basis for the assertion) that physicians are 'required to refer the patient to a willing colleague, but as yet this is only an ethical, not a legal, obligation' (Bernheim et al. 2014, p. 524).

[9] A distinction may be made between hospitals and nursing homes. There are some nursing homes with policies which do not allow euthanasia between their walls (Lemiengre et al. 2009). Nevertheless, nursing homes have come under increasing pressure to conform. In December 2015, the newly installed Archbishop of Mechelen-Brussels, Jozef De Kesel was strongly criticised for his assertion that Catholic institutions had a right to refuse to facilitate or accommodate euthanasia. MPs Jean-Jacques De Gucht and Valerie Van Peel asserted that the right not to participate with euthanasia extended to individual physicians but not to institutions (Burger 2016). The current legal tolerance of a diversity of institutional policies on euthanasia is threatened by a case taken by Nadine Engelen in January 2016. She successfully sued the Sint-Augustinus rest home in Diest for its refusal to permitted lethal injection of Mariette Buntjens within the home (Caldwell 2016, Heneghan 2016).

to the physical pains of terminal illness, or in relation to the frustration of preferences. Someone who receives euthanasia can hardly be said to be happy or to enjoy the satisfaction of his or her preferences, but someone denied euthanasia may be both dissatisfied and in pain. Euthanasia may also alleviate the suffering of those who care for the person who is terminally ill and might allow resources, otherwise spent on keeping someone alive, to be spent instead on making other people happy. Hence the comments of Baroness Mary Warnock in making her case for euthanasia, 'nor can I tolerate the thought of outstaying my welcome, an increasing burden on my family, so that no one can be truly sorry when I die and they are free' (Warnock 2014, p. 133).

On the other hand, the very strength of such economic arguments may lead to fear and insecurity among people who are disabled and in need of health care and other support. This concern is well expressed, by the Australian bioethicist, Nicholas Tonti-Filippini, writing of his own experiences:

> For several years, until I objected, I received from my health insurer a letter that tells me how much it costs the fund to maintain my health care. I dreaded receiving that letter and the psychological reasoning that would seem to have motivated it ... If euthanasia were lawful, that sense of burden would be greatly increased for there would be even greater moral pressure to relinquish one's hold on a burdensome life.
>
> (Tonti-Filippini 2012, p. 112)

This pressure may not be personal but it can shape the practices and ethos of a health care system and have a distorting effect on the way best-interest decisions are made. Part of the utility of the prohibition on euthanasia is in preventing harms that could arise because of overt or covert economic pressures. The philosopher Bernard Williams has remarked that, '"He would be better off dead" can be said for many dubious reasons: the most dubious is that we would be better off if he were dead' (Williams 1985, p. 42). Bernard Williams was a critic of utilitarianism but a similar thought could be framed in utilitarian terms. A society in which people were less secure about why decisions were made about them would, to this extent, lack utility.

Furthermore, while euthanasia cuts off future suffering it also cuts off the possibility of future happiness. Again, Bernard Williams helps articulate this. He argues that death 'tends to be either too early or too late ... If that is any sort of dilemma, it can, as things still are and if one is exceptionally lucky, be resolved, not by doing anything, but just by dying shortly before the horrors of not doing so become evident' (Williams 1973, p.100). An advocate of euthanasia could argue that, rather than 'not doing anything' we could improve our chances by deciding for ourselves when to end our life. However, by taking this irreversible action we also risk dying earlier than would have optimised our happiness.

The evidence from Belgium is of continual increases in rates of euthanasia, and not only official euthanasia but unreported euthanasia, and not only reported and unreported euthanasia but non-voluntary euthanasia (death by LAWER). In addition to all these overt and intentional acts of ending life the evidence shows an increase in the use of sedation as a covert means of euthanasia. Indeed, this general rise and the widening scope and increasing variety of forms of death by physician are true not only of Belgium but of every jurisdiction that has legalised euthanasia or assisted suicide. The total number of deaths has climbed steadily and, it seems, uncontrollably. There are some divergences, for example, the rate of assisted dying is higher among euthanasia states than among those that have decriminalised assisted suicide (Gamondi et al, 2014, p. 127). Nevertheless, beyond such differences there is a common feature, of seemingly inexorable rises. Among these jurisdictions, Belgium not only has the highest rate of assisted death, but also, a significant body of academic research in Flanders has disclosed the presence of other forms of intervention by doctors that are intended to shorten life, either with or without consent.

It is not possible from the gross number of such deaths to deduce whether these are, on average, beneficial or harmful in relation to utility. Nevertheless, it can be stated with confidence that increasing rates of euthanasia increase the risk that some people will die 'too early' when they would still have future happiness ahead of them. This effect is compounded by the increasing proportion of non-cancer deaths, and especially psychiatric and other non-terminal conditions. For example, between 2010 and 2015 the prevalence of euthanasia in Belgium for 'neuropsychiatric disorders' and for 'multiple pathologies' (a term which can cover the ill health of old age), increased from a combined 41 cases (4.3 per cent of euthanasia) to 272 cases (13.5 per cent of euthanasia), as is evident in the FCECE Reports for the respective years. Such conditions are more susceptible to external influence, for good or ill, and have trajectories that are far harder to predict.[10] It is therefore widely

---

[10] While the Seventh Report 2016 shows a further increase in cases of euthanasia where death is not 'foreseen' (*prévisible/afzienbare*), for the first time since reporting started,

252 DAVID ALBERT JONES

acknowledged that, as well as a continuing rise in overall numbers, the official euthanasia reports show 'an increase in cases often considered as more controversial' (Dierickx et al. 2016. p. 7). Commenting on recent data (Dierickx et al. 2015), Barron Lerner and Arthur Caplan detect 'worrisome trends'. Not only are applicants now listing 'tiredness of life' in their requests but 'the fastest-growing populations receiving euthanasia include those potentially vulnerable to discrimination and stigma' (Lerner and Caplan 2015, p. 1641).

Another shift that has occurred in euthanasia practice in Belgium is an increasing willingness to grant euthanasia requests. Between 2007 and 2013, the percentage of requests granted has increased from approximately 55 per cent to around 77 per cent (Chambaere et al. 2015a; Dierickx et al. 2015; Lerner and Caplan 2015).

Utilitarian considerations neither favour nor oppose euthanasia a priori. Utilitarian judgements are always a posteriori, based on estimates of overall utility or disutility. What makes the Belgian euthanasia data most problematic from a utilitarian perspective is the rapidly rising numbers and the continually shifting nature of practice. There is no sense of having reached a stable outcome from which to base one's estimate of the net utility. It is like trying to assess the effects of a bush fire before a fire has burnt itself out. Euthanasia in Belgium is a fire that is still expanding and affecting increasing numbers and increasing categories of people. It is therefore necessary to be cautious in making a judgement and also to consider not only present numbers but also the direction of change, and what may occur.

these represent a smaller proportion of euthanasia deaths than in the previous report (from 17.2% in 2013 down to 14.8% in 2015). It seems paradoxical that a large rise in the proportion of deaths with multiple pathologies (from 6% in 2013 to 10.3% in 2015), and a continuing, if modest, increase in non-cancer deaths more generally (from 31.2% in 2013 to 32.3% in 2015), should be accompanied by an increase in 'foreseen death'. Prognosis from cancer is typically more predictable than other causes of death and thus one would expect a decrease in cancer deaths to correlate with a decrease in foreseen death. As there is no legal or agreed definition of 'foreseen', it may be asked whether this term is being interpreted consistently over time or whether the interpretation is shifting as the practice shifts. It may also be noted that, while the French version of the law states that death is foreseen 'in a short time' (à brève échéance) there is no equivalent to this phrase in the Dutch-language version of the law nor in the Dutch-language version of the FCECE reports. In a Flemish context, the meaning of 'foreseen' (afzienbare) seems particularly open to expansion. Hence, one should view the figure for 'foreseen' death with some caution and rely more on data drawing on specific diagnostic categories.

It can at least be said that all the changes evident in Belgium point in the same direction, which is not only to expanding numbers but also to lowering of thresholds to access euthanasia and to increasing indications including non-terminal conditions. There is an evident shift from euthanasia to address intractable physical symptoms in people with terminal conditions, which are the best candidates for prospective net utility, towards ever more uncertain and more subjective criteria. These changes all increase the risks of missing out on months or years of future life, and missing the possibility of future remission. While there is no confidence about how far these changes will go, and certainly there is no indication at present of them having reached their furthest extent, the Belgian experiment of legalisation of euthanasia cannot be pronounced to be a success in utilitarian terms.

Euthanasia in Belgium: A Libertarian Perspective

From a libertarian perspective, the fundamental justification for euthanasia is as a form of self-determination. This is evident in earlier quotation of Batavia 'The value central to those of us who support a right to assisted suicide is autonomy' (Batavia 2000, p. 557). In the early and mid-twentieth century, as in the work of Glanville Williams, euthanasia was defended primarily on utilitarian grounds rather than by appeal to liberty or autonomy. Nevertheless, from the 1960s liberty or autonomy has increasingly become the dominant rationale for a change in the law.

From this perspective, the evidence of ongoing deaths by LAWER in Belgium is of great concern. Between 1998 and 2001 the prevalence of such acts markedly declined in frequency (from 3.2 per cent to 1.5 per cent), but since legalisation of euthanasia, deaths by LAWER have remained stable at 1.8 per cent/ 1.7 per cent, a level slightly higher than the 2001 figure (Chambaere et al. 2015, p. 1180). Intentional ending of life without request still accounts for approximately 1,000 deaths a year in Flanders alone. In addition to this enduring practice, other forms of life-shortening decision have increased since the legalisation of euthanasia, most prominently continuing deep sedation until death. It is not clear in the cases of sedation which aimed to shorten life what percentage was at the request of the patient. However, only 12.7 per cent of cases of continuous deep sedation until death in Belgium were at the request of the patient, and only 24% without request but at least with the consent of the patient (Papavasiliou et al. 2014, table 4, combining the data for GPs and medical specialists). Taking these different forms of life shortening together, it seems certain that there has been an increase in life ending without request since 2002.

One response to such data is to argue that figures for death by LAWER overstate this phenomenon. Research indicates that in more than a third of LAWER cases the patient had 'at some point expressed a wish for life to be ended (implicitly or explicitly, but not as a formal euthanasia request)' (Chambaere et al. 2014). Be that as it may, there is no equivalence between expressing a wish that the end-of-life be hastened and requesting euthanasia. Even if the expressed wish were serious, explicit and unambiguous, it would not thereby be a request, which is a kind of speech act, what JL Austin (1975) termed a 'performative utterance'.

The research in question was also flawed in asking if a patient 'ever express[ed]' such a wish, for this would include people who at one time expressed such a wish but later expressed the opposite wish. When it comes to a sometime previous wish for life to be ended that is said to be 'expressed. . . but not explicitly', we are in even more ambiguous territory. Such reports are clearly wholly dependent on the interpretation given by the one listening. If this category is intended to provide reassurance it has the opposite effect. From a libertarian perspective, the deliberate ending of someone's life, other than in response to his or her explicit request, simply is non-voluntary termination of life. The attempt to gloss as quasi-voluntary those deaths that are 'in accordance with a patient's wish to die (albeit not in the form of a legally prescribed euthanasia request)' aggravates the problem by seeming to excuse the practice.[11]

The extension of the Act in 2013 to cover minors, without lower age limit, and proposals debated in 2013 (though not in fact passed) to give legal force to advance euthanasia directives in cases where people have dementia, both raise difficult questions for libertarians in relation to people with compromised mental capacity. On the one hand, it is arguably a wish to honour autonomy that has led to the extension of euthanasia. The law, as framed, does not allow the euthanasia of children unless they have 'capacity of discernment'. On the other hand, the extension of the law to minors takes away a layer of protection for those

---

[11] Chambaere et al. 2014. The same move was made by van Delden in response to those who expressed shock about the 1,000 deaths by LAWER identified by the 1990 Remmelink report. He denies that such deaths occurred 'without any request at all' on the basis that '600 (59%) of these patients were involved in some way or other, although not in the sense of explicitly requesting their end of life to be hastened' (van Delden et al. 1993, pp. 328–329). Again, from a libertarian perspective, such special pleading only serves to make matters worse, for it seems to belittle the importance of 'explicitly requesting'.

who may appear to have the requisite capacity but do not possess it consistently or without impulsivity. A similar point may be made about the increase in euthanasia for people with 'neuropsychiatric disorders' (from 25 in 2010 to 63 in 2015),[12] as evidenced in the respective FCECE. Is it respecting autonomy to offer euthanasia to someone who is suffering with a psychiatric condition and who may be struggling against suicidal ideation? What is communicated by such an offer? Such cases show the tension between different conceptions of autonomy.

A further issue that is more difficult to quantify, is whether the increasing prevalence of euthanasia creates an expectation on people that they should consider this as an option. Choice is not exercised in a vacuum but against expectations that are partly determined by social practices. It would be paradoxical if a proposal put forward in the name of liberty, resulted in the curtailment of liberty, but such paradoxes can occur. Certainly, the evidence from Belgium shows that the rise in rates of euthanasia has been accompanied by a rise also in non-voluntary life-terminating acts and has even seen some researchers seeking to excuse such non-voluntary deaths. From a libertarian perspective, an extension of the range of choices in death is certainly desirable, per se, but not at the cost of an increase in intentional ending of life by doctors without the request or even the consent of the patient. This is what seems to have happened in Belgium.

Euthanasia in Belgium: From Rival Traditions to a Defensible Conclusion

The traditions described here are not wholly distinct and indeed many clinicians will take elements from different moral traditions. Nevertheless, there are both different priorities in the way these traditions rank their principles and also difference of understanding. It is precisely for this reason that they can be taken as distinct perspectives which might contrast with or complement one another.

It is not implied by this approach that these three traditions are equally true (or equally false) or that there is no hope of deciding between them on rational grounds. On the contrary, they make incompatible claims, for example, in relation to the justice of killing or the criteria of moral goodness, and these claims cannot all be equally true. Nor are these three exhaustive of the possibilities available to a student of moral philosophy in

---

[12] Reported euthanasia for this indication peaked at 67 in 2013 but the figures for 2014 and 2015 remain higher than any year before 2013 (See FCECE Seventh Report 2016).

a modern university (to say nothing of previous perspectives of previous ages). Nevertheless, these three traditions are prominent in academic and in popular culture. They are each invoked frequently in relation to the morality and law of killing. They are each supported by various aspects of modern professional, economic or political life and none is in danger of imminent departure from Western intellectual culture.

Faced, then, with simultaneous disagreement on principles and on interpretation of evidence, there has been merit in considering the evidence from one country but examined in three ways. This method results in a conclusion that is more compelling because it is not dependent on an ethical framework which is subject to dispute.

This enquiry has shown that euthanasia practice in Belgium raises grave concerns within Hippocratic, utilitarian and libertarian frames. These frames have indeed picked out distinct concerns and vary in relation to the strength of the concern and the degree of certainty. Nevertheless, there is convergence on a central practical conclusion, that from none of these three perspectives does the evidence show the Belgian euthanasia experiment to have been successful.

It is not only that the practice of euthanasia is incompatible with a fundamental element of traditional Hippocratic medical ethics, but also that Belgium shows how accepting this practice has had an impact on other aspects of medical decision making. This is evident not least in relation to the practice of sedation *with the intention to shorten life*. From a utilitarian perspective, a firm conclusion is harder to attain, because the figures keep rising, it is a practice in flux. Nevertheless, the evidence to date gives a strong indication of the direction of change. This involves the increasing likelihood of ending lives months or years before their time and based on increasingly subjective and uncertain indications. Finally, an examination of the practice from a libertarian perspective has seen not only a rise in unjustifiable non-voluntary life-ending acts, and an expansion to people whose capacity may be compromised, but also moves to tolerate or even excuse such acts.

The convergence among these three traditions on this practical point is in part a reflection of the context of this issue. It seems that the simultaneous presence of utilitarian and libertarian rationales for the practice has produced simultaneous movements in opposite directions.[13]

---

[13] As argued by Keown (2002), though the structure of the argument developed here is distinct in various ways from that of Keown, and has sought not to presuppose a single agreed moral-philosophical framework.

The Hippocratic prohibition on intentional hastening of death serves both to inhibit intending death without request and to inhibit the ending of life on a subjective basis of people who are not terminal. When this Hippocratic prohibition is removed, the practice of voluntary euthanasia is subject to pressures that expand it in both directions, and both within and outside the legal framework. Thus, utilitarian concerns and libertarian concerns are both, in practice, safeguarded by medical adherence to the Hippocratic prohibition. In the abstract, it might seem that this prohibition could be removed without harm to utility or liberty, but the evidence from Belgium is that, in practice, euthanasia legislation is harmful not only to the maintenance of a Hippocratic ethos but also in relation to utilitarian goals and libertarian aspirations.[14]

---

[14] Arguably, this enquiry illustrates how, more generally, the pursuit of happiness and the pursuit of liberty are both rationally compromised without a commitment to respect basic human goods including the good of human life. In Aristotelian terms this conclusion illustrates the need to pursue and respect diverse aspects of the human good simultaneously, if one is to find that happiness which is eudaimonia. In Kantian terms, it illustrates the relation between the autonomy that is worthy of respect, and the imperative to respect human nature in others and also in ourselves. Indeed, it is for such reasons that Kant did not regard suicide as an authentic expression of autonomy nor assisting suicide as expressing respect for autonomy, though Kant would not have regarded this thesis as the proper subject of an empirical enquiry.

15

Psychiatric Patients and the Culture
of Euthanasia in Belgium

WILLEM LEMMENS

'even the rabble without doors may judge from the noise and clamour, which they hear, that all goes not well within'.

David Hume, *A Treatise of Human Nature*, Introduction

In *JAMA Psychiatry* of April 2014, three Belgian academics of the *Vrije Universiteit Brussel* published a viewpoint article addressing the issue of euthanasia for non-terminal, psychiatric patients suffering from severe mental disorders. This article is remarkable for at least two reasons: first of all, because it admits that in Belgium today euthanasia is increasingly offered to this group of patients; second, because it recognises that the task of deliberating on these euthanasia requests may be 'too hard to deal with for an individual physician' (Deschepper et al. 2014). The authors admit that the emotional, ethical and even physical burden of addressing these requests is considerable. They express the need not only to optimise euthanasia provisions for psychiatric patients that are in the grip of unbearable mental suffering, but also to provide better training for physicians and caretakers engaged in euthanasia for this group of patients.

In what follows, I take the testimony of these major experts as a reference for some critical reflections on the practice of euthanasia as it unfolded in Belgium since its decriminalisation in 2002. In my view, their opinion bears testimony to a concerning shift of culture in end-of-life care in this country due to the euthanasia social experiment. This shift is worrisome because the implementation of the law on euthanasia propagates an ideal of autonomy and self-determination that is difficult to square with the tragic condition of groups of vulnerable patients, such as psychiatric patients suffering from severe mental disorders. Not a few physicians welcome this shift as a break with the paternalism of classical Hippocratic medicine. However, usually hailed as a change for the better, this rupture contains, I believe, possible dangers and threats that have to date received little attention in the medical world and civil society in Belgium.

While my reflection starts from this opinion article, I do not want to offer a head-on answer on the specific practical worries it addresses, nor do I intend to give a personal reaction on the involvement during the past years of its authors in the deployment of euthanasia for psychiatric patients. My aim is rather to present a genealogical reading of this opinion to highlight some features of the euthanasia debate in general as it unfolded over the past decade in Belgium. I concentrate hereby on euthanasia for patients with psychiatric disorders and abstract from other vulnerable groups, such as elderly people with dementia or minors. However, in different respects my critical observations on the Belgian euthanasia practice may well also be applicable to these groups of patients. Further qualitative research and critical reflection should be developed to better understand the specific challenges that the decriminalisation of euthanasia poses to end-of-life care in Belgium in general.

Unbearable Mental Suffering and the Wish to Die

Belgian physicians willing to offer euthanasia are increasingly confronted with the wish to die of psychiatric patients with severe psychological disorders. Deschepper et al. (2014) mentions 100 such cases between 2007 and 2011 and followed up until February 2013. This apparently is a brief reference to a study published recently, where more details are given about a sample of 100 cases of euthanasia requests from psychiatric patients (Thienpont et al. 2015). The 100 patients in this study are categorised as forming one special group on the basis of a diagnosis of 'psychological suffering associated with psychiatric disorders' (Thienpont et al. 2015, p. 3). Of these 100 patients only 23 had a non-fatal somatic disease (such as chronic fatigue or fibromyalgia) in combination with one or more psychiatric disorders. These patients were thus obviously not terminally ill. Nonetheless, each of these patients submitted a request for euthanasia. The psychiatric disorders considered in accordance with the Belgian law as 'untreatable' and the cause of 'unbearable suffering without any prospect of improvement' ranged from treatment-resistant mood disorders and personality disorders to schizophrenia and other psychotic disorders. But Asperger syndrome and obsessive-compulsive disorders were also considered (Thienpont et al. 2015, p. 5).

Of the sample of 100 patients, 38 withdrew their initial request before the start of the euthanasia procedure. Of the remaining 62 cases, 48 got a positive advice, of which 35 died through euthanasia. Of the requests not granted, five ended in suicide. Recently, one of the co-authors of this study and of the *JAMA* article, Dr Distelmans, testified in an interview for the widely read weekly Flemish magazine *Humo* that in 2013 and 2014 some 50 to 60 patients a year (2 to 3 per cent of the 1924 euthanasia cases in 2014) were euthanised for psychiatric reasons (Carpentier and Antonissen 2015).[1]

These patients have often been under medical observance for years and seem to have no hope or prospect of recovery. They testify to being in the grip of unbearable suffering that, according to the authors of the article mentioned, 'is not less severe than physical suffering and is often hard to treat'. The problems physicians are confronted with in these cases are vexing. One can hardly ignore that the request to die from these patients differs in a substantial way from the more regular requests for euthanasia from terminal patients who are at the end of their lives due to an incurable physical illness. The picture sketched in the *JAMA* article of this issue is revealing, but also illustrates a clear evolution in end-of-life care in Belgium since the implementation of the euthanasia law more than a decade ago. In other words, an increasing number of euthanasia applications are granted to patients who are not terminally ill.

The authors introduce their opinion by highlighting the overall positive effects the legalisation or decriminalisation of euthanasia has had in countries such as Belgium and the Netherlands. They also mention 'some states in the United States' where the law permits physicians to actively help patients to die. Remarkably, in the title, the authors already treat euthanasia and physician assisted suicide as identical, conflating them as one legal figure (called Euthanasia/Assisted Suicide EAS).[2]

This is remarkable, because the Belgian Act of 2002 offers, as such, no legal regulation for physician assisted suicide. In Belgian law euthanasia implies the active ending of a person's life by a physician on request of

---

[1] Psychiatrist Lieve Thienpont, a colleague of Dr Distelmans, estimates that since the establishment of their consultation centre ULTeam in 2011, they received 900 patients of whom 50 per cent reflected a 'psychiatric problematic' (Thienpont 2015, p. 204). The author does not mention how many of these 450 patients were granted euthanasia. ULTeam is an acronym for Uitklaring Levenseindevragen Team (i.e., team for the clearance of end-of-life questions).

[2] In the following, I will refer to EAS when I directly comment on the text of the *JAMA* opinion article. Otherwise I just use the term 'euthanasia' as the act of actively ending a human life by a physician on request by the patient (unless I further distinguish between passive and non-passive, or voluntary and non-voluntary euthanasia).

the first. In the spirit of the law the physician should not just be a passive bystander offering help in dying (or in committing suicide). It might be that this apparent discrimination, which is in fact due to the silence of the law, is unconstitutional (Adams and Nys 2005, pp. 9–10). Why the Belgian lawgiver has remained rather silent on assisted suicide is unclear. One might have wanted to avoid any possible confusion of a granted euthanasia, as such, with the act of suicide: while the first comes down to intentional 'mercy killing' by a physician in a specific situation of medical care, the second takes place outside the scope of medical care and is considered a serious societal problem.

As is well known, Belgium has among the highest suicide rates in the Western world. Obviously, the Belgian lawgiver eagerly wanted its euthanasia law not to be contaminated by this gloomy truth. However, the subtle extension of terminology in the *JAMA* article reflects how difficult it is in the sphere of psychiatry to distinguish euthanasia neatly from suicide: here indeed, tragically enough, requests for euthanasia may often contain a hidden suicide threat. In this sense, the blurring of the distinction between euthanasia and physician-assisted suicide is understandable, though perhaps less unproblematic than it might appear at first sight. Apparently, the fact that Belgian experts identify PAS and euthanasia under one legal figure (EAS) reflects how both have become part of the larger euthanasia practice in Belgium, despite the silence of the law on this point.

But why exactly, according to the authors, did the legal regulation of EAS have such a positive impact on the practice of end-of-life care? Here the opinion highlights the standard arguments often heard in Belgium: 'legalization of EAS', so one reads, 'might function as a safeguard to semi-legal (sic) practices'; it generally 'fosters transparency' and 'enables one to verify whether criteria of due care are met', and finally, it 'provides legal safety for the physicians involved'. This is a nice synopsis of the pragmatic considerations that were brought forward in Belgium during the rather short legislative process that preceded the acceptance of the euthanasia act by parliament in 2002. Of course, next to pragmatic considerations, there were more substantial ethical principles that lay at the basis of these legislative initiatives. Briefly summarised, these ethical principles are, (1) respect for the *autonomy* of the patient who can request that his or her life be ended under certain conditions; (2) *mercy* of the physician who wants to assist his or her patient with dying when he or she so requests. 'Autonomy of the patient' and 'mercy of the physician' are, according to the standard view in Belgium, the two ethical pillars that buttress the euthanasia law.

The authors of the opinion in *JAMA Psychiatry* do not dwell explicitly on these moral principles. They take them for granted and, moreover, they assume that the reader knows exactly what is understood by euthanasia in Belgian law. At this point, it is worth stressing that the legal provisions for euthanasia in Belgium in general are quite similar, though not identical, to the ones in the Netherlands and Luxemburg, but quite different from the law on physician-assisted suicide in, for example, Oregon. I dwell no further on these divergences here, but just notice that legal provisions for euthanasia unavoidably ask for interpretation and practical implementation (see Nys, Chapter 1). This is also the case with the Belgian euthanasia act.

Defining euthanasia as the intentional termination of a person's life by someone else at the former's request, Belgian law stipulates that this other should be a physician.[3] In Belgium, physicians that provide euthanasia do so mostly by a lethal injection.[4] Usually, they prefer to be in full control of the deliberation process preceding the terminating act. They may consider it their duty to perform this act themselves or to be in any case present at the final moment (in the rare cases where the patient takes the lethal doses of euthanising medication themselves).[5]

However, insofar that not a few physicians in Belgium are reluctant or even outright unwilling to perform euthanasia, patients may receive the life-ending treatment by another physician than their GP or the specialists that followed them through their disease process. With psychiatric patients suffering from chronic mental disorders this might be even more common. Not only do they often have a long history of therapy and treatment with different physicians, for a definitive granting of their euthanasia request they also need to be seen by a psychiatrist. So, it might well turn out that the final euthanasia procedure is offered to them by a physician other than the one who has been following them during most of their lives. The study, previously mentioned, gives evidence for this: most of the 100 patients with psychiatric afflictions who received

---

[3] For an English version of The Belgian Act on Euthanasia, see the Appendix III of the present volume.

[4] Unfortunately, some physicians delegate the lethal injection to a nurse. This is illegal and betrays, on the side of the physicians, a sense of fleeting ones responsibility (Cohen-Almagor 2013, p. 516).

[5] The psychiatrist, Lieve Thienpont, favours the position that psychiatric patients take the life ending medication orally, that is, by (physician assisted) suicide. She considers this act a symbolic confirmation on the side of the patient of his or her will to die, his or her 'own act of will' (Thienpont 2015, p. 188)

euthanasia were sent to the same psychiatrist by other physicians or therapists (Thienpont et al. 2015).[6] Apparently this psychiatrist was not necessarily in charge of the final euthanasia act, though she offered each time the ultimate advice that made the aid in dying possible.

Next to the pivotal role of the physician, the Belgian law on euthanasia highlights crucially the idea of patient autonomy, be it with an eye for some preconditions. The law first stipulates that the patient should 'be in a medically futile condition of constant and unbearable physical or mental suffering that cannot be alleviated, resulting from a serious and incurable disorder caused by illness or accident'.[7] Further, the law requires that the patient should be well informed about his or her terminal health condition and that there should be 'no reasonable alternative' to his or her situation. The law further asks that the patient should deliberate with his or her physicians over a 'reasonable period of time' about his or her wish to die. Moreover, the law urges for the consultation of one or two other physicians (when death is not imminent or the patient is in coma) and recommends the consultation of the family of the patient.[8] If possible, the nursing team should be involved in the deliberation process. However, in the end, it is the *free* and *voluntary* request of the patient that should determine the final decision of the physician to honour or not the patient's death wish.

Some legal experts in Belgium were, from early on, doubtful about the alleged transparency of the euthanasia Act of 2002 (Adams and Nys 2005). The authors of the *JAMA* opinion article apparently do not share these worries, at least not in the case of euthanasia requests of patients with serious irreversible diseases such as cancer or certain neuromuscular afflictions. However, they admit that the situation with psychiatric patients who suffer from severe and chronic mental disorders is different. They voice some concerns that clearly relate both to the interpretation and to the application of the law. Their testimony appears to be based on personal experience.

First, the authors testify about considerable stress physicians experience when confronted with requests from psychiatric patients who are sometimes 'well-informed, quite assertive, young, well-educated' and,

---

[6] In a Letter to the editor some Belgian experts voiced profound concerns about the pivotal role of one specific psychiatrist in most of the euthanasia cases for psychiatric patients in Belgium (Claes et al. 2015).

[7] The Belgian Act on Euthanasia, chapter II, section 3, §1.

[8] A patient in an irreversible coma and who left a written will not older than 5 years can receive euthanasia. Without such an advance directive, euthanasia is not legally possible.

evidently, 'not terminally ill'. These patients often put pressure on the physician and threaten, occasionally, to commit suicide if the physician or medical team refuses to grant their euthanasia request.[9]

Second, the authors stress the diagnostic uncertainty in the case of serious mental suffering and psychiatric diseases: the physician might 'fail to detect a (treatable) depression or some other kind of mood disorder'. Moreover, so the experts confirm, 'the implementation of laws on EAS is often impeded by ambivalence and by the vagueness of concepts such as "unbearable suffering" and "incurable disease"'.[10]

This brings us to a further complicating factor in the case of euthanasia for psychiatric and/or severely depressed patients. As the experts testify, regularly, relatives put pressure on the physician and the medical team by their emotional reactions and even accusations. These accusations occur on some occasions most vehemently when the physician has offered euthanasia to a patient without consulting the family. Though the law recommends that the family should be consulted in the deliberation process preceding the assisted dying, the physician in charge must respect the autonomy of the patient: if he or she wishes, for whatever reason, that the family is not informed about his or her euthanasia request or be present at the final hour, the physician has to respect this.

For example, early summer 2015 a well-documented article in the *New Yorker* on the euthanasia practice in Belgium paid attention to three cases of euthanasia granted to patients who were not terminally ill, but suffered from a chronic depression.[11] In two of these cases, the children were informed of the death of their mother after the euthanasia was offered. In another case the physician in charge neglected the appeals of a daughter who was opposed to the euthanasia on her mother and wanted at least to be at her mother's bedside when she died. This article caused some disquiet in Belgium, because it revealed that the children felt

---

[9] In Switzerland a similar experience is reported in relation to assisted suicide (Gamondi et al. 2013): 'In some cases, the patients, in response to doubtful relatives, were reported to repetitively threaten to commit suicide. This kind of pressure from the patient was reported as strongly manipulative by relatives, and it forced the relatives to act in support of assisted suicide, which was regarded as qualitatively better than classical suicide.'

[10] On this vagueness see also Rietjens et al. 2009.

[11] The article by the journalist Rachel Aviv was conceived as a sort of testimony of a distant observer, who interviewed dozens of experts in Belgium and gave, at the same time, an empathic 'thick' description of the lived experience of especially the children of some patients who received euthanasia for a non-terminal condition of depression and psychological suffering (cf. Aviv 2015).

seriously harmed by the specific way in which their mother died. In each of these three cases the children found the attitude of the responsible physician towards the family of the patient negligent and condescending.[12]

A fifth and last complication, though not least disturbing, concerns the difficulty the physician must assess the voluntary, well-considered character of the request for euthanasia. The authors of the *JAMA* article admit that especially psychiatric patients and patients suffering from severe depression may have their capacity of judgement impaired. This makes it hard 'to differentiate between a request based on a genuine and constant form of unbearable suffering and a request as a symptom of a severe depression'. Apparently, the physician here has to rely on the subjective 'perception and complaints' of the patient himself or herself to judge how severely and unbearably he or she suffers. Moreover, the physician must find a way to differentiate between a death wish that is merely a symptom of depression, and one that can be canonised as an expression of free will.

The authors appear to be convinced that this distinction can be made, though often 'after a long and time-consuming process' of dialogue with the patient and a close follow-up of his or her general mental state. The authors thus appear to agree with the *Diagnostic and Statistical Manual of Mental Disorders* (DSM-V) that a death wish forms often a clear indication in the diagnosis of major depression. At the same time, they act in accordance with the directive of the Dutch association of psychiatrists (*Nederlandse Vereniging voor Psychiatrie*) that stipulates that in cases of chronic depression, a wish to die can become durable and should be considered the expression of the well-considered rational choice of the patient.[13] In these cases, so the authors of the *JAMA* article agree, the physician may come to the conclusion that 'all the available treatments have not resulted in any improvement' of the patient's condition. In this case, the verdict may be that the patient fulfils all the criteria for euthanasia. According to the authors, honouring the patient's desire to die thus becomes an act of mercy. It means the recognition of his or her dignity and autonomy.[14]

---

[12] The testimonies in the *New Yorker* reveal that, in the opinion of the children, it is obvious that their mothers could still be alive if they would not have met physicians to help them with their euthanasia requests.

[13] Nederlandse Vereniging voor Psychiatrie 2009. *Richtlijn omgaan met het verzoek om hulp bij zelfdoding door patiënten met psychiatrische stoornis.* Utrecht: de Tijdstroom.

[14] This is also the view of Thienpont in her rather personal testimony as a psychiatrist (Thienpont 2015). This emphasis on patient autonomy as the decisive feature of human dignity is generally stressed in the public debate on euthanasia in Belgium (see also Bernheim et al. 2014).

Recommendations and Worries

The testimony of the experts of the *Vrije Universiteit Brussel* concludes with a few recommendations to enhance the euthanasia practice for psychiatric patients with chronic mental afflictions. Overall, these recommendations are vague and create more questions than answers. Of course, this succinct article was obviously not meant to delve deep into the issue at stake: in the first place, it wanted to highlight the psychological and practical difficulties that physicians might experience when confronted with euthanasia requests of a specific group of vulnerable patients. As the title of the opinion indicates: this is an expression of worry, even a cry of distress by physicians that feel 'vulnerable' themselves when confronted with the euthanasia request of psychiatric patients that are not terminally ill. However, I believe the vagueness of the recommendations as such hides some deeper difficulties that I would like to unpack a bit further. For they relate, in my opinion, to a fundamentally problematic feature of the Belgian euthanasia social experiment. Namely, a too exclusive and uncritical propagation of the ethical principle of respect for autonomy and self-determination.

In fact, the recommendations of the experts in the *JAMA* article to increase the quality of euthanasia provisions for psychiatric patients come down to one: better training of the physicians involved in euthanasia. How should we understand this recommendation? Allegedly, a multidisciplinary team may help to alleviate the stress physicians experience when confronted with stubborn patients and families that suffer emotionally or utter accusations before or after the euthanasia on a loved one: 'such a team can make decisions in a transparent way and can allow caregivers to share responsibility and find support in each other'. The authors of the *JAMA* article are convinced that a shared responsibility and mutual mental support and consultation might make them feel less vulnerable. Even for psychiatric patients, euthanasia might thus become a more integrated part of a broader praxis of end-of-life care. In this sense, the experts further urge that training in end-of-life care should become part of the general medical education. They add that even in countries where euthanasia is not legalised, this sort of training should be implemented since, in these countries, physicians might also be confronted with demands for euthanasia on psychiatric grounds.[15] These recommendations square well with those of a recent article by Belgian experts

---

[15] The authors refer to the following study for evidence about such demands: van der Heide et al. 2003.

(one of them is also author of the *JAMA* opinion) who believe euthanasia should become an integral part of palliative care giving Belgium a guiding role to play for the rest of the world.[16]

In fact, this recommendation takes a lot for granted. It implicitly suggests that a liberal legal regulation of euthanasia is *ipso facto* to the benefit of patients that are in the grip of chronic mental suffering and express the wish to die. Of course, physicians who already decided they should follow these patients in their death wish might feel strengthened by a supportive team and an open, cooperative pro euthanasia culture. The exchange of feelings, thoughts and experiences may alleviate the psychological and mental pressure on care teams involved in euthanasia, especially on patients that are non-terminal ill. Perhaps, working in a team may further help to form a psychological bulwark against too oppressive patients or accusing family members. Moreover, as the authors suggest, the more physicians are trained to offer euthanasia, the smaller the risk becomes that colleagues get overburdened. In the case of psychiatric patients this last challenge is most pressing, as a majority of Belgian psychiatrists appears to be rather reluctant, if not unwilling to perform euthanasia (Claes et al. 2015).[17]

But these recommendations do not meet the more profound worries the authors also highlight. For teamwork is not at all the legitimate answer to the diagnostic uncertainty involved in the treatment of patients with severe mental afflictions who ask for euthanasia, nor does it take away the highly subjective standard for determining the degree of suffering of these patients. Also the difficulty of distinguishing between a pathological death wish and a genuine voluntary euthanasia request remains highly controversial. Why would a team of physicians reach a reliable clinical verdict on this point, when it is agreed that the making of the distinction is not based on an objective, evidence based criterion other than the subjective expression of the wish of the patient as such? Indeed, the authors of the *JAMA* article assure the reader that they have a

---

[16] Bernheim et al. 2014. The full subtitle of the article is: '"Eu-Euthanasia": The Close Historical, and Evidently Synergistic Relationship between Palliative Care and Euthanasia in Belgium: An Interview with a Doctor Involved in the Early Development of Both and Two of his Successors.'

[17] In October 2015, an opinion article criticising the current Belgian practice of euthanasia in psychiatric patients and patients suffering from merely psychic afflictions was signed by more than 40 experts, physicians as well as psychologists, ethicists and legal experts. The majority of these were psychiatrists and clinical psychologists (16) of all Belgian language communities (cf. Bazan 2015).

reliable method or procedure to determine the clinical ground for making this distinction cases. However, certainly not all psychiatrists or clinical psychologists trust that such a reliable method or procedure actually exists (Bazan et al. 2015; Claes et al. 2015).

In this perspective, it becomes understandable that most physicians in countries that have legalised euthanasia, specialists as well as GP's, neatly distinguish between the acceptability of euthanasia for psychiatric patients and euthanasia in the case of patients with a terminal physical disease, such as cancer or a fatal neurodegenerative disease. In a recent opinion study among Dutch physicians a considerable majority found it conceivable to grant euthanasia to patients with cancer (85%) or another physical disease (82%). Of this same group, this willingness decreased in case of patients with psychiatric diseases (34%), early-stage dementia (40%), advanced dementia (29–33%) or patients tired of living (27%) (Bolt et al. 2015). A reason for this reluctance may be the difficulty to judge unequivocally about the 'well-considered' character of the wish to die of these last groups of patients. That adds up to the uncertainty and vagueness of criteria like 'untreatable' and 'unbearable suffering' in the case of psychiatric patients.

There are other problems the opinion article does not address. One of the main issues is of course the questionable exclusion of the family from the euthanasia decision process and the final act of putting the patient to death.[18] How can, on closer inspection, physicians justify a decision that causes such tragic and traumatic controversies? It is not so much the physician who appears to be vulnerable here, but rather the families that are left behind with the loss of a loved one. Their complaints show that these family members feel traumatised not only by the attitude of the physicians involved, but also by society because it ignores *by its very laws* the genuine nature of their traumatic suffering.

No concerns about this are mentioned by the authors of the *JAMA* article: they rather complain that on a few occasions family members of euthanasia patients contacted the Belgian media with accusations, without the physicians being able to defend themselves, given the duty of medical confidentiality.[19] It remains a bit puzzling, however,

[18] Belgian physicians testify confidentially of cases where quarrels occurred at the bedside of patients, whereby euthanasia is offered against the wish of some family members, also in the case of psychiatric patients. These testimonies confirm some cases that reach public attention, as in Aviv 2015.
[19] The authors mention physical threats by family members and interrogations by an attorney. However, they remain silent about the complaints laid down by a few patients since 2013 to the *Orde van artsen* (previously *Orde van geneesheren*), i.e., the *Medical*

how medical confidentiality can be an excuse for the dismissal or condescending negligence of the grief and complaints of the family of euthanasia patients. In reaction to the testimonies of children in the *New Yorker*, two leading pro euthanasia figures in Belgium, the philosopher Etienne Vermeersch and the retired oncologist Jan Bernheim, even went so far as to suggest that these children suffered from 'pathological mourning' and needed psychiatric assistance (Bernheim and Vermeersch 2015). The insensitivity of such allegations is appalling, but unfortunately reflects the zeal with which important public figures try to silence any critique of the euthanasia law and practice in Belgium. It is striking that no one among the pro euthanasia experts ever seems to consider the possibility that there might be something wrong with a law that creates such emotional and existential havoc. Indeed, the euthanasia law insists on the duty to respect the autonomy of the patient and only *recommends* consulting the family: the law here probably undermines an ethics of due medical care.

Admittedly, the authors of the *JAMA* article are not wholly insensitive to the need for extra caution. They do signal that, in the case of psychiatric patients, physicians should be more reluctant and take a longer decision procedure than with more regular euthanasia cases. In fact, the Belgian law requires this. It stipulates that, when the patient is not expected to die soon, a period of a month should pass between the initial written request and the act of euthanasia. Next to this, the law ordains that, in these cases, a third physician should be consulted who is a psychiatrist or a specialist in the disorder in question.[20] This third consultation comes above the second opinion which, in every case of euthanasia, is required by the law. These safeguards invite caution and well-considered judgement on the side of the physician.

However, in the case of psychiatric patients or people with severe mental disorders a period of reflection of only one month between the request and the euthanasia act appears futile from a diagnostic perspective. Moreover, the law makes it possible to leave the family wholly out of sight. All the weight is laid on the *colloque singulier* between physician and patient. The physician is the one who takes the final decision after having listened carefully to his or her patient.

Council that preserves the deontology and honour of the medical profession. These two complaints come from children that also contributed with their testimony to the article in the *New Yorker* (Aviv 2015).
[20] The Belgian Act on Euthanasia, Chapter 2, § 3, 1.

Of course, here too, the additional consultation of colleagues could offer some guidance. Remarkably, however, in Belgian law there need be *no* unanimity between the consulted physicians that consider a euthanasia request including in the case of psychiatric patients. Physicians may judge differently the question whether there is further treatment available or whether there has been sufficient consultation of the family and loved ones. Equally, psychiatrists might differ in opinion on whether the patient, who requests euthanasia, is in the grip of a symptomatic mood disturbance rather than being able to choose to die freely and in full awareness.[21] In short, for the Belgian law giver the responsibility for a positive answer to a euthanasia request lies, in the last instance, with the physician who commits the final act: he or she is also in charge of the consultation with colleagues and the dialogue with the patient before a definitive verdict is made.

Despite all these vexing issues, during the past decade, the number of euthanasia cases among patients with psychiatric or severe mental disorders in Belgium has clearly increased. In an interview for the popular press, Dr Distelmans, one of the authors of the *JAMA* article, leaves no doubt as to his opinion that euthanasia for psychiatric patients should be seen as fully warranted within the conditions stipulated by Belgian law (Carpentier and Antonissen 2015). Not a few Belgian GPs and psychiatrists, but also clinical psychologists, see this as a worrisome evolution. Euthanasia requests from their core patients have become part of the medical culture in Belgium, despite the fact that only a minority of psychiatrists might experience this evolution as unequivocally positive (Claes et al. 2015; Bazan et al. 2015).[22]

---

[21] Different studies on the Belgian situation confirm that, as to the acceptability of the euthanasia request, a lack of unanimity between the consulting physicians is structural. Cohen-Almagor concludes that euthanasia consultation in Belgium is 'inadequate' (Cohen-Almagor 2013, p. 516).

[22] To my knowledge, there is no empirical data yet on the opinion of Belgian psychiatrists. Some Belgian psychiatrists share the worries in Claes et al. 2015 or Bazan et al. 2015, but are open to a care culture where euthanasia would be granted in very exceptional cases. Cf.: Vandenberghe et al. 2013. Some international studies give evidence that worldwide psychiatrists are reluctant towards euthanasia in the case of psychiatric diseases, even if they are neutral on the acceptability of euthanasia for other groups of diseases (McCormack and Fléchais 2012).

The Euthanasia Culture in Belgium: Reasons for Concern

In Belgium, the euthanasia Act of 2002 is often portrayed as a considerable step forward in the quality of the end-of-life care and the protection of the rights of terminally ill patients or those who face unbearable suffering, including mental suffering. Pro euthanasia physicians and experts, such as the authors of the *JAMA* article, vigorously defend this view. In the foregoing, I have tried to point out why I believe this view is overstated when it comes to euthanasia for psychiatric patients with severe mental disorders. Especially for this group of vulnerable patients, the legal regulation of euthanasia has inaugurated some evolutions in the Belgian end-of-life care that are worrisome. These evolutions have hitherto not received due attention and should be investigated further.

First, the authors of the *JAMA* article defend the position that the legalisation of euthanasia in 2002 was a major clinical and ethical step forward because it honours the *autonomy* of the patient. This right to self-determination (the right to 'write the last script of one's life oneself' as one often hears in Belgium), is the cornerstone of the euthanasia law of 2002. Respect for autonomy and self-determination are decisive, in the end, in comparison to other considerations that might interfere when it comes to grant a euthanasia request. However, as the testimony of some pro euthanasia experts reveals, especially in the case of psychiatric patients, these extra considerations are vexing: there is the possible pressure of both patient and family; the intrinsic vagueness of the clinical criteria to determine whether a mental disorder is untreatable or the condition of the patient is really hopeless and without prospect; and last but not least, the difficulty, if not the impossibility, to distinguish in an objective way a genuine and well-considered request to have one's life ended from a mere symptomatic death wish.

This brings under attention a second cause of concern with relation to the Belgian euthanasia social experiment in general. The implementation of the euthanasia law in 2002 has caused a radical transformation of the classical Hippocratic ethics that, since ages past, undergirds the relation between physician and patient in Western medicine (Dowbiggin 2005). Though the Hippocratic oath has its own history, from the beginning it contained the famous clause that no physician should actively use his or her knowledge and skill to help a patient end his or her life. The first and imperative task for a physician, according to the Hippocratic oath, is to care for the bodily well-being and flourishing of his or her patient, to heal the sick: not to end lives by intentional killing.

The legalisation of euthanasia, as stipulated in the Belgian law, however, significantly extends the role of the physician. Unwillingly the law forces, so to speak, any physician in Belgium to at least consider seriously a genuine expression of a wish to die by the patient, whether he or she is terminally ill or not: for it is the physician that is privileged to help the patient with dying. The decriminalisation of euthanasia thus casts its shadow on the medical culture, whether the physician likes it or not. Of course, the Belgian law leaves the decision of granting euthanasia to the physician's conscience in that no physician can be forced to actively end the life of his or her patient. But the very fact that there exists, on the side of the patient, the right to *ask* for euthanasia has in a subtle way overruled in specific circumstances all other ethical principles of good medical care and forms an indirect but almost permanent pressure on the physician's conscience.

Remarkably, this role on the side of the physician in the case of euthanasia exceeds the boarders of strict clinical care. Here the physician enters, as a medical expert, the existential realm that concerns the end-of-life of a human being. Apparently, the Belgian euthanasia law legitimises this role insofar as it allows the physician to actively help the patient in his or her wish to die. But the physician cannot treat this wish as a clinical symptom that could, possibly, be healed. He or she rather must listen to it as the expression of an existential choice on the side of the patient. The right *to ask to be helped to die* has thus become a core ethical principle underpinning the relation between patient and physician. Not surprisingly, this right has been often transformed implicitly into a sort of fundamental *human right*, to wit, *the right to die as such*: the Belgian law on euthanasia of 2002 thus risks giving this right an almost inalienable status. This is especially of great consequence in the sphere of psychiatry, where mental suffering is so closely interwoven with existential and spiritual needs as well as fears.

Of course, with chronic psychiatric afflictions, the expression of the wish to die might, in the specific care context, not immediately silence all other considerations. But the caring and helping attitude on the side of the physician *does* undergo a radical shift from the moment *the patient begins to see his or her suffering as unbearable and intolerable.* Then, so the Belgian law requires, the physician should take the death wish seriously: it should receive a place in the care path, even in the case of psychiatric patients that are not terminally ill. Thus, from the position of a healer, the physician becomes a sort of existential counsellor or even judge who helps the patient to 'clear up' the question whether one's life still has value or not. Again, it is the principle of autonomy that here undergirds a shift in care culture, the consequences of which are often underestimated.

This brings us to a further cause of concern about the Belgian euthanasia experiment: the blurring (or ignoring) of the distinction between euthanasia and assisted suicide. One of the authors of the *JAMA* article, Dr Distelmans, is convinced that euthanasia should be seen as a form of suicide prevention. In an interview he confirms that euthanasia remains too much of a taboo 'as long as there remain people who lie down in front of a train or jump from a building' (Maas 2015a). In another interview, he shows himself confident that the euthanasia practice in Belgium testifies how an experienced physician can distinguish, in an objective manner, a merely symptomatic death wish from a patient's genuine, rational wish to die by euthanasia (Carpentier and Antonissen 2015). Distelmans gives the example of a bipolar personality disorder, whereby in a condition between the deepest depression and the highest exaltation a patient can decide, based on his or her experience, that he or she wants to die to stop this infernal circle of a life full of suffering. This moment 'in between' appears to ground a solid, well-considered euthanasia request.

As I mentioned, it remains questionable whether this sort of diagnosis of a genuine, well-considered death wish is ever objectively warranted in the case of psychiatric patients. At least, one should be very cautious about the huge impact of the environment, especially in the case of psychiatric suffering, on the formation of this wish. Not only is the therapeutic relation highly sensitive for mechanisms of transfer and counter transfer between patient and therapist or psychiatrist, but there is also the highly symbolic and expressive force of suicide (assisted or not) on the level of the care environment, and even the larger civil society. Indeed, mimetic behaviour can become epidemic among psychiatric patients.

This mimetic nature of the wish to die is bluntly ignored in the argument that euthanasia might function as a form of suicide prevention. As some psychiatrists in Belgium defend: the mere possibility of receiving euthanasia gives patients confidence and a feeling of control. In other words, being taken seriously in one's euthanasia request would function as a recognition of one's autonomy: exactly this therapeutic freedom would allow vulnerable psychiatric patients to postpone suicide and sometimes change their minds. Concomitantly advocates suggest that failure to legalise euthanasia or assisted suicide 'forces' people to commit suicide as the only remaining option.

However, there is no evidence that the legalisation of euthanasia or physician assisted suicide for mental illness reduces unassisted suicide. In the *BMJ* open study of 100 requests mentioned before, 35 patients were euthanised, while one patient died through palliative sedation: of the 64 others, 6 patients died through suicide and one by anorexia. This is hardly evidence that the ability to die through euthanasia for some might decrease the willingness to commit suicide by others. One could as well conclude, that having been offered the possibility for euthanasia (or PAS), more patients were pulled over the line than might have been the case with a less liberal pro euthanasia or PAS law. Some experts claim that unassisted suicides might be caused by delays in the positive answer to requests for euthanasia or PAS (Schuklenk 2015). This might be questioned since one might as well argue that offering aid in dying effectively validates the suicidal ideation and thus encourages suicide. In fact, recent research indicates that legalising PAS in some states of the USA was associated with significant increases in suicide.[23]

It should cause no surprise that not a few physicians in Belgium are starting to wonder why they should take up this new role of being an accomplice in suicide. Indeed, it makes physicians - especially psychiatrists - vulnerable when they do so, but for reasons that lie beyond the physician's strictly medical expertise. If physicians could still rely on a law that utterly forbids them to terminate intentionally the life of their patients, they would be protected automatically from the sort of allegations and double-bind relations that now haunts them. For physicians that are familiar with the Hippocratic tradition, this consideration speaks almost for itself. However, to date in Belgium, it has become inappropriate or even provocative to remind the medical world of the liberating force that a clear ethical taboo often contains.

In this sense, the case of euthanasia for psychiatric patients with severe mental disorders illustrates that the decriminalisation of euthanasia may not automatically imply more certainty in practice, even only in a legal sense. As the authors of the *JAMA* article admit, the application of the Belgian euthanasia act to psychiatric patients stretches the interpretation of the law to its edges. As we have seen, the diagnostic and procedural puzzles that emerge in clinical practice are considerable. Therefore, almost automatically, so the *JAMA* opinion article testifies, physicians are pushed in the direction of the one remaining legal criterion that

[23] Jones and Paton 2015; see also Kheriaty 2015.

appears to give some guidance to handle euthanasia requests: the *testimony* of the patient concerning the alleged unbearable character of his or her suffering, in short, his or her *autonomous wish* to die. As Deschepper, Distelmans and Bilsen admit: they must rely on the 'patient's own reporting' to assess the degree of suffering, often 'without there being any "objectively" measurable symptoms'. But this exclusive attention for the subjective sense of suffering on the side of the patient, only adds to the diagnostic uncertainty of the physician, especially in the case of psychiatric patients or patients suffering from mental afflictions. The fulfilling of the euthanasia wish may then easily appear as the safest solution from a procedural point of view. Whether this guarantees necessarily also the best clinical-ethical option, however, remains doubtful.

Often pro euthanasia physicians contend that, next to patient autonomy, they rely ultimately on the ethical value of *mercy* to stand with their patients until the very end.[24] The practice of euthanasia in Belgium is from this perspective also hailed as an ultimate expression of love for the patient, of empathy for his or her suffering. Often, this appeal to mercy on the side of the physician is a guarantee that abuse of the law is almost impossible. Mercy would imply automatically trustfulness, as if a doctor who shows mercy is immune from unethical or illegal behaviour.

Of course, no one can ignore the important role that attitudes, such as empathy and mercy, can and should play in the clinical setting, especially at the bedside of patients in the hour of death. What is more questionable is the contention that *only* a positive answer to a euthanasia or suicide request bears the aura of an act of mercy and due medical care. Of course, tragically, in the case of assisted suicide on psychiatric patients the only available option left, appears to be suicide as such – without a physician being present. But even here a cautious attitude on the side of the physician, a calm refusal to honour too rapidly this request, should not be interpreted too easily as a sign of a lack of humanity and empathy. The psychiatrist who shows mercy should also remain a 'judicious spectator' of the specific condition of his or her patient and the social environment in which the patient experiences his or her last days and hours. Mercy without judgement is contrary to an ethics of due medical

---

[24] This is the core motivation that Thienpont gives in her book with the revealing title *Libera Me* to justify euthanasia in psychiatric patients that are not terminally ill (Thienpont 2015).

care. Therefore, a too easy reliance on mercy and empathy as guiding principles for the relation between physician and patient is highly contestable, especially in matters of life or death. In fact, the very idea that we need a law to regulate euthanasia and at least guarantee some safeguards reflects this insight. What due medical care needs, especially at the bedside of the most vulnerable patients, is a richer deontological practice and tradition. Such practice and tradition shall thrive by experience and authority, which a mere legal regulation, nor a spontaneous empathy, can ever provide.

Remarkably, pro euthanasia voices usually combine the plea for more mercy for patients with euthanasia requests with an almost blind trust in the procedures of the law. As I hope to have shown, exactly this combination of a rule-based ethics with an outspoken reliance on a so-called mercy with their patients generates, once euthanasia is legalised, the sort of conflicts and conundrums highlighted in the *JAMA* opinion article. An overly reliance on mercy and love in a clinical context may easily foster attitudes that can be extremely harmful, such as partiality, imaginary over-identification, projection and self-aggrandisement. In addition, vulnerable physicians may end up in the grip of these attitudes, especially in end-of-life care, with its whimsical and heavily existential dynamics. The proliferation of such attitudes may in turn cause misunderstandings and become the source of conflicts and emotional turmoil, especially at the bedside of dying patients.

Trust thus converts into distrust, which in turn leads to the expectation that a law should remedy the unreliability of mere mercy and love at the bedside of the dying. Paradoxically, the practice of euthanasia thus thrives, on the one hand, on a dangerous – because always partial and emotive (even imaginary) – empathy, while on the other hand it needs the law to control this partiality and sentimentality. It remains questionable whether the current Belgian liberal law on euthanasia is strong and impartial enough to fulfil this controlling role. Especially in the case of psychiatric patients who are not terminally ill, but suffer from severe mental disorders and express the wish to die, the reliability of the law as unconditional safeguard for some of the most vulnerable in our society should be contested. For especially here the idea that we do good when we help these people to die, might be a dangerous illusion that ends up undermining the very idea of unconditional duty of care towards the most vulnerable. And yet this very duty remains essential for the maintenance of solidarity and hope in every society.

Acknowledgements

I dedicate this article to Tom Mortier and Kerstin Huygelen, whose testimonies, next to their remarkable serenity and intellectual acuity, were essential for me in understanding some vexing aspects of the Belgian euthanasia experiment. On an earlier version of this chapter, I received invaluable comments and suggestions from David Albert Jones and Chris Gastmans, for which I am most grateful. Of course, I am responsible for all flaws remaining in my argumentation.

Final Conclusions on Final Solutions

DAVID ALBERT JONES, CHRIS GASTMANS AND
CALUM MACKELLAR

The aim of this book has been to examine the diverse ways in which a change in the law on euthanasia or assisted suicide can have an impact on society. It has provided, for the first time, an interdisciplinary study of the practice of euthanasia in Belgium, drawing both on empirical research and personal experience as well as medical, legal and philosophical analysis. In other words, it is now possible to formulate critical considerations regarding the consequences of the legalisation of euthanasia in a country such as Belgium.

Legalising euthanasia and/or assisted suicide is often advocated as a way to bring into the open, the practices already happening so that these can be subject to scrutiny and control. However, in the first chapter of this volume, Herman Nys argued that, from the beginning, the 2002 law has suffered from the 'deficient transparency of the Belgian procedure to evaluate and to control the practice of euthanasia'. For example, he highlights the difficulty that one Commission composed of sixteen part-time members has in seriously considering all the cases, which now number thousands a year.

Another fundamental flaw with the system, well identified by Etienne Montero, is that it relies on self-reporting. Independent research shows that only around 50 per cent of cases of euthanasia are reported, and the unreported cases are those that are more ethically and legally problematic. Furthermore, as Nys has pointed out, of those thousands that have been reported to the Commission, only one was referred to a public prosecutor. The change in the law seems to have brought neither transparency nor control to the practice of euthanasia.

The immediate impact of the law has not seen any reduction of problematic cases but only higher numbers of deaths by euthanasia. Indeed, David Albert Jones, in his chapter in this volume, has demonstrated that this increase in legal euthanasia has in fact been accompanied by 'an increase in life ending without request'. A further consequence of the euthanasia law has been a continuing pressure to expand the practice, for example, to those without a serious and incurable disorder or those whose competence is compromised or even absent. Montero rightly observed that 'the logic that operates in the dynamics of law-making and implementation' has led to 'the so-called "normalisation of euthanasia"'. The terminology of 'normalisation' was taken up at greater length in Chapter 13 of the book by Calum MacKellar. There is no doubt that, since 2002, euthanasia practice in Belgium has expanded in numbers and scope and has become, increasingly, a matter of 'normal practice' or even routine.

This book reproduces an important paper published by Paul Vanden Berghe, Director of the Federation of Palliative Care, Flanders, and colleagues in 2013. The original article had been interpreted by advocates of assisted dying as an unequivocal endorsement of euthanasia practice in Belgium. However, it should be noted that the article also raised concerns about the direction of developments in euthanasia practice in Belgium: 'There is an indication that euthanasia, once the barrier of legalisation is passed, tends to develop a dynamic of its own and extend beyond the agreed restrictions, in spite of earlier explicit reassurances that this would not happen'. As a new postscript makes clear, these concerns have only been reinforced in the subsequent three years. The authors conclude with a series of questions which challenge the very basis of euthanasia practice: 'Which is prior: unbearable suffering for which euthanasia is the ultimate solution? Or does the suffering become unbearable because, henceforth, there is such a way-out as euthanasia? Could it be that, in the long term, unbridled euthanasia thus enhances the suffering it pretends to relieve?'

While some clinicians welcome the integration of palliative care and euthanasia, this approach creates difficulties for patients who need the support of palliative care but who feel threatened by the possibility of euthanasia. Their plight was highlighted by Benoit Beuselinck. He is one of a number of clinicians in Belgium who are concerned about the adverse impact of euthanasia on the understanding of palliative care. It is no doubt the case that a majority of doctors in Belgium have reconciled themselves to the present law. However, Beuselinck represents a continuing critical voice within the professions. In particular, as a clinical oncologist, he has lamented the changes he has seen to the way that end of life care is delivered.

A good example of the impact of euthanasia on other end of life decisions is the pattern of use of continuous deep sedation in Belgium. Beuselinck noted that continuous deep sedation until death was initiated without consent or request, either of the patient or of the family, in around 28 per cent of the cases reported by medical specialists in Belgium. Other research shows that general practitioners who prescribed continuous deep sedation intended or co-intended to shorten life in just over 20 per cent of cases. Chapter 5 in this volume by Sigrid Sterckx and Kasper Raus is important for providing evidence that, in Belgium, continuous sedation at the end of life is sometimes intended as a form of euthanasia. In contrast, doctors in the United Kingdom rarely, if ever, prescribe sedatives with a life-shortening intention. This difference in intention is demonstrated not just by what doctors say but by differences of practice. Doctors in the United Kingdom attempt to increase the dose of sedatives gradually in proportion to symptoms, whereas in Belgium doctors frequently make a particular decision at a particular moment in time to 'sedate to unconsciousness'.

This qualitative work reported by Sterckx and Raus confirms, and also helps to interpret, the results of large-scale surveys in the use of sedation in Belgium and in the United Kingdom. It shows that the legalisation of euthanasia is associated with differences in the way Belgian doctors make decisions in other areas of medical practice in comparison to doctors in the United Kingdom. The explicit intention to shorten life, which is an essential element of euthanasia, has also started to become evident in other areas of end of life care in Belgium affecting varying numbers of individuals.

Continuous deep sedation until death is a relatively common practice, occurring in 12 per cent of deaths in Flanders in 2013, that is approximately 7,400 deaths per year. Changes to this practice may affect hundreds or thousands of people.

In contrast, the practice of organ donation after euthanasia, discussed in this volume by Trevor Stammers, has occurred only once or twice a year when it has occurred at all.

Similarly, since the euthanasia law was amended in February 2014 to allow euthanasia in children, there have been only two reported cases. Yet the legalisation of child euthanasia created international controversy and hence the volume includes a chapter on this topic.

Another controversial possibility that has not yet been included in legislation in Belgium, let alone realised in practice, is euthanasia for dementia on the basis of an advance euthanasia directive. Though it remains illegal, this proposal has been debated more than once in the Belgian legislative chambers and, for this reason, it is important that the book should cover this possibility.

The rationale for discussing euthanasia in relation to organ donation, minors and people with dementia is not that these practises are prevalent, existent or even legal in Belgium. These topics are important because of the attitude they express to the issues involved. Like 'thought experiments' in physics or philosophy they show where the logic of different positions leads to. In relation to the euthanasia of children, for example, what is significant about the change in the law is not that it has been shown to have adversely affected the care of any child nor that any child has been shown to have benefitted. What generated passion within and outside Belgium was the question of whether, in principle, extending the law would represent a potential threat to children or a potential benefit. The move on the part of the Belgian legislature to extend the law, even though there was no obvious unmet clinical need and there have only been two subsequent cases, shows how far attitudes have changed.

Death by euthanasia in Belgium is, generally, no longer regarded as an exception requiring special justification. Instead, it is often regarded as a normal death and a benefit not to be restricted without special justification. Similarly, it seems impossible that euthanasia, the most significant social and political innovation in end-of-life care in Belgium since it was introduced, will leave untouched dementia care, which is the largest social and political challenge in the care of older people in Belgium, as in other Western nations. As death by euthanasia becomes the new normal, it seems highly likely that, at some point, euthanasia legislation will in some way influence the care of people with dementia.

In contrast to organ donors, minors and people with dementia, to whom euthanasia poses little imminent threat, the expansion of euthanasia among people who are physically disabled, or who suffer from a psychiatric condition, or are 'tired of life', is already occurring on a large scale. This expansion immediately affects hundreds of people in Belgium.

In Belgium, as in the Netherlands, there is a debate over whether being 'tired of life' should be sufficient on its own to justify euthanasia, without having to identify any physical or mental disorder. However, it seems unlikely that, in the near future, the law will be changed to include such a proposal. This is because, to allow euthanasia for people 'tired of life' is essentially to abandon any objective or health-related criteria for euthanasia. It would be a very radical change. On the other hand, in practice it seems that euthanasia for people who are tired of life is already legal and practiced in Belgium. This is occurring under the guise of euthanasia for people with 'multiple disorders', which is sufficient to cover anyone with the common diseases of old age, or 'neuropsychiatric disorders' and thus anyone who is depressed because of his or her current situation.

A number of chapters in the volume have examined the ethical impact of euthanasia performed on people with physical disabilities, psychiatric conditions or older people who are tired of life. These issues have been treated slightly differently by Kevin Fitzpatrick and David Albert Jones, Joris Vandenberghe, Willem Lemmens, Daniel Sulmasy and Raphael Cohen-Almagor. Nevertheless, common themes emerge from these different treatments. It is undoubtedly the case that these represent vulnerable groups and that their ability to cope with their condition is dependent on the support they receive as well as on the cultural messages being articulated about how and which lives are valued. It is undoubtedly the case that in Belgium more people in these vulnerable groups are dying of euthanasia.

Belgium offers clear lessons for other jurisdictions which are considering the legalisation of assisted suicide or euthanasia. One of these is that legislation that was promoted as giving greater clarity, transparency and control to end-of-life practices, has not fulfilled its expectations. Independent research into end-of-life decision making in Belgium offers some insight into what is occurring, and other jurisdictions should consider doing similar research. There is no independent research in Oregon, for example, which could assess what proportion of physician-assisted suicides are, in fact, reported. However, in contrast to this independent research in Belgium, the system of official reports and the work of the Federal Commission offer neither transparency nor control. It seems to provide only the illusion of control.

The clear evidence from Belgium is that once the barrier of legalisation is passed, the practice tends to develop a dynamic of its own but it does not show that such consequences must follow. Rather, the evidence shows that these consequences can follow, and that this was in line with what was predicted to happen, despite reassurances to the contrary. In the United States the ongoing resistance to assisted suicide in most States acts as a powerful inhibiter on the expansion of practice in Oregon, Washington, Montana, Vermont and California as advocates are still seeking to persuade other States. Nevertheless, the only secure way to avoid these consequences is to resist calls to legalise euthanasia or assisted suicide and instead invest in palliative care as well as research into end-of-life practices while reemphasising the preciousness of human life.

This book aimed to draw lessons for other countries but also to provide an opportunity for Belgian lawyers, philosophers, bioethicists and clinicians to reflect and speak to one another and in addition to a wider Belgian audience. As was stated in the introduction, the contributors in this volume do not all take the same view on the ethics of euthanasia and assisted suicide. Where authors are critical of current practice this does not imply that they believe the euthanasia law should be abolished. There are differences of view about what should happen, though there is more agreement about the need to question the direction in which their country is currently travelling.

It is important to stress that, while the book has identified mechanisms in medical practice and society that encourage the expansion of euthanasia and the overcoming of restrictions, such changes are not inevitable. A change in direction is always possible and, if it should occur, this will be because of the words and actions of people who have expressed dissatisfaction with the status quo. It is our hope that this book will promote renewed debate within Belgium and internationally about laws on euthanasia or assisted suicide and give heart to those who resist their normalisation. In the words of G.K. Chesterton, 'A dead thing can go with the stream, but only a living thing can go against it'.

Appendix I

Wet Betreffende de Euthanasie 28 Mei 2002
(The Belgian Act on Euthanasia, Dutch-language Version)

Raadpleging van vroegere versies vanaf 22-06-2002 en tekstbijwerking tot 12-03-2014

Artikel 1

Deze wet regelt een aangelegenheid als bedoeld in artikel 78 van de Grondwet.

HOOFDSTUK I: Algemene bepalingen

Art. 2

Voor de toepassing van deze wet wordt onder euthanasie verstaan het opzettelijk levensbeëindigend handelen door een andere dan de betrokkene, op diens verzoek.

HOOFDSTUK II: Voorwaarden en procedure

Art. 3

§ 1. De arts die euthanasie toepast, pleegt geen misdrijf wanneer hij er zich van verzekerd heeft dat:
- [de patiënt een handelingsbekwame meerderjarige, of een handelingsbekwame ontvoogde minderjarige, of nog een oordeelsbekwame minderjarige is en bewust is op het ogenblik van zijn verzoek;][1]
- het verzoek vrijwillig, overwogen en herhaald is, en niet tot stand gekomen is als gevolg van enige externe druk;
- de [meerderjarige of ontvoogde minderjarige][1] patiënt zich in een medisch uitzichtloze toestand bevindt van aanhoudend en ondraaglijk fysiek of psychisch lijden dat niet gelenigd kan worden, en dat het gevolg is van een ernstige en ongeneeslijke, door ongeval of ziekte veroorzaakte aandoening;

[1] W 2014-02-28/03, art. 2, 003; Inwerkingtreding: 22-03-2014

284

– [de minderjarige patiënt die oordeelsbekwaam is, zich in een medisch uitzichtloze toestand bevindt van aanhoudend en ondraaglijk fysiek lijden dat niet gelenigd kan worden en dat binnen afzienbare termijn het overlijden tot gevolg heeft, en dat het gevolg is van een ernstige en ongeneeslijke, door ongeval of ziekte veroorzaakte aandoening;][1]
– en hij de in deze wet voorgeschreven voorwaarden en procedures heeft nageleefd.

§ 2. Onverminderd bijkomende voorwaarden die de arts aan zijn ingrijpen wenst te verbinden, moet hij vooraf en in alle gevallen:

1° de patiënt inlichten over zijn gezondheidstoestand en zijn levensverwachting, met de patiënt overleg plegen over zijn verzoek tot euthanasie en met hem de eventueel nog resterende therapeutische mogelijkheden, evenals die van de palliatieve zorg, en hun gevolgen bespreken. Hij moet met de patiënt tot de overtuiging komen dat er voor de situatie waarin deze zich bevindt geen redelijke andere oplossing is en dat het verzoek van de patiënt berust op volledige vrijwilligheid;

2° zich verzekeren van het aanhoudend fysiek of psychisch lijden van de patiënt en van het duurzaam karakter van zijn verzoek. Daartoe voert hij met de patiënt meerdere gesprekken die, rekening houdend met de ontwikkeling van de gezondheidstoestand van de patiënt, over een redelijke periode worden gespreid;

3° een andere arts raadplegen over de ernstige en ongeneeslijke aard van de aandoening en hem op de hoogte brengen van de redenen voor deze raadpleging. De geraadpleegde arts neemt inzage van het medisch dossier, onderzoekt de patiënt en moet zich vergewissen van het aanhoudend en ondraaglijk fysiek of psychisch lijden dat niet gelenigd kan worden. Hij stelt een verslag op van zijn bevindingen.

De geraadpleegde arts moet onafhankelijk zijn ten opzichte van zowel de patiënt als de behandelende arts en bevoegd om over de aandoening in kwestie te oordelen. De behandelende arts brengt de patiënt op de hoogte van de resultaten van deze raadpleging;

4° indien er een verplegend team is, dat in regelmatig contact staat met de patiënt, het verzoek van de patiënt bespreken met het team of leden van dat team;

5° indien de patiënt dat wenst, het verzoek van de patiënt bespreken met zijn naasten die hij aanwijst;

6° zich ervan verzekeren dat de patiënt de gelegenheid heeft gehad om over zijn verzoek te spreken met de personen die hij wenste te ontmoeten.

[7° indien de patiënt een niet-ontvoogde minderjarige is, bovendien een kinder- of jeugdpsychiater of een psycholoog raadplegen en hem op de hoogte brengen van de redenen voor deze raadpleging.

De geraadpleegde specialist neemt kennis van het medisch dossier, onderzoekt de patiënt, vergewist zich van de oordeelsbekwaamheid van de minderjarige en attesteert dit schriftelijk.

De behandelende arts brengt de patiënt en zijn wettelijke vertegenwoordigers op de hoogte van het resultaat van deze raadpleging.

Tijdens een onderhoud met de wettelijke vertegenwoordigers van de minderjarige bezorgt de behandelende arts hen alle in § 2, 1°, bedoelde informatie, en vergewist hij zich ervan dat zij hun akkoord geven betreffende het verzoek van de minderjarige patiënt.][1]

§ 3. Indien de arts van oordeel is dat de [meerderjarige of ontvoogde minderjarige][1] patiënt kennelijk niet binnen afzienbare tijd zal overlijden, moet hij bovendien:

1° een tweede arts raadplegen, die psychiater is of specialist in de aandoening in kwestie, en hem op de hoogte brengen van de redenen voor deze raadpleging. De geraadpleegde arts neemt inzage van het medisch dossier, onderzoekt de patiënt en moet zich vergewissen van het aanhoudend en ondraaglijk fysiek of psychisch lijden dat niet gelenigd kan worden, en van het vrijwillig, overwogen en herhaald karakter van het verzoek. Hij stelt een verslag op van zijn bevindingen. De geraadpleegde arts moet onafhankelijk zijn ten opzichte van zowel de patiënt als de behandelende arts en de eerste geraadpleegde arts. De behandelende arts brengt de patiënt op de hoogte van de resultaten van deze raadpleging;

2° minstens één maand laten verlopen tussen het schriftelijke verzoek van de patiënt en het toepassen van de euthanasie.

§ 4. [Het verzoek van de patiënt, alsook de instemming van de wettelijke vertegenwoordigers indien de patiënt minderjarig is, worden op schrift gesteld.][1] Het document wordt opgesteld, gedateerd en getekend door de patiënt zelf. Indien de patiënt daartoe niet in staat is, gebeurt het op schrift stellen door een meerderjarige persoon die gekozen is door de patiënt en geen materieel belang mag hebben bij de dood van de patiënt.

Deze persoon maakt melding van het feit dat de patiënt niet in staat is om zijn verzoek op schrift te formuleren en geeft de redenen waarom. In dat geval gebeurt de opschriftstelling in bijzijn van de arts en noteert die persoon de naam van die arts op het document. Dit document dient bij het medisch dossier te worden gevoegd.

De patiënt kan te allen tijde het verzoek herroepen, waarna het document uit het medisch dossier wordt gehaald en aan de patiënt wordt teruggegeven.

[§ 4/1. Nadat de arts het verzoek van de patiënt heeft behandeld, wordt aan de betrokkenen de mogelijkheid van psychologische bijstand geboden.][1]

§ 5. Alle verzoeken geformuleerd door de patiënt, alsook de handelingen van de behandelende arts en hun resultaat, met inbegrip van het (de) verslag (en) van de geraadpleegde arts(en), worden regelmatig opgetekend in het medisch dossier van de patiënt.

{Art. 3bis

De apotheker die een euthanaticum aflevert, pleegt geen misdrijf wanneer hij handelt op basis van een voorschrift waarop de arts uitdrukkelijk vermeldt dat hij handelt in overeenstemming met deze wet.

De apotheker levert persoonlijk het voorgeschreven euthanaticum aan de arts af. De Koning bepaalt de zorgvuldigheidsregels en voorwaarden waaraan het voorschrift en de aflevering van geneesmiddelen die als euthanaticum worden gebruikt, moeten voldoen.

De Koning neemt de nodige maatregelen om de beschikbaarheid van euthanatica te verzekeren, ook in officina-apotheken die toegankelijk zijn voor het publiek.}[2]

HOOFDSTUK III: De wilsverklaring

Art. 4

§ 1. Elke handelingsbekwame meerderjarige of ontvoogde minderjarige kan, voor het geval dat hij zijn wil niet meer kan uiten, schriftelijk in een wilsver-klaring zijn wil te kennen geven dat een arts euthanasie toepast indien deze arts er zich van verzekerd heeft:
– dat hij lijdt aan een ernstige en ongeneeslijke, door ongeval of ziekte veroorzaakte aandoening;
– hij niet meer bij bewustzijn is;
– en deze toestand volgens de stand van de wetenschap onomkeerbaar is.

In de wilsverklaring kunnen één of meer meerderjarige vertrouwensper-sonen in volgorde van voorkeur aangewezen worden, die de behande-lende arts op de hoogte brengen van de wil van de patiënt. Elke vertrouwenspersoon vervangt zijn of haar in de wilsverklaring vermelde voorganger in geval van weigering, verhindering, onbekwaamheid of overlijden. De behandelende arts van de patiënt, de geraadpleegde arts en de leden van het verplegend team kunnen niet als vertrouwenspersoon optreden.

[2] ingevoegd bij W 2005-11-10/68, art. 2; ED: 23-12-2005

De wilsverklaring kan op elk moment worden opgesteld. Zij moet schriftelijk worden opgemaakt ten overstaan van twee meerderjarige getuigen, van wie er minstens een geen materieel belang heeft bij het overlijden van de patiënt en moet gedateerd en ondertekend worden door degene die de verklaring aflegt, door de getuigen en, in voorkomend geval, door de vertrouwensperso(o)n(e)n.

Indien de persoon die een wilsverklaring wenst op te stellen fysiek blijvend niet in staat is om een wilsverklaring op te stellen en te tekenen, kan hij een meerderjarig persoon, die geen enkel materieel belang heeft bij het overlijden van de betrokkene, aanwijzen, die zijn verzoek schriftelijk opstelt, ten overstaan van twee meerderjarige getuigen, van wie er minstens een geen materieel belang heeft bij het overlijden van de patiënt. De wilsverklaring vermeldt dat de betrokkene niet in staat is te tekenen en waarom. De wilsverklaring moet gedateerd en ondertekend worden door degene die het verzoek schriftelijk opstelt, door de getuigen en, in voorkomend geval, door de vertrouwenspersoon of vertrouwenspersonen.

Bij de wilsverklaring wordt een medisch getuigschrift gevoegd als bewijs dat de betrokkene fysiek blijvend niet in staat is de wilsverklaring op te stellen en te tekenen.

Met de wilsverklaring kan alleen rekening gehouden worden indien zij minder dan vijf jaar vóór het moment waarop betrokkene zijn wil niet meer kan uiten, is opgesteld of bevestigd.

De wilsverklaring kan op elk moment aangepast of ingetrokken worden.

De Koning bepaalt hoe de wilsverklaring wordt opgesteld, geregistreerd en herbevestigd of ingetrokken en via de diensten van het Rijksregister aan de betrokken artsen wordt meegedeeld.

§ 2. De arts die euthanasie toepast, tengevolge een wilsverklaring zoals voorzien in § 1, pleegt geen misdrijf indien deze arts er zich van verzekerd heeft dat de patiënt:

– lijdt aan een ernstige en ongeneeslijke, door ongeval of ziekte veroorzaakte aandoening;
– hij niet meer bij bewustzijn is;
– en deze toestand volgens de stand van de wetenschap onomkeerbaar is;

en hij de in deze wet voorgeschreven voorwaarden en procedures heeft nageleefd.

Onverminderd bijkomende voorwaarden die de arts aan zijn ingrijpen wenst te verbinden, moet hij vooraf:

1° een andere arts raadplegen over de onomkeerbaarheid van de medische toestand van de patiënt en hem op de hoogte brengen van de redenen voor deze raadpleging. De geraadpleegde arts neemt inzage van het medisch

dossier en onderzoekt de patiënt. Hij stelt een verslag op van zijn bevindingen. Indien in de wilsverklaring een vertrouwenspersoon wordt aangewezen brengt de behandelende arts deze vertrouwenspersoon op de hoogte
van de resultaten van deze raadpleging.

De geraadpleegde arts moet onafhankelijk zijn ten opzichte van
zowel de patiënt als de behandelende arts en bevoegd om over de
aandoening in kwestie te oordelen;

2° indien er een verplegend team is dat in regelmatig contact staat met de
patiënt, de inhoud van de wilsverklaring bespreken met het team of leden
van dat team;

3° indien in de wilsverklaring een vertrouwenspersoon wordt aangewezen, het
verzoek van de patiënt met hem bespreken;

4° indien in de wilsverklaring een vertrouwenspersoon wordt aangewezen, de
inhoud van de wilsverklaring bespreken met de naasten van de patiënt die
door de vertrouwenspersoon zijn aangewezen.

De wilsverklaring, alsook alle handelingen van de behandelende arts en
hun resultaat, met inbegrip van het verslag van de geraadpleegde arts,
worden regelmatig opgetekend in het medisch dossier van de patiënt.

HOOFDSTUK IV: Aangifte

Art. 5

De arts die euthanasie heeft toegepast, bezorgt binnen vier werkdagen het
volledig ingevulde registratiedocument bedoeld in artikel 7 van deze wet aan
de in artikel 6 bedoelde federale controle- en evaluatiecommissie.

HOOFDSTUK V: De Federale Controle- en Evaluatiecommissie

Art. 6

§ 1. Er wordt een Federale Controle- en Evaluatiecommissie ingesteld
inzake de toepassing van deze wet, hierna te noemen "de commissie".

§ 2. De commissie bestaat uit zestien leden. Zij worden aangewezen op basis
van hun kennis en ervaring inzake de materies die tot de bevoegdheid van de
commissie behoren. Acht leden zijn doctor in de geneeskunde, van wie er
minstens vier hoogleraar zijn aan een Belgische universiteit. Vier leden zijn
hoogleraar in de rechten aan een Belgische universiteit, of advocaat. Vier leden
komen uit kringen die belast zijn met de problematiek van ongeneeslijk zieke
patiënten.

Het lidmaatschap van de commissie is onverenigbaar met het mandaat van lid van een van de wetgevende vergaderingen en met het mandaat van lid van de federale regering of van een gemeenschaps- of gewestregering.

De leden van de commissie worden, met inachtneming van de taalpariteit - waarbij elke taalgroep minstens drie kandidaten van elk geslacht telt - en op grond van pluralistische vertegenwoordiging, bij een koninklijk besluit vastgesteld na overleg in de Ministerraad, benoemd uit een dubbele lijst, voorgedragen door [Kamer van volksvertegenwoordigers],[3] voor een termijn van vier jaar, die kan worden verlengd. Het mandaat wordt van rechtswege beëindigd indien het lid de hoedanigheid waarin hij zetelt verliest. De kandidaten die niet als effectief lid zijn aangewezen, worden tot plaatsvervanger benoemd, in de orde van opvolging die volgens een lijst bepaald wordt. De commissie wordt voorgezeten door een Nederlandstalige en een Franstalige voorzitter. Deze voorzitters worden verkozen door de commissieleden van de desbetreffende taalgroep.

De commissie kan slechts geldig beslissen als twee derden van de leden aanwezig zijn.

§ 3. De commissie stelt haar huishoudelijk reglement op

Art. 7

De commissie stelt een registratiedocument op dat door de arts, telkens wanneer hij euthanasie toepast, ingevuld moet worden. Dit document bestaat uit twee delen. Het DEEL I moet door de arts worden verzegeld. Het bevat de volgende gegevens:

1° de naam, de voornamen en de woonplaats van de patiënt;

2° de naam, de voornamen, het registratienummer bij het RIZIV en de woonplaats van de behandelende arts;

3° de naam, de voornamen, het registratienummer bij het RIZIV en de woonplaats van de arts(en) die over het euthanasieverzoek is (zijn) geraadpleegd;

4° de naam, de voornamen, de woonplaats en de hoedanigheid van alle personen die de behandelende arts heeft geraadpleegd, en de data van deze raadplegingen;

5° indien er een wilsverklaring is waarin een of meer vertrouwenspersonen worden aangewezen, de naam en de voornamen van de betrokken vertrouwensperso(o)n(en).

(6° de naam, de voornamen, het registratienummer bij het RIZIV en het adres van de apotheker die het euthanaticum heeft afgeleverd, de afgeleverde producten en hun hoeveelheid en eventueel het overschot dat aan de apotheker werd terugbezorgd.)[4]

---

[3] W 2014-01-06/63, art. 21, 002; Inwerkingtreding: 25-05-2014
[4] Errata, zie B.St. 21-03-2016, p. 19410

Dit DEEL I is vertrouwelijk en wordt door de arts aan de commissie overgezonden. Er kan alleen inzage van worden genomen na beslissing van de commissie. In geen geval kan de commissie zich hierop baseren voor haar evaluatietaak.

Het tweede deel is eveneens vertrouwelijk en bevat de volgende gegevens:

1° het geslacht, de geboortedatum en de geboorteplaats van de patiënt [en, met betrekking tot de minderjarige patiënt, of hij ontvoogd was];[5]
2° de datum, de plaats en het uur van overlijden;
3° de aard van de ernstige en ongeneeslijke, door ongeval of ziekte veroorzaakte aandoening waaraan de patiënt leed;
4° de aard van de aanhoudende en ondraaglijke pijn;
5° de redenen waarom dit lijden niet gelenigd kon worden;
6° op basis van welke elementen men zich ervan heeft vergewist dat het verzoek vrijwillig, overwogen en herhaald is en niet tot stand is gekomen als gevolg van enige externe druk;
7° of aangenomen kon worden dat de patiënt binnen afzienbare termijn zou overlijden;
8° of er een wilsverklaring is opgemaakt;
9° de procedure die de arts gevolgd heeft;
10° de hoedanigheid van de geraadpleegde arts of artsen, het advies en de data van die raadplegingen;
11° de hoedanigheid van de personen die door de arts geraadpleegd zijn en de data van die raadplegingen;
12° de wijze waarop de euthanasie is toegepast en de gebruikte middelen.

Art. 8

De commissie onderzoekt het volledig ingevulde registratiedocument dat haar door de behandelende arts is overgezonden. Zij gaat op basis van het tweede deel van het registratiedocument na of de euthanasie is uitgevoerd onder de voorwaarden en volgens de procedure bepaald in deze wet. In geval van twijfel kan de commissie bij gewone meerderheid besluiten om de anonimiteit op te heffen. Zij neemt dan kennis van het DEEL I van het registratiedocument. De commissie kan aan de behandelende arts elk element uit het medisch dossier dat betrekking heeft op de euthanasie opvragen.

De commissie spreekt zich binnen twee maanden uit.

Is de commissie van oordeel bij beslissing genomen door een tweederde meerderheid dat de in deze wet bepaalde voorwaarden niet zijn nageleefd, dan

---

[5] W 2014-02-28/03, art. 3, 003; Inwerkingtreding: 22-03-2014

zendt zij het dossier over aan de procureur des Konings van de plaats van overlijden van de patiënt.

Als bij het opheffen van de anonimiteit blijkt dat er feiten of omstandigheden bestaan waardoor de onafhankelijkheid of de onpartijdigheid van het oordeel van een lid van de commissie in het gedrang komt, zal dit lid zich verschonen of kunnen gewraakt worden bij de behandeling van deze zaak in de commissie.

Art. 9

Ten behoeve van de Wetgevende Kamers stelt de commissie de eerste keer binnen twee jaar na de inwerkingtreding van deze wet en nadien tweejaarlijks:

a) een statistisch verslag op waarin de informatie is verwerkt uit het tweede deel van het volledig ingevulde registratiedocument dat de artsen haar overeenkomstig artikel 8 hebben overgezonden;

b) een verslag op waarin de toepassing van de wet wordt aangegeven en geëvalueerd;

c) in voorkomend geval, aanbevelingen op die kunnen leiden tot een wetgevend initiatief en/of andere maatregelen inzake de uitvoering van deze wet.

Teneinde deze opdrachten te vervullen, kan de commissie alle bijkomende inlichtingen inwinnen bij de diverse overheidsdiensten en instellingen. De inlichtingen die de commissie inwint zijn vertrouwelijk. Geen van deze documenten mag de identiteit vermelden van personen die genoemd worden in de dossiers die aan de commissie zijn overgezonden in het kader van haar controletaak zoals bepaald in artikel 8.

De commissie kan besluiten om aan universitaire onderzoeksteams die een gemotiveerd verzoek daartoe doen, statistische en zuiver technische gegevens mee te delen, met uitsluiting van alle persoonsgegevens. Zij kan deskundigen horen.

Art. 10

De Koning stelt een administratief kader ter beschikking van de commissie voor het uitvoeren van haar wettelijke opdrachten. De formatie en het taalkader van het administratief personeel worden bij koninklijk besluit vastgesteld na overleg in de Ministerraad, op voordracht van de minister bevoegd voor de Volksgezondheid en de minister bevoegd voor de Justitie.

Art. 11

De werkingskosten en de personeelskosten van de commissie, alsook de vergoeding van haar leden, komen voor de ene helft ten laste van de begroting van de minister bevoegd voor de Volksgezondheid en voor de andere helft ten laste van de begroting van de minister bevoegd voor de Justitie.

Art. 12

Eenieder die, in welke hoedanigheid ook, zijn medewerking verleent aan de toepassing van deze wet, is verplicht tot geheimhouding van de gegevens die hem in de uitoefening van zijn opdracht worden toevertrouwd en die hiermee verband houden. Artikel 458 van het Strafwetboek is op hem van toepassing.

Art. 13

[Binnen zes maanden na het indienen van het eerste verslag en, in voorkomend geval, van de aanbevelingen van de commissie, bedoeld in artikel 9, vindt hierover een debat plaats in de Kamer van volksvertegenwoordigers. Die termijn van zes maanden wordt geschorst gedurende de periode dat de Kamer van volksvertegenwoordigers is ontbonden en/of dat er geen Regering is die het vertrouwen heeft van de Kamer van volksvertegenwoordigers.]⁶

HOOFDSTUK VI: Bijzondere bepalingen

Art. 14

Het verzoek en de wilsverklaring bedoeld in de artikelen 3 en 4 van deze wet hebben geen dwingende waarde.

Geen arts kan worden gedwongen euthanasie toe te passen.

Geen andere persoon kan worden gedwongen mee te werken aan het toepassen van euthanasie.

Weigert de geraadpleegde arts euthanasie toe te passen, dan moet hij dit de patiënt of de eventuele vertrouwenspersoon tijdig laten weten waarbij hij de redenen van zijn weigering toelicht. Berust zijn weigering op een medische grond dan wordt die in het medisch dossier van de patiënt opgetekend.

De arts die weigert in te gaan op een euthanasieverzoek moet, op verzoek van de patiënt of de vertrouwenspersoon, het medisch dossier van de patiënt meedelen aan de arts die is aangewezen door de patiënt of de vertrouwenspersoon.

---

⁶ W 2014-01-06/63, art. 22, 002; Inwerkingtreding: 25-05-2014

Art. 15

Een persoon die overlijdt ten gevolge van euthanasie toegepast met toepassing van de voorwaarden gesteld door deze wet, wordt geacht een natuurlijke dood te zijn gestorven wat betreft de uitvoering van de overeenkomsten waarbij hij partij was, en met name de verzekeringsovereenkomsten

De bepalingen van artikel 909 van het Burgerlijk Wetboek zijn mede van toepassing op de in artikel 3 bedoelde leden van het verplegend team.

Art. 16

Deze wet treedt in werking ten laatste drie maanden nadat ze in het Belgisch Staatsblad is bekendgemaakt.

Appendix II

Loi Relative à L'Euthanasie 28 Mai 2002
(The Belgian Act on Euthanasia, French-language Version)

Consultation des versions antérieures à partir du 22-06-2002 et mise à jour au 12-03-2014

Article 1

La présente loi règle une matière visée à l'article 78 de la Constitution.

CHAPITRE I: Dispositions générales

Art. 2

Pour l'application de la présente loi, il y a lieu d'entendre par euthanasie l'acte, pratiqué par un tiers, qui met intentionnellement fin à la vie d'une personne à la demande de celle-ci.

CHAPITRE II: Des conditions et de la procédure

Art. 3

§ 1er. Le médecin qui pratique une euthanasie ne commet pas d'infraction s'il s'est assuré que:

– [le patient est majeur ou mineur émancipé, capable ou encore mineur doté de la capacité de discernement et est conscient au moment de sa demande;][1]
– la demande est formulée de manière volontaire, réfléchie et répétée, et qu'elle ne résulte pas d'une pression extérieure;
– le patient [majeur ou mineur émancipé][1] se trouve dans une situation médicale sans issue et fait état d'une souffrance physique ou psychique constante et insupportable qui ne peut être apaisée et qui résulte d'une affection accidentelle ou pathologique grave et incurable;

[1] L 2014-02-28/03, art. 2, 003; En vigueur: 22-03-2014

– [le patient mineur doté de la capacité de discernement se trouve dans une situation médicale sans issue de souffrance physique constante et insupportable qui ne peut être apaisée et qui entraîne le décès à brève échéance, et qui résulte d'une affection accidentelle ou pathologique grave et incurable;][1]

et qu'il respecte les conditions et procédures prescrites par la présente loi.

§ 2. Sans préjudice des conditions complémentaires que le médecin désirerait mettre à son intervention, il doit, préalablement et dans tous les cas:

1° informer le patient de son état de santé et de son espérance de vie, se concerter avec le patient sur sa demande d'euthanasie et évoquer avec lui les possibilités thérapeutiques encore envisageables ainsi que les possibilités qu'offrent les soins palliatifs et leurs conséquences. Il doit arriver, avec le patient, à la conviction qu'il n'y a aucune autre solution raisonnable dans sa situation et que la demande du patient est entièrement volontaire;

2° s'assurer de la persistance de la souffrance physique ou psychique du patient et de sa volonté réitérée. A cette fin, il mène avec le patient plusieurs entretiens, espacés d'un délai raisonnable au regard de l'évolution de l'état du patient;

3° consulter un autre médecin quant au caractère grave et incurable de l'affection, en précisant les raisons de la consultation. Le médecin consulté prend connaissance du dossier médical, examine le patient et s'assure du caractère constant, insupportable et inapaisable de la souffrance physique ou psychique. Il rédige un rapport concernant ses constatations.

Le médecin consulté doit être indépendant, tant à l'égard du patient qu'à l'égard du médecin traitant et être compétent quant à la pathologie concernée. Le médecin traitant informe le patient concernant les résultats de cette consultation;

4° s'il existe une équipe soignante en contact régulier avec le patient, s'entretenir de la demande du patient avec l'équipe ou des membres de celle-ci;

5° si telle est la volonté du patient, s'entretenir de sa demande avec les proches que celui-ci désigne;

6° s'assurer que le patient a eu l'occasion de s'entretenir de sa demande avec les personnes qu'il souhaitait rencontrer.

[7° en outre, lorsque le patient est mineur non émancipé, consulter un pédopsychiatre ou un psychologue, en précisant les raisons de cette consultation.

Le spécialiste consulté prend connaissance du dossier médical, examine le patient, s'assure de la capacité de discernement du mineur, et l'atteste par écrit.

Le médecin traitant informe le patient et ses représentants légaux du résultat de cette consultation.

Le médecin traitant s'entretient avec les représentants légaux du mineur en leur apportant toutes les informations visées au § 2, 1°, et s'assure qu'ils marquent leur accord sur la demande du patient mineur.][1]

§ 3. Si le médecin est d'avis que le décès [du patient majeur ou mineur émancipé][1] n'interviendra manifestement pas à brève échéance, il doit, en outre:

1° consulter un deuxième médecin, psychiatre ou spécialiste de la pathologie concernée, en précisant les raisons de la consultation. Le médecin consulté prend connaissance du dossier médical, examine le patient, s'assure du caractère constant, insupportable et inapaisable de la souffrance physique ou psychique et du caractère volontaire, réfléchi et répété de la demande. Il rédige un rapport concernant ses constatations. Le médecin consulté doit être indépendant tant à l'égard du patient qu'à l'égard du médecin traitant et du premier médecin consulté. Le médecin traitant informe le patient concernant les résultats de cette consultation;
2° laisser s'écouler au moins un mois entre la demande écrite du patient et l'euthanasie.

§ 4. [La demande du patient, ainsi que l'accord des représentants légaux si le patient est mineur, sont actés par écrit.][1] Le document est rédigé, daté et signé par le patient lui-même. S'il n'est pas en état de le faire, sa demande est actée par écrit par une personne majeure de son choix qui ne peut avoir aucun intérêt matériel au décès du patient.

Cette personne mentionne le fait que le patient n'est pas en état de formuler sa demande par écrit et en indique les raisons. Dans ce cas, la demande est actée par écrit en présence du médecin, et ladite personne mentionne le nom de ce médecin dans le document. Ce document doit être versé au dossier médical.

Le patient peut révoquer sa demande à tout moment, auquel cas le document est retiré du dossier médical et restitué au patient.

[§ 4/1. Après que la demande du patient a été traitée par le médecin, la possibilité d'accompagnement psychologique est offerte aux personnes concernées.][1]

§ 5. L'ensemble des demandes formulées par le patient, ainsi que les démarches du médecin traitant et leur résultat, y compris le(s) rapport(s) du (des) médecin(s) consulté(s), sont consignés régulièrement dans le dossier médical du patient.

{Art. 3bis

Le pharmacien qui délivre une substance euthanasiante ne commet aucune infraction lorsqu'il le fait sur la base d'une prescription dans laquelle le médecin mentionne explicitement qu'il s'agit conformément à la présente loi.

Le pharmacien fournit la substance euthanasiante prescrite en personne au médecin. Le Roi fixe les critères de prudence et les conditions auxquels doivent satisfaire la prescription et la délivrance de médicaments qui seront utilisés comme substance euthanasiante.

Le Roi prend les mesures nécessaires pour assurer la disponibilité des substances euthanasiantes, y compris dans les officines qui sont accessibles au public.}[2]

CHAPITRE III: De la déclaration anticipée

Art. 4

§ 1er. Tout majeur ou mineur émancipé capable peut, pour le cas où il ne pourrait plus manifester sa volonté, consigner par écrit, dans une déclaration, sa volonté qu'un médecin pratique une euthanasie si ce médecin constate:
- qu'il est atteint d'une affection accidentelle ou pathologique grave et incurable;
- qu'il est inconscient;
- et que cette situation est irréversible selon l'état actuel de la science.

La déclaration peut désigner une ou plusieurs personnes de confiance majeures, classées par ordre de préférence, qui mettent le médecin traitant au courant de la volonté du patient. Chaque personne de confiance remplace celle qui la précède dans la déclaration en cas de refus, d'empêchement, d'incapacité ou de décès. Le médecin traitant du patient, le médecin consulté et les membres de l'équipe soignante ne peuvent pas être désignés comme personnes de confiance.

La déclaration peut être faite à tout moment. Elle doit être constatée par écrit, dressée en présence de deux témoins majeurs, dont l'un au moins n'aura pas d'intérêt matériel au décès du déclarant, datée et signée par le déclarant, par les témoins et, s'il échet, par la ou les personnes de confiance.

Si la personne qui souhaite faire une déclaration anticipée, est physiquement dans l'impossibilité permanente de rédiger et de signer, sa déclaration peut être actée par écrit par une personne majeure de son choix qui ne peut avoir aucun intérêt matériel au décès du déclarant, en présence de deux témoins majeurs, dont l'un au moins n'aura pas d'intérêt matériel au décès du déclarant. La déclaration doit alors préciser que le déclarant ne peut pas rédiger et signer, et en énoncer les raisons. La déclaration doit être datée et signée par la

[2] inséré par L 2005-11-10/68, art. 2; En vigueur: 23-12-2005

personne qui a acté par écrit la déclaration, par les témoins et, s'il échet, par la ou les personnes de confiance.

Une attestation médicale certifiant cette impossibilité physique permanente est jointe à la déclaration.

La déclaration ne peut être prise en compte que si elle a été établie ou confirmée moins de cinq ans avant le début de l'impossibilité de manifester sa volonté.

La déclaration peut être retirée ou adaptée à tout moment.

Le Roi détermine les modalités relatives à la présentation, à la conservation, à la confirmation, au retrait et à la communication de la déclaration aux médecins concernés, via les services du Registre national.

§2. Un médecin qui pratique une euthanasie, à la suite d'une déclaration anticipée, telle que prévue au §1er, ne commet pas d'infraction s'il constate que le patient:

– est atteint d'une affection accidentelle ou pathologique grave et incurable;
– est inconscient;
– et que cette situation est irréversible selon l'état actuel de la science;

et qu'il respecte les conditions et procédures prescrites par la présente loi.

Sans préjudice des conditions complémentaires que le médecin désirerait mettre à son intervention, il doit préalablement:

1° consulter un autre médecin quant à l'irréversibilité de la situation médicale du patient, en l'informant des raisons de cette consultation. Le médecin consulté prend connaissance du dossier médical et examine le patient. Il rédige un rapport de ses constatations. Si une personne de confiance est désignée dans la déclaration de volonté, le médecin traitant met cette personne de confiance au courant des résultats de cette consultation.

Le médecin consulté doit être indépendant à l'égard du patient ainsi qu'à l'égard du médecin traitant et être compétent quant à la pathologie concernée;

2° s'il existe une équipe soignante en contact régulier avec le patient, s'entretenir du contenu de la déclaration anticipée avec l'équipe soignante ou des membres de celle-ci;

3° si la déclaration désigne une personne de confiance, s'entretenir avec elle de la volonté du patient;

4° si la déclaration désigne une personne de confiance, s'entretenir du contenu de la déclaration anticipée du patient avec les proches du patient que la personne de confiance désigne.

La déclaration anticipée ainsi que l'ensemble des démarches du médecin traitant et leur résultat, y compris le rapport du médecin consulté, sont consignés régulièrement dans le dossier médical du patient.

CHAPITRE IV: De la déclaration

Art. 5

Le médecin qui a pratiqué une euthanasie remet, dans les quatre jours ouvrables, le document d'enregistrement visé à l'article 7, dûment complété, à la Commission fédérale de contrôle et d'évaluation visée à l'article 6 de la présente loi.

CHAPITRE V: La Commission fédérale de contrôle et d'évaluation

Art. 6

§ 1er. Il est institué une Commission fédérale de contrôle et d'évaluation de l'application de la présente loi, ci-après dénommée "la commission ".

§ 2. La commission se compose de seize membres, désignés sur la base de leurs connaissances et de leur expérience dans les matières qui relèvent de la compétence de la commission. Huit membres sont docteurs en médecine, dont quatre au moins sont professeurs dans une université belge. Quatre membres sont professeurs de droit dans une université belge, ou avocats. Quatre membres sont issus des milieux chargés de la problématique des patients atteints d'une maladie incurable.

La qualité de membre de la commission est incompatible avec le mandat de membre d'une des assemblées législatives et avec celui de membre du gouvernement fédéral ou d'un gouvernement de communauté ou de région.

Les membres de la commission sont nommés, dans le respect de la parité linguistique - chaque groupe linguistique comptant au moins trois candidats de chaque sexe - et en veillant à assurer une représentation pluraliste, par arrêté royal délibéré en Conseil des Ministres, sur une liste double présentée par [la Chambre des représentants],[3] pour un terme renouvelable de quatre ans. Le mandat prend fin de plein droit lorsque le membre perd la qualité en laquelle il siège. Les candidats qui n'ont pas été désignés comme membres effectifs sont nommés en qualité de membres suppléants, selon une liste déterminant l'ordre dans lequel ils seront appelés à suppléer. La commission est présidée par un président d'expression française et un président

[3] L 2014-01-06/63, art. 21, 002; En vigueur: 25-05-2014

d'expression néerlandaise. Les présidents sont élus par les membres de la commission appartenant à leur groupe linguistique respectif.

La commission ne peut délibérer valablement qu'à la condition que les deux tiers de ses membres soient présents.

§ 3. La commission établit son règlement d'ordre intérieur.

Art. 7

La commission établit un document d'enregistrement qui doit être complété par le médecin chaque fois qu'il pratique une euthanasie. Ce document est composé de deux volets. Le premier volet doit être scellé par le médecin. Il contient les données suivantes:

1° les nom, prénoms et domicile du patient;

2° les nom, prénoms, numéro d'enregistrement à l'INAMI et domicile du médecin traitant;

3° les nom, prénoms, numéro d'enregistrement à l'INAMI et domicile du (des) médecin(s) qui a (ont) été consulté(s) concernant la demande d'euthanasie;

4° les nom, prénoms, domicile et qualité de toutes les personnes consultées par le médecin traitant, ainsi que les dates de ces consultations;

5° s'il existait une déclaration anticipée et qu'elle désignait une ou plusieurs personnes de confiance, les nom et prénoms de la (des) personne(s) de confiance qui est (sont) intervenue(s).

(6° les nom, prénoms, numéro d'enregistrement à l'INAMI et adresse du pharmacien qui a délivré la substance euthanasiante, le nom des produits délivrés et leur quantité ainsi que, le cas échéant, l'excédent qui a été restitué au pharmacien.)[4]

Ce premier volet est confidentiel. Il est transmis par le médecin à la commission. Il ne peut être consulté qu'après une décision de la commission, et ne peut en aucun cas servir de base à la mission d'évaluation de la commission.

Le deuxième volet est également confidentiel et contient les données suivantes:

1° le sexe et les date et lieu de naissance du patient [et, en ce qui concerne le patient mineur, s'il était émancipé];[5]

2° la date, le lieu et l'heure du décès;

---

[4] <Errata, voir M.B. 21-03-2016, p. 19410>
[5] L 2014-02-28/03, art. 3, 003; En vigueur: 22-03-2014

3° la mention de l'affection accidentelle ou pathologique grave et incurable dont souffrait le patient;

4° la nature de la souffrance qui était constante et insupportable;

5° les raisons pour lesquelles cette souffrance a été qualifiée d'inapaisable;

6° les éléments qui ont permis de s'assurer que la demande a été formulée de manière volontaire, réfléchie et répétée et sans pression extérieure;

7° si l'on pouvait estimer que le décès aurait lieu à brève échéance;

8° s'il existe une déclaration de volonté;

9° la procédure suivie par le médecin;

10° la qualification du ou des médecins consultés, l'avis et les dates de ces consultations;

11° la qualité des personnes consultées par le médecin, et les dates de ces consultations;

12° la manière dont l'euthanasie a été effectuée et les moyens utilisés.

Art. 8

La commission examine le document d'enregistrement dûment complété que lui communique le médecin. Elle vérifie, sur la base du deuxième volet du document d'enregistrement, si l'euthanasie a été effectuée selon les conditions et la procédure prévues par la présente loi. En cas de doute, la commission peut décider, à la majorité simple, de lever l'anonymat. Elle prend alors connaissance du premier volet du document d'enregistrement. Elle peut demander au médecin traitant de lui communiquer tous les éléments du dossier médical relatifs à l'euthanasie.

Elle se prononce dans un délai de deux mois.

Lorsque, par décision prise à la majorité des deux tiers, la commission estime que les conditions prévues par la présente loi n'ont pas été respectées, elle envoie le dossier au procureur du Roi du lieu du décès du patient.

Lorsque la levée de l'anonymat fait apparaître des faits ou des circonstances susceptibles d'affecter l'indépendance ou l'impartialité du jugement d'un membre de la commission, ce membre se récusera ou pourra être récusé pour l'examen de cette affaire par la commission.

Art. 9

La commission établit à l'intention des Chambres législatives, la première fois dans les deux ans de l'entrée en vigueur de la présente loi, et, par la suite, tous les deux ans:

a) un rapport statistique basé sur les informations recueillies dans le second volet du document d'enregistrement que les médecins lui remettent complété en vertu de l'article 8;

b) un rapport contenant une description et une évaluation de l'application de la présente loi;

c) le cas échéant, des recommandations susceptibles de déboucher sur une initiative législative et/ou d'autres mesures concernant l'exécution de la présente loi.

Pour l'accomplissement de ces missions, la commission peut recueillir toutes les informations utiles auprès des diverses autorités et institutions. Les renseignements recueillis par la commission sont confidentiels. Aucun de ces documents ne peut contenir l'identité d'aucune personne citée dans les dossiers remis à la commission dans le cadre du contrôle prévu à l'article 8.

La commission peut décider de communiquer des informations statistiques et purement techniques, à l'exclusion de toutes données à caractère personnel, aux équipes universitaires de recherche qui en feraient la demande motivée. Elle peut entendre des experts.

Art. 10

Le Roi met un cadre administratif à la disposition de la commission en vue de l'accomplissement de ses missions légales. Les effectifs et le cadre linguistique du personnel administratif sont fixés par arrêté royal délibéré en Conseil des Ministres, sur proposition des ministres qui ont la Santé publique et la Justice dans leurs attributions.

Art. 11

Les frais de fonctionnement et les frais de personnel de la commission, ainsi que la rétribution de ses membres sont imputés par moitié aux budgets des ministres qui ont la Justice et la Santé publique dans leurs attributions.

Art. 12

Quiconque prête son concours, en quelque qualité que ce soit, à l'application de la présente loi, est tenu de respecter la confidentialité des données qui lui sont confiées dans l'exercice de sa mission et qui ont trait à l'exercice de celle-ci. L'article 458 du Code pénal lui est applicable.

Art. 13

[Dans les six mois du dépôt du premier rapport et, le cas échéant, des recommandations de la commission, visés à l'article 9, la Chambre des représentants organise un débat à ce sujet. Ce délai de six mois est suspendu pendant la période au cours de laquelle la Chambre des représentants est dissoute et/ou au cours de laquelle il n'y a pas de gouvernement ayant la confiance de la Chambre des représentants.][6]

CHAPITRE VI: Dispositions particulières

Art. 14

La demande et la déclaration anticipée de volonté telles que prévues aux articles 3 et 4 de la présente loi n'ont pas de valeur contraignante.

Aucun médecin n'est tenu de pratiquer une euthanasie.

Aucune autre personne n'est tenue de participer à une euthanasie.

Si le médecin consulté refuse de pratiquer une euthanasie, il est tenu d'en informer en temps utile le patient ou la personne de confiance éventuelle, en en précisant les raisons. Dans le cas où son refus est justifié par une raison médicale, celle-ci est consignée dans le dossier médical du patient.

Le médecin qui refuse de donner suite à une requête d'euthanasie est tenu, à la demande du patient ou de la personne de confiance, de communiquer le dossier médical du patient au médecin désigné par ce dernier ou par la personne de confiance.

Art. 15

La personne décédée à la suite d'une euthanasie dans le respect des conditions imposées par la présente loi est réputée décédée de mort naturelle pour ce qui concerne l'exécution des contrats auxquels elle était partie, en particulier les contrats d'assurance.

Les dispositions de l'article 909 du Code civil sont applicables aux membres de l'équipe soignante visés à l'article 3.

Art. 16

La présente loi entre en vigueur au plus tard trois mois après sa publication au Moniteur belge.

---

[6] L 2014-01-06/63, art. 22, 002; En vigueur: 25-05-2014

Appendix III

The Belgian Act on Euthanasia of 28 May 2002[1] (Unofficial Translation)

Section 1

This present Act regulates a matter addressed in article 78 of the Constitution.

Chapter I: General Provisions

Section 2

For the purposes of the present Act, euthanasia is understood to be the act which intentionally terminates the life of a person at his/her request and which is carried out by an individual other than the person in question.

Chapter II: Conditions and procedure

Section 3

§1. The physician who performs euthanasia does not commit an offence if he/she ensures that:

- [The patient has reached the age of majority or is an emancipated minor with capacity or is a minor with the ability of discernment and is conscious at the moment of making his/her request;][2]
- The request is expressed in a recurring manner which is voluntary, well-considered and is not the result of any external pressure;

---

[1] Consolidation of previous versions from 22-06-2002 to 12-03-2014, an unofficial translation. This translation has been provided primarily by Calum MacKellar working from the French text. It also draws from the translation of the 2002 law provided by Dale Kidd under the supervision of Prof. Herman Nys, Centre for Biomedical Ethics and Law, Catholic University of Leuven (Belgium) that was printed in the *European Journal of Health Law*, 2003, 329–355.

[2] Law 2014-02-28/03, art. 2, 003; Effective from 22-03-2014.

- The patient [who has reached the age of majority or emancipated minor][3] is in a medically hopeless condition experiencing constant and unbearable physical or mental suffering that cannot be alleviated, resulting from a serious and incurable disorder caused by illness or accident;
- [the patient who is a minor with the capacity of discernment is in a medically hopeless condition of constant and unbearable physical suffering resulting from a serious and incurable disorder caused by illness or accident, that cannot be alleviated and that will result in death in the near future;][4]

and he/she respects the conditions and procedures stipulated in the present Act.

§2. Without prejudice to any supplementary conditions the physician may want to provide to his/her intervention, he/she must, beforehand, and in each case:

1) Inform the patient about his/her state of health and life expectancy, discuss with the patient his/her request for euthanasia and mention the therapeutic possibilities which may still be envisaged as well as the possibilities offered by palliative care and their consequences. He/She must come to the conviction, together with the patient, that there is no reasonable alternatives in his/her condition and that the patient's request is completely voluntary;
2) Ascertain the continued physical or mental suffering of the patient and of the recurring nature of his/her request. To this end, the physician has several conversations with the patient over a reasonable period of time, taking into account the evolution of the patient's condition;
3) Consult another physician about the serious and incurable nature of the disorder specifying the reasons for this consultation. The physician consulted takes note of the medical records, examines the patient and ascertains the constant, unbearable nature of the physical or mental suffering that cannot be alleviated. The physician consulted drafts a report about the results of this consultation.

    The physician consulted must be independent of the patient as well as the attending physician and must be competent to give an opinion about the disorder in question. The attending physician informs the patient about the results of this consultation;
4) If a nursing team exists that has regular contact with the patient, discuss the request of the patient with the nursing team or its members;

[3] Law 2014-02-28/03, art. 2, 003; Effective from 22-03-2014.
[4] Law 2014-02-28/03, art. 2, 003; Effective from 22-03-2014.

5) If the patient so desires, discuss his/her request with those close to the patient whom he/she appoints;
6) Verifies that the patient has had the opportunity to discuss his/her request with the persons that he/she wanted to meet.
7) [furthermore, when the patient is an un-emancipated minor, consult a child psychiatrist or a psychologist, specifying the reasons for this consultation.

The consulted specialist takes note of the medical records, examines the patient, verifies the capacity of discernment of the minor and certifies this in writing.

The attending physician informs the patient and his or her legal representatives of the results of this consultation.

The attending physician has a discussion with the legal representatives of the minor while providing them with all the information specified in §2, 1° and verifies that they convey their agreement with the request of the patient who is a minor.][5]

§3. If the physician is of the opinion that the death of [the patient who has reached the age of majority or is an emancipated minor][6] is clearly not expected in the near future, he/she must also:

1) Consult a second physician, who is a psychiatrist or a specialist in the disorder in question, specifying the reasons for the consultation. The physician consulted takes note of the medical records, examines the patient and ascertains the constant, unbearable nature of the physical or mental suffering, which cannot be alleviated, and of the voluntary, well-considered and recurrent nature of the request. The physician consulted drafts a report on his/her findings. The physician consulted must be, all at the same time, independent from the patient, the attending physician and the first physician consulted. The attending physician informs the patient about the results of this consultation;
2) Allow at least one month between the patient's written request and the performance of euthanasia.

§4. [The request of the patient and, if the patient is a minor, the agreement of the legal representatives, are to be recorded in writing.][7] The document is drawn up, dated and signed by the patient himself/herself. If the patient is incapable of doing this, his/her request is recorded in writing by a person of

[5] Law 2014-02-28/03, art. 2, 003; Effective from 22-03-2014.
[6] Law 2014-02-28/03, art. 2, 003; Effective from 22-03-2014.
[7] Law 2014-02-28/03, art. 2, 003; Effective from 22-03-2014.

his/her choice who has reached the age of majority and who cannot have any material interest in the death of the patient.

This person mentions that the patient is incapable of formulating his/her request in writing and indicates the reasons. In this case, the request is recorded in writing in the presence of the physician and this same person mentions the name of the physician on the document. This document must be annexed to the medical records.

The patient may revoke his/her request at any time, in which case the document is removed from the medical records and returned to the patient.

[§4/1. After the physician has addressed the request of the patient, the persons in question are offered the possibility of psychological assistance.][8]

§5. All of the requests formulated by the patient as well as any measures taken by the attending physician and their results, including the report(s) of the consulted physician(s), are regularly entered into the patient's medical records.

{Section 3bis

The pharmacist who delivers an euthanaticum does not commit an offence when he/she does so on the basis of a prescription in which the physician explicitly mentions that this is taking place in conformity with the present Act.

The pharmacist delivers the prescribed euthanaticum, in person, to the physician. The Crown determines the rules of good practices and the conditions to be satisfied for the prescription and delivery of the euthanaticum.

The Crown takes the necessary measures in order to guarantee that the euthanatica are available including in dispensaries which are accessible to the public.}[9]

Chapter III: The advance directive

Section 4

§1. Every person who has reached the age of majority or who is an emancipated minor can, in the case where he/she is no longer able to express his/her will, record in writing in an advance directive his/her wishes that a physician perform euthanasia if this physician recognises that:
– he/she is affected by a serious and incurable disorder, caused by illness or accident;
– he/she is unconscious;
– and that the condition is irreversible given the current state of science.

---

[8] Law 2014-02-28/03, art. 2, 003; Effective from 22-03-2014.
[9] Inserted 2005-11-10/68, art. 2; Effective from 23-12-2005.

The advance directive can designate one or more person(s) of confidence, who have reached the age of majority, named in order of preference, who inform(s) the attending physician about the patient's will. Each person of confidence replaces his or her predecessor in the advance directive, in the case of refusal, hindrance, incapacity or death. The patient's attending physician, the physician consulted and the members of the nursing team cannot be designated as persons of confidence.

The advance directive may be drafted at any moment. It must be recorded in writing, prepared in the presence of two witnesses who have reached the age of majority, at least one of whom has no material interest in the death of the patient, and be dated and signed by the person in question, the witnesses and, if applicable, by the person(s) of confidence.

If the person who wishes to draft an advance directive is permanently physically incapable of writing and signing, his/her advance directive may be recorded in writing by a person of his/her choice who has reached the age of majority and who cannot have any material interest in the death of the person in question, in the presence of two witnesses who have reached the age of majority, at least one of whom has no material interest in the death of the person in question. The advance directive must then specify that the person in question is incapable of writing and signing and gives the reasons. The advance directive must be dated and signed by the person who has recorded in writing the directive, by the witnesses and, if applicable, by the person(s) of confidence. A medical certificate is annexed to the advance directive certifying this permanent physical incapacity.

The advance directive can only be taken into account if it has been drawn up or confirmed no more than five years prior to the beginning of the time when the wishes could no longer be expressed.

The advance directive may be amended or revoked at any time.

The Crown determines the manner in which the advance directive is presented, stored, confirmed, revoked, and the manner in which it is communicated to the relevant physicians via the offices of the National Register.

§2 A physician who performs euthanasia following an advance directive as provided for in §1, does not commit an offence when he recognises that the patient:

– is affected by a serious and incurable disorder, caused by illness or accident;
– is unconscious;
– and that the condition is irreversible given the current state of science;

and when he/she respects the conditions and procedures stipulated in the present Act.

Without prejudice to any supplementary conditions the physician may want to provide to his/her intervention, he/she must beforehand:

1) consult another physician about the irreversibility of the patient's medical condition while informing him/her about the reasons for this consultation. The physician consulted takes note of the medical records and examines the patient. He/she drafts a report on his/her findings.

   If the advance directive names a person of confidence, the attending physician informs this person of confidence about the results of this consultation.

   The physician consulted must be independent of the patient as well as of the attending physician and be competent as regards to the disorder in question;

2) if a nursing team exists that has regular contact with the patient, discuss the content of the advance directive with that team or its members;

3) if a person of confidence is named in the advance directive, discuss the wishes of the patient with that person;

4) if a person of confidence is named in the advance directive, discuss the contents of the advance directive of the patient with those close to the patient that the person of confidence designates.

The advance directive as well as all the measures taken by the attending physician and their results, including the report of the consulted physician are regularly entered into the patient's medical records.

Chapter IV: Notification

Section 5

The physician who performed the euthanasia submits, within four working days, the duly completed registration form mentioned in Section 7, to the Federal Control and Evaluation Commission mentioned in Section 6 of the present Act.

Chapter V: The Federal Control and Evaluation Commission

Section 6

§1 A Federal Control and Evaluation Commission is established to implement the present Act, hereafter referred to as "the commission".

§2 The Commission is composed of sixteen members, appointed on the basis of their knowledge and experience on the matter relevant to the remit of the commission. Eight members are physicians, of whom at least four are professors at a university in Belgium. Four members are professors of law at a university in Belgium, or solicitors. Four members are drawn from groups responsible for addressing the challenges faced by patients affected by an incurable illness.

Membership of the commission is incompatible with the mandate of member of one of the legislative bodies and with that of a member of the federal government or one of the regional or community governments.

While respecting language parity – where each linguistic group has at least three candidates of each sex – and ensuring pluralistic representation, the members of the commission are appointed by royal decree considered by the Council of Ministers from a double list of candidates put forward by [the Chamber of Representatives][10] for a renewable term of four years. A member's mandate is terminated *de jure* if the member loses the capacity on which he/she sits in the commission. The candidates who are not appointed as sitting members are appointed as substitutes, following a list determining the order in which they will be called as substitutes. The commission is chaired by a Dutch-speaking and a French-speaking member. These chairpersons are elected by the commission members belonging to the respective linguistic group.

The commission is only quorate if two-thirds of its members are present.
§3. The commission establishes its own internal regulation.

Section 7

The commission drafts a registration form that must be completed by the physician each time he/she performs euthanasia. This document consists of two parts. The first part must be sealed by the physician. It includes the following information:

1) The patient's full name and address;
2) The full name, address and health insurance institute registration number of the attending physician;
3) The full name, address and health insurance institute registration number of the physician(s) consulted about the euthanasia request;
4) The full name, address and capacity of all persons consulted by the attending physician, and the date of these consultations;
5) If there exists an advance directive in which one or more persons of confidence are named, the full name of the person(s) of confidence who intervened.
[6] The full name, address and health insurance institute registration number of the pharmacist who issued the euthanaticum, the name and quantity of

---

[10] Law 2014-01-06/63, art. 21, 002; Effective from: 25-05-2014.

the products delivered and, if applicable, the surplus that has been returned to the pharmacist.][11]

The document's first part is confidential, and is forwarded to the commission by the physician. It can only be consulted following a decision of the commission and can never be used as a basis for the evaluation remit of the commission.

The second part is also confidential and includes the following information:

1) The patient's sex, date and place of birth; [and, for the patient who is a minor, whether he/she was emancipated];[12]
2) The date, time and place of death;
3) The nature of the serious and incurable condition, caused by accident or illness, from which the patient suffered;
4) The nature of the constant and unbearable suffering;
5) The reasons why this suffering was qualified as being impossible to alleviate;
6) The elements enabling assurances to be provided that the request was expressed in a voluntary, well-considered and recurrent manner, and without any external pressure;
7) Whether it was expected that the patient would die in the near future;
8) Whether an advance directive exists;
9) The procedure followed by the physician;
10) The capacity of the physician(s) consulted, the outcome and the dates of these consultations;
11) The capacity of the persons consulted by the physician, and the date of these consultations;
12) The manner in which euthanasia was performed and the methods used.

Section 8

The commission examines the duly completed registration form sent by the attending physician. On the basis of the second part of the registration form, the commission verifies whether the euthanasia was performed in accordance with the conditions and procedure stipulated by the present Act. In cases of doubt, the commission may decide, by simple majority, to lift anonymity and examine the first part of the registration form. The commission may request the attending physician to provide all the elements in the medical records relating to the euthanasia.

---

[11] Errata, see M.B. 21-03-2016, p. 19410.
[12] Law 2014-02-28/03, art. 3, 003; Effective from: 22-03-2014.

The commission hands down a verdict within two months.

When, in a decision taken by a two-thirds majority, the commission is of the opinion that the conditions laid down in the present Act have not been fulfilled, it forwards the report to the Crown prosecutor of the jurisdiction in which the patient died.

When the lifting of anonymity reveals facts or circumstances which would compromise the independence or impartiality of one of the commission members, this member will explain, or be challenged about, the examination of this matter by the commission.

Section 9

Within two years of this Act's coming into force, and every two years thereafter, the commission will draft the following reports for the benefit of the legislative chambers:

a) A statistical report based on the information obtained from the second part of the completed registration forms submitted by the physicians pursuant to section 8;

b) A report containing a description and evaluation of the workings of the present Act;

c) If appropriate, recommendations that could lead to new legislative and/or other measures concerning the workings of the present Act.

For the purpose of carrying out these tasks, the commission may collect any useful information from the various public services and institutions. The information collected by the commission is confidential. None of these documents may include the identity of any person named in the reports submitted to the commission for the purposes of the review envisaged in section 8.

The commission can decide to communicate statistical and purely technical information, from which any personal information has been removed, to university research teams that make a reasoned request.

The commission can grant hearings to experts.

Section 10

The Crown provides an administrative framework at the disposal of the commission in order to carry out its legal functions. The composition and language framework of the administrative personnel are established by royal decree, considered in the Council of Ministers, on the recommendation of the Ministers whose remits include Public Health and Justice.

Section 11

The commission's operating and personnel costs, including payments to members, are divided equally between the budgets of the Ministers whose remits include Public Health and Justice.

Section 12

Any person who is involved, in whatever capacity, in the implementation of the present Act is required to maintain confidentiality regarding the data entrusted to him/her in the exercise of his/her function and which are related to the exercise of this function. He/she is subject to section 458 of the Penal Code.

Section 13

[Within six months of submitting the first report and, if applicable, the commission's recommendations referred to in section 9, a debate is to be held on the topic in the Chamber of Representatives. This six-month period is suspended during the time that the Chamber of Representatives is dissolved and/or during the time where there is no government having the confidence of the Chamber of Representatives.][13]

Chapter VI: Special Provisions

Section 14

The request and the advance directive referred to in sections 3 and 4 of the present Act do not have a legally binding nature.

No physician can be compelled to perform euthanasia.

No other person can be compelled to participate in euthanasia.

Should the physician consulted refuse to perform euthanasia, he/she must inform, in a timely fashion, the patient or the potential persons of confidence while explaining his/her reasons. If the refusal is based on a medical reason, this is then entered into the patient's medical records.

The physician who refuses to proceed with a euthanasia request must communicate, when asked by the patient or the person of confidence, the patient's medical records to the physician designated by the patient or the person of confidence.

---

[13] Law 2014-01-06/63, art. 22, 002; Effective from: 25-05-2014.

Section 15

The person who died as a result of euthanasia performed in accordance with the conditions established by the present Act is deemed to have died of natural causes with respect to the execution of contracts for which he/she was a party, in particular insurance contracts.

The provisions of section 909 of the Civil Code apply to the members of the nursing team referred to in section 3 of this Act.

Section 16

The present Act comes into force no later than three months following its publication in the *Official Belgian Gazette*.

REFERENCES

'93-year-old Belgian woman on hunger strike', 2009. *Dying with Dignity* 25 March, www.dwdnsw.org.au/ves/index.php/93-year-old-belgian-woman-on-hunger-stri#more387 (accessed 24 October 2016).

Adaljarnardottir, S. and L.G. Hafsteinsson, 2001. 'Adolescents' perceived parenting styles and their substance use: concurrent and longitudinal analyses', *Journal of Research on Adolescence* 11: 401–423.

Adams, M. and H. Nys, 2005. 'Euthanasia in the Low Countries: comparative reflections on the Belgian and Dutch Euthanasia Act', in P. Schotmans and T. Meulenbergs (eds.), *Euthanasia and Palliative Care in the Low Countries.* Louvain: Peeters, 5–33.

Agich, G., 2003. *Dependency and Autonomy in Old Age: An Ethical Framework for Long-Term Care.* Cambridge: Cambridge University Press.

Alaluf, V. et al., 2012. '*Dix ans d'euthanasie: un heureux anniversaire!*' [Ten years of euthanasia: A Happy Birthday!], *La Libre Belgique* 20 June 2012.

Alexander, L., 1949. 'Medical science under dictatorship', *New England Journal of Medicine* 241(2): 39–47.

Alvargonzalez, D., 2012. 'Alzheimer's disease and euthanasia', *Journal of Aging Studies* 26: 377–385.

Alzheimer's Disease International, 2013. *World Alzheimer Report 2013: Journey of Caring. An Analysis of Long-Term Care for Dementia,* www.alz.co.uk/research/worldalzheimerreport2013.pdf (accessed 24 October 2016).

'Amelie Van Esbeen est décédée par euthanasia', 2009. *Lalibre.be* 1 April, www.lalibre.be/actu/belgique/article/492830/amelie-van-esbeen-est-decedee-par-euthanasie.html (accessed 24 October 2016).

American Psychiatric Association, 2013. *Diagnostic and Statistical Manual of Mental Disorders – 5th ed. DSM-V-TR.* Washington DC: American Psychiatric Publications, Inc.

Advisory National Council of the Belgian National Order of Physicians, 2003. '*Advies betreffende palliatieve zorg, euthanasie en andere medische beslissingen omtrent het levenseinde*' ['Opinion on palliative care, euthanasia and other medical decisions concerning the end of life'], *Tijdschrift Nationale Raad* 100: 5.

Anquinet, L., K. Raus, S. Sterckx, T. Smets, L. Deliens and J.A.C. Rietjens, 2013. 'Continuous sedation until death not always strictly distinguished from euthanasia: a focus group study in Flanders, Belgium', *Palliative Medicine* 27(6): 553–561.

Anquinet, L., J. Rietjens, C. Seale, J. Seymour, L. Deliens and A. van der Heide, 2012. 'The practice of continuous deep sedation until death in Flanders (Belgium), The Netherlands, and the UK: a comparative study', *Journal of Pain and Symptom Management* 44(1): 33–43.

Anscombe, G.E.M., 2005. 'Murder and the morality of euthanasia', in M. Geach and L. Gormally (eds.), *Human Life, Action and Ethics: Essays by G.E.M. Anscombe*. Exeter, UK: Imprint Academic.

Anthony, W., 1993. 'Recovery from mental illness: the guiding vision of the mental health service system in the 1990s', *Psychosocial Rehabilitation Journal* 16: 11–23.

APF, 2008. 'Euthanasie: l'écrivain belge Hugo Claus a choisi sa sortie' [Euthanasia: The Belgian writer Hugo Claus has chosen this exit], *La Depeche* 19 March 2008.

Appelbaum, P.S., 2016. 'Physician-assisted death for patients with mental disorders —reasons for concern', *JAMA Psychiatry* 73(4): 325–326.

Appelbaum, P.S. and T. Grisso, 2001. *MacCAT-CR: MacArthur Competence Assessment Tool for Clinical Research*. Sarasota, FL: Professional Resource Press.

Armstrong-Esther, C., K. Browne and J. McAffee, 1999. 'Investigation into nursing staff knowledge and attitude to dementia', *International Journal of Psychiatric Nursing Research* 4: 489–497.

Arnett, J.J., 2000. 'Emerging adulthood: a theory of development from the late teens through the twenties', *American Psychologist* 55: 469–480.

Ars, B. et al., 2012. '*Dix ans d'euthanasie: un heureux anniversaire?*' [Ten years of euthanasia: A Happy Birthday?], *La Libre Belgique* 12 June 2012.

Austin, J.L., 1975. *How to Do Things with Words*. Oxford:. Oxford University Press.

'Assisted dying debate: the key questions', 2015. *BBC* 10 September, www.bbc.co .uk/news/health-28310868 (accessed 24 October 2016).

Aviv, R., 2015. 'Letter from Belgium. The death treatment. When should people with a non-terminal illness be helped to die?' *The New Yorker* 22 June 2015, www.newyorker.com/magazine/2015/06/22/the-death-treatment (accessed 24 October 2016).

Bacchi, U., 2014. 'Frank Van Den Bleeken: Belgian serial rapist and murderer wins right to die', *International Business Times* 14 September 2014, www .ibtimes.co.uk/frank-van-den-bleeken-belgian-serial-rapist-murderer-wins-right-die-1465667 (accessed 24 October 2016).

Balaguer, A., C. Monforte-Royo, J. Porta-Sales, A. Alonso-Babarro, R. Altisent, A. Aradilla-Herrero, M. Bellido-Pérez, W. Breitbart, C. Centeno, M.A. Cuervo, L. Deliens, G. Frerich, C, Gastmans, S. Lichtenfeld, J.T. Limonero, M.A. Maier,

L.J. Materstvedt, M. Nabal, G. Rodin, B. Rosenfeld, T. Schroepfer, J. Tomás-Sábado, J. Trelis, C. Villavicencio-Chávez, R. Voltz, 2016. 'An international consensus definition of the wish to hasten death and its related factors', *PLoS One* 11(1): e0146184. doi: 10.1371/journal.pone.0146184.

Bandura, A., 2002. 'Selective moral disengagement in the exercise of moral agency', *Journal of Moral Education* 31(2): 101–119.

Barina, R. and J. Bishop, 2013. 'Maturing the minor, marginalizing the family: on the social constitution of the mature minor, sexual politics, and the family', *The Journal of Medicine and Philosophy* 38: 300–314.

Basnett, I., 2001, 'Health care professionals and their attitudes toward decisions affecting disabled people', in G.L. Albrecht, K. Seelman and M. Bury (eds.), *Handbook of Disability Studies*. Thousand Oaks, CA: Sage Publications, 450–467.

Batavia, A. 2000. 'The relevance of data on physicians and disability on the right to assisted suicide: can empirical studies resolve the issue?' *Psychology, Public Policy, and Law* 6: 546–558.

Battin, M. 2007. 'Right question, but not quite the right answer: whether there is a third alternative in choices about euthanasia in Alzheimer's disease', *The American Journal of Bioethics* 7(12): 58–60.

——— 2008. 'Terminal sedation: pulling the sheet over our eyes', *Hastings Center Report* 38(5): 27–30.

——— 2013. 'Terminal sedation: recasting a metaphor as the *ars moriendi* changes', in K. Raus, S. Sterckx and F. Mortier (eds.), *Continuous Sedation at the End of Life*. Cambridge: Cambridge University Press, 240–249.

Battin, M.P., A. van der Heide, L. Ganzini, G. van der Wal and B.D. Onwuteaka-Philipsen, 2007. 'Legal physician-assisted dying in Oregon and the Netherlands: evidence concerning the impact on patients in "vulnerable" groups', *Journal of Medical Ethics* 33(10): 591–597.

Bayertz, K., 1996. 'Human dignity: philosophical origin and scientific erosion of an idea', in K. Bayertz (ed.), *Sanctity of Life and Human Dignity*. Dordrecht: Kluwer, 73–90.

Bazan, A., G. Van de Vijver, W. Lemmens, N. Renuart et al., 2015. 'Euthanasie pour souffrance psychique: un cadre légal discutable et des dommages sociétaux', *Le Journal du Medecin* n° 2420: 42 (Dutch version in: *Artsenkrant*, n° 2420: 42).

Beauchamp, T.L. and J.F. Childress, 2001. *Principles of Biomedical Ethics*. Oxford: Oxford University Press.

——— 2013. *Principles of Biomedical Ethics*. Oxford: Oxford University Press.

Beel, V., 2013a. 'Artsen schuiven euthanasie als een hete aardappel door' ('Doctors transfer the request for euthanasia to each other'), *De Standaard*, 24 June 2013.

——— 2013b. 'Wie wil sterven moet daarvoor kunnen kiezen' ('Those who want to die, must be able to choose for it'), *De Standaard* 22 October 2013.

Beel, V. and E. Bergmans, 2013. 'Euthanasie na strijd van 25 jaar tegen anorexia' ('Euthanasia after the 25 year fight against anorexia'), *Nieuwsblad* 28 January 2013.

Beel, V. and L. Sioen, L., 2013. 'In de VS zat ik al lang achter de tralies, en jij met mij' ('In the United States, I would be in jail, and you with me'), *De Standaard* 21 December 2013.

Bekelman, J.E., et al., 2016. 'Comparison of site of death, health care utilization, and hospital expenditures for patients dying with cancer in 7 developed countries', *JAMA* 315(3): 272–283.

'Belgian euthanasia, controversy is served again', 2009. *Just Another WordPress. com Weblog* 31 March.

'Belgian euthanasia doctor could face criminal charges', 2015. *SBS* 19 November 2015, www.sbs.com.au/news/dateline/article/2015/10/29/belgian-euthanasia-doctor-could-face-criminal-charges (accessed 24 October 2016).

'Belgian woman dead after fighting for assisted suicide', 2009. *Expatica.com* 3 April, www.expatica.com/be/news/local_news/Belgian-woman-dead-after-fighting-for-assisted-suicide_51240.html# (accessed 24 October 2016).

'Belgian woman, 93, gets the help to die that she wanted', 2009. *Assisted-Suicide Blog* 4 April, http://assistedsuicide.org/blog/2009/04/04/belgium-woman-93-gets-the-help-to-die-that-she-wanted/ (accessed 24 October 2016).

Belgisch Staatsblad, 2014. http://mailsystem.palliatief.be/accounts/15/attachments/wetgeving/wet__euthanasie_minderjaringen_bs12_03_2014.pdf (accessed 24 October 2016).

Bentham, J., 1977. 'A comment on the commentaries and a fragment on government', in J. H. Burns and H. L. A. Hart (eds.), *The Collected Works of Jeremy Bentham*. London.

Berger, S., 2007. 'Singapore's compulsory organ transplants', *Daily Telegraph* 2 March 2007. www.telegraph.co.uk/news/1544379/Singapores-compulsory-organ-transplants.html (accessed 24 October 2016).

Berghmans, R., G. Widdershoven and I. Widdershoven-Heerding, 2013. 'Physician-assisted suicide in psychiatry and loss of hope', *International Journal of Law and Psychiatry* 36(5–6): 436–443.

Bernat, J.L., 2013. 'Life or death for the dead donor rule?' *NEJM* 369: 1289–1291.

Bernheim J. et al., 2008. 'Development of palliative care and legalisation of euthanasia: antagonism or synergy?', *BMJ* 336: 864–867.

et al., 2012. 'Het Belgisch model van integrale levenseindezorg: palliatieve zorg en wettelijke euthanasie als aanvullende, niet-tegenstrijdige ontwikkelingen. I. Historische, epidemiologische en regulatorische gegevens', *Tijdschrift voor Geneeskunde* 68(11): 539–548.

et al., 2014. 'Questions and answers on the Belgian model of integral end-of-life care: Experiment? Prototype?', *Bioethical Inquiry* 11: 507–529.

Bernheim, J. and E. Vermeersch, 2015. 'Overhaaste euthanasia? Geloof niet alles wat The New Yorker schrijft', *De Morgen* 26 June 2015, www.demorgen.be/opinie/overhaaste-euthanasie-geloof-niet-alles-wat-the-new-yorker-schrijft-b4c8f813/ (accessed 24 October 2016).

Billings, A. and S.D. Block, 1996. 'Slow euthanasia', *Journal of Palliative Care* 12(4): 21–30.

Bilsen, J., J. Cohen, K. Chambaere, G. Pousset, B. Onwuteaka-Philipsen, F. Mortier and L. Deliens, 2009. 'Medical end-of-life practices under the euthanasia law in Belgium', *New England Journal of Medicine* 361(11): 1119–1121.

Bioethics Advisory Committee of Belgium, 2014. 'Avis n° 59 du 27 janvier 2014 relatif aux aspects éthiques de l'application de la loi du 28 mai 2002 relative à l'euthanasie' (Opinion No. 59 of 27 January 2014 on ethical aspects of the application of the Law of 28 May 2002 concerning Euthanasia).

Biskin, R.S., 2015. 'The lifetime course of borderline personality disorder', *The Canadian Journal of Psychiatry* 60(7): 303–308.

Bittel, N., H. Neuenschwander and F. Stiefel, 2002. 'Euthanasia: a survey by the Swiss Association for Palliative Care', *Support Care Cancer* 10: 265–271.

Bluebond-Langner, M., 1977. 'Meanings of death to children', in H. Feifel (ed.), *New Meanings of Death*. New York: McGraw-Hill, 48–66.

Boer, T.A., 2007. 'Recurring themes in the debate about euthanasia and assisted suicide', *Journal of Religious Ethics* 35(3): 527–555.

Bolt, E.E., M.C. Snijdewind, D.L. Willems, A. van der Heide and B.D. Onwuteaka-Philipsen, 2015. 'Can physicians conceive of performing euthanasia in case of psychiatric disease, dementia or being tired of living?' *Journal of Medical Ethics* 41(8): 592–598.

Boyle, J., 2004. 'Medical ethics and double effect: the case of terminal sedation', *Theoretical Medicine* 25: 51–60.

Brassington, I., 2014. 'Would the Falconer Bill increase the suicide rate?' *JME Blog* 8 Dec 2014, http://blogs.bmj.com/medical-ethics/2014/12/08/would-the-falconer-bill-increase-the-suicide-rate/ (accessed 24 October 2016).

Breitbart, W., B. Rosenfeld, C. Gibson, M. Kramer, Y. Li, A. Tomarken, C. Nelson, H. Pessin, J. Esch, M. Galietta, N. Garcia, J. Brechtl and M. Schuster, 2010. 'Impact of treatment for depression on desire for hastened death in patients with advanced AIDS', *Psychosomatics* 51(2): 98–105.

Bridgens, R., 2009. 'Disability and being "normal": a response to McLaughlin and Goodley: response', *Sociology* 43(4): 753–761. doi:10.1177/0038038509105419.

Brodaty, H., M. Breteler, S. DeKosky, P. Dorenlot, L. Fratiglioni, C. Hock, P.-A. Kenigsberg, P. Scheltens and B. De Strooper, 2011. 'The world of dementia beyond 2020', *Journal of the American Geriatrics Society* 59: 923–927.

Broeckaert, B., 2001. 'Belgium: towards a legal recognition of euthanasia', *European Journal of Health Law* 8(2): 95–107.

2002. 'Palliative sedation: ethical aspects', in C. Gastmans (ed.), *Between Technology and Humanity: The Impact of Technology on Health Care Ethics*. Leuven: Leuven University Press, 239–255.

Broeckaert, B. The Flemish Palliative Care Federation, 2009. 'Treatment decisions in advanced disease: a conceptual framework', *Indian Journal of Palliative Care* 15: 30–36.

Broeckaert B., R. Janssens, 2003. 'Palliative care and euthanasia: Belgian and Dutch perspectives', *Ethical Perspectives* 9: 147–164.

Broeckaert, B., A. Mullie, J. Gielen, M. Desmet and P. Vanden Berghe, 2010. *Guideline Palliative Sedation*. Ethics Steering Committee of the Federation for Palliative Care Flanders [Sedation]. Available at www.pallialine.be/template.asp?f=rl_palliatieve_sedatie.htm (accessed 24 October 2016).

Bruinsma, S.M., J.A.C. Rietjens, S.J. Swart, R.S.G.M. Perez, J.J.M. van Delden and A. van der Heide, 2014. 'Estimating the potential life-shortening effect of continuous sedation until death: a comparison between two approaches', *Journal of Medical Ethics* 40: 458–462.

Buchanan, R.T., 2015. 'Right to die: Belgian doctors rule depressed 24-year-old woman has right to end her life', *Independent* Thursday 2 July 2015, www.independent.co.uk/news/people/right-to-die-belgian-doctors-rule-depressed-24-year-old-woman-has-right-to-end-her-life-10361492.html (accessed 24 October 2016).

Buchen, L. 2012. 'Science in court: arrested development', *Nature* 484(7394): 304–306.

Burger, J., 2016. 'Belgian Bishop criticized for tough stand against euthanasia in Catholic hospitals'. *Aletia* 6 January 2016, http://aleteia.org/2016/01/06/belgian-prelate-criticized-for-tough-stand-against-euthanasia-in-catholic-hospitals/ (accessed 24 October 2016).

Burgess, J.A., 1993. 'The great slippery-slope argument', *Journal of Medical Ethics* 19: 169–174.

Caldwell, S., 2014. 'Elderly couple to die together by assisted suicide even though they are not ill', *Daily Mail* 26 September 2014, www.dailymail.co.uk/news/article-2770249/Healthy-OAP-couple-die-assisted-suicide-Husband-wife-support-three-children.html (accessed 24 October 2016).

2016. 'Catholic care home sued for refusing euthanasia', *Catholic Herald* 8 January 2016.

Callahan, S., 1991. *In Good Conscience: Reason and Emotion in Moral Discourse*. New York: Harper.

Callebert, A., 2014. '*De herstelvisie als antwoord op de euthanasievraag bij ondraaglijk psychisch lijden?*' ['Does a recovery perspective offer an answer to the question of euthanasia in unbearable mental suffering?'], *Tijdschrift Klinische Psychologie* 44(1): 35–41.

Callebert, A., C. Van Audenhove, I. De Coster, 2012. *Euthanasie bij ondraaglijk psychisch lijden*. Leuven, Belgium: ACCO.

Calman, N.S., 2004. 'So tired of life', *Health Affairs* 23(3) (May): 228–232.

Cameron, N., 1991. *The New Medicine: The Crisis in Medicine and the Hippocratic Oath*. London: Hodder and Soughton.

Campbell, J., 2016. 'Kevin Fitzpatrick obituary: disability campaigner who played a big part in shaping the 2006 Equality Act', *Guardian* 17 February 2016.

Carpentier, N. and J. Antonissen, 2015. 'Jaarlijks vijftig keer euthanasie om psy-chiatrische redenen' [Every year fifity cases of euthanasia for psychiatric reasons], *Humo* 20 March 2015, www.humo.be/actua/326521/jaarlijks-vijf tig-keer-euthanasie-om-psychiatrische-redenen (accessed 24 October 2016).

Cassem, E.H., 1995. 'Depressive disorders in the medically ill: an overview', *Psychosomatics* 36: S2–S10.

Catherwood J., 2006. 'Tearing Down the Slippery Slope', *Journal of Northern Ireland Ethics Forum* 3: 42–51.

Cerel, J., J.R. Jordan and P.R. Duberstein, 2008. 'The impact of suicide on the family', *Crisis* 29(1): 38–44.

Chambaere, K., J. Bernheim, J. Downar and L. Deliens, 2014. 'Characteristics of Belgian "life-ending acts without explicit patient request": a large-scale death certificate survey revisited', *CMAJ Open* 2 December 2014, 2(4): E262–E267.

Chambaere, K., J. Bilsen, J. Cohen, B. Onwuteaka-Philipsen, F. Mortier, and L. Deliens, 2011a. 'Trends in medical end-of-life decision making in Flan-ders, Belgium 1998–2001–2007', *Medical Decision Making* 31: 500–510.

Chambaere K., J. Bilsen, J. Cohen, G. Pousset, B. Onwuteaka-Philipsen, F. Mortier, L. Deliens, 2008. 'A post mortem survey on end-of- life decisions using a representative sample of death certificates in Flanders', *BMC Public Health* 8: 299.

Chambaere, K., J. Bilsen, J. Cohen, J.A.C. Rietjens, B. Onwuteaka-Philipsen, F. Mortier and L. Deliens, 2010. 'Continuous deep sedation until death in Belgium: a nationwide survey', *Archives of Internal Medicine* 170(5): 490–93.

Chambaere, K., C. Centeno, E.A. Hernández et al., 2011b. 'Palliative care devel-opment in countries with a euthanasia law', Briefing paper for the Commis-sion on Assisted Dying of the European Association for Palliative Care.

Chambaere, K., J. Cohen, L. Robijn, S. Bailey and L. Deliens, 2015. 'End-of-life decisions in individuals dying with dementia in Belgium', *Journal of the American Geriatrics Society* 63: 290–296.

Chambaere K., R. Vander Stichele, F. Mortier, J. Cohen, L. Deliens, 2015. 'Recent trends in euthanasia and other end-of-life practices in Belgium', *New England Journal of Medicine* 372(12): 1179–1181.

Chamber Commission of Justice. [2001– 2002]. [50–1488/9]: 217.

Chen, J.H., J.L. Lamberg, Y.C. Chen, D.K. Kiely, J.H. Page, C.J. Person and S.L. Mitchell, 2006. 'Occurrence and treatment of suspected pneumonia in long-term care residents dying with advanced dementia', *Journal of the American Geriatrics Society* 54: 290–295.

Cheng, Q., H. Li, V. Silenzio and E.D. Caine, 2014. 'Suicide contagion: a systematic review of definitions and research utility', *PLoS ONE* 9: e108724.

Cherny, N. and L. Radbruch, 2009. 'European Association for Palliative Care (EAPC) recommended framework for the use of sedation in palliative care', *Palliative Medicine* 23(7): 581–593.

Cherry, M., 2013. 'Ignoring the data and endangering children: why the mature minor standard for medical decision making must be abandoned', *The Journal of Medicine and Philosophy* 38: 315–331.

Chochinov, H.M., K.G. Wilson, M. Enns, N. Mowchun, S. Lander, M. Levitt and J.J. Clinch, 1995. 'Desire for death in the terminally ill', *The American Journal of Psychiatry* 152(8): 1185–1191.

Cholbi, M., 2015. 'Kant on euthanasia and the duty to die: clearing the air', *Journal of Medical Ethics* 41: 607–610.

Claes, S., L. Vanbouwel et al., 2015. 'Euthanasia for psychiatric patients: ethical and legal concerns about the Belgian practice', Letter to the editor, *BMJ Open* 6 November 2015. http://bmjopen.bmj.com/content/5/7/e007454/reply#content-block (accessed 24 October 2016).

Claessens, P., J. Menten, P. Schotsmans and B. Broeckaert, 2008. 'Palliative sedation: a review of the research literature', *Journal of Pain and Symptom Management* 36(3): 310–333.

Claessens, P., J. Menten, P. Schotsmans, B. Broeckaert and Palsed Consortium, 2011. 'Palliative sedation, not slow euthanasia: a prospective, longitudinal study of sedation in Flemish palliative care units', *J Pain Symptom Manage* 41(1): 14–24.

Cohen, J., J. Bilsen, S. Fischer, R. Löfmark, M. Norup, A. van der Heide, G. Miccinesi and L. Deliens, 2007. 'End-of-life decision-making in Belgium, Denmark, Sweden and Switzerland: does place of death make a difference?' *Journal of Epidemiology and Community Health* 61: 1062–1068.

Cohen, L.M., M.D. Steinberg, K.C. Hails, S.K. Dobscha and S.V. Fischel, 2000. 'Psychiatric evaluation of death-hastening requests: lessons from dialysis discontinuation', *Psychosomatics* 41(3): 195–203.

Cohen, J., P. Van Landeghem, N. Carpentier and L. Deliens, 2014. 'Public acceptance of euthanasia in Europe: a survey study in 47 countries', *International Journal of Public Health* 59(1): 143–56. doi: 10.1007/s00038-013-0461-6.

Cohen, J., Y. Van Wesemael, T. Smets, J. Bilsen, L. Detiens, 2012. 'Cultural differences affecting euthanasia practice in Belgium. One law but different attitudes and practices in Flanders and Wallonia', *Social Science & Medicine* 75(5): 845–853.

Cohen-Almagor, R., 1996. 'The patients' right to die in dignity and the role of their beloved people', *Annual Review of Law and Ethics* 4: 213–232.

——— 2001. *The Right to Die with Dignity: An Argument in Ethics, Medicine, and Law.* Piscataway, NJ: Rutgers University Press.

——— 2002. 'Dutch perspectives on palliative care in the Netherlands', *Issues in Law & Medicine* 18(1): 111–126.

——— 2004. *Euthanasia in the Netherlands: The Policy and Practice of Mercy Killing.* Dordrecht: Springer-Kluwer.

——— 2009a. 'Belgian euthanasia law: a critical analysis', *Journal of Medical Ethics* 35(7): 436–439.

——— 2009b. 'Euthanasia policy and practice in Belgium: Critical observations and suggestions for improvement', *Issues in Law and Medicine* 24: 187–218.

——— 2011. 'Fatal choices and flawed decisions at the end-of-life: lessons from Israel', *Perspectives in Biology and Medicine* 54(4) (Autumn): 578–594.

——— 2013. 'First do no harm: pressing concerns regarding euthanasia in Belgium', *International Journal of Law and Psychiatry* 36: 515–521.

——— 2015. 'First do no harm: intentionally shortening lives of patients without their explicit request in Belgium', *Journal of Medical Ethics* 41(8): 625–629.

——— 2016. 'First do no harm: Euthanasia of patients with dementia in Belgium', *Journal of Medicine and Philosophy* 41(1): 74–89.

Coombs Lee, B., 2014. 'Oregon's experience with aid in dying: findings from the death with dignity laboratory', *Annals of the New York Academy of Sciences* 1330: 94–100.

Coons, C., and N. Levin, 2011. 'The dead donor rule, voluntary active euthanasia, and capital punishment', *Bioethics* 25: 236–243

Crawford, P., 2002. *Politics and History in William Golding.* Columbia, MO: University of Missouri Press.

Csillag, C., 1998. 'Brazil abolishes "presumed consent" in organ donation', *Lancet* 352: 1367.

Davis, A., 2004. 'A disabled person's perspective on euthanasia', *Disability Studies Quarterly* 24(3).

De Boer, M., C. Hertogh, R.-M. Dröes, C. Jonker and J. Eefsting, 2010a. 'Advance directives in dementia: issues of validity and effectiveness', *International Psychogeriatrics* 22: 201–208.

De Boer, M., R.-M. Dröes, C. Jonker, J. Eefsting and C. Hertogh, 2010b. 'Advance directives for euthanasia in dementia: do law-based opportunities lead to more euthanasia?' *Health Policy* 98: 256–262.

——— 2011. 'Advance directives for euthanasia in dementia: how do they affect resident care in Dutch nursing homes? Experiences of physicians and relatives', *Journal of the American Geriatrics Society* 59: 989–996.

De Ceulaer, J., 2013. 'Tweelingbroers kiezen voor euthanasie' [Twin brothers opt for euthanasia], *De Standaard* 14 January 2013.

De Diesbach, E., M. De Lose, C. Brochier and E. Montero, 2012. *Euthanasia in Belgium: 10 Years on* European Institute of Bioethics, www.ieb-eib.org/en/pdf/20121208-dossier-euthanasia-in-belgium-10-years.pdf (accessed 24 October 2016).

Degnin, F.D. 1997. 'Levinas and the Hippocratic oath: a discussion of physician-assisted suicide', *The Journal of Medicine and Philosophy* 22(2): 99–123.

De Graeff, A. and M. Dean, 2007. 'Palliative sedation therapy in the last weeks of life: a literature review and recommendations for standards', *Journal of Palliative Medicine* 10(1): 67–85.

Deliens, L., F. Mortier, J. Bilsen, M. Cosyns, R. Vander Stichele, J. Vanoverloop and K. Ingels, 2000. 'End-of-life decisions in medical practice in Flanders, Belgium: A Nationwide Survey', *Lancet* 356: 1806–1811.

Delpierre, F., 2011. 'Jeanne – "Ma mère ne répondait pas aux critères pour être euthanasiée"' [Jeanne – My mother did not meet the criteria for euthanasia], *Le Soir* 15 January 2011, 12.

Den Hartogh, G., 2009. 'The slippery slope argument', in H. Kuhse, P. Singer (eds.), *Companion to Bioethics*. Malden, MA: Wiley–Blackwell, 321–332.

2013. 'The authority of advance directives', in Y. Denier, C. Gastmans, A. Vandevelde (eds.), *Justice, Luck & Responsibility in Health Care: Philosophical Background and Ethical Implications for End-of-Life Care*. Dordrecht: Springer, 167–188.

Dening, K., L. Jones and E. Sampson, 2012. 'Preferences for end-of-life care: a nominal group study of people with dementia and their family carers', *Palliative Medicine* 27: 409–417.

De Paepe, N., 2012. 'Suis-je un tueur en série légal?' ('Am I a serial killer?'), *Le journal du Médecin* 18 December 2012, 2287.

Deschepper, R., W. Distelmans and J. Bilsen, 2014. 'Request for euthanasia/physician-assisted suicide on the basis of mental suffering: vulnerable patients or vulnerable physicians?' *JAMA Psychiatry* 71(6): 617–618.

Detry, O., S. Laureys, M-E. Faymonville, A. De Roover et al., 2008. 'Organ donation after physician-assisted death', *European Society for Organ Transplantation* 28: 915.

Dierickx, S., L. Deliens, J. Cohen and K. Chambaere, 2015. 'Comparison of the expression and granting of requests for euthanasia in Belgium in 2007 vs 2013', *JAMA Internal Medicine* 175(10): 1703–1706.

2016. 'Euthanasia in Belgium: trends in reported cases between 2003 and 2013', *Canadian Medical Association Journal* cmaj-160202.

Dijon, X., 2016. 'Euthanasie: les limites s'effacent', *La Libre* 3 March 2016.

Distelmans, W., 2011a. 'Open brief aan Di Rupo: "Pas euthanasiewet eindelijk aan"', *Artsenkrant* 2198(15 November 2011): 6.

2011b. 'An interview with Wim Distelmans', *Le Soir* 22 January 2011

2013a. 'An interview with Wim Distelmans', *De Standaard* 16 October 2013.

2013b. 'An interview with Wim Distelmans', *De Standaard* 21 December 2013.

Dopchie, C., 2014. '*L'euthanasie tue-t-elle les soins palliatifs?*' [Is euthanasia killing palliative care?], *Les Cahiers francophones de soins palliatifs*, 13(2): 28–41.

Dowbiggin, I., 2005. *A Concise History of Euthanasia: Life, Death, God, and Medicine*. Lanham, MD: Rowman & Littlefield.

Draper, B., C. Peisah, J. Snowdon and H. Brodaty, 2010. 'Early dementia diagnosis and the risk of suicide and euthanasia', *Alzheimer's & Dementia* 6: 75–82.

Dresser, R., 1995. 'Dworkin on dementia: elegant theory, questionable policy', *Hastings Center Report* 25(6): 32–38.

Driesse et al., 1988. 'Euthanasia and the law in the Netherlands', *Issues Law Med* 3: 385–397.

Dunn, L.B., M.A. Nowrangi, B.W. Palmer, D.V. Jeste and E.R. Saks, 2006. 'Assessing decisional capacity for clinical research or treatment: a review of instruments', *Am J Psychiatry* 163(8): 1323–1334.

Dutch Association of Clinical Geriatrics, 2005. *Diagnostiek en medicamenteuze behandeling van dementie [Diagnostics and medicinal treatment of dementia]*. Alphen aan de Rijn: Van Zuiden Communications.

Dutch Ministry of Justice and Dutch Ministry of Health, Welfare and Sports, 2001. *Wet Toetsing Levensbeëindiging op verzoek en hulp bij zelfdoding* [The Act on Termination of Life on Request and Assisted Suicide of 12 April, 2001].

Dworkin, G., 2002. 'Patients and prisoners: the ethics of lethal injection', *Analysis* 62: 181–189.

2003a. 'Lethal injection, autonomy and the proper ends of medicine: a response to David Silver', *Bioethics* 17: 212–214.

Dworkin, R., 2003b. *Life's Dominion: An Argument about Abortion and Euthanasia*. London: Harper Collins.

2006. 'Life past reason', in H. Kuhse and P. Singer (eds.), *Bioethics: An Anthology*. Malden: Blackwell Publishing, 357–364.

Dyer, O., 2014. 'The slow death of lethal injection', *BMJ* 348: 2670.

Economist, 2015. '24 & ready to die', *YouTube* video. www.youtube.com/watch?v=SWWkUzkfJ4M (accessed 24 October 2016).

Eiser, C., 1990. *Chronic Childhood Disease: An Introduction to Psychological Theory and Research*. Cambridge: Cambridge University Press.

Emanuel, E.J., 1999. 'What is the great benefit of legalizing euthanasia or physician-assisted suicide?', *Ethics* 109(3): 629–642.

Emanuel, E.J., E.R. Daniels, D.L. Fairclough and B.R. Clarridge, 1998. 'The practice of euthanasia and physician-assisted suicide in the United States: adherence to proposed safeguards and effects on physicians', *JAMA* 280(6): 507–513.

Emanuel, E.J., D.L. Fairclough and L.L. Emanuel, 2000. 'Attitudes and desires related to euthanasia and physician-assisted suicide among terminally ill patients and their caregivers', *JAMA* 284(19): 2460–2468.

Emanuel, E. J., B.D. Onwuteaka-Philipsen, J.W. Urwin, J. Cohen, 2016. 'Attitudes and practices of euthanasia and physician-assisted suicide in the United States, Canada, and Europe', *JAMA* 316(1): 79–90.

Enoch, D., 2001. 'Once you start using slippery slope arguments, you're on a very slippery slope', *Oxford Journal of Legal Studies* 21(4): 629–647. doi: 10.1093/ojls/21.4.629.

Equal Rights Trust, 2013. 'Case summary: International Federation for Human Rights (FIDH) v. Belgium, Complaint No: 75/2011', www.equalrightstrust.org/ertdocumentbank/Case%20summary-%20FIDH%20vs%20Belgium%20final.pdf (accessed 24 October 2016).

Erikson, E.H., 1968. *Identity: Youth and Crisis*. New York: Norton.

Ernst, M., S. Torrisi, N. Balderston, C. Grillon and E.A. Hale, 2015. 'fMRI functional connectivity applied to adolescent neurodevelopment', *Annual Review of Clinical Psychology* 11: 361–377.

Eurotransplant, 2008. 'Ethics committee recommendations on organ donation after euthanasia', REC01.08 www.eurotransplant.org/cms/mediaobject.php?file=newsletter2121.pdf (accessed 24 October 2016).

'Euthanasie voor ondraaglijk psychisch lijden?' *Terzake* Broadcast 2 February 2016 www.canvas.be/video/terzake/voorjaar-2016/dinsdag-2-februari-2016/euthanasie-voor-ondraaglijk-psychisch-lijden (accessed 24 October 2016).

Evans, N., H. Pasman, D. Deeg and B. Onwuteaka-Philopsen, 2015. 'Older Dutch people's self-reported advance euthanasia directive completion before and after the enactment of the euthanasia law: a time trend study (1998–2011)', *Journal of the American Geriatrics Society* 63: 2217–2219.

Eynikel, H., 1999. *Molokai: The Story of Father Damien*. Staten Island: Alba House.

FCECE, 2004. Commission fédérale de contrôle et d'évaluation de l'euthanasie, Premier rapport aux Chambres législatives (22 septembre 2002 - 31 décembre 2003), [Federal Control and Evaluation Commission on Euthanasia, First report to the legislative chambers].

2006. Commission fédérale de contrôle et d'évaluation de l'euthanasie, Deuxième rapport aux Chambres législatives (années 2004 et 2005), [Second report to the legislative chambers].

2008. Commission fédérale de contrôle et d'évaluation de l'euthanasie, Troisième rapport aux Chambres législatives (années 2006 et 2007), [Third report to the legislative chambers].

2010. Commission fédérale de contrôle et d'évaluation de l'euthanasie, Quatrième rapport aux Chambres législatives (années 2008 et 2009), [Fourth report to the legislative chambers].

2012. Commission fédérale de contrôle et d'évaluation de l'euthanasie, Cinquième rapport aux Chambres législatives (années 2010 et 2011), [Fifth report to the legislative chambers].

2014. Commission fédérale de contrôle et d'évaluation de l'euthanasie, Sixième rapport aux Chambres législatives (2012–2013), [Sixth report to the legislative chambers].

2016. Commission fédérale de contrôle et d'évaluation de l'euthanasie, Septième rapport aux Chambres législatives (2014–2015), [Seventh report to the legislative chambers].

Fenigsen, R., 1991. 'The report of the Dutch governmental committee on euthanasia', *Issues in Law and Medicine* 7: 339–344.

FEPZ, 2008. Federale Evaluatiecel Palliatieve Zorg. *Evaluatierapport palliatieve zorg.* [Belgian Federal Palliative Care Evaluation Committee] Brussel, http://media.wix.com/ugd/b61916_79aa250a422d421781464d542609d277.pdf (accessed 24 October 2016).

2014. Federale Evaluatiecel Palliatieve Zorg. Evaluatierapport palliatieve zorg. [Belgian Federal Palliative Care Evaluation Committee] Brussel, www.palliatief.be/accounts/143/attachments/rapporten/rapport_evaluatiecel_palliatieve_zorg_maart_2014_nl.pdf (accessed 24 October 2016).

Ferri, C.P., M. Prince, C. Brayne, H. Brodaty, L. Fratiglioni, M. Ganguli, K. Hall, K. Hasegawa, H. Hendrie, Y. Huang, A. Jorm, C. Mathers, P.R. Menezes, E. Rimmer and M. Scazufca, 2005. 'Global prevalence of dementia: a Delphi consensus study', *Lancet* 366: 2112–2117.

Feyerabend, P., 1975. *Against Method.* London: New Left Books.

Finley, I.G., V.J. Wheatley and C. Izdebski. 2005. 'The House of Lords Select Committee on the Assisted Dying for the Terminally Ill Bill: implications for specialist palliative care', *Palliative Medicine* 19: 444–453.

Fitzpatrick, K., 2013. 'Qualified to speak: Rush Rhees on the (vexed) subject of euthanasia', *Philosophy* 88(04): 575–592.

Foley, K. and A. Hendin, 2002. 'A medical, ethical, legal and psychological perspective', in K. Foley and A. Hendin (eds.), *The Case against Assisted Suicide: For the Right to End-of-Life Care.* Baltimore: The Johns Hopkins University Press.

Førde, R., L.J. Materstvedt, T. Markestad, U.E. Kongsgaard, S. von Hofacker, S. Brelin, S. Ore and M. Laudal, 2015. 'Palliative sedation at the end of life – revised guidelines', *Tidsskrift for Den norske legeforening* 135(3): 220–221.

Fowler, J.W. and M.L. Dell, 2006. 'Stages of faith from infancy through adolescence: reflections on three decades of faith development theory', in: E.C. Roehlkepartain, P.E. King, L. Wagener and P.L. Benson (eds.), *Handbook of Spiritual Development in Childhood and Adolescence.* Thousand Oaks: Sage, 34–45.

FPCF, 2003. Federation of Palliative Care Flanders. *Omgaan met euthanasie en andere vormen van medisch begeleid sterven* [Dealing with euthanasia and other forms of medically assisted dying], www.palliatief.be/accounts/143/attachments/Pub licaties/euthanasie_-_standpunt_federatie.doc (accessed 24 October 2016).

2006. Federation of Palliative Care Flanders. 'Treatment decisions in advanced disease – A conceptual framework', www.palliatief.be/accounts/143/attach ments/Research/conceptual__framework_bb.pdf (accessed 24 October 2016).

2008. Federation of Palliative Care Flanders. 'End-of-life care: no twin-track policy', www.palliatief.be/accounts/143/attachments/Publicaties/endoflife care_notwintrackpolicy.pdf (accessed 24 October 2016).

2011. Federation of Palliative Care Flanders. *Over palliatieve zorg en euthanasie* [On palliative care and euthanasia], www.palliatief.be/accounts/143/attach ments/Standpunten/visietekst_palliatievezorgeuthanasie_def_26092011.pdf (accessed 24 October 2016).

2012. Federation of Palliative Care Flanders. *Overlijdens met palliatieve zorg in Vlaanderen 2008–2012* [Reported deaths with specialised palliative care in Flanders 2008–2012]. Data collected under supervision of the Flemish government.

Friedman, D., G.N. Holmbeck, C. DeLucia, B. Jandasek and K. Zebracki, 2009. 'Trajectories of autonomy development across the adolescent transition in children with spina bifida', *Rehabilitation Psychology* 54: 16–27.

FSO, 2012. *Cause of Death Statistics 2009: Assisted Suicide and Suicide in Switzerland*. Neuchâtel: Federal Statistical Office.

Gaita, R., 2004. *Good and Evil: An Absolute Conception. 2nd edition*. London: Routledge.

Gallagher, J. and P. Roxby, 2015. 'Assisted dying bill: MPs reject "right to die" law', *BBC* 11 September, www.bbc.co.uk/news/health-34208624 (accessed 24 October 2016).

Gamondi, C., G.D. Borasio, C. Limoni, N. Preston, S. Payne, 2014. 'Legalisation of assisted suicide: a safeguard to euthanasia?' *Lancet* 384: 127.

Gamondi, C., M. Pott and S. Payne, 2013. 'Families' experiences with patients who died after assisted suicide: a retrospective interview study in Southern Switzerland', *Annals of Oncology* 24(6): 1639–1644.

Ganzini, L., S.K. Dobscha, R.T. Heintz and N. Press, 2003. 'Oregon physicians' perceptions of patients who request assisted suicide and their families', *Journal of Palliative Medicine* 6(3): 381–390.

Ganzini, L., E.R. Goy and S.K. Dobscha, 2008a. 'Prevalence of depression and anxiety in patients requesting physicians' aid in dying: cross sectional survey', *BMJ* 337: a1682.

2008b. 'Why Oregon patients request assisted death: family members' views', *Journal of General Internal Medicine* 23(2): 154–157. Erratum in: *Journal of General Internal Medicine* 23(8): 1296.

2009. 'Oregonians' reasons for requesting physician aid in dying', *Archives of Internal Medicine* 169(5): 489–492

Gastmans, C. 2013. 'Dignity-enhancing care for persons with dementia and its application to advance euthanasia directives', in Y. Denier, C. Gastmans and A. Vandevelde (eds.), *Justice, Luck & Responsibility in Health Care: Philosophical Background and Ethical Implications for End-of-Life Care.* Dordrecht: Springer, 145–165.

Gastmans, C. and J. De Lepeleire, 2010. 'Living to the bitter end? A personalist approach to euthanasia in persons with severe dementia', *Bioethics* 24: 78–86.

Gastmans, C. and Y. Denier, 2010. 'What if patients with dementia use decision aids to make an advance euthanasia request?', *The American Journal of Bioethics* 10(4): 25–26.

Gastmans, C., F. Van Neste, P. Schotsmans, 2004. 'Facing requests for euthanasia: a clinical practice guideline', *Journal of Medical Ethics* 30: 212–217.

George, K., 2007. 'A woman's choice? The gendered risk of voluntary euthanasia and physician assisted suicide', *Medical Law Review* 15(1): 1–33.

Gill, C., 2000. 'Health professionals, disability, and assisted suicide: An examination of relevant empirical evidence and reply to Batavia', *Psychology, Public Policy, and Law* 6: 526–545.

Gill, C.J., 2010. 'No, we don't think our doctors are out to get us: responding to the straw man distortions of disability rights arguments against assisted suicide', *Disability and Health Journal* 3(1): 31–38.

Gillett, G, and J. Chamberlain, 2013. 'The clinician's dilemma: two dimensions of ethical care', *International Journal of Law and Psychiatry* 36(5–6): 454–60.

Goering, S., 2007. 'What makes suffering "unbearable and hopeless"? Advance directives, dementia and disability', *The American Journal of Bioethics* 7(4): 62–63.

Gorsuch, N.M., 2006. *The Future of Assisted Suicide and Euthanasia.* Princeton, NJ: Princeton University Press.

Gortmaker, S.L., J.M. Perrin and M. Weitzman, 1993. 'An unexpected success story: transition to adulthood in youth with chronic physical health conditions', *Journal of Research on Adolescence* 3: 317–336.

Griffiths, J., H. Weyers and M. Adams, 2008. *Euthanasia and Law in Europe.* Oxford: Hart.

Groenewoud, J.H., A. Van Der Heide, A.J. Tholen, W.J. Schudel, M.W. Hengeveld, B.D. Onwuteaka-Philipsen, P.J. Van Der Maa and G. Van Der Wal, 2004. 'Psychiatric consultation with regard to requests for euthanasia or physician-assisted suicide', *General Hospital Psychiatry* 26(4): 323–330

Grubb A., 1998. 'Glanville Williams: a personal appreciation', *Medical Law Review* 6(13): 133.

Gruber, P., 2008. *'Jeanne avait décidé de mourir'* [Jeanne had decided to die], Le Vif/L'Express (*Belgique*) 21 January 2008, 36–40.

Gunning, K.F., 1991. 'Euthanasia', *Lancet* 338: 1010.

Hall, M., F. Trachtenberg and E. Dugan, 2005. 'The impact on patient trust of legalising physician aid in dying', *Journal of Medical Ethics* 31(12): 693–697.

Hamilton, G., 2013. '"Suicide with the approval of society": Belgian activist warns of slippery slope as euthanasia becomes "normal"', *National Post (Canada)* 24 November 2013.

Hardwig, J., 1997. 'Is there a duty to die?' *Hastings Center Report* 27(2): 34–42.

Harraz, A.M., A.A. Shokeir, S.A. Soliman, Y. Osman et al., 2014. 'Salvage of grafts with vascular thrombosis during live donor renal allotransplantation: a critical analysis of successful outcome', *International Journal of Urology* 21: 999–1004.

Harris, J., 1995. 'Euthanasia and the value of life', in J. Keown (ed.), *Euthanasia Examined*. Cambridge: Cambridge University Press.

Harvath, T., L. Miller, K.A. Smith, L.D. Clark, A. Jackson and L. Ganzini, 2006. 'Dilemmas encountered by hospice workers when patients wish to hasten death', *Journal of Hospice and Palliative Nursing* 8: 200–209.

Haverkate, I., A. van der Heide, B.D. Onwuteaka-Philipsen, P.J. van der Maas and G. van der Wal, 2001. 'The emotional impact on physicians of hastening the death of a patient', *Medical Journal of Australia* 175(10): 519–522.

Health and Sport Committee of the Scottish Parliament, 2015. *Stage 1 Report on Assisted Suicide (Scotland) Bill*. SP Paper 712, 6th Report, Session 4.

Hein, I.M., P.W. Troost, R. Lindeboom, M.C. de Vries, C.M. Zwaan and R.J. Lindauer, 2012. 'Assessing children's competence to consent in research by a standardized tool: a validity study', *BMC Pediatrics* 12: 156.

Hendin, H., 1995. 'Assisted suicide, euthanasia, and suicide prevention: the implications of the Dutch experience', *Suicide and Life-Threatening Behavior* 25(1): 193–204.

1998. *Seduced by Death: Doctors, Patients, and Assisted Suicide*. New York: WW Norton, 69.

Heneghan, T., 2016. 'Catholic nursing home fined thousands in euthanasia case', *The Tablet* 5 July 2016.

Herremans, J. and P. Galand, 2009. '*Carte blanche, Euthanasie: entre l'application de la loi et son extension*' [Euthanasia: from the application of the law to its extension], *Le Soir* 2 April 2009.

Hertogh, C., 2009. 'The role of advance euthanasia directives as an aid to communication and shared decision-making in dementia', *Journal of Medical Ethics* 35: 100–103.

Hertogh, C., M. De Boer, R.-M. Droës and J. Eefsting, 2007. 'Would we rather lose our life than lose our self? Lessons from the Dutch debate on euthanasia of patients with dementia', *The American Journal of Bioethics* 7(4): 48–56.

Hewitt, J., 2010. 'Schizophrenia, mental capacity, and rational suicide', *Theoretical Medicine and Bioethics* 31(1): 63–77.

2013. 'Why are people with mental illness excluded from the rational suicide debate?', *International Journal of Law and Psychiatry* 36(5–6): 358–365.

Ho, A.O., 2014. 'Suicide: rationality and responsibility for life', *The Canadian Journal of Psychiatry* 59(3): 141–147.

Holm, S., 2013. 'Terminal sedation and euthanasia: the virtue in calling a spade what it is', in K. Raus, S. Sterckx and F. Mortier (eds.), *Continuous Sedation at the End of Life*. Cambridge: Cambridge University Press, 228–239.

Hovine, A. 2009. *'Le douloureux destin d'Amelie Van Esbeen'* [The painful destiny of Amelie Van Esbeen], *La Libre Belgique* 2 April 2009.

2014. *'Il faut reporter le vote sur l'euthanasie des enfants'* [It is necessary to delay the vote on euthanasia of children], *La Libre Belgique* 12 February 2014.

Hughes, J., 2001. 'Views of the person with dementia', *Journal of Medical Ethics* 27: 86–91.

Johnstone, M., 2013. 'Metaphors, stigma and the "Alzheimerization" of the euthanasia debate', *Dementia* 12: 377–393.

Hume, D., 1783. *Of Suicide*. New York: Penguin, 2005.

Humphry, D., 1991. *Final Exit: The Practicalities of Self-Deliverance and Assisted Suicide for the Dying*. New York: Dell Publishing.

Huver, R.M.E., C.M.E. Engel, G. van Breukelen and H. de Vries, 2007. 'Parenting style and adolescent smoking cognitions and behavior', *Psychology and Health* 22: 575–593.

Ide, L., 2013. Oral question from Senator L. Ide to the Minister of Justice on *'les demandes d'euthanasie de la part d'internés'* [Requests for euthanasia from prisoners] (n° 5-791), Annales, Senate, 17 January 2013.

Inghelbrecht, E., J. Bilsen, F. Mortier and L. Deliens, 2011. 'Continuous deep sedation until death in Belgium: a survey among nurses', *Journal of Pain and Symptom Management* 41(5): 870–879.

Iltis, A. 2013. 'Parents, adolescence, and consent for research participation', *The Journal of Medicine and Philosophy* 38: 332–346.

Isometsä E.T., 2001. 'Psychological autopsy studies–a review', *European Psychiatry* 16(7): 379–385.

Jackson, E., 2001. *Regulating Reproduction: Law, Technology & Autonomy*. Oxford: Hart Publishing.

Jaeken, J.P., 2009. *'Mise au point concernant des patients âgés'* [The state of the art concerning elderly patients], *Bulletin de l'ADMD*, n° 112, June 2009.

Jansen-van der Weide M.C., B.D. Onwuteaka-Philipsen, G. van der Wal, 2005. 'Granted, undecided, withdrawn, and refused requests for euthanasia and physician-assisted suicide', *Archives of Internal Medicine* 165 (15): 1698–704.

Janssens, R., J.J.M. van Delden and G.A.M. Widdershoven, 2012. 'Palliative sedation: not just normal medical practice. Ethical reflections on the Royal Dutch Medical Association's Guideline on Palliative Sedation', *Journal of Medical Ethics* 38(11): 664–668.

Jones, D.A., 2003. 'The Hippocratic oath I: its content and the limits to its adaptation', *Catholic Medical Quarterly* 54(3): 9–17.

2006. 'The Hippocratic oath II: modern adaptations of the classical doctors' oath', *CMQ* 56(1): 6–16.

2007. 'The Hippocratic oath III: Hippocratic principles applied to the withdrawal of treatment and the mental capacity act', *CMQ* 57(2): 15–23.

2011. 'Is there a logical slippery slope from voluntary to nonvoluntary euthanasia?', *Kennedy Institute of Ethics Journal*. 21(4): 379–404.

2013a. 'Death by equivocation: a manifold definition of terminal sedation', in K. Raus, S. Sterckx and F. Mortier (eds.), *Continuous Sedation at the End of Life*. Cambridge: Cambridge University Press, 47–64.

2013b. 'Is dignity language useful in bioethical discussion of assisted suicide and abortion?', in C. McCrudden (ed.), *Understanding Human Dignity*. Oxford: Oxford University Press.

Jones, W.H.S., 1924. *The Doctor's Oath*. Cambridge: CUP.

Jones, D.A. and D. Paton, 2015. 'How does legalization of physician-assisted suicide affect rates of suicide?', *The Southern Medical Journal* 108: 599–604.

Kamisar, Y., 1958. 'Some non-religious views against proposed "mercy killing" legislation', *Minnesota Law Review* 42(6): 969–1042.

Kant, I., 1785. *Grounding for the Metaphysics of Morals*. AK 422. Trans. EW Ellington. Indianapolis, IN: Hackett, 1981: 30–31.

Karlamangla, S., 2015. 'End-of- life law may stir ethical debates; Cost controls could emphasize lethal pills over more-expensive life-extending drugs, medical experts say', *LA Times* 18 October 2015.

Kass, L. 1985. *Towards a More Natural Science*. New York: Free Press.

2002. 'I will give no deadly drug: Why doctors must not kill', In K. Foley and H. Hendin (eds.), *The Case against Assisted Suicide*. Baltimore: The Johns Hopkins University Press.

KCE, 2009. Belgian Health Care Knowledge Centre. *Organisation of palliative care in Belgium, 2009*, https://kce.fgov.be/sites/default/files/page_documents/d20091027342.pdf (accessed 24 October 2016).

Kelly, B.J., F.T. Varghese and D. Pelusi, 2003. 'Countertransference and ethics: a perspective on clinical dilemmas in end-of-life decisions', *Palliative & Supportive Care* 1(4): 367–375.

Keown, J., 1992. 'On regulating death', *Hastings Center Report* 22(2): 39–43.

1995. 'Euthanasia in the Netherlands: Sliding down the slippery slope?' in J. Keown (ed.), *Euthanasia Examined: Ethical, Clinical and Legal Perspectives*. Cambridge: Cambridge University Press.

2002. *Euthanasia, Ethics and Public Policy*. Cambridge: Cambridge University Press.

2014. *Physician-Assisted Suicide: Some Reasons for Rejecting Lord Falconer's Bill*. Care Not Killing Alliance.

Keown, J. and D.A. Jones, 2008. 'Surveying the foundations of medical law: a reassessment of Glanville Williams's "The Sanctity of Life and the Criminal Law"', *Medical Law Review* 16(1):85–126.

Keuleneer, F. 2009. *'Puntjes op de 'i' in het euthanasiedebat. Euthanasie veeleer inperken dan uitbreide'* [Dotting the 'i's in the debate on euthanasia: limit rather than extend euthanasia], *Tertio* No. 477, 10.

Kheriaty, A., 2015. 'Social contagion effects of physician-assisted suicide', *Southern Medical Journal* 108(10): 605–606. doi: 10.14423/SMJ.0000000000000346.

Khorrami, K. 2003. 'Die "Euthanasie-Gesetze" im Vergleich. Eine Darstellung der Aktuellen Rechtslage in den Niederlanden und in Belgiën', *Medizinrecht*: 19–25.

Kim, T., S.T. Martin, K.R. Townsend and S. Gabardi, 2014. 'Antibody-mediated rejection in kidney transplantation: a review of pathophysiology, diagnosis, and treatment options', *Pharmacotherapy* 34: 733–744.

Kim S.Y. and T. Lemmens, 2016. 'Should assisted dying for psychiatric disorders belegalized in Canada?', *CMAJ* Jun 21.pii: cmaj.160365. [Epub ahead of print].

Kim, S.Y., De Vries R.G., Peteet J.R., 2016. 'Euthanasia and assisted suicide of patients with psychiatric disorders in the Netherlands 2011 to 2014', *JAMA Psychiatry* 73(4): 362–368.

Kind en Gezin, 2014. 'Het kind in Vlaanderen', www.kindengezin.be/img/kind-in-vlaanderen-2014.pdf (accessed 24 October 2016).

Kitchener, B. and A. Jorm, 1999. 'Conditions required for a law on active voluntary euthanasia: a survey of nurses' opinions in the Australian Capital Territory', *Journal of Medical Ethics* 25: 25–30.

Klein, D., A. Rotarska-Jagiela, E. Genc et al., 2014. 'Adolescent brain maturation and cortical folding: evidence for reductions in gyrification', *PLoS ONE* 9(1): e84914.

KNMG, 2009. *Koninklijke Nederlandse Maatschappij ter bevordering van de Geneeskunde* [Royal Dutch Medical Association] *KNMG-Guideline for palliative sedation (2009)*.

KNMG/KNMP, 2012. *Koninklijke Nederlandsche Maatschappij tot bevordering der Geneeskunst/ Koninklijke Nederlandse Maatschappij ter bevordering der Pharmacie* [Royal Dutch Medical Association/ Royal Dutch Pharmacists Association] *Guidelines for the Practice of Euthanasia and Physician-Assisted Suicide August 2012*.

Koenig, H.G., D. Wildman-Hanlon and K. Schmader, 1996. 'Attitudes of elderly patients and their families toward physician-assisted suicide', *Archives of Internal Medicine* 156(19): 2240–2248.

Kohlberg, L., 1991. *Kohlberg's Original Study of Moral Development. A Compendium*. New York: Garland.

Koostra, G., J.H. Daeman and A.P. Oomen, 1995. 'Categories of non-heart-beating donors', *Transplantation Proceedings* 27: 2893–2894.

Kouwenhoven, P., N. Raijmakers, J. van Delden, J. Rietjens, M. Schermer, G. van Thiel, M.J. Trappenburg, S. van de Vathorst, B.J. van der Vegt, C. Vezzoni, H. Weyers, D.G. van Tol and A. van der Heide, 2013. 'Opinions of health care professionals and the public after eight years of euthanasia legislation in the Netherlands: a mixed method approach', *Palliative Medicine* 27: 273–805.

Kouwenhoven, P., N. Raijmakers, J. van Delden, J. Rietjens, D. van Tol, S. van de Vathorst, N. de Graef, H. Weyers, A. van der Heide and G. van Thiel, 2015. 'Opinions about euthanasia and advanced dementia: a qualitative study among Dutch physicians and members of the general public', *BMC Medical Ethics* 16: 7.

Krag, E. 2014. 'Rich, white, and vulnerable: rethinking oppressive socialization in the euthanasia debate', *The Journal of Medicine and Philosophy* 39(4): 406–429.

Kuin, A., Courtens A.M., Deliens L., et al., 2004. 'Palliative Care Consultation in the Netherlands: a nationwide evaluation study', *Journal of Pain and Symptom Management* 27(1): 53–60.

Lagerwey, W. trans. 1988. 'Guidelines for euthanasia (KNMG)', *Issues in Law & Medicine* 3: 429–437.

Lamensch, M. 2009. 'Amelie Van Esbeen', *Le Soir* 24 March 2009, 19.

Lamensch, M. and F. Soumois, 2009. 'La vieille dame de 93 ans a obtenu l'euthanasie' [The old lady of 93 obtained euthanasia], *Le Soir* 2 April 2009, 8.

Lebel, C. and C. Beaulieu, 2011. 'Longitudinal development of human brain wiring continues from childhood into adulthood', *Journal of Neuroscience* 31(30): 10937–10947.

'Les leçons d'un cas très médiatisé' [Lessons from a highly publicized case], 2009. Editorial, *Le Soir* 2 April 2009, 22.

Leemans, Kathleen, 2014. *Quality Indicators to Improve Palliative Care in Flanders.* Belgium: Development, Evaluation and Implementation Strategy. Doctoral Dissertation. Vrije Universiteit Brussels.

Leget, C., 2013. 'Assisted dying – the current debate in the Netherlands', *European Journal of Palliative Care* 20: 168–171.

Lemiengre, J., B. Dierckx de Casterlé, Y. Denier, P. Schotsmans, C. Gastmans, 2008. 'How do hospitals deal with euthanasia requests in Flanders (Belgium)? A content analysis of policy documents', *Patient Education and Counseling* 71: 293–301.

2009. 'Content analysis of euthanasia policies of nursing homes in Flanders (Belgium)', *Medicine, Health Care and Philosophy* 12(3): 313–322. doi: 10.1007/s11019-008-9176-5. Epub 2009 Jan 11

Lerner, B. and A. Caplan, 2015. 'Euthanasia in Belgium and the Netherlands on the slippery slope?' *JAMA Internal Medicine* 175(10): 1640–1641.

'L'euthanasie des patients âgés' [Euthanasia of elderly patients] 2016 www.admd.be/medecins.html (accessed 24 October 2016).

Levi, P., 1969. *If This Is a Man*, trans. S. Woolf. London: Abacus.

Levinas, E., 1985. *Ethics and infinity*. Trans. RA Cohen. Pittsburgh, PA: Duquesne University Press, 85–88.

Levy, B. and M. Green, 2010. 'Too soon to give up: re-examining the value of advance directives', *The American Journal of Bioethics* 10(4): 2–22.

Lewis, P., 2007. 'The empirical slippery slope from voluntary to non-voluntary euthanasia', *The Journal of Law, Medicine & Ethics* 35(1): 197–210.

Lievens, J., 2013. '*Ter bescherming van de bewoners*' ['Protecting the inhabitants']. EuthanasiaStop 04/07/2013 www.euthanasiestop.be/artikel/ter-bescherm ing-van-de-bewoners-135 (accessed 24 October 2016).

'*L'euthanasie de deux frères sourds et aveugles bouleverse*' [Euthanasia of both deaf and blind brothers upsets], L'Avenir.net 18 January 2013.

Liston, C., R. Watts, N. Tottenham et al., 2006. 'Frontostriatal microstructure modu-lates efficient recruitment of cognitive control', *Cereb Cortex* 16(4): 553–560.

Lloyd, L., 2004. 'Mortality and morality: ageing and the ethics of care', *Ageing and Society* 24: 235–256.

Lossignol, D. 2012. '*Soins palliatifs et euthanasie: la fin du conflit*' [Palliative care and euthanasia: an end to the conflict], *La revue des soins palliatifs en Wallonie* 14: 24.

Lowental, U. 1984. 'Euthanasia: a serene voyage to death', in Amnon Carmi (ed.), *Euthanasia*. Berlin: Springer-Verlag, 180–184.

Luyckx, K., I. Seiffge-Krenke, S.J. Schwartz et al., 2008. 'Identity development, coping, and adjestment in emerging adults with a chronic illness: the sample case of type 1 diabetes', *Journal of Adolescent Health* 43: 451–458.

Maas, S. 2015a. 'Euthanasie is nog steeds niet bespreekbaar genoeg', *De Morgen* 20 June 2015 (interview with Dr Distelmans).

2015b. 'Laura is 24 jaar en fysiek gezond. Ze krijgt deze zomer euthanasie', *DeMorgen* 19 June 2015.

Machnicki G., L. Seriai and M. Schnitzler, 2006. 'Economics of transplantation: a review of the literature', *Transplantation Reviews* 20: 61–75.

Mahoux, P. 2014a. 'La loi doit être appliquée partout' [The law must be applied everywhere], *Le Soir* 25 February 2014.

2014b. 'La loi sur l'euthanasie: un débat à poursuivre' [The law on euthanasie: a debate to watch], *Le Soir* 11 December 2014.

MacIntyre, A. 1988. *Whose Justice Which Rationality*. London: Duckworth.

Marzuk, P.M., K. Tardiff, C.S. Hirsch, A.C. Leon, M. Stajic, N. Hartwell and L. Portera, 1993. 'Increase in suicide by asphyxiation in New York City after the publication of Final Exit', *The New England Journal of Medicine* 329: 1508–1510.

Marzuk, P.M., K. Tardiff and A.C. Leon, 1994. 'Increase in fatal suicidal poisonings and suffocations in the year Final Exit was published: a national study', *The American Journal of Psychiatry* 151: 1813–1814.

Masson, J., 2005. '*L'exception euthanasique en droit belge*' [The euthanasia exception under Belgian law], *Louvain Médical*: 238–245.

Matton, P.A., 2014. '*Une fin de vie, un verre de champagne à la main*', *La Libre Belgique* 7 January 2014.

McCormack, R. and R. Fléchais, 2012. 'The role of psychiatrists and mental disorder in assisted dying practices around the world: a review of the legislation and official reports', *Psychosomatics* 53(4): 319–326.

McCormack, R., M. Clifford and M. Conroy, 2011. 'Attitudes of UK doctors towards euthanasia and physician-assisted suicide: a systematic literature review', *Palliative Medicine* 26(1): 23–31.

McKethan, A. and A.K. Jha, 2014. 'Designing smarter pay-for-performance programs', *JAMA* 312(24): 2617–2618.

Mcpherson, C., K. Wilson and M. Murray, 2007. 'Feeling like a burden to others: a systematic review focusing on the end of life', *Palliative Medicine* 21: 115–128.

Merrill, J.P., J.E. Murray, J.H. Harrison and W.R. Guild, 1958. 'Successful homotransplantations of human kidneys between identical twins', *The American Journal of Surgery* 148: 343.

Miles, S.H., 1994. 'Physicians and their patients' suicides', *JAMA* 271(22): 1786–1788. 1995. 'Physician-assisted suicide and the profession's gyrocompass', *Hastings Center Report* 25(3): 17–19.

Mitchell, S. 2007. 'A 93-year-old man with advanced dementia and eating problems', *Journal of the American Medical Association* 298: 2527–2536.

Mitchell, S., D.K. Kiely, S.C. Miller, S.R. Connor, C. Spence and J.M. Teno, 2007. 'Hospice care for patients with dementia', *Journal of Pain and Symptom Management* 34: 7–16.

Mitchell, S., J. Teno, D. Kiely, M.L. Shaffer, R.N. Jones, H.G. Prigerson, L. Volicer, J.L. Givens and M.B. Hamel, 2009. 'The clinical course of advanced dementia', *New England Journal of Medicine* 361: 1529–1538.

Montero, E., 2013. *Rendez-vous avec la mort. Dix ans d'euthanasie légale en Belgique* [*An appointment with death. Ten years of legal euthanasia in Belgium*]. Limal: Anthemis.

Moody, H., 1992. *Ethics in an Aging Society*. Baltimore: The Johns Hopkins University Press.

Nuffield Council on Bioethics, 2009. *Dementia: Ethical Issues*. London: Nuffield Council on Bioethics.

Moonen, C., J. Lemiengre and C. Gastmans, 2016. 'Dealing with existential suffering of patients with severe persistent mental illness: experiences of psychiatric nurses in Flanders (Belgium)', *Archives of Psychiatric Nursing* doi:10.1016/j.apnu.2015.10.005.

Morita, T., S. Tsuneto and Y. Shima, 2002. 'Definition of sedation for symptom relief: a systematic literature review and a proposal of operational criteria', *Journal of Pain and Symptom Management* 24(4): 447–453.

Morita, T., J. Tsunoda, S. Inoue and S. Chihara, 2001. 'Effects of high dose opioids and sedatives on survival in terminally ill cancer patients', *Journal of Pain and Symptom Management* 21(4): 282–289.

Morrison, R.S., and D.E. Meier, 2004. 'Palliative care', *New England Journal of Medicine* 350(25): 2582–2590.

Mortier, T., 2013. 'Life issues: Belgium euthanasia experience teaches bitter lessons', *News Weekly* 21 December 2013.

Moskowitz, E.H., 1997. 'Mental illness, physical illness, and the legalization of physician-assisted suicide', *Fordham Urban Law Journal* 24(4): 781–794.

Murray, S.A., K. Boyd and I. Byock, 2008. 'Continuous deep sedation in patients nearing death: Imprecise taxonomy makes interpreting trends difficult', *BMJ* 336: 781–782.

Mutlu, A.K., M. Schneider, M. Debbane, D. Badoud, S. Eliez and M. Schaer, 2013. 'Sex differences in thickness, and folding developments throughout the cortex', *Neuroimage* 82: 200–207.

Nash, S.S., L.K. Kent and P.R. Muskin, 2009. 'Psychodynamics in medically ill patients', *Harvard Review of Psychiatry* 17(6): 389–397.

National Council of the Order of Physicians, 2003. Opinion of 22 March 2003 on palliative care, euthanasia and other medical decisions concerning the end of life, *Bulletin* XI, June 2003.

Nederlandse Vereniging voor Psychiatrie, 2009. *Richtlijn omgaan met het verzoek om hulp bij zelfdoding door patiënten met psychiatrische stoornis.* Utrecht: de Tijdstroom.

Newell, C., 2006. 'Disability, bioethics, and rejected knowledge', *Journal of Medicine and Philosophy* 31(3): 269–283.

Norwood, F., 2009. *The Maintenance of Life. Preventing Social Death through Euthanasia Talk and End-of-Life Care – Lessons from The Netherlands.* Durham, NC: Carolina Academic Press.

NOS, 2014. http://nos.nl/artikel/609971-euthanasie-kind-beslist-mee.html (accessed 24 October 2016).

Nowak, R., 1992. 'The Dutch way of death', *New Scientist* 135(20 June): 28–30.

Nuttin, B, H. Wu, H. Mayberg, M. Hariz, L. Gabriëls et al., 2014. 'Consensus on guidelines for stereotactic neurosurgery for psychiatric disorders', *Journal of Neurology, Neurosurgery, and Psychiatry* 85(9): 1003–1008.

Nys, H., 2013a. 'Medicalisering van levenseinde neemt toe', in Y. Nuyens and H. De Ridder (eds.), *Dokter, ik heb ook iets te zeggen.* Tielt: Uitgeverij Lannoo NV, 174–186.

Nys, T. 2013b. 'The wreckage of our flesh: dementia, autonomy and personhood', in Y. Denier, C. Gastmans and A. Vandevelde (eds.), *Justice, Luck & Responsibility in Health Care: Philosophical Background and Ethical Implications for End-of-Life Care.* Dordrecht: Springer, 189–203.

Nys, H. and M. Adams, 2005. 'Euthanasia in the low countries. Comparative reflections on the Belgian and Dutch euthanasia act', in P. Schotsmans and T. Meulenberghs (eds.), *Euthanasia and Palliative Care in the Low Countries*. Leuven: Peeters Ethical Perspectives Monograph Series, 5–33.

OECD, 2012. 'Suicide', in *Health at a Glance: Europe 2012*. OECD Publishing. http://dx.doi.org/10.1787/9789264183896-10-en (accessed 24 October 2016).

Oldham, R.L., S.K. Dobscha, E.R. Goy and L. Ganzini, 2011. 'Attachment styles of Oregonians who request physician-assisted death', *Palliative & Supportive Care* 9(2): 123–128.

Olesen, P.J., Z. Nagy, H. Westerberg and T. Klingberg, 2003. 'Combined analysis of DTI and fMRI data reveals a joint maturation of white and grey matter in a fronto-parietal network', *Brain Research. Cognitive Brain Research* 18(1): 48–57.

Oliver, M., A. Woywodt, A. Ahmed and I. Saif, 2011. 'Organ donation, transplantation and religion', *Nephrology Dialysis Transplantation* 26: 437–444. doi: 10.1093/ndt/gfq628.

Onwuteaka-Philipsen, B., A. Brinkman-Stoppelenburg, C. Penning, G.J.F. de Jong-Krul, J.J.M. van Delden and A. van der Heide, 2012. 'Trends in end-of-life practices before and after the enactment of the euthanasia law in the Netherlands from 1990 to 2010: a repeated cross-sectional survey', *The Lancet* 380(9845): 908–915.

Oregon Department of Public Health, 2015. 'Death with dignity annual reports. Oregon's Death with Dignity Act—2014', http://public.health.oregon.gov/ProviderPartnerResources/EvaluationResearch/DeathwithDignityAct/Pages/ar-index.aspx (accessed 24 October 2016).

Osborn, A., 2001. 'Belgians follow Dutch by legalising euthanasia', *The Guardian* 26 October 2001.

Oxford English Dictionary, 2016a. 'tired, adj.' *OED Online*. Oxford University Press, June 2016. Web.

2016b. 'normal, adj. and n.' *OED Online*. Oxford University Press, June 2016. Web.

Palmer B.W. and Harmell A.L., 2016. 'Assessment of healthcare decision-making capacity', *Archives of Clinical Neuropsychology* 31(6): 530–540.

Papadimitriou J.D., et al., 2007. 'Euthanasia and suicide in antiquity: viewpoint of the dramatists and philosophers', *Journal of the Royal Society of Medicine* 100(1): 25–28.

Papastavrou, E., A. Kalokerinou, S.S. Papacostas, H. Tsangari and P. Sourtzi, 2007. 'Caring for a relative with dementia: family caregiver burden', *Journal of Advanced Nursing* 58: 1–12.

Papavasiliou, E.E., K. Chambaere, L. Deliens, S. Brearley, S. Payne, J. Rietjens, R. Vander Stichele and L. Van den Block, 2014. 'Physician-reported practices on continuous deep sedation until death: A descriptive and comparative study', *Palliative Medicine* 28(6): 491–500.

Parker, M., 2005. 'End Games: Euthanasia under interminable scrutiny', *Bioethics* 19(5–6): 523–536.

Partridge, B.C., 2013. 'The decisional capacity of the adolescent: an introduction to a critical reconsideration of the doctrine of the mature minor', *The Journal of Medicine and Philosophy* 38: 249–255.

Pasman, H.R.W., M.L. Rurup, D.L. Willems and B. D. Onwuteaka-Philipsen, 2009. 'Concept of unbearable suffering in context of ungranted requests for euthanasia: qualitative interviews with patients and physicians', *BMJ* 339 (16 November): b4362.

Peace, W.J., 2013. 'Euthanasia in Belgium: The untold story', *Bioethics Forum 02/11/2013*, www.thehastingscenter.org/euthanasia-in-belgium-the-untold-story/ (accessed 24 October 2016).

Pearlman, M., K.C. Cain, D.L. Patrick, M. Appelbaum-Maizel, H.E. Starks, N.S. Jecker and R.F. Uhlmann, 1993. 'Insights pertaining to patient assessments of states worse than death', *Journal of Clinical Ethics* 4: 33–41.

Pellegrino, E., 2001. 'Physician-assisted suicide and euthanasia: Rebuttal of rebuttals – the moral prohibition remains', *Journal of Medicine and Philosophy* 26(1): 93–100.

Pereira, J., 2011. 'Legalizing euthanasia or assisted suicide: the illusion of safeguards and controls', *Current Oncology* 18(2): e38–45.

Pereira, J., D. Anwar, G. Pralong, J. Pralong, C. Mazzocato and J.M. Bigler, 2008a. 'Assisted suicide and euthanasia should not be practiced in palliative care units', *Journal of Palliative Medicine* 11(8): 1074–1076.

Pereira, J., P. Laurent, B. Cantin, D. Petremand and T. Currat, 2008b. 'The response of a Swiss university hospital's palliative care consult team to assisted suicide within the institution', *Palliative Medicine* 22: 659–667.

Petanjek, Z., M. Judas, G. Simic et al., 2011. 'Extraordinary neoteny of synaptic spines in the human prefrontal cortex', *Proceedings of the National Academy of Sciences of the United States* 108(32): 13281–13286.

Piaget, J., 1971. 'The theory of stages in cognitive development', in Green DR, Ford MP, Flanner G.B. (eds.), *Measurement and Piaget*. New York: McGraw-Hill.

Pike, G.K. 2010. 'So tired of life'. *Health Affairs* 22(1)(May): 1–3.

'*Plus de 2,000 déclarations d'euthanasie en 2015*', 2016. DH 27 January 2016 www.dhnet.be/actu/sante/plus-de-2-000-declarations-d-euthanasie-en-2015–56a8c4103570ed38955c444d (accessed 24 October 2016).

Pollard, B., 1992. 'Euthanasia in Holland', *Quadrant* (Nov 1992): 42–46.

Pols, H. and S. Oak, 2013. 'Physician-assisted dying and psychiatry: recent developments in The Netherlands', *International Journal of Law and Psychiatry* 36(5–6): 506–514.

Post, S., 1995. 'Alzheimer disease and the "then" self', *Kennedy Institute of Ethics Journal* 4: 307–321.

Prince, M., R. Bryce, E. Albanese, A. Wimo, W. Ribeiro and C.P. Ferri, 2013. 'The global prevalence of dementia: a systematic review and metaanalysis', *Alzheimers Dementia* 9: 63–75.

'*Quatre cas pour dépression majeure irréductible*' [Four cases of untreatable serious depression], 2007. *La Libre Belgique* 2 February 2007.

Rachels, J. 1986. *The End of Life: Euthanasia and Morality*. Oxford: Oxford University Press.

Radbruch, L., Leget, C., Bahr, P., Müller-Busch, Ch., Ellershaw, J., De Conno, F., Vanden Berghe, P., 2015. 'Euthanasia and physician-assisted suicide – A white paper from the European Association for Palliative Care', *Palliative Medicine* November 2015.

Radcliffe Richards, J., 2013. *Careless Thought Costs Lives: The Ethics of Transplants*. Oxford: Oxford University Press.

Raijmakers, N.J., A. van der Heide, P.S. Kouwenhoven, G.J. van Thiel, J.J. van Delden and J.A. Rietjens, 2015. 'Assistance in dying for older people without a serious medical condition who have a wish to die: a national cross-sectional survey', *Journal of Medical Ethics* 41(2): 145–150.

Rassart, J., K. Luyckx, E. Goossens, S. Apers, T.A. Klimstra and P. Moons, 2013. 'Personality traits, quality of life, and perceived health in adolescents with congenital heart disease', *Psychology & Health* 28: 319–335.

Raus, K., S. Sterckx and F. Mortier, 2011. 'Is continuous sedation at the end of life an ethically preferable alternative to physician-assisted suicide?', *American Journal of Bioethics* 11(6): 32–40.

2012. 'Continuous deep sedation at the end of life and the "natural death" hypothesis', *Bioethics* 26(6): 329–336.

2013. 'Can the doctrine of double effect justify continuous deep sedation at the end of life?' in K. Raus, S. Sterckx and F. Mortier (eds.), *Continuous Sedation at the End of Life*. Cambridge: Cambridge University Press, 177–201.

Raus, K., M. De Laat, F. Mortier and S. Sterckx, 2014. 'The ethical and clinical importance of measuring consciousness in continuously sedated patients', *Journal of Clinical Ethics* 25(3): 207–218.

Raznahan, A., J.P. Lerch, N. Lee et al., 2011. 'Patterns of coordinated anatomical change in human cortical development: a longitudinal neuroimaging study of maturational coupling', *Neuron* 72(5): 873–884.

Reichel, W. and A.J. Dyck, 1989. 'Euthanasia: a contemporary moral quandary'. *The Lancet* Dec 2: 1321–1323.

Report of the Chamber Commission of Justice, 2002. *Rapport fait au nom de la Commission de la Justice*, par T. Giet, A. Van De Casteele, A. Barzin et J. Schauvliege, 23 avril 2002, Doc. parl., Ch. repr., session 2001–2002, n° 50 1488/009].

Report of the Chamber Commission on Public Health, 2002. *Rapport fait au nom de la Commission de la santé publique, de l'environnement et du renouveau de la société*, par A.-M. Descheemaeker et J. Vande Walle, annexé au Rapport fait au nom de la Commission de la Justice, *Doc. parl.*, Ch. repr., n° 50 1488/009.

Report of the Joint Commissions for Justice and Social Affairs *Rapport fait au nom des Commissions réunies de la Justice et des Affaires sociales*, par Mesdames Laloy et Van Riet, 9 juillet 2001, Doc. parl., Sénat, session 2000–2001, n° 2-244/22.

Rhees, R., 1999. *Moral Questions*, ed. D.Z. Phillips. Basingstoke: Macmillan.

Rietjens, J. et al., 2009. 'Judgement of suffering in the case of a euthanasia request in The Netherlands', *Journal of Medical Ethics* 35(8): 502–507.

Rijksoverheid, 2014. Available at www.rijksoverheid.nl (accessed 24 October 2016).

Roberts, G., 2014. 'Healthy elderly couple chose to die together by assisted suicide so one not left on own', *Mirror* 26 September, www.mirror.co.uk/news/world-news/healthy-elderly-couple-chose-die-4327743 (accessed 24 October 2016).

Rotman, C. and C. Beal, 2008. '*En Belgique, le départ choisi d'Hugo Claus*' [In Belgium, the departure chosen by Hugo Claus], *Libération* 21 March 2008.

Rurup et al., 2005a. Rurup, M.L., B.D. Onwuteaka-Philipsen, M.C. Jansen-van der Weide, G. van der Wal, 2005. 'When being "tired of living" plays an important role in a request for euthanasia or physician-assisted suicide: patient characteristics and the physician's decision', *Health Policy* 74(2): 157–166.

2005b. 'Requests for euthanasia or physician-assisted suicide from older persons who do not have a severe disease: an interview study', *Psychological Medicine* 35(5): 665–671.

2005c. 'Physicians' experiences with demented patients with advance euthanasia directives in The Netherlands', *Journal of the American Geriatrics Society* 53: 1138–1144.

2006a. 'Frequency and determinants of advance directives concerning end-of-life care in the Netherlands', *Social Science and Medicine* 62: 1552–1563.

2006b. 'Attitudes of physicians, nurses and relatives towards end-of-life decisions concerning nursing home patients with dementia', *Patient Education and Counseling* 61:372–380.

2011. 'Understanding why older people develop a wish to die: a qualitative interview study', *Crisis: The Journal of Crisis Intervention and Suicide Prevention* 32(4): 204–216.

RTBF, 2015. *Procédure d'euthanasie interrompue pour Frank Van den Bleeken*, www.rtbf.be/info/societe/detail_procedure-d-euthanasie-interrompue-pour-frank-van-den-bleeken?id=8720935 (accessed 24 October 2016).

Rys, S., R. Deschepper, F. Mortier, L. Deliens and J. Bilsen, 2014. 'Bridging the gap between continuous sedation until death and physician-assisted death: a focus group study in nursing homes in Flanders, Belgium', *American Journal of Hospice and Palliative Medicine* 2014 Mar 26.

Ryynänen, O.-P., M. Myllykangas, M. Viren and H. Heino, 2002. 'Attitudes towards euthanasia among physicians, nurses and the general public in Finland', *Public Health* 116: 322–331.

Saget, E. 2008. '*L'euthanasie, ma mère et moi*' [Euthanasia, my mother and me], *L'Express* (France), 24 April 2008, www.lexpress.fr/actualite/societe/l-eutha nasie-ma-mere-et-moi_472327.html (accessed 24 October 2016).

Sampson, E., B. Candy and L. Jones, 2009. 'Enteral tube feeding for older people with advanced dementia', *Cochrane Database of Systematic Reviews* 15(2): CD007209.

Sampson, C., I. Finlay, A. Byrne et al., 2014. 'The practice of palliative care from the perspective of patients and carers', *BMJ Supportive & Palliative Care* (7 August).

Schamps, G., M. Van Overstraeten, 2009. '*La loi belge relative à l'euthanasie et ses développements*' [Belgian law on euthanasia and its evolution], in *Liber amicorum Henri-D. Bosly*. Bruges, La Charte, 337–355.

Schenker, Y. and Arnold, R., 2015. 'The next era of palliative care', *JAMA* (3 September).

Scherder, E., J. Oosterman, D. Swaab, K. Herr, M. Ooms, M. Ribbe, J. Sergeant, G. Pickering and F. Benedetti, 2005. 'Recent developments in pain in dementia', *British Medical Journal* 330: 461–464.

Schmithorst, V.J. and W. Yuan, 2010. 'White matter development during adolescence as shown by diffusion MRI', *Brain and Cognition* 72(1): 16–25.

Schrank, B. and M. Slade, 2007. 'Recovery in psychiatry', *Psychiatric Bulletin* 31: 321–325.

Schuklenk, U. and S. van de Vathorst, 2015. 'Treatment-resistant major depressive disorder and assisted dying', *Journal of Medical Ethics* 41(8): 577–83.

Schuklenk, U. et al., 2011. 'End-of-life decision making', *The Royal Society of Canada Expert Panel*, www.rsc-src.ca/en/expert-panels/rsc-reports/end-life-decision-making (accessed 24 October 2016).

Seale, C., 2009a. 'End-of-life decisions in the UK involving medical practitioners', *Palliative Medicine* 23: 198–204.

2009b. 'Legalisation of euthanasia or physician-assisted suicide: survey of doctors' attitudes', *Palliative Medicine* 23: 205–212.

Seale, C., K. Raus, S.M. Bruinsma, A. van der Heide, S. Sterckx, F. Mortier, S. Payne, N. Mathers and J.A.C. Rietjens, 2015. 'The language of sedation in end-of-life care: The ethical reasoning of care providers in three countries', *Health* Epub ahead of print. Doi:10.1177/1363459314555377.

'Second British woman "tired of life" helped to die by Swiss suicide clinic aged 99',
    2014. *The Daily Mail* 13 April, www.dailymail.co.uk/news/article-2603586/
    Second-British-woman-tired-life-helped-die-Swiss-suicide-clinic-aged-99.html
    (accessed 24 October 2016).
Seiffge-Krenke, I., 1998. 'Chronic disease and perceived developmental progression
    in adolescence', *Developmental Psychology* 34: 1073–1084.
Senate, 2013. *Sénat de Belgique. Session de 2013-2014* 4 December 2013,
    www.senate.be/www/?MIval=/publications/viewPub.html&COLL=S&LEG=
    5&NR=2170&VOLGNR=4&LANG=fr (accessed 24 October 2016).
Sepulveda, C., A. Marlin, T. Yoshida and A. Ullrich, 2002. 'Palliative care: the World
    Health Organization's global perspective', *Journal of Pain and Symptom Man-
    agement* 24: 91–96.
Seymour, J., J. Rietjens, J. Brown, A. van der Heide, S. Sterckx and L. Deliens, 2011.
    'The perspectives of clinical staff and bereaved informal care-givers on the
    use of continuous sedation until death for cancer patients: the study protocol
    of the UNBIASED study', *BMC Palliative Care* 10(5): available online.
Shackleton, R., 1972. 'The greatest happiness of the greatest humber: the history of
    Bentham's phrase', *Studies on Voltaire and the Eighteenth Century* 90.
Shariff, M.J., 2012. 'Assisted death and the slippery slope – finding clarity amid
    advocacy, convergence, and complexity', *Current Oncology* 19(3): 143–154.
    doi: 10.3747/co.19.1095.
Sharp, R., 2012. 'The dangers of euthanasia and dementia: how Kantian thinking
    might be used to support non-voluntary euthanasia in cases of extreme
    dementia', *Bioethics* 26: 231–235.
Shaw, D., 2012. 'We should not let families stop organ donation from their dead
    relatives', *BMJ* 345: e5275.
Sheldon, T., 2000. 'Dutch GP cleared after helping to end man's "Hopeless
    Existence"', *BMJ* 321 (11 November): 1174.
    2003. 'Being "tired of life" is not grounds for euthanasia', *BMJ* 326(7380): 71.
    2011. 'Dementia patient's euthanasia was lawful, say Dutch authorities', *BMJ*
    343: d7510.
Sherman, L.E., J.D. Rudie, J.H. Pfeifer, C.L. Masten, K. McNealy and M. Dapretto,
    2014. 'Development of the default mode and central executive networks
    across early adolescence: a longitudinal study', *Developmental Cognitive
    Neuroscience* 10: 148–159.
Silver, D., 2003. 'Lethal injection, autonomy and the proper ends of medicine',
    Bioethics 17: 205–211.
Singer, P., 1993. *Practical Ethics*. Cambridge: Cambridge University Press.
Smets, T., J. Bilsen, J. Cohen, M.L. Rurup, F. Mortier, L. Deliens, 2010. 'Reporting
    of euthanasia in medical practice in Flanders, Belgium: cross sectional
    analysis of reported and unreported cases', *BMJ* 341: 1–8.

Smets, T., J. Bilsen, J. Cohen, M.L. Rurup et al., 2009. 'The medical practice of euthanasia in Belgium and The Netherlands: Legal notification, control and evaluation procedures', *Health Policy* 90: 181–187.

Smets, T., Cohen J. et al., 2011. 'Attitudes and experiences of Belgian physicians regarding euthanasia practice and the euthanasia law', *Journal of Pain & Symptom Management* 41(3): 590.

Smith, K.A., T.A. Harvath, E.R. Goy and L. Ganzini, 2015. 'Predictors of pursuit of physician-assisted death', *Journal of Pain and Symptom Management* 49(3): 555–561.

Snijdewind, M.C., D.L. Willems, L. Deliens, B.D. Onwuteaka-Philipsen and K. Chambaere, 2015. 'A study of the first year of the End-of-Life Clinic for physician-assisted dying in the Netherlands', *JAMA Internal Medicine* 175(10): 1633–1640.

Sosa-Ortiz, A., I. Acosta-Castillo and M. Prince, 2012. 'Epidemiology of dementias and Alzheimer's disease', *Archives of Medical Research* 43: 600–608.

Spindelman, M. 1996. 'Are the similarities between a woman's right to choose an abortion and the alleged right to assisted suicide really compelling?', *University of Michigan Journal of Law Reform* 29(3): 775–856.

Stack, S. and A.J. Kposowa, 2008. 'The association of suicide rates with individual-level suicide attitudes: a cross-national analysis', *Social Science Quarterly* 89(1): 39–59.

Stevens, K.R., 2006. 'Emotional and psychological effects of physician-assisted suicide and euthanasia on participating physicians', *Issues in Law & Medicine* 21(3): 187–200.

Suarez-Almazor, M.E., C. Newman, J. Hanson and E. Bruera, 2002. 'Attitudes of terminally ill cancer patients about euthanasia and assisted suicide: predominance of psychosocial determinants and beliefs over symptom distress and subsequent survival', *Journal of Clinical Oncology* 20(8): 2134–2141.

Steck, N. et al., 2014. 'Suicide assisted by right-to-die associations: a population based cohort study', *International Journal of Epidemiology* doi: 10.1093/ije/dyu010.

'Steeds meer Belgen willen levenseinde zelf bepalen' [More and more Belgians want to define life itself], *De Standaard* 16 February 2015.

Steinberg, L., 2013a. 'Does recent research on adolescent brain development inform the mature minor doctrine?', *The Journal of Medicine and Philosophy* 38: 283–299.

2013b. 'The influence of neuroscience on US Supreme Court decisions about adolescents' criminal culpability', *Nature Reviews Neuroscience* 14(7): 513–518.

Steinbock, B., 2005. 'The case for physician assisted suicide: not (yet) proven', *Journal of Medical Ethics* 31: 235–241.

Steindal, S.H., I. Schou Bredal, L. Wergeland Sørbye and A. Lerdal, 2011. 'Pain control at the end of life: a comparative study of hospitalized cancer and noncancer patients', *Scandinavian Journal of Caring Sciences* 25(4): 771–779.

Sulmasy, D.P., B.P. Linas, K. Gold and K. Schulman, 1998. 'Physician resource use and willingness to participate in assisted suicide', *Archives of Internal Medicine* 158: 974–978.

Swart, S.J., A. van der Heide, L. van Zuylen, R.S.G.M. Perez, W.W.A. Zuurmond, P.J. van der Maas, J.J.M. van Delden and J. Rietjens, 2012. 'Considerations of physicians about the depth of palliative sedation at the end of life', *Canadian Medical Association Journal* 184(7): E360–E366.

Sykes, N. and A. Thorns, 2003. 'Sedative use in the last week of life and the implications for end-of-life decision making', *Archives of Internal Medicine* 163: 341–344.

Syristová, E., 2010. *A Contribution to Phenomenology of the Human Normality in the Modern Time*. Dordrecht: Springer Science + Business Media.

Tack, S., 2013. *'Recht op (uitvoering van) euthanasie?'* [Right to (performance of) euthanasia?] *Instellingsbeleid en de professionele autonomie van de arts* [Institutional policy and the professional autonomy of the physician], *Revue de droit de la santé* 12: 7–22.

Tal Young, I., A. Iglewicz, D. Glorioso, N. Lanouette, K. Seay, M. Ilapakurti and S. Zisook, 2012. 'Suicide bereavement and complicated grief', *Dialogues in Clinical Neuroscience* 14(2): 177–186.

Tännsjö, T., 2004a. 'Terminal sedation: a subsitute for euthanasia?' in T. Tännsjö (ed.), *Terminal Sedation: Euthanasia in Disguise?* Dordrecht: Kluwer Academic Publishers, 15–30.

— (ed.), 2004b. *Terminal Sedation: Euthanasia in Disguise?* Dordrecht: Kluwer Academic Publishers.

Ten Have, H.A.M.J., and J.V.M. Welie, 1992. 'Euthanasia: normal medical practice?', *Hastings Center Report* 22(2): 34–38.

— 2014. 'Palliative sedation versus euthanasia: an ethical assessment', *Journal of Pain and Symptom Management* 47(1): 123–136.

Thienpont, L. 2015. *Libera Me: Over Euthanasie en Psychisch Lijden*. Witsand Uitgevers.

Thienpont, L., M. Verhofstadt, T. Van Loon, W. Distelmans, K. Audenaert and P.P. De Deyn, 2015. 'Euthanasia requests, procedures and outcomes for 100 Belgian patients suffering from psychiatric disorders: a retrospective, descriptive study', *British Medical Journal (BMJ Open)* 5: doi: 10.1136/bmjopen-2014-007454.

Thirion, et al., 2013, *'Actualisons la loi sur l'euthanasie'* [Let us modernize the law on euthanasia], *Le Soir* 14 June 2013.

Tholen et al., 2009. 'Physician-assisted suicide for a patient with a psychiatric disorder: guidelines for psychiatrists.' [in Dutch]. Utrecht, The Netherlands: De Tijdstroom.

Tomlinson, S., 2013. 'Deaf Belgian twins bought new suits and shoes before killing themselves, reveals brother who was with them when they died . . . but couldn't talk them out of it', *Daily Mail* 15 January 2013, www.dailymail.co.uk/news/article-2262630/Brother-deaf-Belgian-twins-killed-euthanasia-describes-final-words-reveals-live-learning-going-blind.html (accessed 24 October 2016).

Tomlinson, E. and J. Stott, 2015. 'Assisted dying in dementia: a systematic review of the international literature on the attitudes of health professionals, patients, carers and the public, and the factors associated with these', *International Journal of Geriatric Psychiatry* 30: 10–20.

Tomlinson, E., A. Spector, S. Nurock and J. Stott, 2015. 'Euthanasia and physician-assisted suicide in dementia: a qualitative study of the views of former dementia carers', *Palliative Medicine* 29: 720–726.

Tonti-Filippini, N. 2012. *About Bioethics: Volume 2 – Caring for People who are Sick or Dying*. Ballan VIC: Conor Court Publishing.

Toshiro, U. 1989. 'Transplants forbidden', *Japan Quarterly* 146–154.

Tulsky, J. 2005. 'Beyond advance directives: importance of communication skills at the end of life', *Journal of the American Medical Association* 294: 359–365.

UK Government Cabinet Office, 2013. Review of cross-government horizon scanning, Cabinet Office, 21 January 2013.

Ulrich, L.P., 1999. *The Patient Self-Determination Act*. Washington, DC: Georgetown University Press.

'Une euthanasie après une opération ratée de changement de sexe', 2013. *La Libre* (Belgique) 1 October 2013.

'Un prisonnier belge a été euthanasié', 2012. *Le Soir* 13 September 2012 www.lesoir.be/85926/article/actualite/belgique/2012-09-13/un-prisonnier-belge-a-été-euthanasié (accessed 24 October 2016).

van Delden, J.J.M., L. Pijnenborg and P.J. Van Der Maas, 1993. 'Reports from the Netherlands: dances with data', *Bioethics* 7: 323–329.

van Delden, J.J.M., 2007. 'Terminal sedation: source of a restless ethical debate', *Journal of Medical Ethics* 33(4): 187–188.

van den Bos, W., E. van Dijk, M. Westenberg, S.A. Rombouts and E.A. Crone, 2011. 'Changing brains, changing perspectives: the neurocognitive development of reciprocity', *Psychological Science* 22(1): 60–70.

Vandenberghe, J., 2011. 'The "good death" in Flemish psychiatry', [in Dutch]. *Tijdschriftvoor Psychiatrie* 53 (8): 551–553.

2012. 'Euthanasia in patients with intolerable suffering due to a psychiatric condition: ethical considerations', *European Congress of Psychiatry*. Prague, Czech Republic, 3–6 March 2012.

2013. 'Euthanasia in patients with intolerable suffering due to an irremediable psychiatric illness' [in Dutch], 40–50 pp. in: J. De Lepeleire, B. Broeckaert, C. Gastmans, M. Keirse, J. Menten, H. Nys, A. Vandevelde, J. Vandenberghe, R. Vandenberghe, S. Van Gool, *Euthanasia and human vulnerability. Metaforum vision statement 11.* [in Dutch], 1–52 pp. Werkgroep Metaforum KU

Leuven:Leuven, Belgium, www.kuleuven.be/metaforum/docs/pdf/wg_9_ n.pdf (accessed 24 October 2016).

et al., 2013. 'Euthanasie bij ondraaglijk lijden als gevolg van een ongeneeslijke psychiatrische aandoening', in *Euthanasie en Menselijke Kwetsbaarheid.* Visietekst Metaforum Katholieke Universiteit Leuven, 39–49.

Vanden Berghe, P., A, Mullie, M. Desmet and G. Huysmans, 2013. 'Assisted dying – the current situation in Flanders: euthanasia embedded in palliative care', *European Journal of Palliative Care* 20(6).

Van De Perre, K. and W. Daenen, 2016. 'I don't want to live anymore, but give me time to die'. [in Dutch]. *De Morgen* 6 February 2016, www.demorgen.be/ lifestyle/-ik-wil-niet-meer-leven-maar-geef-me-tijd-om-te-sterven-be13a7e3/ (accessed 24 October 2016).

van der Heide, A., L. Deliens, K. Faisst et al., 2003. 'End-of-life decision-making in six European countries: descriptive study', *The Lancet* 362(9381): 345–350.

van der Heide, A., B.D. Onwuteaka–Philipsen, M.L. Rurup, H.M. Buiting, J.J. van Delden, J.E. Hanssen-de Wolf, A.G. Janssen, H.R. Pasman, J.A. Rietjens, C.J. Prins, I.M. Deerenberg, J.K. Gevers, P.J. van der Maas, G. van der Wal, 2007. 'End-of-life practices in the Netherlands under the *Euthanasia Act*', *The New England Journal of Medicine* 356: 1957–1965.

Van der Heyden, J., 2012. Gezondheidsenquete België 2008. Chronische aandoeningen. Available at https://his.wiv-isp.be/nl/Gedeelde%20%20documenten/ MA_NL_2008.pdf (accessed 24 October 2016).

van der Maas, P.J. et al., 1991. *Medische Beslissingen Rond het Levenseinde. Het Onderzoek Voor de Commissie Onderzoek Medische Praktijk Inzake Euthanasia.* Gravenhage: SDU Uitgeversij Plantijnstraat.

1996. 'Euthanasia, physician-assisted suicide, and other medical practices involving the end of life in the Netherlands, 1990–1995', *The New England Journal of Medicine* 335: 1699.

Van der Steen, J., 2010. 'Dying with dementia: what we know after more than a decade of research', *Journal of Alzheimers Disease* 22(1): 37–55.

Van der Steen, J., L. Radbruch, C. Hertogh, M. de Boer, J. Hughes, P. Larkin, A. Francke, S. Jünger, D. Gove, P. Firth, R. Koopmans and L. Volicer and on behalf of the European Association for Palliative Care, 2014. 'White paper defining optimal palliative care in older people with dementia: a Delphi study and recommendations from the European Association for Palliative Care', *Palliative Medicine* 28: 197–209.

Van der Wal, G. and P.J. van der Maas, 1996. *Euthanasia and Other Medical Decisions Concerning the End of Life: Practice and Reporting Procedure.* Den Haag: SDU Uitgevers.

Van Gool, S. et al., 2014. '*Fin de vie des enfants: une loi inutile et précipitée*' [Children's end of life: a useless and premature law], *La Libre Belgique* 29 January 2014.

Van Holsteyn, J. and M. Trappenburg, 1998. 'Citizens' opinions on new forms of euthanasia: a report from the Netherlands', *Patient Education and Counseling* 35: 63–73.

Van Raemdonck, D.V., A. Neyrinck, W. Coosemans et al., 2013. 'Lung transplantation with grafts recovered from euthanasia donors', Abstract O-099 *21st European Conference on General Thoracic Surgery, Birmingham, UK 26–29 May 2013*, www.estsmeetings.org/2013/images/documents/ests-abstracts-2013.pdf (accessed 24 October 2016).

Van Raemdonck, D.V., G.M. Verleden, L. Dupont et al., 2011. 'Initial experience with transplantation of lungs recovered from donors after euthanasia', *Applied Cardiopulmonary Pathophysiology* 15: 38–48.

Van Tol, D., J. Rietjens, A. van der Heide, 2010. 'Judgment of unbearable suffering and willingness to grant a euthanasia request by Dutch general practitioners', *Health Policy* 97: 166–172.

Van Veldhuizen, A.M. and B.F. Last, 1991. *Children with Cancer: Communication and Emotions.* Amsterdam/Lisse.

van Wesemael, Y., J. Cohen, J. Bilsen, T. Smets, B. Onwuteaka-Philipsen and L. Deliens, 2011. 'Process and outcomes of euthanasia requests under the Belgian act on euthanasia: a nationwide survey', *Journal of Pain and Symptom Management* 42(5): 721–733.

Van Wijngaarden, E., C. Leget, A. Goossensen, 2014. 'Experiences and motivations underlying wishes to die in older people who are tired of living: a research area in its infancy', *Omega* 69(2): 191–216.

——— 2015. 'Ready to give up on life: the lived experience of elderly people who feel life is completed and no longer worth living', *Social Science & Medicine* 138: 257–264.

Varelius, J., 2007. 'Execution by lethal injection, euthanasia, organ donation and the proper ends of medicine', *Bioethics* 21: 140–149.

——— 2015. 'On the moral acceptability of physician-assisted dying for non-autonomous psychiatric patients', *Bioethics* DOI: 10.1111/bioe.12182.

Varghese, F.T. and B. Kelly, 2001. 'Countertransference and assisted suicide', *Issues in Law & Medicine* 16(3): 235–258.

Velleman, D.J., 1999. 'A right of self-termination', *Ethics* 109(3): 606–628.

Vellinga, A. and J. Vandenberghe, 2010. 'Decision-making capacity', [in Dutch] in R. van der Mast, T. Heeren, M. Kat, M. Stek, M. Vandenbulcke, F. Verhey (eds.), *Handboek Ouderenpsychiatrie*, Chapt. 13.1. De Tijdstroom: Utrecht, The Netherlands, 167–182.

Verhagen, E., P.J. Sauer, 2005. 'The Groningen protocol – euthanasia in severely ill newborns', *The New England Journal of Medicine*, 352(10): 959–962.

Vincent, J.L., 2014. '*Maintenons la santé, mais pas la vie à tout prix*' [Let us preserve health, but not life at any price], *Le Soir* 25 February 2014.

Vincent, J.L., I. Kahn, A.Z. Snyder, M.E. Raichle and R.L. Buckner, 2008. 'Evidence for a frontoparietal control system revealed by intrinsic functional connectivity', *Journal of Neurophysiology* 100(6): 3328–3342.

Vincent J.L., M. Schetz, J.J. De Waele, S. Clément de Cléty, I. Michaux, Th. Sottiaux, E. Hoste, D. Ledoux, A. De Weerdt, A. Wilmer. On behalf of the Belgian Society of Intensive Care Medicine, 2014. 'Piece of mind: end of life in the intensive care unit – statement of the Belgian Society of Intensive Care Medicine', *Journal of Critical Care* 29: 174–175.

Volker, D., 2001. 'Oncology nurses' experience with requests for assisted dying from terminally ill patients with cancer'. *Oncology Nursing Society* 28: 39–49.

Volokh, E., 2003. 'The mechanisms of the slippery slope', *Harvard Law Review* 116: 1026–1137. doi: 10.2307/1342743.

Vox Europe, 2013. Available at www.voxeurop.eu/nl/content/news-brief/4298761-euthanasie-voor-kinderen-nu?xtor=RSS-18 (accessed 24 October 2016).

Wagner, B., J. Müller and A. Maercker, 2012. 'Death by request in Switzerland: posttraumatic stress disorder and complicated grief after witnessing assisted suicide', *European Psychiatry* 27(7): 542–546.

Walsh, F., 2015. 'The assisted dying debate', *BBC* 26 May, www.bbc.co.uk/news/health-32893689.

Warnock, M., 2014. 'Easeful death for the very elderly', in C. Brewer and M. Irwin (eds.), 2014. *I'll See Myself Out, Thank You*. Newbold, Warwickshire: SkyScraper.

Waterfield, B., 2015. 'Son challenges Belgian law after mother's "mercy killing"', *Telegraph* 2 February 2015.

Weber, W., 2001. 'Belgian euthanasia bill gains momentum', *Lancet* 357: 372.

Wesley, P., 1993. 'Dying safely', *Issues in Law & Medicine* 8(4): 467–485.

Widdershoven, G. and R. Berghmans, 2001. 'Advance directives in dementia care: from instructions to instruments', *Patient Education and Counseling* 44: 179–186.

Wijsbek, H., 2012. '"To thine own self be true": on the loss of integrity as a kind of suffering', *Bioethics* 26(1): 1–7.

Wilhelms, E. and V. Reyna, 2013. 'Fuzzy trace theory and medical decisions by minors: differences in reasoning between adolescents and adults', *The Journal of Medicine and Philosophy* 38: 268–282.

Wilkinson, D. and J. Savulescu, 2012. 'Should we allow organ donation euthanasia? Alternatives for maximising the number and quality of organs for transplantation', *Bioethics* 26: 32–48.

Williams, B., 1985. *Ethics and the Limits of Philosophy*. London: Fontana.
    1973. *Problems of the Self*. Cambridge: Cambridge University Press.

Williams, G., 1957. *The Sanctity of Life and the Criminal Law*. New York: Knopf.

Williams, N., C. Dunford, A. Knowles and J. Warner, 2007. 'Public attitudes to life-sustaining treatments and euthanasia in dementia', *International Journal of Geriatric Psychiatry* 22: 1229–1234.

Wilson, K.G., T.L. Dalgleish, H.M. Chochinov, S. Chary, P.R. Gagnon, K. Macmillan, M. De Luca, F. O'Shea, D. Kuhl and R.L. Fainsinger, 2014. 'Mental disorders and the desire for death in patients receiving palliative care for cancer', *BMJ Supportive & Palliative Care* DOI: 10.1136/bmjspcare-2013-000604.

Wilson, K.G., M. Lander and H.M. Chiochinov, 2009. 'Diagnosis and management of depression in palliative Care', in H.M. Chochinov and W. Breitbart (eds.), *Handbook of Psychiatry in Palliative Medicine*, 2nd ed. New York: Oxford University Press, 39–68.

Withnall, A., 2014. 'Retired British art teacher ends life at Dignitas "because she couldn't adapt to modern world"', *The Independent* 6 April, www.independent.co.uk/ news/uk/home-news/retired-british-art-teacher-ends-life-at-dignitas-because-she-couldnt-adapt-to-modern-world-9242053.html (accessed 24 October 2016).

Wittgenstein, L., 1958. *Philosophical Investigations*. trans. G.E.M. Anscombe, Oxford: Blackwell.

Wittwer, H., 2013. 'The problem of the possible rationality of suicide and the ethics of physician-assisted suicide', *International Journal of Law and Psychiatry* 36(5–6): 419–426.

Woolhead, G., M. Calnan, P. Dieppe and W. Tadd, 2004. 'Dignity in old age: what do people in the United Kingdom think?', *Age and Ageing* 33: 165–170.

World Health Organization, 2014. *Preventing Suicide: A Global Imperative.* World Health Organisation.

2015. *World Report on Ageing and Health.* Geneva: World Health Organization.

2016. 'Definition of palliative care', World Health Organisation website, www.who.int/cancer/palliative/definition/en/ (accessed 24 October 2016).

Wurz, J., 2014. 'The ethics of new organ donation methods', www.swissinfo.ch/eng/ the-ethics-of-new-organ-donation-methods/41103306 (accessed 24 October 2016).

Ysebaert, D., G. Van Beeumen, K. De Greef et al., 2009. 'Organ procurement after euthanasia: Belgian experience', *Transplantation Proceedings* 41: 585.

Jonathan Ives, Michael Dunn and Alan Cribb (eds)
Empirical Bioethics: Theoretical and Practical Perspectives

Alan Merry and Warren Brookbanks
Merry and McCall Smith's Errors, Medicine and the Law: Second Edition

Donna Dickenson
Property in the Body: Feminist Perspectives, Second Edition

Rosie Harding
Duties to Care: Dementia, Relationality and Law

Ruud ter Meulen
Solidarity and Justice in Health and Social Care

David Albert Jones, Chris Gastmans and Calum MacKellar
Euthanasia and Assisted Suicide: Lessons from Belgium

Lightning Source UK Ltd.
Milton Keynes UK
UKHW02n0231181117
312908UK00013B/309/P

9 781107 198869

Refs.

Beauchamp
Shannon
O'Neil
Savulescu
Kant
Foster
Herring
Watt
David Albert Jones
Kukla

? Disability Issues ?

? Walton.
Wyatt.
Jackson.

—legal Cases—
- Bills -

Quill/Baltin

N. Biggar

K. Mannix

Keown

Finnis

Pope JP 2.